THUCYDIDES, PERICLES, AND THE IDEA OF ATHENS IN THE PELOPONNESIAN WAR

Thucydides, Pericles, and the Idea of Athens in the Peloponnesian War is the first comprehensive study of Thucydides' presentation of Pericles' radical redefinition of the city of Athens during the Peloponnesian War. Martha Taylor argues that Thucydides subtly critiques Pericles' vision of Athens as a city divorced from the territory of Attica and focused, instead, on the sea and the empire. Thucydides shows that Pericles' reconceptualization of the city led the Athenians both to Melos and to Sicily. Toward the end of his work, Thucydides demonstrates that flexible thinking about the city exacerbated the Athenians' civil war. Providing a critique and analysis of Thucydides' neglected book 8, Taylor shows that Thucydides praises political compromise focused on the traditional city in Attica. In doing so, he implicitly censures both Pericles and the Athenian imperial project itself.

Martha Taylor is an associate professor of classics at Loyola University Maryland. A Fellow of the American School of Classical Studies in Athens, she is the author of *Salamis and the Salaminioi: The History of an Unofficial Athenian Demos*.

THUCYDIDES, PERICLES, AND THE IDEA OF ATHENS IN THE PELOPONNESIAN WAR

Martha C. Taylor

Loyola University Maryland

CAMBRIDGE UNIVERSITY PRESS
Cambridge, New York, Melbourne, Madrid, Cape Town, Singapore,
São Paulo, Delhi, Dubai, Tokyo

Cambridge University Press
32 Avenue of the Americas, New York, NY 10013-2473, USA

www.cambridge.org
Information on this title: www.cambridge.org/9780521765930

First published 2010

Printed in the United States of America

A catalog record for this publication is available from the British Library.

Library of Congress Cataloging in Publication data

Taylor, Martha C. (Martha Caroline)
Thucydides, Pericles, and the idea of Athens in the Peloponnesian War / Martha C. Taylor.
p. cm.
Includes bibliographical references and indexes.
ISBN 978-0-521-76593-0 (hbk.)
1. Thucydides. History of the Peloponnesian War. 2. Pericles, ca. 495–429 B.C. 3. City and town life – Greece – Athens – History. 4. Athens (Greece) – History. 5. Athens (Greece) – Politics and government. 6. Greece – History – Peloponnesian War, 431–404 B.C. 7. City and town life – Greece – Athens – Historiography. 8. Athens (Greece) – Historiography. 9. Athens (Greece) – Politics and government – Historiography. 10. Greece – History – Peloponnesian War, 431–404 B.C. – Historiography. I. Title.
DF229.T6T39 2009
938′.05 – dc22 2009014507

ISBN 978-0-521-76593-0 Hardback

For Nicholas,

James,

and Mike

Contents

List of Maps

Acknowledgments

This book began as a three-page paper for a junior-year course on Thucydides with Richard Hamilton at Bryn Mawr College. It was then reincarnated as a final paper for a seminar on Herodotus, Thucydides, and the Greek Enlightenment with Carolyn Dewald when she was at Stanford University. It is to these classes and these exemplary teachers that this book owes its genesis and most of what is good in it.

Many other individuals were crucial to my work. Early on, Mark Munn gave wise advice on the direction of the project, and Mike Jameson offered crucial encouragement and vision. I wish that he could have seen the final product. Anthony Woodman read an early draft of Chapter 3 and offered many helpful suggestions for further thought and inquiry. Leslie Zarker Morgan, Katherine Stern Brennan, Sharon Nell, and Joe Walsh helped me with translations from Italian, French, and German. Audiences at the American Philological Association's annual meetings, Bryn Mawr College, the University of Virginia, the University of North Carolina at Chapel Hill, and the University of Pennsylvania honed my argument with their comments and questions. I am grateful to Mark Munn, Rick Hamilton, John Dillery, James Rives, and Jeremy McInerney for the invitations to speak. The Milton S. Eisenhower Library at The Johns Hopkins University was very generous in offering affiliate access to its collection, and Margaret Field in the Interlibrary Loan Office of the Loyola University/Notre Dame College Library proved indispensable. Finally, the anonymous readers of Cambridge University Press and my exemplary editors there saved me from numerous errors and greatly enhanced the whole work.

For the time free from teaching that was crucial to the completion of this project, I am grateful to the Center for the Humanities at Loyola University Maryland for the grant of a Junior Faculty Sabbatical in 1997–1998, and to the provost and dean of the College of Arts and Sciences at Loyola University Maryland and to its Research and Sabbaticals Committee for the grants of a half-year sabbatical in 1999–2000 and a full-year sabbatical in 2006–2007. These last sources also offered numerous summer grants over the (long) life of this project. For both the time and the financial assistance I am deeply grateful to all these individuals and groups.

Katherine Stern Brennan, Nora Chapman, Angela Christman, Amy Cohen, Christine De Vinne, Virginia De Vinne, Kathy Forni, Janet Headley, Barbara Jutila, Phil McCaffrey, Marsh McCall, Tom McCreight, Gayla McGlamery, Bob Miola, James Rives, Jennifer Tobin, and especially Joe Walsh were constant sources of personal and professional encouragement.

Finally, I am grateful to the directors of the Society for the Promotion of Hellenic Studies for permission to reuse in Chapter 4 elements of an argument that appeared in an article published in the *Journal for Hellenic Studies* (Taylor 2002).

The dedication records my greatest debt – to my husband, who read the entire manuscript many, many times and never flagged in his belief in it, and to my sons, who provided a respite from it.

Introduction: Foundation Levels

Every student of Greek history knows that in the Persian wars of 480–479 B.C., the Athenians abandoned their *polis* but fought on to victory at Salamis from their ships. In the Peloponnesian War fifty years later (431–404 B.C.), Pericles urged the Athenians to use a similar strategy. In accord with Pericles' vision of Athens as "the sea and the city," the Athenians abandoned the land and houses of Attica and adopted a defensive war strategy designed to take advantage of Athenian naval superiority.

Thucydides chronicled this long war between Athens and Sparta. Despite all that has been written about Thucydides and Pericles, however, no work has yet focused on Thucydides' critique of Pericles' radical redefinition of Athens as a city divorced from its traditional homeland of Attica. That critique is the subject of this book.

Thucydides, I argue, repeatedly questions and discredits the Periclean vision.

He demonstrates that this vision of Athens as a city separated from Attica and coextensive with the sea leads the Athenians both to Melos and to Sicily. After Sicily, flexible notions of the city greatly exacerbate civil strife in Athens, and the end of Thucydides' (preserved) text praises political compromise and reconciliation focused on the traditional city in Attica. Thucydides' final comments prize that city over even empire itself and implicitly censure Pericles for ever directing the Athenians' gaze toward another city.

We begin with an analysis of Thucydides' presentation of Pericles' radical redefinition of the city in books 1 and 2 of his *History*. Thucydides suggests that Athens' strength lies in intangibles. Both the Corinthians and the Athenians at the Spartan congress before the war present the Athenians' ability to conceptualize their city and divorce it from their territory as a source of strength. The Corinthians, in particular, stress the restlessness and boundary confusion of the Athenians and show that they make no distinction between their "home" territory and that of others. (This is part of what makes them such worrisome neighbors.) Furthermore, in his account of the fifty years between the Persian War and the beginning of his war, Thucydides shows that the Athenians grew powerful because of their willingness to be away from home.

When he comes to describe Pericles' vision of the city, however, Thucydides reveals that it is even more radical than the idea of the city for which the Athenians fought at Salamis, in part because it does not seem to seek eventually to regain the land-bound city in Attica. Pericles sees Athens as a city with no connection to Attica. He deems the land and houses of Attica valueless, because he sees other land that (in his eyes) can take Attica's place. In his last speech, Pericles tells the Athenians that they are "absolute masters" of the watery half of the world, and he directs their attention away from Attica, and their traditional city there, to the sea and everything it touches. Thucydides questions whether the Athenians can or should accept Pericles' new city and the policy dependent on it. He associates Pericles' policy with civil strife and details the difficulty experienced by the Athenians during their move into Athens from their country homes and country life. Pericles offers to replace their houses and Attica itself with his vision of a limitless city on the sea. Thucydides prompts his reader to ask whether they will find this just compensation.

Thucydides asserts that Pericles' successors "did the opposite of Pericles with regard to all points of his advice" (2.65.7),[1] but his narrative makes it clear that the Athenians after Pericles fully embraced his vision of a city divorced from Attica and focused on the sea. Thucydides shows that in the years after Pericles' death, the Athenians and others fully accept Pericles' vision of Athens. The Spartans make an equivalence between the Spartans' "own land" and the Athenians' allied territory (4.80.1) and so indicate that they recognize that the Athenians' "own land" is not in Attica but in the empire. In their complaint about the Athenians' breach of a treaty, the Argives employ a definition

[1] All translations are my own unless otherwise indicated.

of Athenian "territory" that includes, indeed equates it with, the sea (5.56.2). Finally, the Athenians' response to the revolt of Scione demonstrates that the Athenians feel particular ownership over islands (and coastal places that the Athenians could imagine were islands), perhaps even those not in alliance with Athens (4.122.5).

The city view on display in Pericles' last speech, at Scione, and in the treaty dispute with Argos leads logically to aggressive campaigns like that against Melos. The attack on Melos is no aberration but a logical step in Athens' assertion of its rule of the sea. Two echoes of Pericles here underscore that the attack on Melos is not the result of the new policies of Pericles' deficient successors. Melos does not diverge from Pericles' policy; it follows the city view articulated in his last speech exactly.

As time and the narrative progess, Thucydides demonstrates that the Athenians' ability to abandon their homes and their real city in Attica – an ability that was so important to their earlier success – is a liability. The Athenians' conception of a city at sea, for example, leads them to their ill-fated invasion of Sicily. Thucydides presents the Sicilian Expedition as madness and lays some of the blame at Pericles' feet, because Pericles' boast that Athens ruled the sea – and his exhortation to the Athenians to abandon their land and their houses – encouraged the "mad longing for the far off" that fuels this "longest voyage from home ever attempted" (6.31.6). Pericles helped to sever the tie to home that might have kept the Athenians away from Sicily.

Furthermore, Thucydides shows that the Athenians' investment in the Sicilian city endangered the Athens at home. Thucydides repeatedly characterizes the army as a city during the Sicilian narrative and suggests that the Athenians, following Pericles' model, ultimately abandoned the city in Attica in favor of the Sicilian city. Thucydides criticizes this as muddled thinking and a confusion of priorities. The disastrous end to the expedition culminates in a symbolic tribute payment from the Sicilian Athens that reverses the imperial result of Salamis (and invites contrast with that earlier abandonment of Attica). Thucydides' final words on Sicily – "out of many, few returned home" – relate to the Athenians' failure to distinguish "home" from foreign in books 1 and 2 and underscore that the men in Sicily had real homes that were not in Sicily. Thucydides' commentary criticizes the imaginary city conjured for the Sicilian expedition and the Athenians' (and Pericles') failure to recognize where their city truly lay.

The Athenians' disconnection from Attica also fuels civil strife and seems to change the very nature of the Athenians. In his account of the rise of the oligarchy of the Four Hundred, Thucydides' narrative deliberately contradicts his assertion that it was difficult to end the Athenians' liberty. He depicts the Athenians, instead, as remaining quiet in the face of oligarchy and putting up little fight for their "ancient liberty." He thereby invites his readers to reexamine their own assumptions and expectations about Athens. If Athens is by nature democratic, it ought to have been hard to introduce an oligarchy there. But Thucydides shows that it was relatively easy, and so implies that democracy is not essential to Athens. On the other hand, after the fleet on Samos rejects oligarchy, the Athenians on Samos vehemently insist on the importance of democracy and, because they support democracy, claim that they (and not those oligarchs in Athens) are the true Athenians.

Thucydides disapproves of this position, however. The newborn Athenian democrats on Samos insist that Athens, to be Athens, must be democratic, but Thucydides' consistently negative portrayal of them undermines their claims. Thucydides especially emphasizes how the ideological purity of the Samian factioneers endangers the city in Attica because of the ease with which they denigrate that city and imagine abandoning it in favor of a new, democratic city elsewhere (8.76.6). Although most modern commentators see them as heroic patriots, Thucydides charges that they would destroy the city, not save it. In doing so, Thucydides criticizes all Athenian redefinitions that encourage men in crisis to follow their own idea of their city rather than compromise with their fellow citizens.

Indeed, throughout his account of the return to democracy, Thucydides emphasizes reconciliation, not partisanship. He stresses the unity of the two groups, democrats and oligarchs, and favors political compromise, not ideological purity – compromise focused, moreover, on the city in Attica. In the last hypothetical in his work, Thucydides implies that the loss of the empire would be worth it – indeed, even compulsory – if it was necessary to preserve the Athens in Attica from the Spartans (8.96.4). It seems that for Thucydides that city in Attica, and that alone, was the city.

Thucydides does not baldly state any of this in his own words. Instead, as Hobbes noted long ago, "the narration itself doth secretly instruct the reader, and more effectually than can possibly be done by precept."[2] Passages of Thucydides' text echo and invoke other passages in his work, so that it is impossible to proceed through the narrative without being repeatedly reminded of earlier passages and thereby invited to confirm or revise judgments those earlier passages had suggested.[3] Thucydides "needs to be turned over line by line, and his hidden thoughts read as clearly as his words: there are few poets so rich in hidden thoughts," as Friedrich Nietzsche asserts.[4] We will, then, be reading carefully and (I hope) well, reading (in Nietzsche's words) "slowly, deeply, looking cautiously before and aft," looking for echoes and resonances, "dramatic juxtapositions," internal allusions, and ironic commentary.[5] Such a reading assumes that, although he did not finish it, Thucydides had carefully revised much, if not most, of his work after the war to represent the events of the whole war and the judgments he had reached at its conclusion.[6] This is not to say that I think that all books show the same degree of polish.[7] Rather, I recognize what John Finley described as the "tightness of texture" of the work."[8]

Such a reading assumes, furthermore, that these echoes, resonances, "dramatic juxtapositions," internal allusions, and ironic commentary are deliberate – that Thucydides meant for readers to see and contemplate them. I assume, in other words, that "Thucydides . . . is a real writer,

[2] Hobbes 1843, xxii.

[3] Cf. Morrison (2006b, 266): "in many instances . . . Thucydides uses memorable phrases, striking metaphors, or recurrent polarities – Athenians-as-islanders, Athens the tyrant-city, land and sea, the opposition of Athenian and Spartan character – which provide Thucydides' audience (whether reader or auditor) with touchstones that offer coherence and unity for the *History*."

[4] Nietzsche, *"What I Owe the Ancients,"* 2 in *Twilight of the Idols* (trans., Lange).

[5] Nietzsche, *Daybreak*, preface 5 (trans., Hollindale). Connor (1984, 64) uses the phrase "dramatic juxtaposition" to describe Thucydides' placement of the Funeral Oration and plague narrative. J. Finley (1938/1967, xii) speaks of the "internal allusiveness" of Thucydides' text.

[6] Although some have suggested that perhaps the text we have ends where Thucydides wished it to end, most scholars agree that the text is unfinished. See below, chapters 4 and 5, for more on this point.

[7] See Andrewes' "Appendix 1. Indications of Incompleteness" in Gomme et al. 1981.

[8] J. Finley 1938/1967, xii.

who addresses directly, perhaps for the first time in history, a reading audience,"[9] and that Thucydides "created a work designed primarily for – indeed, only fully comprehensible by – the reflective reader."[10] No doubt I am overreading in some instances, but not in all, I think.

I hope that this book will be of interest not just to classicists but also to political theorists, not least because I myself am indebted as much to the latter (such as Peter Euben, Steven Forde, Clifford Orwin, Michael Palmer, and Leo Strauss) as to the former. I also hope that this book will appeal both to specialists and to more general readers. To that end, I have translated all foreign quotations in the text, and I assume no knowledge of the Peloponnesian War or Thucydides' account of it in my discussion. I have also tried to limit my quotations of Thucydides' Greek to those places where it is absolutely necessary. At the same time, my argument fully engages the specialists' debates, though I have confined that conversation, as much as possible, to the footnotes.[11]

This is not a work of history. I do not claim here to prove anything about the policy of the historical Pericles or the real Athenians' reaction to it. Rather, by careful analysis of Thucydides' text, I hope to elucidate Thucydides' presentation of the Athenians' "theoretical thinking" about the *polis*[12] and to show that Thucydides levels serious criticism at it. To the extent that we depend on Thucydides for our historical understanding of Pericles and the Athenians, this elucidation will also have historical significance, but it is, first and foremost, a study of what Thucydides has to say.[13]

[9] Bakker 2006, 109.

[10] Crane 1996, 7. Rhodes (1998, unpaginated), in contrast, argues that "with Thucydides we are not yet far from an oral culture in which cross-referencing is difficult and when possible is avoided."

[11] These footnotes, furthermore, must not be read as an exhaustive record of the vast scholarship on Thucydides. I do not cite the opinion or even the name of every scholar who ever discussed the Melian Dialogue, or mention every book or article I have read. Instead, I have confined my notes to instances where I must acknowledge a direct debt to another scholar on a particular point, where I must note a contrary argument, or where a commentator's formulation is so elegant it must be quoted.

[12] The phrase is Euben's (1986, 361).

[13] I agree with Abbott (1925, vi) that students should "take for their principal instructor in Thucydides Thucydides himself."

1 Pericles' City

THE POWER OF CITIES IS NOT EASY TO JUDGE

The goal of this chapter is the elucidation of Pericles' city, or more precisely, Pericles' radical redefinition of the city of Athens. This redefinition is crucial not only to Pericles' war strategy but also to Thucydides' presentation and assessment of Pericles. Although Thucydides does not introduce Pericles and his new vision of the city until the end of his first book, he signals his interest in cities and what constitutes them from the very beginning of the work. He thus primes his readers (when they reach it) to judge Pericles' understanding of the city carefully and critically. In the so-called *Archaeology*, for example – Thucydides' brief account of events in Greece until the Persian War (1.2–1.19) – Thucydides encourages his readers to focus on the intangibles that lead to power – especially in Athens.

The *Archaeology* surveys the earliest history of Greece known to Thucydides. It seeks to put the Peloponnesian war in context and to justify Thucydides' claim that the war he described was "a great war and more worthy of report than those that came before it" (1.1.1). Part of what makes the Peloponnesian War so important for Thucydides is the greatness of the cities involved, and so the *Archaeology* aims also to define what makes a city great. The first answer that Thucydides provides is walls; indeed, walls seem to be an essential element of a city for Thucydides. In a curious passage, Thucydides talks of pirates falling on "unwalled cities inhabited as villages" (πόλεσιν ἀτειχίστοις καὶ κατὰ κώμας οἰκουμέναις, 1.5.1). These unwalled "cities" seem both to be and yet not to be cities, as they are, after all, made up only of "villages." The absence of walls (and perhaps also the absence of a single center) makes Thucydides hesitate to call these habitations cities.[1]

Thucydides begins his definition of a city with a physical, tangible example of power – a city's walls. He then goes on to develop a thesis that it is navies that allow a city to grow and, especially, to acquire other territory: "those who tended their navies gained the greatest strength in both revenue and rule over others for they sailed to the islands and overcame them" (1.15.2). By developing general trends in history that explain how and why a naval state will be powerful, the *Archaeology* supports a perception of imperial Athens as naturally (and actually) powerful.

Yet Thucydides is not interested only in physical manifestations of power. In a famous passage, he argues that one would misjudge the power of Athens and Sparta if one tried to ascertain it from their physical remains alone:

> If, for example, the city of the Lacedaemonians were to be deserted, but the temples and the foundations of buildings were left, after much time had passed, I think that later generations would have great skepticism about their power in contrast to their reputation. And yet they occupy two-fifths of the Peloponnesus and lead the whole of it and many allies outside it. Nevertheless because their city is not a grand central one, and they have no temples or expensive buildings, but live in villages in the ancient Hellenic way, they would appear inferior. If, on the other hand, the Athenians were to suffer the same thing, their power would be reckoned to have been double what it is because of the remarkable appearance of their city (ἀπὸ τῆς φανερᾶς ὄψεως τῆς πόλεως ἢ ἔστιν, 1.10.2).[2]

At the end of this passage, Thucydides insists that "it is unreasonable not to believe [my account of Mycenae's power], and unreasonable to

[1] As Garlan (1968, 255f) concludes in the Classical period "the idea of a circuit wall is inseparable from the idea of the city." Modern archaeologists agree. Cf. Camp (2000, 47): "I would still be inclined to argue that a substantial circuit wall was the *sine qua non* of the Greek *polis*."

[2] In this passage Thucydides speaks of the Spartans as Lacedaemonians. Lacedaemon is the territory in which the city of Sparta lies. Although "Spartan" ("Spartiate") is properly a technical term for full Spartan citizens (as opposed to lesser-status free residents of Lacedaemon), I will use the two terms interchangeably in my text.

examine the appearances of cities rather than their powers" (τὰς ὄψεις τῶν πόλεων μᾶλλον σκοπεῖν ἢ τὰς δυνάμεις, 1.10.3). Thucydides warns that judging the power of a city is difficult; one can be deceived by show.[3] Furthermore, it is showy, naval Athens, Thucydides insists, whose power is likely to be judged as greater than it is. This warning serves as a counterpoint to the *Archaeology*'s apparent general thesis that naval powers are the strongest.[4]

Furthermore, the appearance of a city includes not just dazzling landmarks like Athens' Acropolis with its solid marble temples, but also city walls, harbor fortifications, and ship sheds – the very things on which Thucydides' *Archaeology* had focused up to this point, and led the reader to believe are of prime importance to the power of a city. By de-emphasizing the "look" of a city and insisting that to judge well one must look not at appearances but at power, Thucydides encourages his reader to think that "power" may reside as much in intangibles as in the walls and naval strength on which the *Archaeology* seems to focus. Sparta, after all, was famously unwalled (and it was surely this that Thucydides thought would lead a later critic to misjudge its power). Yet Sparta the unwalled defeated Athens of the many walls (circuit walls, Long Walls, "wooden walls" of ships). Athens, although materially powerful, eventually lost the war. The power of cities, Thucydides insists, is not easy to judge – especially the power of Athens. Indeed, despite its emphasis here on the impressive "look" of Athens, Thucydides' history argues that the power of Athens lay, more than for any other city, in the intangible and the invisible – in the character of its men and in their ability to conceptualize and redefine their *polis* in difficult circumstances. This ability, which was essential to Pericles' war strategy and which he

[3] As Kallet (2001, 57) observes, in Thucydides' view, "his contemporaries were inclined to mistake displays of wealth for accurate indicators of power." See Kallet 56–59 for the ways in which 1.10 resonates with 6.31, Thucydides' description of the effect on the spectators of the impressive appearance of the Sicilian expedition.

[4] Furthermore, as Ober (1998, 90, n. 76) points out, the *Archaeology* itself recounts the history of the Ionians, whose sea power was thwarted and contained by the rise of Persia, a major land power (1.16). The *Archaeology*, then, raises questions about the essential strength of naval and land powers. Cf. Foster (2001, 125) on Corinth.

nurtured and encouraged, was the Athenians' greatest strength, but, Thucydides contends, it ultimately helped to destroy them.

The defeat of Athens and the destruction of its walls is ever in the background of Thucydides' text. Although Thucydides tells his reader that he began to write "as soon as the war broke out" (1.1), it is clear from the so-called second preface, in which Thucydides states he recorded events "until the Lacedaemonians and their allies put an end to the empire of the Athenians and occupied the Long Walls and the Piraeus" (5.26), that Thucydides lived to see the end of the war and (because his text is unfinished) was still writing and revising his text after Athens lost the war.[5] Part of his purpose is to explain how Athens lost. In his only explicit statement on the matter, Thucydides judges that the Athenians "did not give in until, falling afoul of each other in their private disagreements, they were overthrown" (2.65.12). It was an intangible that destroyed them, according to Thucydides – "private disagreements." Over the course of his text, Thucydides shows that the most important disagreement in Athens was about the definition of the city.

It is fitting, then, that Thucydides begins his narrative of the war with an account of the *stasis* (or civil strife) in Epidamnus, a colony of Corcyra on the edges of the Greek world (see Map 1).[6] Thucydides says he recounts the story of Epidamnus because it was one of three "publicly expressed accusations" between the belligerents before the war. The Peloponnesians did not go to war over any of these, however. According to Thucydides, the "truest motivation" was "the increasing strength of the Athenians, which engendered fear in the Lacedaemonians, and compelled them to war" (1.23.6). The dispute over Epidamnus, then, was openly expressed but not of fundamental importance for the war. Thucydides recounts it anyway, in part because it allows him to focus his readers' attention from the very start of the war on the dissolution of cities.[7]

[5] Although some have argued that Thucydides chose his end point, most scholars agree that he probably died before he could complete his text.

[6] Epidamnus lay on the mainland north of Corcyra (present-day Corfu) at the site of modern Durrës, Albania.

[7] Furthermore, as Ober (1998, 71) notes, civil conflict in one city, Epidamnus, leads to intervention by Corcyra and eventually to intervention by Athens and civil strife in Corcyra as well. The pattern suggests that civil strife will come

Thus the beginning of Thucydides' work focuses on the city from two opposite points of view: In the introductory *Archaeology*, Thucydides provides a discussion of the birth of cities and how they rise to greatness, and at the beginning of the war narrative itself, he offers a picture of a city's self-destruction. The *Pentekontaetia*, Thucydides' twenty-nine-chapter excursus on how Athens reached the height of power that terrified Sparta into war, serves as a kind of *Archaeology* for Athens. And Thucydides' whole work chronicles how Athens' ability to redefine itself left it vulnerable to *stasis*.

Thucydides' account of the *stasis* in Epidamnus details the breakdown of a city. The dissolution of Epidamnus is evident even in the language that Thucydides uses to discuss its civil war. Thucydides tells us that the *demos*, or common people of Epidamnus, drove out the upper classes (1.24.5). The upper classes then joined forces with non-Greeks in the area and made attacks on the democrats. Thucydides describes these democrats as "those in the city" (τοὺς ἐν τῇ πόλει, 1.24.5) and also as "the Epidamnians in the city" (οἱ δὲ ἐν τῇ πόλει ὄντες Ἐπιδάμνιοι, 1.24.6). But Thucydides doesn't call the upper classes "the Epidamnians in exile" but merely "the exiles" (τούς τε φεύγοντας, 1.24.6), and he soon calls the democrats simply "the Epidamnians" (1.25.1, 2). The upper classes, having been pushed out by the democrats, were no longer "in the city," and Thucydides' language suggests that they were, consequently, no longer of the city, that is, no longer "Epidamnians." Having lost their place in the city, they have lost their claim to it, and their claim to the name "Epidamnian." But to the exiles, surely, *they* were the "real" Epidamnians; they constituted the real city of Epidamnus, not the usurping *demos* who happened to find themselves in possession of the physical city.

Later in the war, *stasis* came also to Epidamnus' mother-city, Corcyra, and Thucydides' account of the Corcyran Revolution contains the more famous passage on the language of civil war (3.83). Thucydides documents how the factioneers "exchanged their usual verbal evaluations of actions for new ones in the light of what they thought justified."

eventually to Athens. Thucydides judges that Athens lost the war through *stasis*, and the loss of the war led to the great *stasis* of the Thirty Tyrants. Thus the story that little Epidamnus begins runs through to the very end of the history Thucydides wrote and lived.

Map 1. Greece and the Aegean.

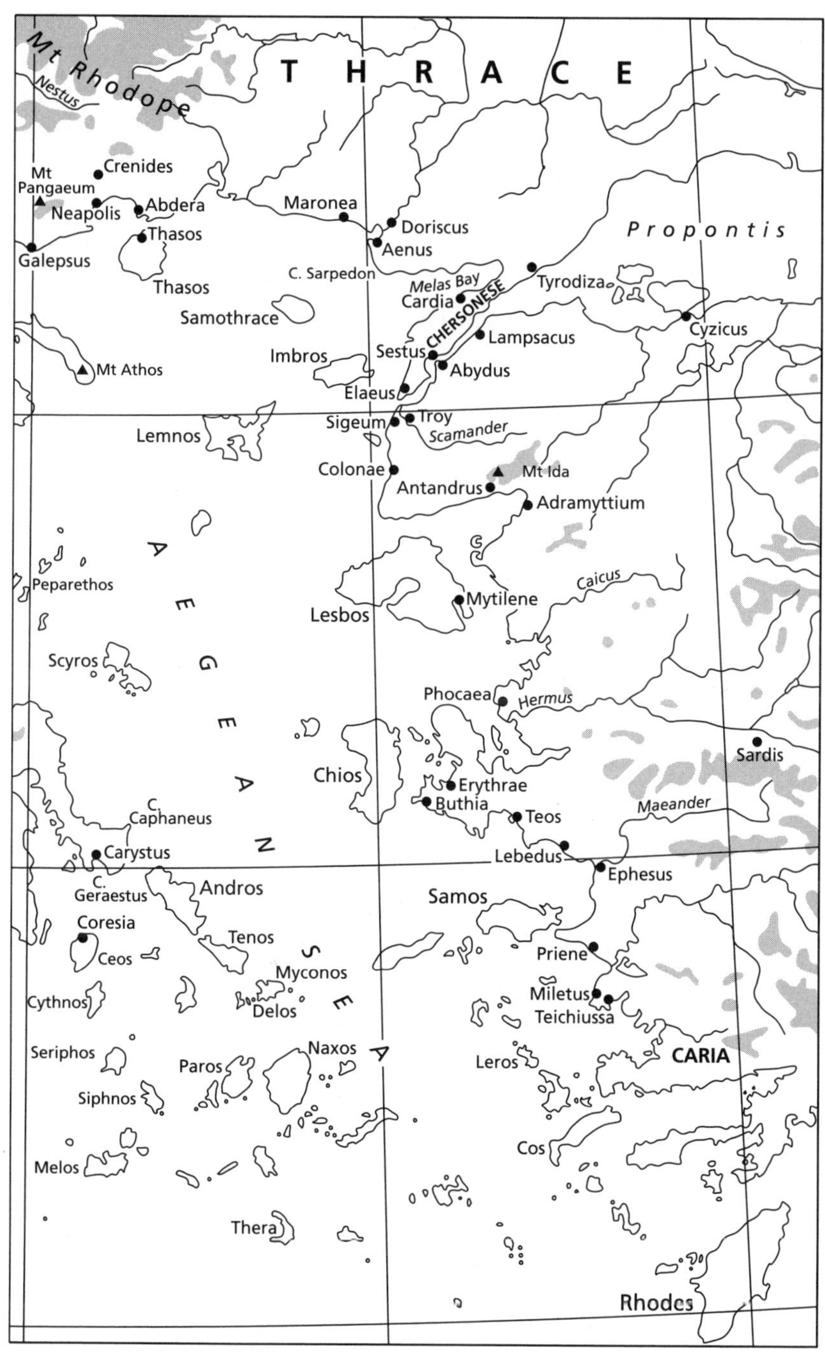
Mt Rhodope
Nestus
THRACE
Mt Pangaeum
Crenides
Neapolis
Abdera
Thasos
Galepsus
Thasos
Samothrace
Maronea
Doriscus
Aenus
C. Sarpedon
Melas Bay
Cardia
CHERSONESE
Tyrodiza
Propontis
Cyzicus
Lampsacus
Sestus
Abydus
Imbros
Mt Athos
Elaeus
Sigeum
Troy
Scamander
Lemnos
Colonae
Mt Ida
Antandrus
Adramyttium
AEGEAN SEA
Peparethos
Lesbos
Mytilene
Caicus
Scyros
Phocaea
Hermus
Sardis
Chios
Erythrae
Buthia
Teos
Maeander
C. Caphaneus
Carystus
Lebedus
Ephesus
C. Geraestus
Andros
Samos
Coresia
Tenos
Ceos
Myconos
Priene
Cythnos
Delos
Miletus
Teichiussa
Seriphos
Naxos
Paros
Leros
CARIA
Siphnos
Cos
Melos
Thera
Rhodes

He notes, for example, that "irrational daring was considered courage and loyalty to one's party" (3.82.4). The slippery language of the Epidamnian Revolution, although less well discussed, is perhaps even more revealing, asking, as it does, who counts as Epidamnian. The language Thucydides uses for the Epidamnian factioneers encourages his readers to ask who and what constitute a city, on what criteria, and in whose judgment? These questions are important because it is clear from the speeches Thucydides gives us from the belligerents on the eve of the war that Athens is a unique city. The speeches confirm Thucydides' hint in the *Archaeology* that Athens' strength lies as much in intangibles as in material sources of power. Furthermore, we learn that the Athenians are distinguished especially by their ability to conceptualize their city and to divorce their idea of it from its actual territory. The story of Epidamnus' dissolution encourages readers to wonder if all Athenians view their city so distinctively, and also to consider what happens to a people who voluntarily separate themselves from their home territory.

ATHENS' POWER IS INTANGIBLE

After recounting the "publicly expressed accusations" between Athens and the Peloponnesians regarding Epidamnus, Corcyra, and Potidaea, Thucydides presents four speeches from a congress held at Sparta in 432 to determine if the Athenians had broken the terms of the Thirty Years' Peace that ended the so-called First Peloponnesian War in 446. Although many Peloponnesian allies raised grievances against Athens, Thucydides gives an account only of the speech of the Corinthians, who were angered because the Athenians had helped Epidamnus' mother-city Corcyra in its dispute with Corinth over Epidamnus. The Corinthians' speech paints the Athenians as a dangerous and alien people, unique in their daring and their unorthodox attitudes.[8]

The Corinthians complain of "insolence" they have suffered from the Athenians (1.68.2), but they lay the blame on the Spartans. "You are the

[8] As Kagan (1969, 290) remarks, the Corinthians' speech is exaggerated. Nevertheless, as Edmunds puts it (1975, 89–90), it "provides the terms and the concepts by which both Thucydides in his own voice . . . and also the actors of the *History* understand events."

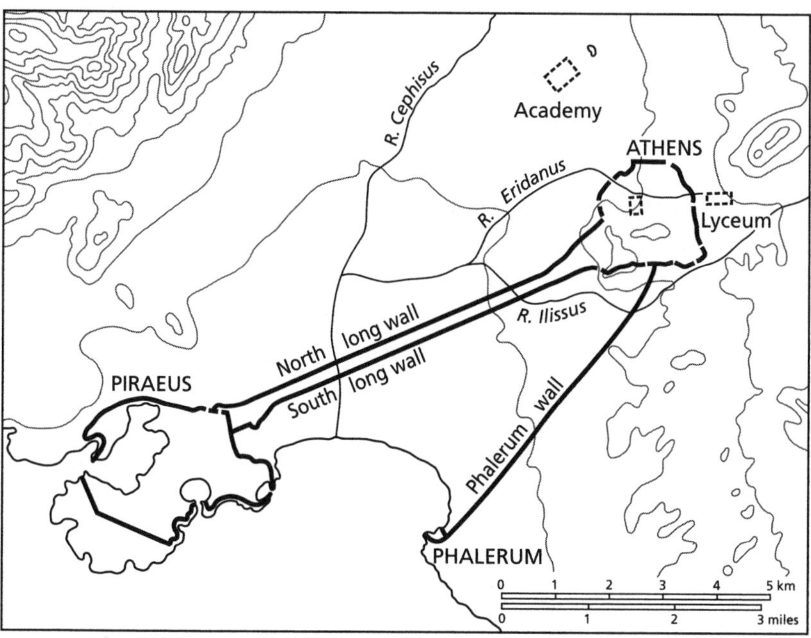

Map 2. Athens, Piraeus, and the Long Walls.

ones responsible for these things," they complain. "For you in the first place allowed them to fortify their city after the Persian war and later to build the Long Walls" (1.69.1). The Corinthians' first image of Athens focuses on its material strength – the fortification walls of the city center, the *asty*, and the so-called "Long Walls" that ran down from the *asty* to the Athenians' harbor towns of Piraeus and Phaleron (see Map 2). The Corinthians thus follow the initial focus of the *Archaeology*, which stresses the prime importance of walls and physical strength. Yet just as Thucydides undercuts the importance of the physical when he says in the *Archaeology* that one would mistake the power of Sparta and Athens if one judged by appearances, so too the Corinthians shift their focus. The Spartans' greatest fault, according to the Corinthians, was that they "seem never to have reckoned up against what sort of people the contest against the Athenians will be and how much and how completely they differ from you" (1.70.1). The real danger to Sparta, and the real source of Athens' power, that is, comes from the distinctive character of its people, according to the Corinthians.

The Corinthians then go on to classify how different the Athenians are from the Spartans. The Corinthians single out in particular the Athenians' devotion to their city – and their willingness to sacrifice themselves for it – and their daring and innovative qualities of mind. Athenians, according to the Corinthians, are "revolutionaries, quick both to contrive things and to put them into effect" (1.70.2). The Spartans, on the other hand, "never discover anything and don't even accomplish what's necessary" (1.70.2). The Athenians take risks. "They are bold beyond their power, take risks beyond good judgment, and are confident even in the midst of dangers," the Corinthians charge, whereas it is the Spartans' nature "to do less than your power would have allowed, and as far as resolution goes, to trust not even in certainties, and to think that you will never be free of dangers" (1.70.3). The Athenians' intangible character, that is, allows them to use their power to greater effect than the Spartans. Where the Athenians are quick, the Spartans delay; where the Spartans are "complete homebodies" (ἐνδημοτάτους), the Athenians are "always abroad" (ἀποδημηταὶ, 1.70.4). Furthermore, according to the Corinthians, "the Athenians use their bodies for their city's sake as if they were utterly foreign" (ἔτι δὲ τοῖς μὲν σώμασιν ἀλλοτριωτάτοις ὑπὲρ τῆς πόλεως χρῶνται, 1.70.6). And if they fail to accomplish something they have set their minds on, the Athenians "consider themselves to have been robbed of their household property" (οἰκείων στέρεσθαι ἡγοῦνται, 1.70.7).

The Corinthians here employ a particularly Thucydidean usage of the adjective *oikeios* – "belonging to the house or household" and thus by extension "one's own." As Gregory Crane has shown, Thucydides uses *oikos* (house or household) "relatively infrequent[ly]";[9] his focus on the political does not include much talk of actual houses or families.[10] By contrast, Thucydides uses *oikeios* (belonging to the house or household) quite often, but in a very particular way. More than 60 percent of the time, Thucydides applies it "to one's homeland or ethnic group as a whole (rather than simply one's personal home or family)." Thus, "in most cases when Thucydides says that a thing or person is *oikeios*, he

[9] Crane 1996, 24.

[10] Crane 1996, 25. Kinship shows up only to make dramatic points about "disaster . . . or a breakdown in society."

means that this entity belongs to a particular polis."[11] Thucydides uses *oikeios* "in such a way as to assert the primacy of *polis* over *oikos*, and to imply that the city-state has subsumed the individual household."[12]

The Corinthians' use of *oikeios* here, however, has a further peculiarity. They say that the Athenians "consider themselves to have been robbed of their household property" if they don't accomplish something they have set their minds on. The Corinthians certainly use *oikeios* to mean belonging to the *polis* of Athens rather than to an individual. What is especially striking in their image, however, is their use of this "belonging" word for things that emphatically do not belong to Athens. The Athenians feel robbed, but of things that are not theirs – things that they have failed to attain. In the Corinthians' presentation, wishing and planning for something makes the Athenians think it is already theirs; if, in the end, they don't get it, they feel robbed "of their household property." The Athenians may be led to feel so because, according to the Corinthians, "they alone both hope for and have equally whatever they set their minds on because of the speed of their attempt upon whatever they decide" (1.70.7). However, what the Athenians feel robbed of – what they consider their "household property" – actually belongs to someone else. With this image, the Corinthians manage to convey that the Athenians do not judge well what belongs to them and what does not.

This sense of confusion is confirmed by what the Corinthians say about the Athenians' bodies. According to the Corinthians, the Athenians use their bodies on behalf of the *polis* "as if they were utterly foreign" (ἔτι δὲ τοῖς μὲν σώμασιν ἀλλοτριωτάτοις ὑπὲρ τῆς πόλεως χρῶνται). That which is most personal, that which most belongs to them as individuals – their own bodies – the Athenians give over to the city "as if utterly foreign." Furthermore, they treat their minds as "most belonging to the house" – read *polis* – "for action on the city's behalf" (τῇ δὲ γνώμῃ οἰκειοτάτῃ ἐς τὸ πράσσειν τι ὑπὲρ αὐτῆς, 1.70.6). The Corinthians here clearly foreshadow Pericles' image of the *polis* of Athens as "a city now conceived as primary, over and against both the family and piety."[13] Yet they also suggest that the Athenians have no

[11] Crane 1996, 145.
[12] Crane 1996, 24.
[13] Orwin (1994, 15, n. 1), citing Edmunds (1975, 44–70).

clear boundary between things that are theirs or their city's and things that are not. In contrast to the "homebody" Spartans, the Athenians, after all, are "always abroad." "It is a city of such a sort," the Corinthians tell the Spartans in summary, "that stands opposed to you" (1.71.1).[14]

The Corinthians' presentation of the Athenians is particularly revealing because the Athenians they describe seem to ignore or transcend the dichotomy of "the near and the far." David Young first discussed the common theme of "the superiority of the near or present to the far or absent" in relation to Pindar's Third Pythian ode.[15] In that poem, Pindar tells the story of Coronis, the mother of Asclepius, who, "like many another . . . hungered for things remote." Pindar describes such foolish folk thus: "There are some, utterly shiftless, who always look ahead, scorning the present, hunting the wind of doomed hopes."[16] Coronis's particular version of this failing was to lie "in the arms of a stranger," although she had already lain with Apollo.[17] As Young describes it, the theme "assumes a variety of forms: indigenous/foreign, one's own property/others' property, inside the house/outside, present time/future time, etc."[18] The *topos* argues that in contrast with those who "indulge in a fatal passion for what [they] do not have,"[19] wise men "refrain[] from wishes for distant, impossible things while using to the full what is possible and accessible."[20]

If read against this dichotomy, the Athenians, who, according to the Corinthians, are always abroad and confuse their own and others' things, would seem to be living dangerously. But the Corinthians do

[14] Both Greenwood (2006, 49) and Rood (1998b, 45) emphasize that as the narrative progresses, it will reveal that the Athenians and Spartans are not quite so different as the Corinthians claim. Nowhere, however, does the narrative suggest that the Peloponnesians in any way share the Athenians' conflation of their own and others' things.

[15] Young 1968, 49, n. 1.

[16] Pindar, Pythian 3.21–23, Nisetich, trans.

[17] Pindar, Pythian 3.27.

[18] Young 1968, 49, n. 1. Young catalogues a number of examples of the theme in his Appendix 1. He includes Thucydides in his appendix, but lists only a few passages from books 5 and 6.

[19] Kitto (1966, 327) in reference to Pindar's and Nicias' warnings. Kitto, too, focuses for the theme on the later books of Thucydides.

[20] Young 1968, 49.

not suggest that the Athenians are fools or that they will suffer for this failing.[21] Rather, the Athenians' restlessness and boundary confusion are two of the sources of the Athenians' threatening power. The Corinthians make it clear that it is by acting this way and being such a city that the Athenians have attained such strength, "for they believe that they will acquire something by being away . . . and when they conquer their enemies they go forth the furthest but when they are bested they fall back the least" (1.70.4).

In the *Pentekontaetia* that follows soon after the Corinthians' speech, Thucydides confirms their analysis precisely with regard to the connection the Corinthians draw between the Athenians' strength and their willingness to be away from home. First, Thucydides tells us that after the great battle of Mycale, Leotychides, king of the Lacedaemonians and the leader of the Greek forces at Mycale, "returned home" (ἀπεχώρησεν ἐπ' οἴκου), but the Athenians and the Ionians remained abroad to besiege Sestos. Only after they captured it did they sail home (1.89.2). Then, after Pausanias was recalled in disgrace and the allies would no longer accept a Spartan in command, the Lacedaemonians decided not to send any more men out, "fearing that those going abroad (οἱ ἐξιόντες) would be corrupted" (1.95.7). Finally, Thucydides tells his readers that the Athenians were able to assume control of the Hellenic league because the allies shirked campaigns. Instead of contributing ships, the allies contributed money, which merely served to increase the Athenians' navy, all because the allies "did not want to be away from home" (ἵνα μὴ ἀπ' οἴκου ὦσι, 1.99.3). In Thucydides' fundamental account of how Athens acquired its empire, home looms large.[22] Repeatedly, Thucydides makes it clear that the Athenians' strength grew from their unusual willingness to be away from home.

The Corinthians do give some hint that the Athenians may be overreaching. The Athenians, they say, are "bold beyond their power, take risks beyond good judgment and are hopeful even in the midst of

[21] Cf. Crane (1992, 245): "the Corinthians exhibit no confidence that ἄτη [rash madness] will put a stop to Athenian success."

[22] Cf. Rood 1998b, 235. The Spartans' lack of interest in an overseas empire is not the result only of innate moderation, however. The Spartans must be "homebodies" because of the constant danger of a helot revolt. Cf. Bruell (1974, 15).

dangers" (αὖθις δὲ οἱ μὲν καὶ παρὰ δύναμιν τολμηταὶ καὶ παρὰ γνώμην κινδυνευταὶ καὶ ἐν τοῖς δεινοῖς εὐέλπιδες, 1.70.3). This, if true, might suggest that the Athenian character will lead to disaster, especially if we read "hope" here as the destructive hope that figures as part of the *logos/ergon* (word/deed) antithesis elucidated by Adam Parry. In his reading, word stands against deed, truth stands against fiction, that which is here and now (*huparchonta/paronta*) stands against that which may be in the future (*mellonta*),[23] and "blind hope in an uncertain future" stands against the present reality.[24] *Huparchonta* "are the real things that are, and are at hand now. *Mellonta* are things one plans, hopes to get, things that exist only in conception."[25]

Later, especially in the Sicilian Expedition, the Athenians will be done in by hope, and Thucydides wields the "theme of the near and the far" against them with great art. For example, in his description of its departure for Sicily, Thucydides says that the doomed Athenian fleet was celebrated in part "because it was the longest voyage from home ever attempted and with the greatest hope for the future in contrast to the present circumstances" (ἐπὶ μεγίστῃ ἐλπίδι τῶν μελλόντων πρὸς τὰ ὑπάρχοντα ἐπεχειρήθη, 6.31.6). This comment is not designed to allay worries. As Young notes, Thucydides' use of the theme "emerges magnificently" in the Sicilian books,[26] and it spells doom for the Athenians. Yet in the Corinthians' speech it is not the Athenians who will suffer for hoping; rather, those who trust in the Spartans have already suffered because of the Spartans' failure to recognize brute reality: "In fact, placing hopes on you has already destroyed men who were unprepared on account of trusting you" (1.69.5). The Athenians, by contrast, tellingly merge hope and actuality. For "they alone," according to the Corinthians, "both hope and have in like manner whatever they set their minds on because of the speed of their attempt upon whatever they decide" (1.70.7). The Athenians' innate quickness allows them to bridge the gap between hoping and having. Thucydides closely links the two verbs in his sentence in order to underscore the point, as if to

[23] In this element, of course, the *logos/ergon* antithesis is a variant on the theme of the "near and the far" which, as Young (1968, 49, n. 1) notes, exists in one form as "present time/future time."

[24] Parry 1981, 186–87.

[25] Parry 1981, 74.

[26] Young 1968, 120, n. 18.

suggest that for the Athenians alone there is no dichotomy between hoping and having: μόνοι γὰρ ἔχουσί τε ὁμοίως καὶ ἐλπίζουσιν ἃ ἂν ἐπινοήσωσι.[27] The Athenians' (only apparent?) liberation from the constraints of "the theme of the near and the far" serves to underscore how very different they are from their neighbors.[28]

In their speech, the Corinthians do not spend much time rehearsing their grievances against Athens or detailing the military resources that the Spartans will need to overcome. Their focus is on the people of Athens and their psychological and spiritual resources, all of which the Corinthians anthropomorphize into the "sort of city" Athens is. According to the Corinthians, the real power of Athens lies in something quite different from the sources of strength that Thucydides detailed in the *Archaeology*. They focus on the Athenians' speed and daring and on their apparent ability to transcend the boundaries between their own and others' things, between near and far, between hope and fact.[29]

"WE ROSE UP FROM A CITY THAT NO LONGER EXISTED"

Thucydides' text contrives to validate the Corinthians' assessment of the intangible nature of Athens' strength and the Athenians' rejection of traditional boundaries. Thucydides reports that certain Athenian

[27] Ober (1998, 90), as if echoing the Corinthians' assessment, remarks that "Athenian sea power narrowed to the disappearing point the gap between desire and fact, between the wish of the policymaker that something should occur and the accomplishment of that wish in the material world."

[28] Crane (1992, 255) comments, "Athens was a historical phenomenon which had, at least temporarily, shattered the conditions which bound others to follow the traditional subsistence ethic of the pre-industrial agrarian society," and explains that (253) "independence from the agricultural produce of their own land was almost as novel as if they had suddenly acquired the ability to fly. . . . " Thus the Corinthians are correct in arguing that the Athenians are a wholly new and different people.

[29] The Athenians the Corinthians describe have been variously read. Parry (1981, 129) remarks that "one could not have asked for a more sympathetic account of the Athenian temper." Palmer (1992, 47) argues that "readers cannot but sense that the Corinthians, begrudgingly to be sure, admire their dynamic adversary." Cornford (1907, 167), on the other hand, calls the Athenian character "a dangerous temperament . . . peculiarly liable to be carried away in the flush of success."

ambassadors "happened" to be in Sparta at the time of the congress, and they asked leave to address the gathering after the Corinthians had spoken. In the speech that Thucydides gives them (1.73–78), the Athenians adopt a point of view similar to that of the Corinthians. What the Peloponnesians needed to understand, according to the Athenians, was "against what sort of a city the contest will be set for you if you do not deliberate well" (1.73.3). Like the Corinthians, the Athenians suggest that their city is unique and perhaps not fully comprehended by the Spartans.

In his explanatory introduction to this speech, Thucydides says that the Athenians' purpose was "to demonstrate how great the power of their city was" (1.72). Yet the Athenians detail no resources and make no specific comparisons between the power of Athens and the Peloponnesians (as the Spartan king Archidamus, the Corinthians, and Pericles all will do in later speeches). Instead, they begin their speech with a focus on the daring and innovation they showed in the Persian wars. The contrast between Thucydides' prefatory statement and the Athenians' focus at the beginning of their speech reinforces the notion that a great part of Athens' power consists not in resources but in spirit.[30] Apparently the Athenians never tired of telling the story of the Persian wars because it provided so important a lesson about Athens and its power: "It is absolutely necessary to speak of the Persian wars and all those things which you know well," they insisted, "even if it is rather annoying for us always to be bringing it up" (1.73.2). The lesson the Athenians teach focuses on their radical decision to abandon their city in Attica in the face of the Persians' advance yet to fight them from their ships.

[30] De Romilly (1947/1963, 267–70) claimed that because the theme of "the importance of Athenian power" was absent, this meant that Thucydides later replaced the portion of the speech that covered that topic with the second half of the speech we now possess. Stahl (1966/2003, 44) is doubtful, and most such compositional arguments are rejected today. Orwin (1994, 45), following L. Strauss (1964, 170–172), argues that the Athenians *are* expressing their power "through the very boldness of that defense." Strauss himself (170) points out that the Athenians at Sparta spoke on their own initiative. That is, it is not just the words of their speech that demonstrate boldness, but also their independent decision to make one.

"We and our whole people," they remind their listeners, "went on board ship and joined in the battle for Salamis" (ἐσβάντες ἐς τὰς ναῦς πανδημεὶ ἐν Σαλαμῖνι ξυνναυμαχῆσαι, 1.73.4). They go on:

When no one came to help us on land, with all the states up to us already enslaved, after abandoning our city and sacrificing our household property we thought it right that we should not desert the common cause of the remaining allies or, by scattering, become useless to them, but thought it right that we go on board ship and face the danger (1.74.2).

The Ambassadors then define exactly what was so special about the Athenians' actions:

You came to help from cities that were still inhabited and for the sake of living in them in the future, since you were afraid for yourselves for the most part and not for us (when we were still whole, at least, you didn't appear). We, on the other hand, rose up from a city that no longer existed, and facing the danger on behalf of a city that had little hope of existing, we joined in saving both you and ourselves (1.74.3).

And they remind their audience how important the Athenians' courage was to all of Greece:

If, like others, fearing for our territory we had made terms with the Mede[31] earlier or if later, thinking ourselves lost, we had not dared to go on board ship, there would have no longer been any need for you to fight at sea, since you did not have sufficient ships, but the war would have proceeded easily for him just as the barbarian wished (1.74.4).

The Athenians remark that they provided "three very useful elements: the largest number of ships, the most intelligent general and the most courageous zeal" (1.74.1). They later repeat that they "displayed the utmost zeal and daring" (1.74.2) and sum up this part of their speech with the question, "On account of our zeal then and the intelligence of our judgment, are we not then worthy, Lacedaemonians, of the empire we have and not to be so excessively resented by the Hellenes?" (1.75.1).

[31] The Greeks often call the Persians as a group "the Mede," although "Medes" are properly only a subgroup of the Persian empire.

The Athenians' speech focuses on their daring, resolution, and ability. They do not define power by physical resources.[32]

The Athenians' proof of their zeal is their radical and daring decision to abandon their city in the face of the Mede's advance, take to their ships, and fight on despite the loss of their territory. The city survived because the Athenians, urged on by Themistocles, recognized that the true city lay, in some way, in the men and in their identification with it. The Athenians and Themistocles conceptualized the city and recognized that "the city" could continue to exist despite the devastation of its territory and the destruction of its walls. Thucydides' language is very strong. The Athenians "abandoned their city" (ἐκλιπόντες τὴν πόλιν) and "sacrificed their household property, their *oikeia*" (τὰ οἰκεῖα διαφθείραντες). They fought on, in fact, on behalf of "a city that no longer existed" (ἀπό τε τῆς οὐκ οὔσης ἔτι).[33]

No other city saw the possibility that the Athenians did of freeing themselves from concern for their land and fighting for a lost city – a "city that no longer existed."[34] When faced with the apparently overwhelming onslaught of the Persians, almost all of the states north of Athens capitulated when their land was lost. Not so the Athenians, for Themistocles had, in effect, freed their city from physical bonds. Even if the city were razed to the ground, the *polis* would still continue as an idea held in the minds of the Athenians themselves. As Steven Forde explains, "perhaps one of the things they discovered as a body on their ships was the enormous potential of what we may call purely human power, standing on its own and bereft of its traditional supports,

[32] Cf. L. Strauss (1964, 171): "these qualities – the superior intelligence of their leaders and the daring zeal of the people – they intimate, and not the navy, are the core of Athens' power." Forde (1986, 434) emphasizes how closely the Athenians are linked to "daring." Daring "seems to describe precisely the frenetic, astoundingly bold, even reckless quality the Athenians display in their many far-flung enterprises."

[33] The so-called "Themistocles decree," which at least purports to be a copy of the evacuation order of 480, by contrast uses a "euphemism" (Jameson 1960, 202, n. 6) when it claims to "entrust the city to Athena the Protectress of Athens...." (trans. Jameson 1963, 386, modified). The city does not here "not exist." It rests in the hands of the gods. Furthermore, some men remain on the acropolis. The entire city, that is, is not abandoned.

[34] Only the Athenians, as Euben (1986, 361) writes, could "think theoretically."

terrestrial or otherwise."[35] The Athenians were able to seize their only chance of success in the Persian war and fight on behalf of a city "that no longer existed." And this daring act allowed their small hope that it would exist again to become a reality.

There are important points of contact between the Athenians' portrait of themselves and the immediately preceding characterization of the Corinthians. The Athenians, of course, confirm the Corinthians' claim that they are quick, innovative, and daring. They also confirm that they have a particular view of household property and a special relation to hope. As we learned above, the Corinthians charge that if the Athenians fail to get something that actually belongs to someone else, they react as if they have been "robbed of their household property (*oikeia*)" (1.70.7). This reveals both an innate acquisitiveness and a confusion on the part of the Athenians regarding what is theirs and what is not. This implies, in turn, both a stronger-than-normal connection to others' goods as well as a weaker-than-normal connection to their own. In the Athenians' speech, we find both confirmation and explanation for this phenomenon.

The Athenians alone were able to bring themselves to "abandon their city" and "sacrifice their *oikeia*." They did not, "like others, fear for their territory" (1.74.4). The Athenians already show here a unique ability to separate themselves from their land and *oikeia*. The success of their radical thinking would, in turn, only exacerbate this tendency. The Athenians' Persian experience would also tend to confirm in them the power of beneficent hope. Because they were not tied to their land or *oikeia*, the Athenians did not despair or give in but chose to hope. Rising up "from a city that no longer existed," they "faced the danger on behalf of a city that had little hope of existing." But their hope prevailed.

These phrases resonate with the "theme of the near and the far." Yet the Athenians' experience again confounds the axiom. By the terms of the pattern, men who put their hope in things that do not exist are bound to fail. Thus later in the war, when the Athenians try to persuade the Melians to join the Athenian empire voluntarily because they have no means of resistance, yet the Melians resist anyway, the Athenians complain that "you alone, as you seem to us from these debates at least, judge things to come to be more clear than what you can see and in your

[35] Forde 1989, 25.

wishful thinking gaze at things unseen as if they have already occurred" (5.113). But at Salamis the Athenians bet their all on their hope in an insubstantial future and won. Hence the Corinthians judge that the Athenians both "hope and have" (1.70.7).

Three times in this speech the Athenians use the same phrase to describe their daring, transformative action. They "went on board ship" (ἐσβῆναι ἐς τὰς ναῦς). Tim Rood calls this one of the "catch-phrases that emerged from Athens' resistance to Persia" and argues that when Thucydides uses it for Athenians elsewhere in his work, he means to suggest a continuity in both strategy and policy with "the spirit of 480."[36] That spirit, as the Athenians at Sparta revealed, was the ability to redefine the *polis* as the people themselves, and leave land and homes behind in order to "go on board ship" to fight for a city that they somehow carried with them.[37] This power of conception, then, becomes one of Athens' collective strengths: "the Athenian capacity to think of the world as other than it is is a resource Sparta lacks."[38]

Thucydides' Athenians are careful to link this spirit to all of the Athenians and to present Athens as united in the daring redefinition of the city: "We and our whole people (πανδημεί) went on board ship and joined in the battle for Salamis" (1.73.4). This presentation of the decision, of course, does not conform to Herodotus' version of the story. According to Herodotus, Themistocles' interpretation of an oracle from Delphi persuaded the majority of Athenians to stake all on "the wooden wall" of the fleet and a naval battle at "divine Salamis" (Hdt. 7.141–143). However, Themistocles did not persuade everyone, and not all Athenians "went on board ship" to face the danger. Some Athenians thought the oracle's "wooden wall" referred not, as Themistocles said, to Athens' ships, but to an archaic structure on the Acropolis, so they barricaded themselves there in the expectation that it alone would be "a stronghold" for Athens (7.141.3–142). All the Athenians in Herodotus do not "abandon the *polis*."

[36] Rood 1999, 151–52.

[37] Gomme, 1945, *s.v.* 1.74.2, by contrast, calls it "a very trite phrase on Athenian lips," but concedes it "marks the turning-point in Athenian history." So Forde (1989, 20): "it seems that this particular moment or action somehow transformed the character of the city of Athens."

[38] Euben 1986, 376.

As Simon Hornblower points out, Thucydides "knew Herodotus' text very well." There are "occasions, in narrative and speeches, when Thucydides would be barely intelligible, or actually unintelligible, to a reader who did not know Herodotus very well."[39] Thucydides, that is, "expects his readers to be familiar with Herodotus."[40] Thus Thucydides would presumably expect his readers to be aware of Herodotus' dramatic story of dissension in Athens regarding how best to defend (and understand) the *polis*. If so, the way Thucydides tells the story is all the more significant. The story in Thucydides emphasizes (if it does not exaggerate) the totality of the abandonment of the city, land, and *oikeia*, as well as the degree of cohesion in the city regarding this radical decision. There is no disagreement, and no one hopes to preserve the land. The city is united, and all Athenians display "the spirit of 480."[41] Nevertheless, even here there are hints that if the city is portable or carried in the men, there is the danger of disagreement, dissolution, and the end of the Athens in Attica.

Directly after the Athenians remind their audience that they alone abandoned their city and sacrificed their *oikeia*, they say that they "thought it right that we should not desert the common cause of the remaining allies or, by scattering, become useless to them" (1.74.2). According to Herodotus (8.62), in order to compel the Peloponnesian forces to fight at Salamis instead of making a stand with the land forces further south, below Athens, at the isthmus of Corinth, Themistocles threatened to remove the Athenian forces (and the Athenians) not only from the war, but from Greece itself. There was an oracle, he said, that decreed that the Athenians must colonize the city of Siris in Italy, and if the Greeks did not fight to save Athens, Themistocles warned, the Athenians would pack up their households and immediately sail there. Themistocles threatened, that is, that the reconceptualized, portable Athenian *polis* might abandon Greece altogether and relocate in Italy.

39 Hornblower 1992, 141. For Thucydides' allusions to Herodotus, see now Rood 1998a and 1999 and Rogkotis 2006.

40 Hornblower 1991, *s.v.* 1.74.1.

41 Euben (1986, 364) points out that Aeschylus, too, told a different story than did Thucydides. The messenger in the *Persians* (349) says that "the ramparts of the city remain impregnable." Euben explains, "Greek power and freedom remains tied to the land, household and ancestral hearth."

The Athenians in Thucydides hint at an even worse possibility – that the "city that no longer existed" might actually cease to exist if the Athenians did not remain united (πανδημεί) but took different positions and "scattered."

Indeed, as Hornblower notes, the Athenians' claim at Sparta that their ancestors had fought "for a city that no longer existed" "recalls the sneer of Adeimantus the Corinthian at Themistocles as a 'man without a city'" recounted by Herodotus (8.61.1).[42] Adeimantus wanted to prevent Themistocles from participating in the debate over where to meet the Persians because he was a city-less man. In Adeimantus' view, the loss of Attica and the physical city of Athens meant the loss of the city. Themistocles and the Athenians, however, were well able to conceive of a city existing even when it did not. This ability saved Athens (and, indeed, Greece) in the Persian wars. Nevertheless, Adeimantus' taunt hints again at the dangers inherent in the Athenians' flexible conception of Athens. Might not all Athenians become "city-less"?[43]

There is another curious element in the Athenians' treatment of "the spirit of 480." When discussing their subjects, the Athenians say, "Under the Mede, of course, they endured far more terrible sufferings, but for our rule to seem harsh is only natural; it is always the present situation that is oppressive for subjects" (1.77.5). As Hans-Peter Stahl notes, "the Athenians freely admit that *they themselves have taken on the role of the Persians, the arch-enemy* of the Greeks (against whom their acceptance of hegemony was originally directed – for the freedom of the Greeks!)."[44] The Athenians' speech at Sparta describes "the turning point in Athenian history"[45] but suggests that in addition to making the Athenians nautical, it set forces in motion that transformed the

[42] Hornblower 1991, *s.v.* 1.74.3.

[43] So Forde (1989, 24): "It would be a real question within Greek piety whether a city could have any being at all under such circumstances; and this in fact seems to be behind the anonymous Athenians' emphasis on the fact that the Athenians did not simply disperse, did not consider the city to have been ruined or dissolved, and joined the common fight although they were issuing in effect from a city that was no more (1.74.2–4)."

[44] Stahl 1966/2003, 49. Italics Stahl.

[45] Gomme 1945, *s.v.* 1.74.2.

Athenians into their enemies.[46] The Athenians' speech links "the spirit of 480" fundamentally with the Athenians' ability to redefine their *polis* and sever their connection to their land and households. At the same time, their speech intimates that their very strength holds within it dangers for the Athenians and their city.[47]

THE ATHENIANS WILL NOT BE "SLAVES TO THEIR LAND"

The first two speeches at the Spartan congress, those of the Corinthians and Athenians, focused more on the character of the Athenians than on their military resources. The next speaker, King Archidamus of Sparta, who spoke only after the Lacedaemonians asked all outsiders to depart, does give an account of the resources of both sides, and he includes as one of their strategic resources the Athenians' unusual attitude to their land. He makes explicit what the Corinthians had only insinuated.[48]

Archidamus begins with a focus on the equipment of war. He reminds the Peloponnesians that the Athenians, in addition to their wide naval experience, were very experienced at sea and most excellently equipped in all other things, with wealth both public and private, with ships, and horses and weapons and with a population as big as exists in no other land in Hellas, and furthermore they have many allies who pay them tribute (1.80.3).

The Spartans, on the other hand, had no navy, no wealth, and no public funds. What was worse, their clear superiority in heavy infantry would get them nowhere, according to Archidamus, because merely invading and devastating Attica would not win the war for them. "Perhaps someone might take heart because we have the advantage of them in weapons and numbers, so that we can repeatedly plunder their land" (1.81.1), Archidamus says. But he immediately discounts this thinking when he notes that the Athenians "have a great deal of other land which

[46] The assimilation of the Athenians to the Persians is a major theme of the Sicilian books.

[47] So Forde (1989, 23) says that by becoming nautical, "the Athenians severed in some way their connections with all the fixed things that the life of a city normally revolves around, that normally serve as its stable conservative base."

[48] See Tompkins 1993 for a stylistic analysis of this speech.

they rule and they import by sea what they lack" (1.81.2). Archidamus here suggests that this other land can compensate for land lost to or damaged by Spartan invasion, and he warns that the Athenians will never become "slaves to their land" (μήτε τῇ γῇ δουλεῦσαι, 1.81.6).

In the next chapter Archidamus seems to switch course a bit when he suggests that if the Spartans prepare better in future, "perhaps seeing our preparation and our words they would be liable to yield, when they have their land still undamaged and they are taking counsel concerning present goods that are not yet destroyed" (1.82.3). Yet this scenario is "two or three" years in the future, with a Sparta strengthened by additional allies and with increased naval and financial resources (1.82.1). And even then the Athenians' land is a "hostage" that the Spartans would do well to "spare as long as possible" lest they make the Athenians "harder to catch by driving them to desperation" (1.82.4). The result of plundering Attica, then, even after two to three years of further preparations will not be concessions but a more difficult war, according to Archidamus. If the Spartans plunder the Athenians' land now, "while we are unprepared," Archidamus fears the result will be "more shameful and harder to deal with for the Peloponnesians" (1.82.5). Archidamus is thus consistent in his belief in this speech that the Athenians will not be "slaves to their land."[49] Archidamus argues that the Athenians' ideas about their city, and their attitude to their land, gives them the strength to nullify the Spartans' tangible superiority in infantry.

The account of the Persian wars that the Athenian ambassadors had just given supports Archidamus' point. The Persians invaded Attica twice but to no avail. The Athenians emphasized in their speech that at that time they were happy to "abandon their city and sacrifice their *oikeia*" rather than give in (1.74.2). A. W. Gomme remarks that "the speaker might have added that they were ready to do the same again now rather than yield to an enemy."[50] The Athenians' account is "a veiled threat,"[51] but Thucydides leaves it to Archidamus (and then later

[49] I disagree, therefore, with Pelling's (1991, 125) judgment that these two parts of Archidamus' speech "sit[] uncomfortably" together. See below for the blatant contradiction between Archidamus' speech here and his thoughts and actions during the march in Attica.

[50] Gomme 1945, *s.v.* 1.74.2.

[51] Stahl 1966/2003, 46.

to Pericles) to make the connection and warn that the Spartans should not think that things would be any different for them now if they invaded.[52] This also enables Thucydides to have Pericles (and not some unnamed Athenian ambassadors) articulate and announce the Athenian abandonment of their city for this war.

Archidamus' description of the Athenians' unwillingness to be "slaves to their land" is striking in its suggestion that it is weak and slavish to care for one's land and territory, and that the Athenians will easily rise above such impulses.[53] This is especially noteworthy because it comes from an enemy and the king of a people whom Pericles will define, simply, as "farmers" (αὐτουργοί, 1.141.3). Archidamus' phrasing is consistent, on the other hand, with the generally positive presentation of the Athenians' redefinition of their city and their ties to their land and households in the early part of book 1. The so-called *Pentekontaetia* that follows Thucydides' account of the Spartan congress, however, builds on the hints Thucydides has already given that there are dangers inherent in the Athenians' redefinitions.

Thucydides describes the so-called *Pentekontaetia* (his brief narrative of the "fifty years" between the Persian and Peloponnesian Wars) as an account of the way in which the Athenians "came into the circumstances in which they became more powerful" (1.89.1). He refers here to the power that he claims terrified the Spartans into voting for war at the Spartan congress. The first episode Thucydides recounts in the *Pentekontaetia* is the rebuilding of the circuit walls around the city center of Athens, which the Persians had destroyed. The rebuilding occurred despite intense Spartan opposition, according to Thucydides.

52 Archidamus is a tragic "warner" figure like Artabanus in Herodotus, whose advice goes unheeded. For "wise advisors," see Bischoff 1932 and Lattimore 1939.

53 Ober (1985, 182) notes that this passage "suggest[s] that the desire to defend one's land was indeed an unworthy, even slavish, impulse" and implies that this was Thucydides' belief. According to Ober, Pericles was compelled to compromise with his people and so used the cavalry to try to protect rural land. Thucydides, however, in Ober's view, concealed this because "Thucydides' Pericles could not be depicted as making a deal with the rural citizens over a concern so negligible in the greater scheme of things as rural property." Rather, if the argument of this chapter is correct, Thucydides is suggesting that Pericles overlooked the real importance of the Athenians' ties to their land.

Thucydides tells the story in elaborate detail and devotes some one-sixth of the entire *Pentekontaetia* to it. As Richard McNeal notes, "for Thucydides the wall is the ultimate symbol of power." For McNeal, this alone explains the space that Thucydides devotes to this story. "Small wonder," he says, "that he should be so fascinated with Athens' wall and that the description of this prophetic symbol should preface an account of the city's rise to empire."[54] True. But there is more to it than this.

Some scholars, for example, have found Thucydides' account of Sparta's displeasure with Athens' rebuilding suspect. Virtually all cities in Greece were walled except for Sparta, and it is hard to believe that the Spartans would have tried to prevent the Athenians from rebuilding their walls.[55] Furthermore, although Thucydides claims that the Spartans "were secretly vexed" when they learned that the walls had been built, he nevertheless admits that "the Lacedaemonians did not indicate their anger openly to the Athenians" (1.92.1). Thucydides thus claims to know secret Spartan feelings that contradicted their open words and actions. This (suspect?)[56] Spartan anger has no consequences at this point in the history, so there is no point in mentioning it aside from beginning the *Pentekontaetia* on a note of hostility between Athens and Sparta that associates Spartan fear of Athens and the threat of war with the first essential element of radical Athens – the circuit wall of the *asty* or city center of Athens (see Map 2 for the rough location of this circuit wall). The Corinthians, too, in their speech at Sparta began with this point. "You are the ones responsible for these things," they accused the Spartans, "for you in the first place allowed them to fortify their city after the Persian war and later to build the Long Walls" (1.69.1). Walls do signify power, as McNeal notes. In the *Pentekontaetia*, however, they look toward war and even hint at civil war.

According to the *Pentekontaetia*, after the rebuilding of the *asty*, Themistocles next persuaded the Athenians to complete the fortification of the Piraeus with its three excellent natural harbors. The Piraeus was a large Athenian village on the west coast of Attica not far from the

[54] McNeal (1970, 312), cited approvingly by Hornblower (1991, 135), for "Thucydides' motive for including so much on these walls."

[55] See, e.g., Sealey 1976, 240.

[56] Sealey (1976, 240) calls this one of the "suspicious features" of the story. Nevertheless, he thinks the story "more probably distorted than invented."

asty (see Map 2). Themistocles' walls fortified the harbors themselves as well as the village, making the whole highly defensible from attack by land. Thucydides tells us that Themistocles persuaded the Athenians to fortify the Piraeus because, "now that they had become a naval people, he thought that it would be a great help in their acquiring power." Indeed, Thucydides tells us that it was Themistocles "who first dared to tell the Athenians that they had to cleave to the sea" (1.93.3). And so, we are told, were the foundations of the walls of Athens and of the Athenian empire laid.[57]

Thucydides gives a strong hint in this passage, however, that this future on the sea might require divisive sacrifices and changes to the contemporary understanding of Athens:

> Themistocles considered the Piraeus more useful than the upper-city and he regularly advised the Athenians that if they should ever be hard pressed on land they should go down to it and withstand all enemies with their ships (1.93.7).

Themistocles is said here to have prized the Piraeus above the Acropolis and city-center, and he urged the abandonment of the *asty* to preserve a naval vision of Athens based at the Piraeus.[58] This was, of course, Themistocles' strategic judgment of what would best help the city survive a military emergency. Yet Themistocles' apparent ability to easily disregard the city-center of Athens, with its shrines and temples and sacred places, is surprising, and one may wonder whether many Athenians would have been able to follow him in his view.

The Athenians' next renovation project answers this question in the negative. In 458–457, the Athenians decided to build two "Long Walls," one of which would run from Athens down to Piraeus and the other from Athens down to the coast south of Phaleron, thus joining the two fortified sites (1.107.1).[59] The Athenians thus recognized the wisdom

[57] Orwin (1994, 51) notes that Thucydides' Greek here emphasizes the connection between Themistocles' walls and the empire.

[58] Cf. Orwin (1994, 51): "Themistocles appears to have concluded that the success of the city-fleet implied the conversion of the city itself into something resembling a fleet."

[59] The first two "Long Walls" ran from Athens to Piraeus and from Athens to the harbor of Phaleron. Later, "perhaps c. 444–442" (Gomme 1945, *s.v.* 1.107.1), a third "Long Wall" was built parallel to the Piraeus wall, more strictly linking Piraeus with Athens.

of Themistocles' strategic vision and the importance of their port town and their navy to their ambitions, but they were unwilling to abandon the Acropolis and urban center for his vision. The answer was to make the *asty* an adjunct to the Piraeus by tying them together with the Long Walls (see Map 2).

Both Themistocles' judgment of the supreme importance of the Piraeus and the Athenians' decision to build the Long Walls highlight the physical divisions of the *polis* of Athens into *asty*, Piraeus, and countryside. Not surprisingly, Thucydides' *Pentekontaetia* soon gives us intimations of political divisions in Athens as well. All Athenians did not support the new Athens and its dependence on the sea, and this new vision of Athens led not to the increased security that Themistocles had predicted, but rather to *stasis* or factional strife.

When the Spartans were campaigning in central Greece to aid the city of Doris, Thucydides tells us that certain Athenians took advantage of their proximity and "were in communications with them in secret, hoping to put an end to the democracy and to the Long Walls being built" (1.107.4). Scholars have tended to deny or minimize this event. Ernst Badian, for example, is "inclined to doubt [Thucydides'] allegation."[60] Hornblower thinks "some concrete facts surely lay behind the 'allegation'" but remains wary about the motive Thucydides ascribes to the Athenian plotters.[61] Gomme, on the other hand, accepts that the event occurred but downplays its significance by describing the men in question as "a few desperate oligarchs." He does, however, identify their motive when he notes that "the Long Walls meant for them the permanent domination of the democracy by making Athens dependent on the sea."[62]

The Long Walls, of course, did not themselves make Athens dependent on the sea. Rather, the Long Walls assume a reliance on the sea; they imply abandonment of everything outside them to unopposed enemy infantry. Furthermore, reliance on the sea encourages democracy because the masses were necessary to the manning of the ships of Athens' fleet,

[60] Badian 1988, 318, n. 43.

[61] Hornblower 1991, *s.v.* 1.107.4: "we should always be wary when Thucydides gives a statement about motive."

[62] Gomme 1945, *s.v.* 1.107.4.

and the masses, recognizing their importance to the state, demanded a share in its governance.[63] Oligarchs would have every reason to regard the building of the Long Walls as a threat. It seems precipitous, then, to accuse Thucydides of inventing the incident, as Badian does, or to doubt the motive Thucydides reports, as Hornblower does. It is also unclear why Gomme has characterized the "desperate oligarchs" involved as only "a few." Thucydides himself gives no clear indication of the number of Athenians disaffected by the new vision of Athens. He merely refers to "men of the Athenians" (1.107); he does not say how many.

We should wonder, however, why Thucydides chose to include this event in his *Pentekontaetia* (especially if one suspects he has invented it or mistaken the motive). The secret negotiations with the Spartans had no result. The disgruntled Athenians (however many there were) did not betray Athens to an invading Spartan army, and we hear nothing more about the plot. The incident, that is, seems to be wholly without historical effect. Why, then, did Thucydides include it when he had to leave so much that happened out of his text (especially in the *Pentekontaetia*, which covers some forty-five years in sixteen pages in a standard edition)?[64] H. D. F. Kitto judged that "one of [Thucydides'] chief preoccupations must have been to leave things out"; he was "a carver, not a modeler."[65]

Why, then, did Thucydides decide not to carve this apparently insignificant incident away? The answer surely lies in the fact that this passage is Thucydides' first description of faction fighting in Attica (although it does not use any of the Greek verbs or nouns for factional strife per se). Athens had suffered from civil war before the building of the Long Walls, of course. The most notable occasions are Cylon's attempt at tyranny in the seventh century and the faction fighting surrounding the rise of the tyrant Peisistratus and the introduction of democracy in the late sixth century. Although they occurred earlier

[63] The Pseudo-Xenophantic "Old Oligarch" explains it this way (1.2): "there the poor and the people generally are right to have more than the highborn and wealthy for the reason that it is the people who man the ships and impart strength to the city" (trans. Bowersock 1925).

[64] The *Oxford Classical Text*, edited by H. S. Jones. Gomme's "Notes on the *Pentekontaetia*" (Gomme 1945, 361–413) document the many omissions.

[65] Kitto 1966, 261.

chronologically than the event with the Long Walls, none of those events has yet figured in Thucydides' main text when he tells this story.[66]

Thucydides thus contrives that his first mention of political division in Attica (division so wide that it leads to treating with Sparta) arises from a new conception of the city: walled and dependent on the sea rather than on the countryside. The vision of a walled, naval Athens is divisive. Walls here lead not to strength, as in the *Archaeology*, but to division. In the *Archaeology*, in his first mention of Attica in his work, Thucydides notes that the same people had always inhabited the territory, and that it was, because of the poverty of its soil, remarkably free from *stasis* or factional strife (1.2.5). He calls it *astasiaston* (ἀστασίαστον) or "least inclined to *stasis*." The first vision of Athens that Thucydides gives his readers is one of the rooted unity of the people. Themistocles' naval vision of the city, however, counteracts the effect of Attica's soil. This passage links the Long Walls and the vision of Athens dependent on them to *stasis*. It further charges that the new vision of the city changed an essential and beneficial characteristic of Athens. The new conception of Athens, exemplified by the Long Walls, is divisive and results in fundamental and dangerous changes to the city.

Thucydides charges that the tipping point was the building of the Long Walls. The Athenian ambassadors at Sparta, for example, insist that all Athenians joined together in the decision to abandon the city to fight the Persians: "We and our whole people (πανδημεί) went on board ship" (1.73.4). Especially given that Herodotus' account of the same events does not show all Athenians abandoning the physical city, we see an emphasis here on the unity of Athens in its redefinition. That sense of unity continues through the rebuilding of the circuit walls after the war. Thucydides reports that Themistocles told "all the Athenians in the city, altogether (πανδημεί) to build the wall" (1.90.3) and confirms that "in this way the Athenians fortified their city in a brief time" (1.93.1). Thucydides underscores the truth of his account with a rare appeal to visible and tangible proofs: The style of the masonry of the walls, he says, "still now" makes it "clear that the construction was done in a rush"

[66] The murder of Hipparchus by Harmodius and Aristogeiton figures very briefly in the *Archaeology* (1.20.2–3), but the emphasis is not on civil war but on the Athenians' ignorance of the details of the event.

(1.93.2).[67] Thucydides thus gives his readers every reason to believe him when he says that all Athenians joined together in building the circuit wall of Athens as fast as they could. He emphasizes the unity of the city in his dramatic story. "The narrative invites the reader to imagine the pain and the ambition of the Athenians as they tore down what was left of tombs, homes and temples to fortify their ruined city."[68] Yet because nearly all cities had circuit walls, and their rebuilding did not necessarily entail a radical vision of Athens, all the people might well join together to build them. It was radical, however, for Themistocles to judge the Piraeus more important than the *asty.* The Long Walls, furthermore, imagine an Athens that will, in war, abandon Attica for the *asty*-Piraeus corridor and the sea. In this revisioning, Thucydides insists, all Athenians did not concur.

Interestingly, the new vision of Athens was never fully realized before the Peloponnesian War, although the potential to abandon Attica and "go down to the Piraeus and withstand all enemies with their ships," in Themistocles' words, existed as soon as the Long Walls were completed. However, Thucydides demonstrates that when the Athenians were hard-pressed soon after the completion of the Long Walls, they did not follow Themistocles' vision even though they had Pericles to encourage it.

Towards the end of the *Pentekontaetia*, Thucydides reports a serious challenge to Athens' power (1.114–115). In 446, both Megara and Euboea revolted from the Athenian Empire. Pericles crossed over to Euboea to deal with that island's revolt and then learned that in addition to everything else, the Peloponnesians were on the point of invading Attica. Pericles, Thucydides tells us, "quickly brought the army back from Euboea" (1.114.1). The Peloponnesians, under the command of King Pleistoanax, invaded Attica and laid waste the country as far as Eleusis and Thria but then they returned home without going any further (1.114.1–2). In a later point in his text, Thucydides reveals that the Spartans came to believe that King Pleistoanax had been bribed to retreat from Attica during this invasion (2.21.1). However, Thucydides

67 By contrast with Herodotus, Thucydides includes far fewer objects and artifacts in his text. This is in part because, according to Crane (1996, 7), Thucydides wanted his book to be useful in the future, and to retain that usefulness "the text must stand by itself and, as much as possible, contain its own evidence."

68 Stadter 1993, 44.

makes no mention of that belief at this point in his text. Nor does he provide any specific explanation for why the Spartans left Attica. He brings Pericles back from Euboea and then describes the Peloponnesians' invasion as far as Thria and their departure in one sentence. He adds another sentence in which Pericles returns to Euboea and sets things in order and then goes on immediately to explain: "Not long after they returned from Euboea they concluded a thirty-year truce with the Lacedaemonians and their allies, giving back Nisaea, Pagae, Troezen, and Achaea; these places the Athenians held in the Peloponnesus" (1.115.1). Thucydides separates the Spartan withdrawal and the peace by only one sentence and surely expects his readers to require no explicit explanation from him to see that instead of fighting the Spartans in Attica or leaving all of Attica to their devastation and "going on board ship," the Athenians made territorial concessions to them. "The real bribe," as Gomme states, "was the offer to surrender, or to discuss the surrender of, Megara, Troizen, and Achaea."[69] Instead of fighting or withdrawing behind the walls, Athens "had to give up her land empire and some valuable individual possessions."[70]

This event was only fourteen years in the past when Archidamus stirringly warned his Peloponnesian audience at the Spartan congress not to expect the Athenians to be "slaves to their land" (1.81.6). The story the Athenian ambassadors had told about their abandonment of Attica in the Persian wars gave strength to Archidamus' warning. The account Thucydides gives late in the *Pentekontaetia*, on the other hand, undercuts Archidamus' judgment and the Athenian speakers' implicit warning. When Pleistoanax invaded, Thucydides' text reveals, the Athenians were, in fact, slaves enough to their land to cede their "land empire" in order to protect Attica. Why would they not do the same now?[71]

[69] Gomme, 1956a, *s.v.* 2.21.1.

[70] Hornblower 1991, *s.v.* 1.115.1.

[71] Brunt (1965, 264–65) argues that it is reasonable to suppose that the Spartans on the eve of war thought just like this: "they could argue that the invasion of Attica in 446, half-hearted as it seemed to some, had even after the completion of the Long Walls coerced the Athenians into important concessions, and that more systematic and persistent devastations might result in Athens' surrender. . . . It was . . . quite reasonable for them to think that Archidamus' warnings were refuted by the success of 446." Cf. Kelly 1982, 27.

The *Pentekontaetia*, then, offers a powerful corrective to the vision of Athens presented at the Spartan congress, where the ability to redefine the city seemed unrestricted and an (almost) unequivocal source of strength. In the *Pentekontaetia's* story of the building of the Long Walls, however, we see the redefinition of Athens leading to *stasis.* In the last story of the revolt of Euboea and the Spartan invasion, we learn that perhaps Athens is not actually willing to put this radical strategic vision into practice. The *Pentekontaetia* thus primes the readers, as they move into Thucydides' account of the second Spartan congress, to be very curious about whether or not the Athenians will be slaves to their land and with what consequences for their city.

The Spartans called this second congress of their allies to determine whether they should go to war against Athens. This congress reinforces the sense that we must think again about Athens and its strengths and weaknesses. From this congress Thucydides gives his readers a second Corinthian speech that is very different from their first speech. Like Archidamus at the first assembly, the Corinthians focus this time on material strength; but unlike Archidamus, they insist that victory will belong to Sparta and its allies.

The Peloponnesians were superior "in numbers and in experience of war," the Corinthians insist (1.121.2). The Peloponnesians could overcome the Athenians' superiority in naval strength by building up their navy with money from the offerings at Olympia and Delphi. "By taking out such loans," the Corinthians argue, "we could entice away their foreign seamen with higher pay" (1.121.3). Furthermore, the Peloponnesians would soon be able to match the Athenians in naval skill. The Corinthians also suggest specific tactics to the allies. "There are other paths of warfare available to us," they insist, "including causing their allies to revolt . . . and building a fortification in the Attic countryside" (1.122.1).

The Corinthians here counter Archidamus' speech at the earlier Spartan congress and directly challenge the idea that the Athenians will not be "slaves to their land." Whereas the Corinthian speech at the earlier congress had detailed the power of Athens, here they recite the strengths of their own side and rebut Archidamus' gloomy predictions. In particular, they deny Archidamus' contention that invasion will not avail. In doing so, the Corinthians offer a new vision of invasion. They propose a year-round fortification, not the temporary invasion

Archidamus envisioned (or the Persians effected) and also suggest that attacks elsewhere than Attica will bring Athens to its knees. This point–counterpoint between the Corinthians and Archidamus regarding the efficacy of invasion focuses attention on the Athenians' ties to their land and leads the reader to wonder if a fortification like that proposed by the Corinthians would, indeed, make the Athenians "slaves to their own land" (which Archidamus insisted was impossible).

In effect, Archidamus denies that the Athenians are normal and can be defeated by recourse to the traditional military tactics of invasion and hoplite infantry battle in Attica. The Corinthians, by contrast, insist that the Athenians are normal, even if they have to propose an innovative tactic like a permanent fortification or urge focusing on other land entirely in order to counteract their unusual qualities. Thus the two congresses highlight for the reader the issue of how important the land of Attica is to Athens and to the Athenians. The Athenians' ability to redefine their city seems like a source of strength in the Corinthans' first speech and in Archidamus' speech, but the *Pentekontaetia* suggests that it is dangerous and divisive and also that the Athenians may not be as willing to pursue their radical strategic vision as Archidamus expects. Finally, the Corinthians' second speech suggests that there may be ways of countering the Athenians' redefinition and striking at Athens' unorthodox *polis*. All of this serves as background to Thucydides' initial presentation of Pericles and his vision of Athens.

"WE MUST ABANDON OUR LAND AND HOUSES AND SAFEGUARD THE SEA AND THE CITY"

As a result of the second congress, the Spartans sent ambassadors to bring an ultimatum to Athens that there need not be war if the Athenians would "leave the Hellenes free and independent" (1.139.3). This amounted to a Spartan demand that the Athenians give up their "empire" of subject, tribute-paying states. It is only at this point, toward the end of his first book, that Thucydides finally brings Pericles on stage in a speaking role.[72] Thucydides calls Pericles "the first man of

[72] Pericles appears twice in the *Pentekontaetia* in brief accounts in which he does not speak (1.111, 1.114–117).

the Athenians during that time and most able both in speech and in action" (1.139.4) and presents a speech of advice that Pericles gave to the Athenians about the Spartan ultimatum (1.140–144). Because Thucydides uncharacteristically gives Pericles no opposing speaker, he seems, according to Leo Strauss, "unrivalled even among the Athenians of his time."[73]

Pericles' first words emphasize the constancy of his opinion and underscore that the Athenians have heard it all before: "My judgment, Athenians, is always the same." (1.140.1). Thus, in contrast to the Peloponnesians, who argued among themselves about the wisdom of going to war and the best tactics for doing so, Thucydides' Athenians seem to speak, through Pericles, with one unchanging voice.[74] Pericles' constant view was that war was inevitable. Pericles nevertheless argued that the Athenians could accept the coming war without fear, because, he assured them, they would win it. Pericles based this judgment partly on his assessment of Athenian and Peloponnesian material resources. He judged the Athenians as far superior to their enemies because of their financial advantages and their experience in overseas naval warfare.

In its accounting, Pericles' speech echoes or "answers" several of the points made earlier by the Corinthians or Archidamus.[75] Thus Pericles notes (1.141.3), as had Archidamus (1.80.4), that the Peloponnesians had no wealth. They were, furthermore, "inexperienced in lengthy or oversea wars" (1.141.3). Pericles thus confirms the Corinthian accusation that the Spartans were "the most home-bound" (1.70.4). As if to counter the Corinthian claim that the Peloponnesians would soon learn seamanship and could thereby nullify the Athenians' advantage in that area (1.121.2), Pericles remarks that "they will not easily gain expert status on the sea. Not even you who have been practicing ever since the Persian wars have completely accomplished that" (1.142.6–7). Pericles

[73] L. Strauss (1964, 213). West (1973a, 6, and n. 3) emphasized that Pericles' speeches were not so much paired as "complementary."

[74] The speech of the unnamed Athenians at the Spartan congress tends to the same impression. That they are unnamed makes them seem to be generic "Athenians." This, in turn, suggests that Athenians speak with one voice and are of one mind. The narrative, however, shows this impression to be false.

[75] Cf. Grundy (1948, 437), who remarks that Pericles' speech is "to a certain extent" a "paragraph by paragraph" response to the Corinthian speech. See also Bloedow's (1981) useful comparison of Archidamus' and Pericles' first speech.

also "answers" the Corinthian suggestion that the Peloponnesians should build a fort in Attica with the incorrect (as it was discovered) claim that "neither their fortification-building nor their navy is worth worrying about" (1.142.2).[76] Finally, Pericles even imagines a response to the daring possibility he foresees that the Peloponnesians might "remove the money at Olympia or Delphi and try to seduce our foreign seamen away with higher pay" (1.143.1) – a possibility that the Corinthians also suggested at Sparta (1.121.3). "That would be a serious thing," he concedes, "if going on board we ourselves together with our resident aliens were not an equal to them" (1.143.1). Thus Pericles agrees with Archidamus' accounting that judged Athens the more powerful and has ready answers for the suggestions the Corinthians made to reach their decision that the Peloponnesians would prevail.

Pericles also agrees with Archidamus' judgment about the efficacy of invasion. He asserts as emphatically as possible that, as Archidamus said, the Athenians would not be "slaves to their land":

> If they invade our country by land, we will sail against theirs, and it will not be a similar thing for some portion of the Peloponnesus to be cut off and the whole of Attica. For they will not be able to lay hold of other territory without fighting for it but we have plenty of land both in the islands and on the mainland. For sea power is of great importance (1.143.4).

Pericles denies that a Spartan invasion will have any effect, even if "the whole of Attica" were to be cut off. He urges the Athenians to abandon

[76] The connection between Pericles' speech and that of the Corinthians' caused some scholars to argue that the two speeches must be written wholly by Thucydides for his own purposes and, because the idea of a permanent fortification seems to foretell the damaging fortification by the Spartans of the Athenian village of Decelea in 413, to argue that Thucydides must have written them after that event. However, as Adcock (1947, 5–6 and 1951, 8–9) argued, a permanent fortification is not an anachronism; it was tried repeatedly during the Archidamian War. Furthermore, as Connor (1984, 49, n. 58) notes, it is not unlikely that Pericles would learn what the Corinthians said at Sparta and wish to reply. (Cf. Hornblower 1987, 59). Nevertheless, as Connor (1984, 50, n. 59) points out, even if the speech need not be written after Decelea, "a post-war reader would certainly be reminded, as the scholiast in 1.122.1 was, of Decelea," and Thucydides "must have been willing to let the reminder of Decelea stand."

their land and their houses and focus instead on the empire and the navy. In this way they will "safeguard the sea and the city." This time, Pericles makes clear, the threat of invasion will wrest no concessions from the Athenians. They will not be "slaves to their land." They will abandon it instead. Pericles uses a daring comparison to describe his vision of Athens:

> Consider this. If we were islanders, who would be harder to catch? We must now think as nearly like this as possible and abandon our land and our houses and safeguard the sea and the city (τὴν μὲν γῆν καὶ οἰκίας ἀφεῖναι, τῆς δὲ θαλάσσης καὶ πόλεως φυλακὴν ἔχειν) and not fight against the much greater numbers of the Peloponnesians because we are enraged over these . . . nor make lament over houses and land but over lives (τήν τε ὀλόφυρσιν μὴ οἰκιῶν καὶ γῆς ποιεῖσθαι, ἀλλὰ τῶν σωμάτων, 1.143.5).

Pericles' daring strategy seems clever and powerful, but there are reasons for unease. First, the central simile Pericles uses to justify his strategy does not apply to the situation at hand and thus underscores how radically Pericles is forced to remake his *polis*. Pericles claims that if the Athenians were "islanders," no one would be "harder to catch," and he urges the Athenians to think "as nearly like" islanders as possible. To "think like an islander," according to Pericles, means "to abandon our land and our houses and safeguard the sea and the city." The island Pericles will protect, therefore, includes neither the land nor the houses of Attica but only "the sea and the city." The walled *asty*/Piraeus corridor is Pericles' island city. Real islanders, however, protect both *asty* and land with the "walls" of the sea. They protect everything and abandon nothing beyond the "walls" of their island. Pericles' comparison to islanders implies that if they follow his plan, the Athenians will be embarking on a tried-and-true, naturally powerful strategy. Yet there is no comparison to what Pericles is urging his citizens to do. If they follow Pericles, the Athenians will not be acting *like* anyone at all. The mismatch of Pericles' example underscores the radical nature of Pericles' city, which he redefines here as an entity divorced from the houses and land of Attica.[77]

[77] The problem, that is, goes far beyond the fact that, as Connor (1984, 51) notes, "Athens is not an island and will find it difficult to pretend to be one."

Pericles' false comparison to islanders has a counterpart in the appearance of a precedent for Pericles' strategy in the Athenian abandonment during the Persian War. But like the (absent) island analogy, the precedent is really no precedent at all and so serves to underscore how different Pericles' vision is. In their speech at Sparta, the Athenian ambassadors said that their ancestors "abandoned the *polis*." They fought on behalf of a *polis* "that no longer existed" and that had "little hope of existing" (1.74.3). The Athenians at Salamis took their *polis* on their ships, but as the ambassadors' words show, their goal was to reconstitute their same abandoned *polis* in Attica. Pericles, by contrast, redefines the existing *polis* and claims that even with the land and homes of Attica lost, the Athenians will be "safeguard[ing] the sea and the city." For Pericles, the truncated, emergency, island city *is* the city.

Pericles sees no value in lands and homes. The Athenians must not "lament" over these.[78] Pericles is also particularly dismissive of the importance of Attica, claiming,

> If they invade our country by land, we will sail against theirs, and it will not be a similar thing for some portion of the Peloponnesus to be cut off and the whole of Attica. For they will not be able to lay hold of other territory without fighting for it but we have plenty of land both in the islands and on the mainland (1.143.4).

Pericles begins with a clear equivalence between "their" (ἐκείνων) and "our" (ἡμῶν) territory but immediately broadens the definition of "ours" well beyond Attica when he says that "we have plenty of land both in the islands and on the mainland." Pericles here presumably means, at least in part, subject territory from which the Athenians could import food while hoping to defeat the Spartans and regain Attica. This is

[78] Longo (1974, 11) underscores the "lexical incompatibility" in Pericles' use of "lament" in regard to houses and land, for a lament is proper only for persons – the lives that Pericles mentions. Pericles' use of "lament," then, highlights the error he wants to prevent his people from making: valuing land and things over men. At the same time, however, the dramatic nature of the "lexical incompatibility" – that the Athenians would "lament" over their land and houses – underscores the depth of their feeling.

how Gomme explains the passage; Pericles does not, Gomme insists, mean "that there was actual Athenian territory abroad."[79] Yet Gomme's formulation is not consistent with what Pericles says. Pericles speaks calmly of the destruction of "the whole of Attica" and claims that this would not be so bad because the Athenians have plenty of other land.[80] It seems that Pericles recognizes no difference between Attica and any other Athenian possessions – as though the historical, emotional, and religious importance of the territory of Attica means nothing. It can easily be replaced.[81]

This devaluing of Attica is particularly intriguing if we remember the Athenians' myth of autochthony – that they were born from and have always inhabited this land that Pericles suggests was just like any other. Thucydides, in the *Archaeology*, takes care to recount the view that unlike most of the Greeks, the Athenians had always inhabited their land (1.2.5), and in his Funeral Oration, Pericles himself alludes to this belief (2.36.1). We should also recall the way in which the Athenian political system tied the Athenians to the land. When Kleisthenes introduced his democratic reforms in 507 B.C., he based citizenship in the scattered villages of Attica. All Athenian men were citizens by virtue of their belonging to one of these 148 political units. Each man carried a name in addition to his given name and patronymic that was derived from the name of his village (called a "demotic" after *demos*, the Greek word for these political villages). When an Athenian went abroad

[79] Gomme 1945, *s.v.* 1.143.4.

[80] Foster (2001, 152) notes that Pericles only once refers to Attica by name and more regularly uses "houses and land" or simple demonstratives to refer to it. As Foster remarks, "if Attica is just houses and land, any other land is just as useful."

[81] B. Strauss (1986, 52), in contrast to Gomme, argues that "there is every reason to take [Pericles] literally," noting (53) that of the men who had their property confiscated because of their involvement in the mutilation of the Herms, seven owned land and property abroad. See also Longo (1974, 19–20) who speaks of "a compensatory exchange between Attica, abandoned to the enemy, and the territories (including in the form of cleruchies) that Athens was able to administer in the districts of the empire. . . . " He states, "the *chora* (land) of Athens will no longer be Attica but will be the Athenian empire itself."

as, for example, a *cleruch* to a conquered Athenian territory, he remained an Athenian and kept his demotic name and village affiliation that tied him to the territory of Attica.[82] This is the land that Pericles suggests the Athenians should calmly see devastated because they have "plenty of land" around the Aegean.

Certain ideas in Pericles' speech are echoed in the so-called "Old Oligarch's" "Constitution of the Athenians," a text wrongly attributed to the historian Xenophon from (approximately) the 430s or 420s.[83] The Old Oligarch writes of the Athenians, "If they were *thalassocrats* ("sea-rulers") living on an island, it would be possible for them to inflict harm, if they wished, but as long as they ruled the sea, to suffer none – neither the ravaging of their land nor the taking on of enemies" (2.14).[84] This correspondence is close enough[85] that (unless we follow Hornblower and put the Old Oligarch in the fourth century and make him copy Thucydides[86]) either the Old Oligarch must be echoing an actual speech of Pericles (which Thucydides accurately reports) or Thucydides/Pericles and the Old Oligarch are echoing a notion common in Athens in the 430s or later.[87]

The similarity in the island image that both the Old Oligarch and Pericles use makes their differences appear all the more interesting. First, and most importantly, when the Old Oligarch employs his island image, he suggests that being "*thalassocrats* and living on an island" would allow the Athenians to suffer no harm. He specifically says that for this reason, they would *not* have to endure "the ravaging of their

[82] See, e.g., Merritt, Wade-Gery, and McGregor 1950, 285, and Whitehead 1986, 68, n. 2.

[83] Bowersock (1968, 465) places it as early as the 440s; De Ste Croix (1972, 310) thinks "the summer of 424 . . . the most likely single date." Frisch (1942) gives a good summary of views and arguments.

[84] All citations of the "Old Oligarch" are from Bowersock's 1968 translation.

[85] Bowersock (1968, 465) calls it "startlingly reminiscent of Thucydides."

[86] Hornblower 2000, 366.

[87] J. Finley (1938/1967, 4), for example, remarks that the parallels between Pericles and the "Old Oligarch" show that "in a few cases at least, Thucydides attributes to the statesman ideas that were apparently commonplaces in the contemporary discussion of democracy and that, as such, Pericles must have known."

land." Pericles, in marked contrast, ties his island image directly to the abandonment of the Athenians' land: "We must think as nearly like this as possible and abandon our land and our houses. . . ." Furthermore, when the Old Oligarch admits that Athens' policy does leave it in danger of suffering, he claims that "the farmers and the wealthy curry favor with the enemy" in order to protect their property and that it is only "the people, knowing that nothing of theirs will be burnt or cut down," who "live without fear and refuse to fawn upon the enemy" (2.14). Thus, for the Old Oligarch, it is only those Athenians with nothing to lose who are willing to abandon Attica and the land to the Spartans. Later, he admits that the people do have something when he writes that "they place their property on islands while trusting in the naval empire and they allow their land to be ravaged, for they realize that if they concern themselves with this, they will be deprived of other greater goods" (γιγνώσκοντες ὅτι εἰ αὐτὴν ἐλεήσουσιν ἑτέρων ἀγαθῶν μειζόνων στερήσονται, 2.16). In the Old Oligarch the Athenians allow their land to be ravaged, not because it is worthless or interchangeable with some other land, but in the interests of other "greater goods." The formulation itself suggests that Attica is a good. Furthermore, there is no suggestion that Attica can simply be replaced by other territory.

From Pericles, by contrast, "we have plenty of land both in the islands and on the mainland." Pericles has no particular tie to his home territory. If the Athenians somehow lost part of this "plenty" of other, non-Attic land, we can well imagine Pericles (and Athenians taught by him) reacting as if they had been "robbed of their household territory," for they see no distinction between Attica and other land. Thus Pericles emphatically confirms Archidamus' warning that the Athenians will not be "slaves to their land" and confirms the Corinthians' characterization of the Athenians as people who have no tie to home and confuse the boundary between their own and others' territory.

Yet there are hints that perhaps Pericles' people might have some difficulty accepting his vision of the city. After he tells the Athenians not to "lament over houses and land," he says, "If I thought I could persuade you, I would urge you to go out yourselves and lay waste your houses and your land and show the Peloponnesians that you will not yield to them for the sake of these things" (1.143.5).[88] Pericles himself admirably acceded to the consequences of his own repudiation of the land by making his own property public; he was no slave to his land (2.13).[89] But Thucydides shows here that he did not hope to persuade the Athenians to do as he did. He knew he could not persuade them. Nevertheless he expects his people to calmly let the Spartans lay waste the land that they themselves would not destroy or repudiate.[90] This glimmer of a difference between leader and people suggests that Pericles' supreme confidence in his plan and in ultimate victory may be misplaced.

THE ATHENIANS SLOWLY AND WITH DIFFICULTY MIGRATE TO THEIR ISLAND CITY

At the completion of his account of Pericles' first speech, Thucydides reports that the Athenians, "considering that he had advised them

[88] Pericles privileges men and the city/empire over land and houses. Connor's (1985) work on *kataskaphe* – the deliberate destruction of houses as a punishment – however, demonstrates that houses are more than mere buildings. The destruction of a house as a punishment, according to Connor (1985, 86), "connotes the extirpation of the individual and his immediate kin from the society." Men and houses, that is, cannot be quite so easily distinguished.

[89] Tsakmakis (2006, 184) notes that here Pericles "suggests an action with a calculable cost, one which has no goal or use other than to create an impression. Image has its own reality."

[90] The calm inactivity required by Pericles' plan is not what one would naturally expect from the Athenians as described by the Corinthians (or by themselves) at Sparta. As L. Strauss writes (1964, 156), whereas Sparta "cherishes rest . . . Athens cherishes motion." Cf. Palmer (1982b, 1992, 19): "Pericles' strategy of sitting tight . . . goes against the very temper of a city at war, but especially against the Athenian temper." Palmer (1982b, 1992, 21) goes on to note that although Pericles' strategy "appears to sacrifice the old Athens to the new, for the sake of preserving the achievements of the new, it rests neither on the old or the new Athens. . . . It is an inglorious, prosaic strategy that requires the old element of Athens to abandon its sacred hearths, temples and monuments in order to move into the city and the new element to suppress its daring and its inclination for motion in order to remain at rest."

best, voted as he had bid them to do" (1.145). As Thucydides' next words show, this refers specifically to the Athenians' response to the Lacedaemonian ambassadors: "They made answer to the Lacedaemonians according to his opinion" (1.145). Thucydides' report that the Athenians considered that Pericles had advised them best refers, presumably, also to Pericles' defensive strategy and his advice about the kind of Athens that would win the war. This comment, that is, seems to close the gap between leader and people by giving the impression that the people accepted Pericles' plan without argument or delay. Thucydides allows this impression to stand because he does not follow Pericles' speech immediately with the Athenians' response to that part of Pericles' advice. Book 1 closes, instead, with a simple summary paragraph of what the book had covered. Book 2 opens with "the actual outbreak of war" and Thucydides' account of its first action – the Theban surprise attack on Plataea, the Athenians' ally in Boeotia (see Map 3).[91] When Thucydides finally moves the scene back to Athens after he reports a speech of encouragement that Archidamus gave to the troops gathered at the isthmus, he provides a speech of Pericles' that shows that the Athenians, quite contrary to this impression, only slowly and with difficulty followed Pericles' advice.

In this speech, Pericles "gave the same advice in these circumstances that he had given before, that they should make preparations for the war, and bring in their property from the fields, that they should not go out to battle, but should come inside the city and guard it" (2.13.2). Pericles also details again Athens' financial and military resources for the war. Confident as it is, the very existence of this speech undercuts Pericles' authority and underscores the disconnect between Pericles and his people.

[91] Rood (1999, 149–151) argues that Thucydides conceived of the Peloponnesian War both as a kind of "reliving" of the Persian War and as a "perversion" of it. Pelling (2000, 68) remarks that Plataea shows that this war is not to be "the old-fashioned open war of large-scale army movements, the sort which might appropriately be introduced by Archidamus' invasion: the dominant notes will be the furtive plotting, the local hatreds, the faction-ridden little town which cannot solve its squabbles without calling in the powerful neighbors, the frustrated planning, the stealth, the dagger in the back in the middle of the night."

Thucydides earlier described Pericles as "the first man in Athens at that time, the ablest in both speaking and acting." He is careful to record no dissenting voice to Pericles' first speech. Unlike other speeches in the work, which are generally paired with those of an opposing speaker, Pericles' speeches stand alone. In this way, Thucydides manages to make Pericles appear "unrivalled even among the Athenians of his time."[92] This contributes to our sense that Athens agrees with Pericles. Why, then, does Pericles have to repeat himself in this speech about his basic strategy? As Thucydides notes, Pericles gives "the same advice in these circumstances that he had given before." Why have the Athenians not already moved into their island city, as Pericles' entire plan for the war requires? Why were the naturally quick Athenians suddenly so slow?

Time has passed since the earlier speech in which Pericles recounted his plan. There has been time for the Lacedaemonian ambassadors who brought the ultimatum to return home (1.146); there has been time for the Theban attack on Plataea, for the Plataean counterattack, and for the Athenians to send a garrison (2.2–6). There has been time for both sides to decide that events at Plataea meant that the war was afoot and for both sides to prepare for war, for the Lacedaemonians to send messengers to Italy and Sicily to order ships, and for the Athenians to closely review the existing alliance (2.7). There has been time for the Lacedaemonians to send messengers around to the allied cities telling them to assemble their armies at the isthmus (2.10). Thucydides encourages his readers to note the passage of time when he remarks that the Peloponnesians set out from Oenoe into Attica "on about the eightieth day after the events at Plataea" (2.19). Pericles "had the winter to work on the minds of his fellow-citizens."[93] Why, then, are the Athenians still in the countryside? Why must Pericles repeat himself at the eleventh hour? Thucydides says that Pericles made his speech "during the time when the Peloponnesians were still assembling at the isthmus and were on the road"; it was not

[92] L. Strauss 1964, 213. Nor does Thucydides, of course, include overt examples of domestic opposition to Pericles such as that covered in Plutarch.

[93] Brunt (1965, 265), making a contrast between 431 and 446 when, perhaps, Pericles had "not enough time to persuade them – the revolt of Megara and the ensuing Peloponnesian invasion was a surprise. . . ."

Map 3. Attica and Boeotia.

at the end of the Peloponnesians' preparations, but it was not at the beginning either.

It is clear, therefore, that when Thucydides writes after Pericles' first speech that the Athenians "voted as he had bid them to do" (1.145), this means only that they answered the Spartan ambassadors as he urged them, not that they immediately put into effect his advice about their land and houses and the kind of city they would preserve in this war. Pericles knew he could not persuade the Athenians to lay waste their own land. Thucydides makes it clear that he has a difficult time getting them even to leave it to the Spartans. The quick Athenians clearly delay before putting Pericles' advice into action. The Spartans even think that Archidamus still had a chance of catching the Athenians in their fields once he finally begins his march, so slow were the Athenians to leave them. There is a strong contrast with the Plataeans who, to prevent the Thebans from using their rural folk as hostages, "quickly brought in everything from the countryside" (2.5.7).

After Pericles' speech in indirect discourse, Thucydides tells us that "the Athenians were convinced and they brought in from the country their children, their women and the equipment they used in the home." Harvey Yunis remarks that the move into the city proceeds "like clockwork" and that Pericles' speech is a "paradigm of instructive political rhetoric."[94] Yet this is true only if we ignore that this is Pericles' *second* speech on the matter. Furthermore, even in his first speech Pericles begins by saying "My judgment, Athenians, is always the same" (τῆς μὲν γνώμης, ὦ Ἀθηναῖοι, αἰεὶ τῆς αὐτῆς ἔχομαι) and continues, "and I see that again now I must give the exact same counsel" (ὁρῶ δὲ καὶ νῦν ὁμοῖα καὶ παραπλήσια ξυμβουλευτέα μοι ὄντα, 1.140.1) so that we have a sense of an endless repetition of exactly similar speeches. Pericles' words are not an example of authoritatively persuasive political rhetoric. On the contrary, he has to make his point repeatedly and still the Athenians barely obey. Only when the Spartans were "on the road" did they finally do as Pericles said.[95] (Did they think that this time, too, Pericles would "bribe" the army away?) This must raise doubts in the reader about whether the people of Athens agree with Pericles' definition of the city. What Thucydides tell us next directly confirms these doubts.

Immediately after his account of Pericles' speech, Thucydides paints a vivid picture of the Athenians putting Pericles' vision of the city into practice:

94 Yunis 1996, 79. Cf. Garlan (1974, 51) who, despite citing *both* speeches, claims that Pericles' point of view "was immediately ratified by the assembly."

95 Allison (1983, 21) remarks that "the actual decision to move the people is not, however, presented as clearly as we might wish." She thus must note that although Thucydides makes it seem as if the "actual decision" occurred after Pericles' first speech, it clearly had not even occurred by his second.

The Athenians heard Pericles' speech and obeyed it and brought in from the fields their children and women and the other property that they used at home, taking down the woodwork from the homes themselves. They sent their sheep and their cattle to Euboea and to the islands lying off the coast. The move was difficult (χαλεπῶς) for them because most of them had always been accustomed to living in the countryside (2.14.1–2).

The stream of displaced villagers on the country tracks and roads must have brought back vivid memories of the evacuation of the Persian War, as would the transportation of the flocks to Euboea. The scene must also have borne some resemblance to that after the defeat of a besieged city, as the displaced inhabitants gathered what belongings they could carry and left their homeland for an uncertain future. Here, of course, the stream was in the opposite direction, as the Athenians flocked inside their city.

This first paragraph of Thucydides' description of the move is curious. As Yunis notes, the concision of Thucydides' statement gives the impression that the Athenians left the assembly at which Pericles gave his speech and immediately went to carry out his advice without question or complaint (although we have the nagging question of why they are just now doing it). Thucydides immediately undercuts this impression, however, and reinforces the import of the Athenians' delay in the last sentence of the paragraph, where he stresses that the move was "difficult" (χαλεπῶς) for them. This explains, to attentive readers, why the move has taken so long. Thucydides then reveals that the move was "difficult" because "most of them had always been accustomed to living in the countryside."

At this point Thucydides inserts a long and fascinating excursus that superficially explains why this move was especially hard on the Athenians (2.15–16). Living in the country, Thucydides reports, was

from earliest times a characteristic of Athenians more than of others. For from the time of Cecrops and the first kings down to the time of Theseus, Attica was always inhabited in cities that had their own magistrates' halls and officials and unless they had something to fear they did not come together to deliberate before the king, but each themselves administered their state and deliberated. And some of these even went to war, as did the Eleusinians with Eumolpus against King Erectheus (2.15.1).

But, Thucydides continues, when Theseus became king, he changed all this, and reorganized the countryside:

He abolished the council-chambers and the magistracies of the other cities; he designated one council-house and magistrates' hall and combined them all into the present city. Although each managed their own affairs just as they had done previously, he compelled them to employ this single city. Since they were all now contributing to it, it became great and was passed down by Theseus to those who came after (2.15.2)

Theseus performed a political synoecism for the Athenians. He did not force the Athenians to come together physically, but he compelled them to use the city center of Athens for their political life.[96] The last sentence of the passage quoted above suggests that for Theseus, like Pericles, the *polis* was the city center. What Thucydides continues to stress as he continues, however, is that this was not the case for the vast majority of Athenians, whose rural lifestyle he details:

For a long time, therefore, the Athenians lived in independent communities throughout the countryside. Even after they were synoecized, nevertheless, because of their habit the majority of them, both those of older generations and those later up until this war, lived in the countryside. And they did not easily make the move of their entire households especially because they had only just recently reestablished them after the Persian War (2.16.1).[97]

Thucydides completes his discussion of the Athenians' move with this comment:

They were oppressed and found it difficult (χαλεπῶς ἔφερον) to leave their homes and the shrines which from the time of their ancient form of government had always been their ancestral places of worship since they were preparing not only

[96] Cf. Moggi (1975, 916–17), who notes that "the amalgamation and absorption of the other *poleis* was realized only at the political level, since the inhabitants of Attica continued to live in their ancient residences."

[97] Nevett (2005, 96) argues that the "organization of space" in houses from Attic deme sites is different from that of houses in the *asty* and concludes that "there were subtle differences between the social lives of households in these communities and those of households in Athens itself." This would suggest that a rural resident might well find Athens-*asty* an alien place.

to change their way of life but each one was doing nothing other than abandoning his own *polis* (καὶ οὐδὲν ἄλλο ἢ πόλιν τὴν αὑτοῦ ἀπολείπων ἕκαστος , 2.16.2).

Thucydides uses the word "difficult" (χαλεπῶς) to link this passage, where Thucydides notes that the Athenians "found it difficult" to leave their homes, to the beginning of the excursus where he recounts that "the move was difficult for them" (2.14). The whole passage is ostensibly an explanation of this difficulty. But not everything in the passage fits that purpose. Thucydides' emphasis on the Athenian rural lifestyle explains why moving to the *asty* was difficult. His focus on Theseus' synoecism, on the other hand, does not. It is, in fact, wholly out of place. Theseus' synoecism should mean that for centuries the Athenians had all thought of the *asty* as the *polis* and the center of their civic life – as, clearly, did Theseus. This should have made the move into that city all the easier for the Athenians. It is no explanation for why it was difficult.[98]

The last words of the last sentence of the excursus are the crux of the matter: "They were oppressed and found it difficult to leave their homes . . . since they were preparing not only to change their way of life but each one was doing nothing other than abandoning his own *polis*."[99] Here, in an emphatic position at the end of the whole passage,

[98] This point has not received the attention it deserves. According to Hunter (1973, 14), "Chapter 15 explains the difficulty: from the time of Theseus and even Kekrops most of them had lived in the countryside." Rusten (1989, 121) says that Thucydides' interest in his "note on the story of the [synoecism] of Attica by Theseus" is "not antiquarian but anthropological." He is interested in the "traditionally rural settlement pattern of Attica" and "the topography of the oldest Athenian temples." Hornblower (1991, 259–260) also does not note how the digression on Theseus undercuts Pericles' synoecism.

[99] Skydsgaard (2000, 229) objects to the introduction of a "subjective aspect" into this sentence, citing, e.g., Whitehead (1986, 222): "what . . . seemed [sc. to each man] to be nothing less than his own polis" and others. This subjective element enters because "we know that many Athenians lived in the demes and the demes were not *poleis*." Nevertheless, Skydsgaard argues that "the former *poleis* continued to exist as nucleated settlements as many would call them today; but Thucydides considered them to be *poleis*." For Skydsgaard, then, this passage tells us of the word Thucydides might normally use for a deme or village settlement. Whitehead (2001, 606), however, although agreeing that the passage does not contain "an explicit, focalized comment upon what each Athenian evacuee *felt* about his home town or village in the Attic countryside,"

Thucydides undercuts Theseus' synoecism. If, for each Athenian, his home village was "nothing other than his own *polis*," Theseus' vision of an Athenian countryside (as Thucydides writes) "compelled" by him "to employ this single *polis*" of Athens is a failure and a fantasy.[100]

Theseus was the great national hero of the Athenians, the counterpart to the Peloponnesian Heracles and font of much of Athens' national mythology. Thucydides did not have to include a discussion of his synoecism in his explanation of the difficulty of the Athenians' move. His account of the Athenians' ties to their home demes would have sufficed. Indeed, his inclusion of Theseus' synoecism runs counter to the purpose of explaining the Athenians' difficulty with their move.[101] Thucydides chose, however, to include a famous past Athenian visionary with new ideas about what the city was in the middle of his account of the implementation of Pericles' vision of the city. Thucydides shows that Theseus' conception was at best partially accomplished. [102] This must presage failure for the civic vision of the mortal Pericles.[103] Thucydides

argues (605) that the "innocent-looking" phrase "nothing other than" is a rhetorical device with the purpose of "flagging up something *not* 'purely' or 'literally' so, but, at most, tantamount to being so." Thus Thucydides knows that the demes or villages are *not* properly called *poleis*. His choice to use *poleis* for demes and villages here (and it is, as Skydsgaard's argument insists, *his* choice, not a usage meant to give only the subjective feeling of the demesmen) is quite deliberate.

[100] Moggi (1975, 916) interprets this passage as showing that "the *poleis* of Attica, distinct and in fact independent political entities, were reduced to a union upon their fusion into Athens, which remained the sole *polis* of the region." It is this last point exactly that Thucydides urges us to question.

[101] Foster (2001, 174) calls the excursus the "narrative of the *demos*" and argues (175) that it "is opposed to Pericles' 'narrative of materials' (2.13) in the same abrupt way that the plague is opposed to the funeral oration."

[102] Walker (1995, 198) discusses dark elements in Thucydides' presentation of Theseus and concludes that "it is extremely significant that Thucydides does not present Theseus as a champion of enlightenment and progress doing battle against the forces of darkness and backwardness. . . . If Theseus started the unification of Attica, Pericles brought it to its awful logical conclusion, by sacrificing the Attic countryside to his ambitions."

[103] Cf. Morrison 2006a, 147–48: "the idea of Attic 'cities' is significant in that it undermines Pericles' idea of the devotion of all citizens to a single object: the polis of Athens. . . . Thucydides has chosen to place this model of potentially

plants the doubt: If Theseus could not compel acceptance of his view of the city, how can Pericles succeed? It also demands the question: What will happen in a city in which there are such profound disagreements about what the *polis* is? Thucydides has already made it clear that the building of the Long Walls led to *stasis* in Athens. He gives us reason now to think that Pericles' vision of the *polis* holds the same dangers. Thucydides' comments about the earliest history of Athens in the *Archaeology* confirm these fears.

In the *Archaeology*, one of the qualities for which Thucydides praised Athens was that it was securely settled: "The same people always dwelled in it" (1.2.5). By contrast, Greece, in general, "was not securely settled in ancient times but there were frequent migrations, with each group easily (ῥᾳδίως) abandoning their territory when they were pushed out by a more numerous people" (1.2.1). The ancients' weak attachments to their land also led people to migrate easily "and on account of this they grew strong neither in the size of their cities nor in other property" (1.2.2). Attica, being free from migrations, received the refugees of other areas and, because it was securely settled, became strong. Thucydides disparages the early migrants in Greece because "believing that they could obtain the daily necessities of food from anywhere they found no difficulty in migrating" (οὐ χαλεπῶς ἀπανίσταντο, 1.2.2). Such thinking did not lead to strength, according to Thucydides. Yet that thinking sounds surprisingly like that of Pericles when he urged the Athenians not to be afraid if all of Attica was destroyed because "we have plenty of land both in the islands and on the mainland" (1.143.4). In addition, when Thucydides criticizes these ancient non-Athenians because they "found no difficulty" in migrating, he uses the same word for "difficulty" that he uses to frame his description of the Athenians' move into the city. The verbal echo to Thucydides' comments in the *Archaeology* suggests that the Athenians were right to find this move difficult and that Pericles was wrong to ask them to make it at all. Early Athens was remarkably free from *stasis* (1.6.1). Thucydides' account of the Athenians' move inside their island city, and the disagreement he

divided loyalties here at the beginning of the war – during the evacuation and before Pericles' Funeral Oration. The effect is that the reader may now question the validity of Pericles' vision." Cf. Palmer (1982b, 827–28; 1992, 21).

reveals over what the *polis* is, suggests that Athens' days of freedom from *stasis* may be coming to an end.

Thucydides' description of the Athenians' move onto their island is crafted to lead readers to question not only the practicality but also the wisdom of Pericles' vision of the city.[104] The Athenians' enemies apparently doubted both. Thucydides' account of the Spartan invasion of Attica continues to undercut readers' confidence in Pericles' vision of the city.

When Archidamus invades Attica, he moves first to the village of Oenoe on the border between Attica and Boeotia and attacks the fort there (see Map 3). Thucydides tells us it was said that Archidamus delayed at Oenoe "expecting that the Athenians would yield in some way while their land was still unharmed, and that they would shrink from looking on while it was plundered" (2.18.5). When the Athenians make no concessions, Archidamus finally invades Attica, ravages the Eleusinian and Thriasian plains, and camps at Acharnae. Thucydides writes that "it was said" that Archidamus delayed at Acharnae because he expected that the Athenians "would come out against him and would not look on while their land was ravaged" (2.20.2). Thucydides does not merely report what people said about Archidamus at Acharnae, however. The passage begins as a report of what was said, but by the end it clearly is Thucydides' own assessment of the situation. It is not evident where the switch happens, so that the whole of the passage comes to have Thucydides' imprimatur. Throughout this discussion, Thucydides indicates that Archidamus could not believe that the Athenians would not come out to defend their land:

It is said that Archidamus stayed around Acharnae drawn up for battle, and did not go down into the plain during the invasion for the following reason. He expected

[104] Palmer (1982a, 1992, 21) notes that "in the name of his strategic policy . . . the soil in which the old, conservative element of Athens is rooted will be sacrificed. . . . Pericles appears to be sacrificing the old Athens to the new Athens. Whether he can do so, and whether he should, may have significant consequences for the Athenians' prosecution of the war, and for their regime." Cf. Bruell (1981, 25): Pericles' strategy "brought about a grave transformation of Athenian life (II.14–17). In this, and perhaps in other ways, Perikles may have unwittingly contributed to the political decline which, in the end, undid his work."

that the Acharnians, abounding as they were in youth and prepared for war as never before, would come out against him and would not look on while their land was ravaged. Since, therefore, they did not oppose him at Eleusis and the Thriasian plain, he camped at Acharnae, and made a trial to see if they might come out against him. For the area seemed a suitable place to make camp and at the same time he thought that the Acharnians, being a large part of the *polis* (for they were 3000 hoplites strong) would not look on at their possessions being ravaged, but would rouse even all the Athenians to battle. And even if the Athenians did not come out against him during this invasion he could ravage the plain and advance right up to the city with greater confidence later. The Acharnians, deprived of their own property, would not be equally zealous on behalf of the property of others and there would be *stasis* in their deliberations. With such reasoning as this Archidamus was at Acharnae (2.20.1–5).

According to Thucydides' account of Archidamus' motives, once he is on the march, he no longer believes either of the points of his speech at Sparta. First, Archidamus expects that the Athenians will be slaves to their land and will not watch it being plundered. Second, he now thinks that losing the leverage of the "hostage" land (which he had earlier said the Spartans must spare as long as possible lest it make the Athenians "harder to catch," 1.82.4) actually would benefit him by causing a part of Athens to be unwilling to come out against him "on behalf of the property of others" and by causing *stasis* in Athens.

Most scholars ignore, downplay, or deny this inconsistency.[105] Christopher Pelling has discussed the contradiction between Archidamus' words in Sparta and Thucydides' account of his thoughts and actions once in Attica. Pelling mutes the contradiction, however, by claiming that Archidamus' hope that the Athenians might come out to

[105] For Rusten (1989, 124), for example, Archidamus' actions in Attica are "entirely consistent with what he had advised from the start." Hornblower (1991, *s.v.* 1.81.2) merely notes that Archidamus takes a "rather different line" in Sparta and in his speech at the isthmus. Westlake (1968, 125–6) acknowledges the difference between Archidamus' two positions but thinks that it can be explained by arguing that Thucydides puts words in Archidamus' mouth in the speech in Sparta whereas Archidamus' words and actions in book 2 more accurately reflect the real man. De Romilly (1962a) ignores altogether the contradiction between Archidamus' speech in Sparta and his actions (and thoughts) in Attica.

fight him "does not go very deep."[106] According to Pelling, despite everything that Archidamus says and does in book 2, he does not really believe that the Athenians will come out to fight. He is "forced," according to Pelling, "to revert to his final strand" of reasoning and "finally clutches" at the hope that the Athenians will come out to fight only at Acharnae. This policy is "second- or even third-best."[107] His "deepest conviction" was "that the Athenians would come over to Pericles' policy."[108]

Pelling calls Archidamus' hope that the Athenians will fight him the "irrationalist" policy but notes that it "very nearly wins success, especially because of the bellicose Athenians." For Pelling, Thucydides' point is to make Archidamus' earlier "certainties" about the Athenians' (lack of) attachment to the land seem "more misguided at 1.81–2."[109] The Spartans complained, according to Thucydides, that if Archidamus had not hesitated at Oenoe before beginning his invasion, he could have caught the Athenians with their possessions still out in the countryside, since they were still moving them in while he waited (2.18.4). Pelling argues that the Spartans were wrong to accuse Archidamus for this because no invasion "could really be so speedy and unexpected." He judges that "unless we are simply supposed to write off the Spartan criticisms as misconceived, Thucydides . . . seems to be straining plausibility to make his point. And that point makes us wonder whether Archidamus should not have been more of an irrationalist after all."[110] "If the ravaging policy had been pursued with more urgency," Pelling concludes, "the first encounter might have gone differently."[111]

[106] Pelling 1991, 127.
[107] Pelling 1991, 127–28.
[108] Pelling 1991, 129.
[109] Pelling 1991, 128.
[110] Pelling 1991, 128. Cf. Rood 1998, 119: "For the invasion in 431, dense temporal correlations help the reader to explore the paradoxical disadvantages of a well-founded strategy: . . . by marching slowly, [Archidamus] did not allow for the possibility that the sight of ravaged land might provoke the Athenians into offering battle – and that his delay might help Pericles to control them." So Stahl (1966/2003, 76): "there is no doubt that Archidamus' plan comes very near to succeeding and that its failure is at least partly due to his own hesitation."
[111] Pelling 1991, 129.

According to Pelling, despite everything that Archidamus says and does in book 2, he does not really believe that the Athenians will come out. He only "clutches" at this possibility as a last resort. But Thucydides does nothing to encourage this interpretation. He does not suggest that Archidamus delayed or did anything because he thought he was on a fool's errand. Six different times Thucydides tells us either what Archidamus said about the Athenians and their land ("it was necessary and absolutely to be expected that the Athenians will come out to battle," 2.11.8), what was said about him (it was said that he delayed at Oenoe "expecting that the Athenians would yield in some way while their land was still unharmed and that they would shrink from looking on while it was plundered," 2.18.5; it was said that he stopped at Acharnae because he "expected that the Acharnians . . . would come out against him and would not look on while their land was ravaged," 2.20.2), or, most tellingly, what Thucydides says Archidamus thought and did (he sent a herald to see "if they were more willing to give in now that they saw the Peloponnesians actually on the move," 2.12.2; he "recognized that the Athenians were not yet yielding anything," 2.12.4; he thought at Acharnae that the Acharnians "would not look on at their possessions being ravaged" and would either get all of Athens to fight for them or, if they were plundered, would cause *stasis* in Athens, 2.20.4–5). In six different places, the text suggests that once he is on the march, Archidamus no longer judges that the Athenians would not be "slaves to their land." He is slow to ravage the land, in fact, not because he thinks his position weak, but because he thinks that the mere threat of ravaging part of Attica would cause the Athenians either to fight him or to make concessions.

Thucydides' Archidamus thus exemplifies two very different viewpoints on Pericles' policy and his redefinition of Athens. In his speech at Sparta when the invasion and devastation of the land of the Athenians and their response to it was still in the future and still abstract, Archidamus echoed Pericles and opined that the pull on the Athenians of the physical, tangible city and their attachment to the land would not be strong. Archidamus expected the Athenians to focus instead on Pericles' abstract city. When the invasion had begun in earnest, however – when it was no longer an idea but a reality of siege action and burnt olive trees – Archidamus could not imagine that the Athenians would let the physical devastation happen to protect Pericles' idea of a city.

We should not try to explain away the contradiction, for Archidamus' change in judgment heightens for readers the question of whether the Athenians can follow Pericles' policy. Archidamus changes from assuming the Athenians will follow the strategy dependent on Pericles' vision of the city to expecting the Athenians to reject it. His change in judgment leads the reader to wonder if the Athenians themselves might (or indeed should) modify their attitude to Pericles' policy as well. Furthermore, the intertwining of Thucydides' accounts of Archidamus' expectations and the Athenians' actions encourages comparison between them. At the very moment that Archidamus was expecting the Athenians to concede to him in order to protect their land, they were finally following Pericles' advice, abandoning the countryside, and moving inside the city. Yet, as Thucydides emphasizes, they found this difficult and did so very slowly. Pelling thinks Thucydides "strain[s] plausibility" in suggesting that if Archidamus had moved more quickly, he might have caught the Athenians still in the fields. But this suggestion is consistent with the information Thucydides has already given us about the Athenians' move, and if Thucydides strains plausibility, he does so, surely, to underscore how slowly and reluctantly the Athenians put Pericles' plan into practice. If the realities of Archidamus' invasion of Attica indicate that his earlier "certainties" that the Athenians would not be slaves to their land were misguided, they indicate that Pericles' certainties in his first speech were misguided as well.

Pelling points out that the narrative demonstrates that Archidamus' ravaging policy almost succeeded. As Thucydides notes,

> When the Athenians saw his army around Acharnae sixty stades from the city, it was no longer bearable. As is reasonable, it seemed terrible to them when their land was being ravaged in plain view which none of the younger men had seen nor the elders except for the ravaging of the Mede. It seemed to many but especially to the youth that they should go out and not look on at this. . . . The city was in a state of every kind of excitement and they were angry at Pericles. And they recalled none of the things that he had earlier advised, but damned him because although he was a general he did not lead them out and they considered him the cause of everything they were suffering (2.21.2).

Yet we need not concede that the ravaging policy was, as Pelling describes it, "irrationalist" – as if the Athenians would be mad to give in to it. Thucydides certainly uses the language of anger and passion when he describes the effect in Athens of Archidamus' ravaging of Acharnae: The people were in "violent disagreement" (ἐν πολλῇ ἔριδι ἦσαν). The whole city was "in every kind of excitement," and they were "angry" at Pericles (παντί τε τρόπῳ ἀνηρέθιστο ἡ πόλις, καὶ τὸν Περικλέα ἐν ὀργῇ εἶχον, 2.21.3). But Thucydides' first description merely says that the people found the sight of the Spartan army so close to the city "no longer bearable" (οὐκέτι ἀνασχετὸν ἐποιοῦντο, 2.21.2) without any pejorative coloration. And he goes on to say that seeing their land being ravaged in full view "seemed terrible to them, as is reasonable" (ὡς εἰκός . . . δεινὸν ἐφαίνετο). The moving description Thucydides has just given of the Athenians' attachment to their countryside *poleis* explains why it was "reasonable" for this to be a terrible sight that might anger even rational men.[112]

Athens had, after all, chosen differently fourteen years before. Thucydides carefully reminds his reader of the earlier policy when he notes that "as long as the army was around Eleusis and the Thriasian plain, the Athenians had a hope that they would not proceed closer, remembering that Pleistoanax, son of Pausanias the king of the Lacedaemonians, when he invaded Attica to Eleusis and Thria, with a Peloponnesian army, fourteen years before this war, withdrew, advancing no further" (2.21.1). Fourteen years earlier, Athens, under Pericles, chose to make concessions to Sparta rather than see its land ravaged. This time, however, Pericles urged the people to go into their island city because he judged that the loss of Attica meant nothing. The Athenians followed Pericles' advice, but only very slowly and reluctantly; Archidamus' ravaging policy almost worked.

Thucydides takes care to show that for many Athenians, it was Pericles' policy that was mad, and as was the case with the Long Walls years before, the result of Pericles' policy in his city was *stasis.* Thucydides does

[112] As Ober (1985, 173) notes, Pericles' policy "was revolutionary and contravened the unwritten rules of agonal combat. It was one matter for the Athenians to abandon Attica in face of the barbarian Persian invaders in 480, quite another for hoplites to refuse the formal challenge to battle by fellow hoplites. . . ."

not use the word *stasis* when he describes the dissension that resulted in Athens over Pericles' vision of the city, but Archidamus does when he predicts the results of his ravishing Acharnae: "There would be *stasis* in their deliberations" (2.20.4). This is the first appearance of the noun itself in the work after the introductory *Archaeology* (and only the fourth use overall).[113] It is meant to be noticed.

The division that Archidamus foresaw and encouraged in Athens was far from complete, of course; no one treated with the Spartans on this occasion, as they had over the Long Walls, and the Athenians did not, in fact, go out to meet Archidamus. The Athenians ultimately confounded Archidamus' expectation and reinforced the point that the Corinthians had made over and over – that the Athenians were different from the Peloponnesians. Yet the episode and the ensuing tension and division in the city illustrate that the Athenians did not follow Pericles' policy easily. They show, furthermore, that the redefinition of the city that Pericles required of his citizens had the possibility of destroying the *polis* altogether.

PERICLES WONDERS AT "THE POWER OF THE CITY AS IT REALLY IS"

Pericles, however, persisted in his vision of an idealized *polis* severed from the Athenians' territory of Attica. In the winter after the Athenians moved into their island and endured seeing the Spartans ravage their lands, they held a state funeral for the men who had died in the first campaigns of the war. The Funeral Oration that Pericles gave is perhaps the most famous passage in Thucydides. Pericles' speech is a paen to his vision of Athens as an immaterial *polis* unbounded by the physical. At the same time, Pericles presents that city as holding a position of supreme importance in mens' lives. The traditional elements of an Athenian funeral oration seem to have included "praise of the ancestors, praise of the fallen warriors, exhortation to citizens, and consolation to relatives," but, as Jeffrey Ruston notes, Pericles' oration "acknowledges such a pattern, but departs strikingly from it by subordinating all these

[113] The others are at 1.2.4, 1.2.5, and 1.12.2, according to Bétant.

themes to the glorification of *contemporary* Athens itself."[114] Pericles' presentation of his city in this speech is eloquent and powerful. However, as we shall see, Thucydides' narrative and elements of Pericles' speech itself undercut his ideas.

Pericles explains the Athenians' form of government, which is administered in the interests of the many and gives all men a chance to serve. He mentions the games and festivals, which provide "rest from toil" for the spirit, praises the Athenians' "attractive private furnishings whose daily delight drives away cares" (2.38), and describes Athens' system of military training. He calls his city an "education for Hellas" and claims that "it is among us, in my opinion, that a single man would provide an individual nimbly and gracefully self-sufficient for all circumstances" (2.41.1).[115] The city, that is, allows the full flowering of each man. The speech is a "hymn to the corporate virtues of Athens, which satisfy the aspirations of its citizens and justify their death in battle as the most desirable communal service."[116]

Pericles' speech is designed for its specific historical occasion. As Rood has pointed out, "the attachment of each individual to his deme as if to 'his native city' (16.2) makes all the more urgent the unified

[114] Rusten 1989, 136 (italics Rusten). See also Loraux (1981/1986, 123) and Ziolkowski (1981, 51). Palmer (1982b, 828; 1992, 21–22) notes (1992, 22) that "Pericles' attitude toward this old Athenian tradition of the funeral oration is but a particular example of his attitude toward ancestral Athens altogether." Furthermore, Palmer (1992, 23) discusses the implications for Athenian imperial expansion in Pericles' deprecation of his ancestors. Because each generation after the ancestors is praised "in ascending order" for their imperial conquests, Palmer asks, "what does this imply must be the task of the next generation if it does not want to fall short of the generation of its own fathers, the Periclean generation?" Sicking (1995, 411, n. 34) remarks that Pericles' refusal to discuss the exploits of the ancestors "must have been something like that of a Christmas preacher announcing to the congregation that he is not going to reiterate the overworked story of Bethlehem." Hornblower (1991, 295), by contrast, is more skeptical of our ability to know how Thucydides' Funeral Oration compares "in form and content with other speeches of the type," because we have no other fifth century examples. He does agree that "Thucydides makes Pericles concentrate to an unusual degree on the present rather than the past, avoiding traditional themes."

[115] This translation is dependent on Ruston 1989, *s.v.* 2.41.1.

[116] Bosworth 2000, 6.

polis values upheld by Pericles."[117] Pericles places the *polis* at the very center of an individual's life. In a famous passage, he tells his fellow citizens, "It is necessary that you, gazing every day at the power of the city as it really is, become its lovers" (τὴν τῆς πόλεως δύναμιν καθ' ἡμέραν ἔργῳ θεωμένους καὶ ἐραστὰς γιγνομένους αὐτῆς, 2.43.1), using the word *erastes*, which means "lovers" in the sense of erotic passion.[118] Pericles "presents the city as satisfying the deepest yearnings of the citizen."[119]

For Pericles, like the Athenian speakers at Sparta, it was the Athenian character that created this city. Pericles begins his speech with a promise to discuss "the character that brought us to our present situation and the government and lifestyle that made it great" (2.36.4). He later remarks, "This is the power of the city which we have won from these characteristics" (2.41.2). Pericles' picture of Athens is idealized and abstract. As Parry explains,

> it is a sustained and realized attitude of the mind, expressing itself in manner of living (τρόποι), in daily practices (ἐπιτήδευσις), in laws (νόμοι) both written and unwritten, and in essential, native courage (τῷ ἐς τὰ ἔργα εὐψύχῳ). And it finds its being (ἐνδιαιτᾶται 43,3) not in actuality, but in the minds of men.[120]

Parry goes farther. Regarding his first speech, Parry says that "Pericles is represented as believing that, with a requisite amount of power and resource, and with the energy and devotion that is inherent in the Athenian nature, the intellect can in large part *make* the world."[121] As Marc Cogan notes, "all of Pericles' statements tend toward one point: . . . that [Athens'] greatness is not to be judged as is the greatness of other cities, and that its strength, greatness and prosperity do not reside (as in other cities) in its material wealth or monuments, but in singular qualities of habit, intellect and will."[122] This idealized,

[117] Rood 1998, 141.
[118] It is not clear of what the Athenians are to be the lovers – Athens or its power?
[119] Orwin 1994, 23. Pericles "would transpose to the public sphere that which is most intensely private."
[120] Parry 1981, 160.
[121] Parry 1981, 152.
[122] Cogan 1981a, 41–42.

abstract presentation of the city responds to the historical reality that the physical, truncated city is now packed with homeless refugees from the countryside. With it, Pericles can "convince the Athenians both to continue the war and to continue it on his terms (for in the city of his speech, what is essential has not yet been threatened)."[123]

Pericles' immaterial, idealized *polis* is not grounded in Attica. Pericles claims that "by our daring we have compelled every sea and land to be open to us" (2.41.4), and when he describes the delights the city offers to its inhabitants, he remarks, "Because of the greatness of the city everything from every land comes in to us and it is our luck to enjoy the goods from here with no more homegrown and familiar a pleasure than the goods of other men" (καὶ ξυμβαίνει ἡμῖν μηδὲν οἰκειοτέρᾳ τῇ ἀπολαύσει τὰ αὐτοῦ ἀγαθὰ γιγνόμενα καρποῦσθαι ἢ καὶ τὰ τῶν ἄλλων ἀνθρώπων, 2.38.2). This is consistent with Pericles' reassurance in his first speech that the loss of all of Attica would not really matter because "we have plenty of land both in the islands and on the mainland" (1.143.4). Pericles makes the same argument here when he implies that the Athenians have no more familiarity with, or connection to, the Athenian olive than to the Megarian eel. Athenians have no home goods because they have no homeland. All the world, Pericles implies, is as much Athens as is Attica.

Pericles says almost as much when he speaks of the sepulcher of the dead men. According to Pericles, the honored dead won

> the most notable tomb, not the one in which they lie, but rather the one in which their reputation remains ever remembered on every occasion for word and deed. The whole earth is the grave of famous men and not only the inscription on the grave-markers in their own land (ἐν τῇ οἰκείᾳ) marks it, but even in land that is unconnected to them (καὶ ἐν τῇ μὴ προσηκούσῃ) an unwritten memorial of their resolution rather than their deed dwells in each man (2.43.2–3).

Given that pointing out the graves of his ancestors in Attic soil was one of the ways a man showed his Athenian citizenship and demonstrated that Athens was *oikeios* to him, the claim that the tombs of the glorious Athenian dead are everywhere suggests that the whole world belongs

[123] Cogan 1981a, 42.

to Athens.[124] As Cogan remarks, Pericles "reveal[s] a city that exists wherever the Athenians may be."[125]

But can such a city exist? Can Pericles' intellect really "make the world"? The plague that follows the Funeral Oration certainly shows the untruths in many of the claims of the speech.[126] In a "dramatic juxtaposition," the grand state funeral gives way to corpses rolling in the streets, and all the laws and institutions of the Funeral Oration collapse.[127] As Foster notes, although the Athens of the Funeral Oration is "no doubt almost as rich as she was when Pericles counted her money at 2.13, a lack of materials turns the Athenians into pyre thieves."[128] Leo Strauss remarks on the contrast between Pericles' speech, which "avoid[s] the words 'death,' 'dying,' or 'dead bodies,'" and Thucydides' account of the plague, which "abounds with mentions of death, dead, dying, and corpses."[129] Thucydides emphasizes the juxtapositions by

[124] The examination for office described in [Arist.] *Ath. Pol.* 55.2–3 includes among the questions asked of a magistrate when he is about to enter into his office the inquiry whether he has family tombs and where they are.

[125] Cogan 1981a, 42. Pericles does this partly by emphasizing oral over written communication and reputation over deed; Cf. Steiner (1994, 141–42) : "The normal virtues of monuments, their permanence and fixity, emerge as so many points in their disfavor. While the grave marker is planted in one place, confined to the native land of the men who have died, *doxa* [reputation] recognizes no such boundaries and makes the whole earth the burial place of the fallen."

[126] As Raaflaub (2006, 197) remarks of 2.40.2–3, "much of this will increasingly prove illusionary." Cf. Palmer (1982b, 1992, 29–33) who argues (32–33) that in the plague, "his own funeral oration," Thucydides "tacitly but forcefully expresses his doubts" about "Pericles' political understanding." Pericles, according to Palmer (32), "suggests that love of glory may be the foundation of a regime that will raise us above our fears." The plague, by contrast, "suggests that fear, especially fear of the gods . . . is a necessary ground of that moderation and stability required for all decent political life." Orwin (1984, 1994, 182–83) contrasts Pericles, who "eulogizes citizens who . . . have emancipated themselves from their bodies and live in anticipation of a glorious immortality," with the plague, which "brings home both the primacy and frailty of the body as well as its centrality to actual political life in Athens as elsewhere." The plague passage demonstrates that "society proves to depend more fundamentally on our hopes and fears for our bodies than . . . on our capacity to overcome these." Thucydides "thus corrects the Funeral Oration."

[127] The phrase is Connor's (1984, 64).

[128] Foster 2001, 186.

[129] L. Strauss 1964, 194–95; see also 229, n. 92.

verbal echoes. For example, Pericles claimed that in Athens "a single man provides an individual nimbly and gracefully self-sufficient (τὸ σῶμα αὔταρκες) for all circumstances" (2.41.1), and he called his city "the most self-sufficient" (αὐταρκεστάτη, 2.36.3). Yet during the plague we learn that "no body type – as concerns strength or weakness – showed itself sufficient against it but it destroyed all sorts" (σῶμά τε αὔταρκες ὂν οὐδὲν διεφάνη πρὸς αὐτὸ, 2.51.3). Rusten thinks Thucydides' choice to use the same "striking" phrase in the plague narrative "like the placement of the entire plague narrative immediately after the *epitaphios* seems almost to mock Pericles' initial optimism."[130] Colin Macleod, furthermore, sees in Pericles' use of the term "self-sufficient" an echo of Solon's warnings to Croesus that "a man cannot combine all advantages in himself. Just as no country can adequately supply itself, but has one thing and lacks another and the one which has most is the best: so no single man's person is independent" (αὔταρκες, 1.32.8). Macleod concludes that "with the plague, we see that Pericles' assertions were as doubtful as Croesus' claim to be the most blessed of men."[131]

Yet it is not just the following narrative of the plague that undercuts the certainties of the Funeral Oration. Thucydides' introduction to the speech plants seeds of doubt about the reality of Pericles' vision. In his oration, Pericles claims that it is memory, and especially foreign memory, that is important, not the physical grave. But as Edith Foster points out, Thucydides is careful to note that in the days before the official speech, "people who knew the dead personally bury the actual bones of the fallen in an especially desirable place in the city they died to defend." As she explains, this passage thus "maintains" what she calls (I think rightly) "Thucydides' anti-Periclean emphasis on the reality of private attachments and the importance of tradition."[132]

[130] Rusten 1989, 159.

[131] Macleod 1983a, 150–51. Trans. Macleod. Raaflaub (2006, 197), by contrast, suggests that the commenting may be going in the other direction. He argues that Herodotus is "possibly countering Athens' (or Pericles', Th. 2.36.3) claim" when he "lets Solon deny that any country or individual can be self-sufficient (1.32.8)."

[132] Foster 2001, 182. The passage insists, that is, on the importance of bodies. Cf. the remarks of Palmer (1982b, 1992) and Orwin (1994) mentioned in n. 126 above.

Furthermore, the speech itself is "self-subversive."[133] First, it glorifies sham heroes. Part of the reason Pericles skips quickly over the traditional praise of the ancestors is that the achievements of the dead who are being honored could not stand the comparison.[134] Dionysius of Halicarnassus blamed Thucydides bitterly for including a Funeral Oration at this point in his text:

> Why then, pray, in the case of the few horsemen who brought neither reputation nor additional power to the city, does the historian open the public graves and introduce the most distinguished leader of the people, Pericles, in the act of reciting that lofty tragic composition; whereas, in honor of the larger number and more valiant who caused the people who declared war against the Athenians to surrender to them, and who were more worthy of obtaining such an honor, he did not compose a funeral oration? (*De Thuc.* 18)[135]

Albert Bosworth comments: "With superb skill Pericles insinuates that the deeds of the fallen are quite outstanding, consistent with the city's glorious heritage, but he wisely refrains from spelling out what those deeds actually were."[136]

In Pericles' oration there is a repeated contrast between the falsity or idealization of the speech and the deeds or the actuality of Athens and its men. Pericles begins his speech by challenging the need for it: "It would have seemed to me to be good for the virtues of men who displayed their worth in deed to be made clear also in deed (ἔργῳ) . . . and that the credibility of the virtues of many men not be risked on whether one man speaks well or poorly" (2.35.1). "By pointing out that his *logos* [speech] is not an *ergon* [deed] Thucydides' Pericles alerts his audience to the element of idealization in his portrait of Athens. . . . The contrast is between false, flowery praise in words (i.e. what Pericles is doing) and

[133] Ober 1998, 86.

[134] Cf. Palmer (1982b, 1992, 21): "certainly no notable military engagement has been the occasion of their deaths."

[135] Trans. Pritchett 1975.

[136] Bosworth 2000, 4, n. 21. Bosworth notes (6) "The dead of 431 had perished in a series of skirmishes, most of them inconclusive, and the major event had been a practically uncontested invasion. Against that background the heroic Athenian forefathers were a downright embarrassment, and it is easy to see why Pericles avoided dwelling on their achievement."

the trustworthy evidence of facts."[137] Yet the *erga* of the dead are not very impressive.[138]

Pericles, furthermore, claims that "with great proofs (σημεία) and a power in no way without witness we will be a marvel to men now and in the future" (2.41.1) But what proofs does Pericles mean? He goes on immediately to deny that Athens needs a Homer. Josiah Ober argues that, for this reason, "the *semeia* [proofs] can hardly be in the form of poetic words." We must, he concludes, "imagine permanent monuments of some sort."[139] However, Thucydides' *Archaeology* specifically argued that such monuments will not allow a correct assessment of a city's power (1.10). Thus Pericles' claim that the monuments of Athens will give future generations a correct image of Athenian power "seems a painfully empty boast."[140]

Pericles' speech is not only boastful; it is dangerous. Pericles' presentation of Athenian power knows no bounds. Athenian daring has compelled "every sea and land to be open to us" (2.41.4), and his speech puts few limits on Athens' men.[141] The Funeral Oration, furthermore, is

[137] Ober 1998, 84–85.

[138] Palmer (1982b, 1992, 27) points out a "crowning irony": "These fallen, by having died for Athens, will gain eternal life through eternal glory, yet Thucydides . . . declines even to mention their names!" On the other hand, Herodotus does not give us the names of all the men who died at Thermopylae. He takes care to let us know he learned the names of all three hundred Spartans who fell, however (7.224), and he does record the names of the men who were most outstanding in the battle and those who were shamed by their survival (7.226–229).

[139] Ober 1998, 85.

[140] Ober 1998, 86. Bruell (1981, 29), in discussing Pericles' deprecation of thought and writing in favor of action, remarks that "Thucydides, who clearly regarded his writing and thought, the substance and outcome of his search for truth (1.20.3), as superior to any possible action on his part, quietly presents the evidence for the alternative view."

[141] Hussey (1985, 124) notes that Pericles, in his speech, "breathes no word" of "individual and collective self-discipline. . . . Instead of crushing the individual personality, the Athenian way of life fails to impose any effective check whatever on it." Palmer (1982b, 1992, 24–25) notes Pericles' exaggerations and, more importantly, points out (1992, 27) that his emphasis on the supreme good of glory demands the question, "Will not the logic of love of glory lead some to

"self-subversive" even in Pericles' most famous and most striking claims about the relation between the Athenians and the new city he shows them. When Thucydides denied that an observer would reach a correct assessment of Athenian and Spartan power from their monuments, he contrasted looking to visual appearances with a consideration of more important evidence: "It is not reasonable to consider the appearances of cities rather than their powers" (οὔκουν ἀπιστεῖν εἰκός, οὐδὲ τὰς ὄψεις τῶν πόλεων μᾶλλον σκοπεῖν ἢ τὰς δυνάμεις, 1.10.3). Here Thucydides uses a favorite word for seeing, *skopeo* , that distinguishes him from Herodotus. Herodotus is very fond of the verb *theaomai* , "to gaze," which connotes the "wondering gaze" of the traveler, and "the hold that striking phenomena exert" on the viewer.[142] By contrast, Thucydides "dwells upon the detached observer. His favorite words for vision are *skeptomai* and *skopeo*, virtually synonymous terms for scrutinizing and studying evidence."[143] Thucydides uses *theaomai* only three times in his text. The first is when Cleon gazes like a traveler at Amphipolis (5.7.4). The second is in a passage we have already encountered where the Athenians wield the "theme of the near and the far" against the Melians: "you alone . . . judge things to come to be more clear than what you can see, and in your wishful thinking gaze (*theasthe)* at things unseen as if they have already occurred" (5.113). As Crane reminds us, "the fascinated gaze reflects the self-deluding foolishness that archaic and classical authors so commonly deride. The effect is emotional, and thus subverts rational analysis."[144]

Thucydides' third use of "the fascinated gaze" is in the Funeral Oration, where he combines it with contemplation (*skopeo*):

> It is necessary that those remaining . . . not contemplating (σκοποῦντας) in word alone (μὴ λόγῳ μόνῳ) the benefit, which someone might draw out for you who know it no less, how many goods there are in warding off the enemy, but rather gazing (θεωμένους) every day at the power of the city as it really is (ἔργῳ), become its lovers (2.43).

want more than others?" For Palmer, this Periclean vision leads to tyrannical individuals like Alcibiades. (Cf. L. Strauss, 1964, 193–95).

142 Crane 1996, 239 and 242.

143 Crane 1996, 241.

144 Crane 1996, 245.

Crane remarks:

> Here, and here alone, a speaker in Thucydides not only brings the two terms together, but he dismisses as inadequate the coolly rational contemplation implied by *skopeo*. When the Thucydidean Pericles presents his idealizing vision of Athens – a vision that reflects less what Athens really was than what it should be – he calls upon all Athenians to shake off the coldly analytical pose of the thinker.[145]

Crane goes on to note Pericles' claim that "we will be a source of wonder to the present and succeeding ages, since we have not left our power without witness, but have shown it by mighty proofs" (2.41.4) and interprets Pericles' words thus:

> Athenian power is not an illusion, but real and demonstrable through external proof. Athens is not some suspect *thauma*, a marvel from the ends of the earth or the distant past that can be described but not substantiated. The greatness of Athens is tangible, its power genuine, and, for this reason, observer and patriot alike can justifiably surrender to their emotions.[146]

However, as Ober has argued, there are no proofs. Pericles' words are simply a "painfully empty boast."[147] Crane himself admits that "Thucydides' narrative undercuts Pericles' ideas" but argues that "it does not so much attack Pericles' stated goals as the gap that separates vision from reality."[148] On the contrary, Thucydides' narrative and the "self-subversive" speech he has given to Pericles suggest that he is wrong to urge Athenians to irrationally wonder at a city that does not exist. Thucydides' use of the wondering *theaomai* here, together with the repeated accusations that the Athenians do not know where their homeland is, begin to wield the theme of the near and the far against the Athenians. The combination suggests that Pericles is encouraging his people in a dangerous, foolish fascination for things distant and insubstantial.[149]

[145] Crane 1996, 246.
[146] Crane 1996, 247.
[147] Ober, 1998, 86.
[148] Crane, 1996, 246.
[149] Cf. Foster 2001, 163–64: Pericles' command "asks people to look at what is in fact invisible. . . . He is asking his hearers to . . . be struck with an irrational devotion that does not calculate."

Thucydides' narrative repeatedly undercuts his presentation of Pericles. Many of Pericles' confident predictions turn out to be wrong. The Spartans do eventually gain naval skill. They do eventually lure Athenian sailors away with higher pay, and the Athenians have to enfranchise their slaves to man their ships for Arginussae. It becomes clear that the Peloponnesians' navy is cause for worry, as is a fortification in Attica that, when the Spartans finally build it, "particularly damaged affairs" and transformed Athens from a city into a "fortress" (7.27.3–28.1).[150] Thucydides' digression on the Athenians' rural lifestyle, with its comparison to Theseus, revealed that Pericles' people only painfully and reluctantly accepted his vision of the city, implying that his synoecism was likely to fail. Finally, Pericles' idealized city of the Funeral Oration falls victim to the physical in the plague. When Pericles turns his citizens away from their real land of Attica toward the whole world, from their real city to an idealized vision that he wants them to gaze at in erotic fascination, there is more than a hint that he is leading them to disaster.

THE MASTERS OF HALF THE WORLD LAMENT THE LOSS OF THEIR HOUSES

Thucydides' deliberate placement of the plague narrative immediately after Pericles' Funeral Oration calls into question Pericles' vision of Athens. The plague also caused the Athenians to challenge Pericles' leadership. The disease was accompanied by a Spartan invasion of Attica. The double calamity of plague and invasion sank the Athenians into utter despondency and caused a marked change in the Athenians' willingness to follow Pericles' plan for the war. The Athenians,

[150] Contrast this to Pericles' claim in his first speech that the Spartans "will not easily gain expert status on the sea" (1.142.6–7) and his reassurance there that it would be "a serious thing" if the Peloponnesians lured their sailors away but only "if going on board we ourselves together with our metics were not an equal to them" (1.143). Finally, Pericles airily claimed that "neither their fortification-building nor their navy is worth worrying about" (1.142.2).

Thucydides writes, "changed their opinions and they cast blame at Pericles because he had persuaded them to go to war and because (they said) it was his fault that they have fallen on these misfortunes" (2.59.1–2). The Athenians sent ambassadors to Sparta to try to make peace, only to have them come away empty-handed. This, of course, only increased their despondency. As Thucydides explains it, "their planning was reduced to despair in every way and they attacked Pericles" (2.59.2). Pericles, observing the bitter feeling against him, called an assembly in order to stoke their courage (2.59.3). Such is the context of Pericles' final speech in Thucydides' text and his final description of his city (2.60–64).

Pericles begins by saying that he expected this outbreak of anger against him and had called the assembly in order "to remind you of some things and also chastise you if there is anything unreasonable in your being angry at me and your yielding to circumstances" (2.60). As many commentators have noticed, there is a striking opposition here between leader and people.[151] Pericles argued that the people were merely giving into their suffering: "You are changing course since it happens that you were persuaded to go to war when you were still unharmed but you repent of it now when things are going badly for you and in your weakness of judgment my policy seems wrong." By contrast, he said of himself, "I am the same, I do not alter" (2.61.2). This echoes Pericles' assertion in his first speech that his judgment "is always the same" (1.140.1). However, his advice to the Athenians, at least in its details and fullness, does change in this speech, as even he emphasizes. Pericles tells his people that they had an advantage they had not yet thought of and that he had never mentioned in his previous speeches. "Indeed," he says, "I would not even now use this argument, since it is a bit boastful, if I did not see that you were unreasonably panic-stricken" (2.62.1). The contrast between Pericles' claim that he is ever the same and his announcement that he will now tell the Athenians something new is surely meant to focus our attention on Pericles' boastful new argument.

[151] As Connor (1984, 65) comments, "'I' and 'you' become the means of discourse."

Pericles gives his people this encouragement:

You think that you hold your *arche* only over your allies, but I tell you that of the two useful parts that the world is divided into, land and sea, you are complete masters over all of the latter, both as much as you now hold and still more if you wish. And there is no one, not the king of Persia nor any other people who now live, who could prevent you sailing with your present naval force. This power of yours is not of the same order as the advantage of houses and of land which you think are important things to be stripped of. Nor is it fitting for you to bear this with difficulty because of them but rather you ought to consider them like a little garden or bauble of wealth and take no heed of them in contrast with this power (οὐδ᾽ εἰκὸς χαλεπῶς φέρειν αὐτῶν μᾶλλον ἢ οὐ κηπίον καὶ ἐγκαλλώπισμα πλούτου πρὸς ταύτην νομίσαντας ὀλιγωρῆσαι, 2.62.2–3).

Pericles' words are indeed boastful; he claims that the Athenians are literally complete masters of half of the world.[152] He specifically denies that he is talking merely of the lands that the Athenians now hold and rule. The Athenians are wrong, he says, when they "think that you hold your *arche* – your imperial power – only over your allies." Pericles insists, by contrast, that the Athenians now rule over and are "complete masters" (κυριωτάτους) over even other territories as well, "if you wish."[153] Thus that which belongs to Athens becomes, in Pericles'

[152] Pericles' vision echoes the word choice of the " Old Oligarch" who repeatedly calls the Athenians "thallasocrats" (2.2, 2.14) or "rulers of the sea." That last term becomes a synonym for the Athenians in this text: 2.3, 2.5, 2.11.

[153] Connor (1984, 70) argues that despite his claim to newness, what Pericles says "develops the conceit alluded to in the Funeral Oration that Athens has by its boldness subordinated both land and sea under the feet of its citizens (40.4)." For this reason, some scholars have supposed that this indicates different periods of composition for the two speeches. Connor (1984, 70, n. 46) calls the problem "specious" because in Pericles' last speech, "Thucydides does not claim that the idea has never before been heard but that no one has taken the idea seriously" and because "he then proceeds to develop the conceit much more elaborately than in the earlier passage." The passages are, however, more different than Connor and other critics admit. In the Funeral Oration, Pericles mentions both land and sea; here the focus is solely on the sea and on the specific replacement of all sea lands both for the empire the Athenians now know and for Attica. As Bloedow (2000, 300) insists, "Pericles clearly indicates that there is something fundamentally new here."

interpretation, all land vulnerable to naval power.[154] The potential is the actual to Pericles.[155]

In his first speech, Pericles said that the Peloponnesians "will not be able to lay hold of other territory without fighting for it but we have plenty of land both in the islands and on the mainland" (1.143.4). Gomme insisted that Pericles did not mean here that there was "actual Athenian territory abroad."[156] Yet that is exactly what Pericles implied in that first speech and what he says explicitly in this last speech. He describes the Athenians as complete masters of the sea. Perhaps the stumbling block in Gomme's disagreement is his focus on "actual Athenian territory," for this suggests that there is real and (somehow) unreal Athenian territory and surely assumes that the "real" Athenian territory is in Attica. However, it is just this calculation that Pericles rejects. The Athenians are complete masters of the sea, not merely the rulers of Attica or even of their present *arche*; they can have whatever they wish, whether they hold it now or not, and Attica means no more to Pericles than does any other territory under Athenian rule.

Thucydides' early presentation of Pericles' city charges that Athenians do not make a distinction between their own possessions and those of others. The Corinthians, in their speech to the Spartan congress, warned the Peloponnesians that if the Athenians set their minds on something

[154] De Romilly (1947/1963, 123) denies that Pericles "intends to encourage the Athenians to undertake new conquests" (in which she is seconded by Rengakos 1984, 44). De Romilly asserts that Pericles "speaks only of the sea, of people sailing on it . . . he really means the water itself. There is no question of seizing islands, coasts, or ports." This cannot be correct (but if true, would seem to hold Pericles open to charges of Xerxes-like hubris). Although I do not doubt that Thucydides meant to imply a certain hubristic sense of "ruling the water," I think it clear that Pericles is, indeed, talking of expanding the area the Athenians "hold their *arche* over" and thus of conquest. Palmer (1992, 35) rightly emphasizes the possible "dramatic effects" of Pericles' "boasts and blandishments" on Athenian understanding of his war policy: "Might Pericles be understood here to condone implicitly endeavors like the Sicilian expedition?"

[155] As Foster (2001, 168) notes, Pericles "quite literally offers the Athenians the world. What was suggested in the Funeral Oration, but perhaps passed for poetry, namely that the Athenians were conquering the sea and the earth, is here claimed as outright fact."

[156] Gomme 1945, *s.v.* 1.143.4.

and failed to obtain it, they reacted as if they "had been robbed of their household property" (1.70.7). This conforms precisely to Pericles' vision in this speech. According to his presentation of the Athenians' control of the watery part of the world, wishing is the only difference between what the Athenians actually have and what they could have. They can have "still more, if you wish."

During the Persian wars, the Athenians refused to be bound by their geography. They transformed themselves into sailors; they uprooted their *polis* and brought it with them as they went on board ship. Pericles has a similar vision of the world in which Athens is not limited by geography. In fact, he recognizes no land boundaries at all, for Athens is as extensive as the sea. Along with the possession of the whole world comes a concomitant rejection of home. The Athenians have no particular "homegrown pleasure" in Attic goods because they do not recognize a single home – certainly not in Attica.[157]

Pericles' last speech powerfully highlights this point because it couples his new concept of Athenian possessions with an especially impressive abandonment and, indeed, deprecation of traditional Athenian territory that even goes beyond what he had said before. In his first speech, Pericles told the Athenians they had to abandon their land and their houses to "safeguard the sea and the city" (1.143.5) and said that if he thought he could persuade them, he would urge them to lay waste their houses and land themselves to show the Peloponnesians that "you will not yield to them for the sake of these things" (1.143.5). Now that the Athenians have seen their land and houses laid waste by the Peloponnesians, Pericles tells them how to respond. The Athenians, he says, should think of their houses and fields as similar to gardens or other baubles of wealth. They are essentially superfluous – nothing really to care about or to get upset about. Anyone who thinks they are is, in some way, both ostentatious and misguided. Foster notes that this is "logical" because "a different value might easily conflict with the fixed value of the empire. If Attica is worth having, then the empire is a

[157] Sicking (1995, 412) underscores that "we should not underestimate the significance of this forthright negation of fundamental assumptions that had guided the Greek world for centuries, and which outside Athens still constituted the standard view of the conditions of existence."

relative value, and can be drawn back out into the sphere of real life in which it is compared to other good or bad things."[158] This, however, Pericles cannot and does not allow.

There are reasons for unease with this vision of the city.[159] First, as Foster remarks, the Athenian Empire was, in fact, "medium-sized," and Pericles "had plenty of contact with sea powers that Athens did not control, as well as the dangerously rebellious allies. Pericles' repeated assurances that Athens controls the sea (1.143.5, 2.41.4, 2.62.2) are thus a replacement of precision with poetic exaggeration "[160] Second, Robert Connor notes, Pericles' vision here rejects the presentation of the city that Pericles gave in the Funeral Oration: "the amenities of Athenian life, confidently recognized as refreshments for the mind (2.38.1) in the Funeral Oration, are now to be cast overboard in the effort to maintain Athens' power."[161] Yet it was the preservation of the city of the Funeral Oration that Pericles used to justify the war. Finally, the text has given ample reason to doubt as to whether the Athenians will be willing to follow Pericles' exhortations here.

Pericles urges the Athenians to judge the loss of their houses and cultivated fields as though they were gardens or baubles of wealth. However, when Thucydides actually describes the Athenians' response to the loss of house and land when he recounts their move into the island city, he writes that they cared so much about their homes and household possessions that they even stripped the decorative woodwork off their houses to save it from Spartan destruction (2.14.1).

This is surely a curious detail for Thucydides to have included in his work. It is all the more noticeable because of Pericles' emphasis on houses in his first and last speeches and his insistence that the Athenians must abandon their houses and treat their loss lightly. Thucydides "all but excludes" from his work the house or *oikos* "both as physical structure and as social unit."[162] Yet this section of the history, and especially this

[158] Foster 2001, 169.

[159] The "extravagance" of Pericles' last speech was so striking to Andrewes (1960, 7) that he used it alone as an argument that the speech "is not based primarily on record or recollection of what Pericles said."

[160] Foster 2001, 161.

[161] Connor 1984, 70.

[162] Crane 1996, 126.

reference to the decorative woodwork, focuses on the Athenians' houses. In this reference the physical houses of the rural Athenians intrude into the text with their stone or stucco walls, the doors and windows framed in the wood the Athenians now carefully remove.

Thucydides' description of the Athenians' move into the city begins and ends with houses. Immediately after Pericles' speech, we learn that "the Athenians . . . brought in from the fields their children and women and the other property that they used at home, taking down the woodwork from the houses themselves" (αὐτῶν τῶν οἰκιῶν καθαιροῦντες τὴν ξύλωσιν, 2.14.1). At the end of his description of the move, Thucydides concludes that "they were oppressed and found it difficult to leave their houses" (οἰκίας τε καταλείποντες, 2.16.2). These Athenians, at least, have a well-developed connection to home and place and do not want to leave them. Crane argues that Thucydides' excursus on rural Attica shows that "Thucydides' Athenians do not so much miss the comfort of their homes as the smaller, more personalized local *poleis* in which they had grown up."[163] Yet Thucydides' first and last sentences focus on houses, not local government, and Thucydides' description of the Athenians removing the woodwork from their houses helps the reader judge how well the Athenians could be expected to accept Pericles' city.

This section of Pericles' last speech makes an emphatic verbal link back to Thucydides' description of the Athenians' move into his city with the word "with difficulty" (χαλεπῶς). Thucydides uses this word at both the beginning and end of his description of the Athenians' move. Its emphasis demonstrates the limited success of Theseus' earlier synoecism and this hints at failure for the physical synoecism of Pericles. Pericles' use of the word in this speech strikes the same chord and focuses our attention on the reluctance of the Athenians to accept the primacy of the *polis* over the *oikos*. Pericles told the Athenians that it is not fitting for them to bear the loss of their houses and lands "with difficulty" (2.62.3). However, Thucydides' text has already told us that they do bear it "with difficulty." The echo underscores that the people and the leader do not think in the same way about houses. Pericles' reference to that (he says unfitting) difficulty here emphasizes that the Athenians are not reconciled to their loss even now. Pericles offers to replace the

[163] Crane 1996, 137.

Athenians' houses and indeed even Attica itself with his vision of a limitless city on the sea. Will they find this just compensation?[164]

This speech is Pericles' last appearance in Thucydides' text, although he lived for almost another year. Thus Thucydides chose this speech and its radical redefinition of the city as the reader's last impression of Pericles. The questions it raises are thus unresolved as Pericles disappears from the text. Thucydides' presentation of Pericles' abstract idea of the island city has shown that it requires divisive sacrifices. With his use of the theme of the near and the far, furthermore, Thucydides intimates that Pericles' radical redefinition of the city is a foolish delusion that holds within it the seeds of *stasis.* The Athenians' ability to redefine their city saved them in the Persian War, but Thucydides shows that Pericles' much more radical redefinition of the city, which trades Attica and the traditional city there for limitless conquest on the sea, may destroy them.

[164] Foster (2001, 178) argues that "the destruction of the houses is also a sign of the dissolution of Attic culture." In the plague that follows the Athenians' move into their fortress city, the Athenians famously become (in Foster's words, 186) "pyre-thieves." We can assume, then, that there was a shortage of wood in the city and that the decorations so lovingly taken from the Athenians' country homes were burned up under the corpses of the dead. Furthermore, Thucydides takes care to note in his plague description that the Athenians who had come into the city from the countryside lived in "huts" because "they had no houses" (οἰκιῶν γὰρ οὐχ ὑπαρχουσῶν, 2.52.2) and so underscores again the Athenians' loss. Pericles had argued that the Athenians must "not make lament over houses and land but over lives" (1.143.5). We may imagine, however, that as the Athenians stood around the pyres lit, in part, from the wood from their country houses, they lamented both their lives and their houses. In following Pericles, the Athenians lost them both.

2 The Sea and the City

THE ATHENIANS CHOOSE PERICLES' CITY

At the completion of Pericles' last speech, in which he disclosed to the Athenians his "quite boastful" vision of an Athens that had traded its land and houses in Attica for control of half of the world, Thucydides segues into the so-called *Epitaph* of Pericles (2.65). Thucydides reveals here that Pericles lived only two years and six months after his speech, and he compares Pericles' leadership of Athens with that of his successors. According to Thucydides, after Pericles died, "his foresight in regard to the war was still more evident." He goes on to explain

> Pericles said that the Athenians would come out on top if they kept quiet and took care of the navy, if they did not add to the empire during the course of the war, and if they did not take risks with the city; others did the opposite of Pericles with respect to all points of his advice, and following personal ambition and personal profit they managed things badly both for themselves and for their allies (2.65.7).[1]

At the end of the *Epitaph*, Thucydides notes that even after Sicily, Pericles' successors held out for years

> against their former enemies and, together with them, those from Sicily and, furthermore, against most of their own allies who had revolted and later against Cyrus the son of the king in addition, who provided money to the Peloponnesians

[1] Connor (1984, 61, n. 27, following Classen/Steup) concludes that Thucydides' "indictment is very general and at least initially is directed as much against the Athenians as a whole as against the politicians."

for their fleet. And they did not give in until falling afoul of each other in their private disagreements they were overthrown (2.65.12).

Thucydides uses the Athenians' ability to hold out as his link back to Pericles: "so great at this time was the abundance of resources at Pericles' disposal, through which he foresaw that the city would very easily prevail in the war over the Peloponnesians alone."

This is a very curious passage. On the one hand, this eulogy of Pericles might seem to preclude the critique of his policy I have argued Thucydides' text to this point offers. As Connor notes, it has been common to read the last sentence in particular as the cry of "the defender of Pericles and his policies against critics who fail to recognize that if only his advice had been followed, Athens could have won."[2] And many modern scholars see Thucydides as the defender of Pericles. Malcolm McGregor, for example, speaks of the "glowing enthusiasm detectable in the Periclean speeches and the estimate of Pericles."[3] Jacqueline de Romilly judged that Thucydides "approved of and admired Pericles."[4] Peter Pouncey calls Pericles Thucydides' "paragon" and his "hero."[5] Hornblower, for his part, argues that "personal prejudice – the spell of Pericles and the nostalgia for Pericles induced by experience of his less stylish successors – stood between Thucydides and a correct assessment" of at least partial Periclean culpability for Athens' defeat.[6] Yunis claims that "given Thucydides' unqualified admiration for Pericles and his leadership of the *demos*, we have no basis for inferring that Thucydides had any reservations about Pericles at all."[7] On the other hand, such readings (of Thucydides and of the *Epitaph*) seem to ignore the

[2] Connor 1984, 73. Cf. Gomme (1951, 75), who notes that it is "customary to assert" that Thucydides wrote the *Epitaph* after the war "with express reference to the final defeat, as a defence of Pericles to his despairing and incredulous fellow citizens."

[3] McGregor 1956, 97.

[4] De Romilly 1965, 558.

[5] Pouncey 1980, 80–81. See now Will (2003): *Thukydides und Perikles. Der Historiker und sein Held.*

[6] Hornblower 1987, 174–75.

[7] Yunis 1996, 69–70.

unavoidable awkwardness and irony of praising Pericles' foresight of victory in a war that was, in fact, lost.[8]

The details of the *Epitaph* cause difficulties as well. Given Thucydides' enumeration of the elements of Pericles' advice and his specific claim that his successors "did the opposite of Pericles with respect to all points" of it, the clear implication of the *Epitaph* is that Pericles' successors failed because they did not keep quiet, did not look after the navy, extended the empire during the war, and took risks with the city. Unfortunately, Thucydides gives no specific examples demonstrating this. Of the "many mistakes" (ἄλλα τε πολλά . . . ἡμαρτήθη) he says were made, Thucydides names only one, the Sicilian Expedition, and even here he does not condemn it because the Athenians were not quiet, risked the fleet, tried to extend the empire, and so endangered the city. Perhaps this is thought to be obvious, but Thucydides' discussion of the Sicilian Expedition suggests otherwise. For example, Thucydides insists that the expedition to Sicily was

> not so much a mistake of judgment about those whom they attacked as much as those who sent the expedition out not making the proper decisions for those who went. Through their individual disputes over the leadership of the *demos* they blunted the effectiveness of the army and for the first time were thrown into confusion with regard to the affairs of the city (2.65.11).[9]

Thucydides here strongly implies that the exact blunder in Sicily is *not* obvious and so raises a measure of doubt about the precise way in which Athens after Pericles diverged from Pericles.

Thucydides further contributes to the confusion because of the way he describes Pericles' policy and foresight. He writes in the *Epitaph*,

[8] As Gribble (1998, 53) points out, 2.65 "adverts to the time of narration. In doing so it merely points explicitly to the knowledge shared by reader and narrator of the way things turned out which has been constantly in the background of the narrative so far." So, too, Palmer (1992, 41) argues of the *Epitaph* that "what begins as praise of Pericles and shifts to blame of his successors and pure democracy ends perhaps, as a critique of Pericles. Suffice it to say that Thucydides' eulogy is by no means as unambiguous as it first appears."

[9] Most scholars see here a reference to the attacks on Alcibiades and his dismissal as one of the commanders of the Sicilian expedition.

"Pericles said that the Athenians would come out on top if they kept quiet and took care of the navy, if they did not add to the empire during the course of the war, and if they did not take risks with the city" (ὁ μὲν γὰρ ἡσυχάζοντάς τε καὶ τὸ ναυτικὸν θεραπεύοντας καὶ ἀρχὴν μὴ ἐπικτωμένους ἐν τῷ πολέμῳ μηδὲ τῇ πόλει κινδυνεύοντας ἔφη περιέσεσθαι, 2.65.7), but his presentation here is not consistent with what he tells us Pericles said in his speeches. Thucydides mimics, with careful verbal echoes, Pericles' assessment from his first speech that "I have many other reasons for my expectation that you will come out on top if you are willing not to add to the empire while you are fighting the war and do not involve yourself in risks of your own making" (πολλὰ δὲ καὶ ἄλλα ἔχω ἐς ἐλπίδα τοῦ περιέσεσθαι, ἢν ἐθέλητε ἀρχήν τε μὴ ἐπικτᾶσθαι ἅμα πολεμοῦντες καὶ κινδύνους αὐθαιρέτους μὴ προστίθεσθαι, 1.144.1). The echo of "come out on top," Thucydides' reference to not adding to the empire during the war, and talk of risks, make it seem as if Thucydides is carefully repeating in the *Epitaph* exactly what he says Pericles said in his first speech. However, although Thucydides echoes Pericles' warning about risks – in Thucydides' formulation in the *Epitaph* he claims that Pericles urged the Athenians not to take risks specifically "with the city" (μηδὲ τῇ πόλει κινδυνεύοντας). According to Thucydides' own account of his speech, however, Pericles had actually been much more general, speaking vaguely only of "risks of your own making" (κινδύνους αὐθαιρέτους).

Thucydides' formulation in the *Epitaph*, by contrast, focuses great attention on "the city." This is highly significant because of Thucydides' emphasis, up to this point, on Pericles' redefinition of the city as an entity without ties to Attica, a redefinition that identifies the city with the navy and the sea. Indeed, when Pericles himself spoke of the city in his warnings to the Athenians, he did not speak of "the city" alone. Rather he told the Athenians to "safeguard the sea and the city" (1.143.5). Therefore, if Pericles at some point really told the Athenians, as Thucydides claims, not to "take risks with the city," the speeches Thucydides has reported suggest that we should really read this to mean "don't take risks with the 'sea-and-the-city.'" This may seem a small distinction, but "the sea-and-the-city" is a far less conservative formulation than Thucydides' wording in the *Epitaph* because it focuses Athenian attention away from the city in Attica to the entire sea-borne empire – or recognizes that the city in Attica, now divorced from its land, is dependent on that sea-borne empire. Not taking risks with *that* city is a bit more complicated.[10]

Thucydides' formulation of Pericles' policy in the *Epitaph* is more conservative than what he has shown us of Pericles himself in another aspect as well. Thucydides begins his presentation of Pericles' strategy in the *Epitaph* by saying, "Pericles said that the Athenians would come out on top if they kept quiet." However, this does not conform to the speech we have just (as it were) "heard" Pericles give. In his last speech, which ends immediately before the *Epitaph*, Pericles did not tell the Athenians to keep "quiet." On the contrary, he told the Athenians, "of the two useful parts that the world is divided into, land and sea, you are complete masters over all of the latter, both as much as you now hold and still more if you wish" (2.62.2).[11] To this image of complete control of the sea, Pericles added no note of quiet or caution.[12] Gomme underlines the "contrast between the cautious, almost Nician tone of 65.7 and the magniloquence and adventurous spirit of the last words given to Pericles, 63–4: 'action and yet more action, and we gain a glorious name even if we fail.'"[13] In this "magniloquent" speech, Pericles gave the Athenians no command not to try to add to the empire during the war. In fact, Pericles' vision seems almost to encourage the Athenians to leave their "little gardens and baubles" behind and seize their city's real territory: the sea and everything it reaches.[14] Pericles' last speech reduces the conflict between his supposed defensive policy and

[10] Though all direct the reader to the earlier passages, neither Gomme 1956a nor Ruston 1989 nor Hornblower 1991 notes the discrepancy I point out here. Gomme (1951, 71, n. 6) judges that "2.65.7 repeats the advice attributed to Pericles in 1.144.1."

[11] Cf. Palmer (1982b, 1992, 38): "the prognosis of Athenian power that is most recent in the reader's mind [when reading the *Epitaph*] is that of Pericles' last speech . . . : illimitable imperial expansion."

[12] See Palmer (1982a, 1982b, 1992) for the consequences for Athens of Pericles' encouragements here.

[13] Gomme 1951, 71, n. 6.

[14] Bloedow (2000, 300), remarks that Pericles' speech could easily have encouraged Athenians to dream of conquest "*unintentionally*. . . . Moreover, if he really did possess the *pronoia* [foresight] with which Thucydides credits him, he ought to have been able to foresee the real implications inherent in his statement."

his people, between "the Periclean demand for restraint and tranquility," as Connor describes it, and "the innately restless character of the Athenians" because Pericles is no longer asking the Athenians to violate their natures by keeping quiet.[15] Thus, if the *Epitaph* is a "defense" of Pericles, the discrepancy between its presentation of Pericles' policy and that policy as articulated in his last speech justifies us in asking, with Gomme, defense "of which Pericles – the prudent strategist, as in 2.65, or the adventurous imperialist"?[16]

Thucydides' presentation of Pericles' policy in the *Epitaph* diverges from what he has shown us of Pericles in two important aspects. Thucydides claims that Pericles insisted on "quiet" and eschewed new acquisitions, but in his last speech, Pericles did no such thing (quite the opposite, in fact). Furthermore, Thucydides suggests that safeguarding "the city" was a straightforward idea, although he has carefully demonstrated that for the Athenians the "city" was a point in dispute, and for Pericles, at least, it meant Athens' sea-borne empire and, it seems, the sea itself. In the *Epitaph*, Thucydides claims that after Pericles, "others did the opposite of Pericles with respect to all points of his advice." Yet he has made it difficult for his readers to judge whether this assessment is correct because of the divergence between his presentation of Pericles' views in the *Epitaph* and his Pericles' formulation of those views in the speeches.[17]

Thucydides has also made it difficult for readers to contrast Athenian action before and after Pericles because of his decision to announce Pericles' death "two years and six months" (2.65.6) before the actual

[15] Connor 1984, 73. Cf. Palmer 1992, 35. Hussey (1985, 125) claims that "Pericles, in spite of his rhetoric in 2.37–43, saw the vital importance of keeping a strict limit on Athens' commitments" and suggests that disaster came only because "his policies were finally thrown overboard." But Pericles' last speech does not seem to include any "limit on Athens' commitments" whatsoever, certainly not a "strict" one. So, too, Rengakos (1984, 44, citing Plenio 1954, 49) claims that Pericles' statements about the ability of Athens to sail wherever it wants are "purely hypothetical.... Its sense is that the Athenians, who are temporarily crowded together in the city, actually possess unlimited scope for activity." I agree with Bloedow (2000, 301) that this is "simply not compelling."

[16] Gomme 1951, 75.

[17] Thus I disagree with Ober (1985, 171) that Thucydides' summary at 2.65.7 is "unambiguous."

event instead of reporting it at the point it occurred in his year-by-year chronicle. He reports it in a dramatic manner. As S. Sara Monoson and Michael Loriaux write, "the narrative leaves the reader asking: 'Wait a minute, did Pericles just die?'"[18] Yet the dramatic recounting makes it difficult for readers to draw a clear line between actions that were carried out under Pericles' guidance and those that were not. For example, Connor argues that the Epitaph "impose[s] over the natural time-scheme of the year-to-year narrative a further chronological division based on the end of Periclean leadership. We are led to view events as before or after Pericles . . . ," but as he notes, Pericles' role in the "several major decisions" the Athenians made between his last appearance in the work and his death in "the autumn of 429" is "quite obscure."[19] For example, although Connor argues that the decision to assure Plataea of full support occurred early enough that Pericles must still have been alive,[20] Badian is able to read the Athenians' "formal promise of aid which they well knew they would not be able to give" as a "first glimpse of the changes in Athens that Thucydides wants us to ascribe to war and the end of Pericles' dominance."[21] Thus the line between events "before and after Pericles" is considerably blurry.

Furthermore, Thucydides undercuts the clear implication of the early part of the *Epitaph* – that the successors of Pericles failed because they did the opposite of what he advised and were restless, did not care for the navy, tried to add to the empire during the war, and took risks with the city – with his later emphasis on *stasis*. For example, Thucydides informs us that the Sicilian Expedition failed not because it was an aggressive, expansive campaign that risked the navy (and the city?), but because the senders "through their individual disputes over the leadership of the

[18] Monoson and Loriaux 1992, 290. As they note, Thucydides "could have included some narration of the circumstances of that death, but in doing so he would have eased the reader into the knowledge of Pericles' loss." Thus "Thucydides empowers us to experience vicariously the shock and confusion that the Athenians of the period must have felt."

[19] Connor 1984, 75–76. We reach a date of autumn 429 for Pericles' death if we take 2.65.6 to mean that he died two years and six months after the start of the war in 431. Cf. Connor 1984, 75, and n. 55.

[20] Connor 1984, 75, n. 56.

[21] Badian 1993, 111.

demos blunted the effectiveness of the army and for the first time were thrown into confusion with regard to the affairs of the city" (2.65.11). Furthermore, Thucydides attributes Athens' eventual defeat to *stasis*: when "coming to grief through individual disputes, they brought about their own overthrow" (2.65.12). In short, if the *Epitaph* is supposed to provide Thucydides' precise opinion of why Athens fell and a succinct explanation of how Pericles' successors diverged from his policy, he has made a rather poor job of it.

It is better to read the *Epitaph* as a prime example of Thucydides offering his reader what appears to be a quick and easy answer while later demonstrating that the situation is far more complex. As Connor explains, "Thucydides' text . . . often achieve[s] its literary effects by subverting assumptions and expectations that it has itself already established."[22] Thucydides' penchant for antithesis "extends to the very structure of the work, to the juxtaposition from phrase to phrase, chapter to chapter, book to book of starkly contrasting images, such that expectations nurtured at one point are dashed at another."[23] In this case, the *Epitaph* responds in part to "a background of hostile public opinion."[24] The "apparent defense of Pericles" is designed to show that "it is too simple to dismiss Pericles or to conclude that Athens should simply have yielded to Peloponnesian demands." The *Epitaph* is meant "to prevent premature and facile judgments about [the war]."[25] It does not provide "an encapsulation of Thucydides' view about the war, or a resolution to the interpretive problem of the text."[26] We should not take it as Thucydides' final judgment on either Pericles or the war.[27] Indeed, the

[22] Connor 1991, 57–58.

[23] Monoson and Loriaux 1992, 286.

[24] Gribble 1999, 189, n. 83. Cf. Schwarz 1929.

[25] Connor 1984, 74–75.

[26] Connor 1984, 74.

[27] We should note with caution, for example, that Thucydides' judgment about the efficacy of Pericles' strategy appears in a contrafactual. It is, as Hunt (2006, 397) writes, "a confident appraisal of a course of action not taken." Hunt argues (399–400) that Thucydides' "frequent consideration of what could have been gives his whole history . . . a greater sense of the possibilities that lay open than some of his interpreters acknowledge." This should give us pause in taking Thucydides' "judgment" about Pericles and his strategy in the *Epitaph* as his final word on the subject.

Epitaph subtly counsels that it is too simple to argue that Pericles' successors diverged entirely from his policy and that if only Pericles had lived, Athens would have won.[28] As Edmund Bloedow notes, Thucydides "presents us with two Pericles, without resolving the contradictions between them." On the one hand, there is Pericles the moderate imperialist, but there is also the man who "in virtually the same breath for the first time brandishes before the minds of the Athenians the notion of unlimited empire." "Given the Athenian temperament," Bloedow goes on, "characterised by a high degree of πολυπραγμοσύνη ["curiosity," "busyness"], which he himself had done much to undergird and to foster, it should surprise no one that his successors combined the two and opted for expansion." Bloedow concludes that "Pericles was, when it came to *Machtdenken* [his philosophy of power], really not basically different from any other Athenian – contemporary or successor." Bloedow claims, nevertheless, that "this picture of Pericles is completely at variance with the one which Thucydides has drawn."[29] In fact, I believe that Thucydides carefully draws his portrait of Pericles to lead us to the very conclusion Bloedow reaches.

In the text that follows the *Epitaph*, Thucydides makes it clear that after Pericles' death, the Athenians did not reject Pericles' vision of the city on the sea. Much of the text up to this point had focused on whether the Athenians would accept Pericles' city or would show themselves "slaves to their land" and go out to fight the Spartans. Archidamus almost goaded them into doing so, and Pericles only barely prevented the Athenians from marching out against him. With Pericles dead, we might expect that the Athenians would revert to valuing their houses and land over Pericles' vision of the city at sea. Furthermore, if the Athenians really "did the opposite of Pericles with respect to all points of his advice," as Thucydides claims, they should have rejected Pericles' radical definition of the city. Yet Thucydides shows that a land-based vision of Athens, which might compel the Athenians to march out against the Spartans, is never again an issue. The Athenians choose Pericles' city.

[28] See Orwin (2000, 862) who argues that the *Epitaph* "implies, in what it says and what it does not, a critique of Pericles." Rasmussen (1995, 41) argues that the *Epitaph* is simply a "political analysis of domestic affairs" and is not "meant to be Thucydides' praise of Pericles."

[29] Bloedow 2000, 308.

The narrative of events immediately after Pericles' disappearance from the text seems subtly to support Pericles' abandonment strategy, but Thucydides' detailed account of the fate of Plataea sounds a discordant note. Thucydides' focus on loss in the Plataean story raises questions about the efficacy and the dangers of city transformations. These questions suggest that the Athenians will lose much, perhaps even their Athenian identity, in redefining their city. The Plataeans' willingness to act Athenian, and the Thebans' charge that Athens causes cities to be like it, demonstrate the expansive power of Athens but also call into question the Athenians' claim to being exceptional. Nevertheless, we see the successors of Pericles take up and use the most expansive vision of the city from his last speech. The Athenians "become victims of their own propaganda."[30] Furthermore, many of Athens' allies and enemies (with the notable exception of Amphipolis) also embrace a vision of Athens that equates it with the sea. Finally, an analysis of the arguments the Athenians use at Melos shows that far from being a break with Pericles' policy, the Melian campaign (and Sicily to follow) is based on a Periclean vision of the city and is entirely consistent with Pericles' injunction to "safeguard the sea and the city" as he understood it.

PLATAEA "ATTICIZES" AND IS DESTROYED

Soon after Pericles disappears from the narrative, however, Thucydides seems to support the wisdom of a Periclean approach to the city in the report he gives about Potidaea, the revolting Athenian ally on the Chalcidice peninsula, the three-pronged peninsula that projects southeastward from Macedonia (see Map 1). In the winter of 430/29, when it became clear that Spartan invasions would not force the Athenians to lift the siege they had held in place since before the war, the Potidaeans surrendered to Athens. Thucydides provides the precise terms of the agreement they made: "the Potidaeans, their children, wives and mercenary troops could march out, each with one cloak – the women

[30] Foster 2001, 172. The Athenians have no choice (187): "[S]ince their older ways are all but destroyed, Pericles' characterization of the city and empire will seem more and more true."

with two – and with a specified amount of silver for the journey. And so they marched out under oath for Chalcidice or wherever each one could go" (2.70.3–4). Thucydides concludes his account of Potidaea's capture by noting that the Athenians "later sent Athenian colonists out to Potidaea and occupied the place" (2.70.4). In Potidaea, that is, we see a city remade.

When discussing the magnitude of his war, Thucydides notes that it was "not only the great length of the war" that "stood out." It was also that

> such sufferings occurred in Hellas as never before in a similar time. For never were so many captured cities left empty, some by Barbarians, others by Hellenes fighting against each other (and there were some which when captured even changed their inhabitants) (1.23.2).

This passage gives to the Athenians' "victory" over Potidaea a sense of irreparable loss. Nevertheless, the background to Potidaea's forced transformation seems to validate the wisdom of flexible definitions of the *polis* (and so of Pericles' vision of Athens and his abandonment policy in Attica). Thucydides tells his readers that at the same time that Potidaea revolted from Athens, Perdiccas of Macedon persuaded other cities of the Chalcidice peninsula to level and abandon their cities and to settle inland at Olynthus, making that into one larger, synoecized city (1.58.2). Various peoples of the Chalcidice destroyed their own cities and moved voluntarily to Olynthus, taking with them, we can be sure, more than one cloak. The Potidaeans, unlike their neighbors, rejected this "big city" in favor of their own city and territory of Potidaea, which they continued to inhabit. Unlike the rural Athenians, who were "doing nothing other than abandoning their own *polis*" (2.16.3), but nevertheless agreed to leave that *polis* and to move into Pericles' city, the Potidaeans rejected synoecism in favor of their own *polis*, and the decision cost them dearly. They lost their city anyway, but instead of making the move at their own pace (having packed up their household goods like the Athenian country deme/*polis*-men), they lost their city in the siege and marched out involuntarily with, as Thucydides underscores, only a cloak or two. The Athenians were angry at their generals for making this arrangement because they "thought they could have won control of the city in any way they wanted" (2.70.4). This implies that the Potidaeans only narrowly escaped being killed or sold into slavery.[31] The fate of Potidaea argues that the Potidaeans should have left their land and joined the big city at Olynthus when they had the chance. The Potidaeans' loss seems to validate the usefulness of nontraditional, flexible, immaterial definitions of the *polis*. The Potidaeans rejected a similar strategy, and so suffered ultimate destruction. This story seems to suggest that Pericles' abandonment strategy is wise.

At the same time, however, the story of Potidaea undercuts a key element of the characterization of the Athenians we have seen up to this point. At the Spartan congress, the Athenians, the Corinthians, and Archidamus all present the Athenians as exceptional, especially in their relation to their city and land. The Athenians insist that it was they alone who were able to separate themselves from their territory and fight on behalf of the idea of their *polis*. The synoecism of the cities around Olynthus, however, shows that the ability to think flexibly about the *polis* is not an exclusively Athenian trait. This calls into question the exceptionalism of the Athenians and asks how secure the separation between Athenians and others really is.

This issue is crucial to the story of Plataea, because the Plataeans, like the synoecizing Chalcidians, seem to embrace an Athenian-like, nonterritorial view of their city. The Plataeans serve in Thucydides' text as a kind of "surrogate Athens."[32] In the summer of 429, despite the Greeks' (and the readers') expectation that the Peloponnesians would once again invade Attica, they instead marched against Plataea. Once there, King Archidamus treated Plataea like Athens in his expectation that they could separate themselves from their land.

In their negotiations with Archidamus, the Plataeans initially asked him to "allow us to live independently, just as Pausanias deemed right" (2.71.4), making reference to the guarantee of independence they say that the Spartan King Pausanias gave them after the battle in their territory during the Persian War. To this request Archidamus retorted that it would "suffice for us" if the Plataeans were to "keep your peace, tending to your own possessions; join neither side but receive both as friends, but neither side for any purpose for the war" (2.72.1). The Plataeans

[31] Cf. Gomme 1956a, *s.v.* 2.70.4.

[32] Morrison (2006a, 54) calls Plataea a "'surrogate' Athens."

responded that it was impossible for them to accede to Archidamus' wishes without consulting the Athenians, because their wives and children were in Athens. They also expressed anxiety that after the Spartans left, "the Athenians might come and not turn control of the city back over to them, or the Thebans, who would be included in the oath's provisions about receiving both sides, might try again to capture their city" (2.72.2).

Archidamus responded with an ingenious suggestion:

> Give over your city and your houses to us the Lacedaemonians after having pointed out the boundaries of your land and the number of your trees and of everything else that can be enumerated. Then you yourselves depart away wherever you wish for as long as the war lasts. And when the time of war has passed, we will give back to you everything that we received. Until that time we will hold it in trust for you, both working the land and paying you whatever stipend seems sufficient (2.72.3).

This is an extraordinary proposal. Archidamus suggests that the Plataeans should voluntarily (and, he at least implies, temporarily) accept the fate that was forced upon the Potidaeans. He suggests that the Plataeans march out from their city and see others march in to live in their houses and cultivate their fields for the duration of the war. The Plataeans themselves should "depart away wherever you wish for as long as the war lasts." In short, Archidamus is urging the Plataeans to act like the Athenians. The very man who judged that the Athenians would not be "slaves to their land" now bids the Plataeans to act like Athenians and hand over their land to the Spartans for the duration of the war.

Even more interestingly, the Plataeans are ready to act like Athenians. They say that they are willing to accept the plan if Athens approves. They are willing to follow Pericles' advice to the inhabitants of Athens and abandon their land and move inside the walls of Athens. In their case, of course, they would not be leaving behind something that was only very similar to their own *polis*, like a resident of rural Attica (2.16.2), but their real *polis*.

Scholars tend to either ignore or downplay the radical nature of Archidamus' proposal.[33] Gomme, for example, although conceding that it is

[33] This is partly because scholars have, in general, ignored the exchange.

"not surprising that Plataea had not much faith in Sparta, and none in Thebes," calls Archidamus' suggestion "apparently a generous offer, for it would enable the Plataeans to retire to Athens, to their wives and children, and there fight."[34] Paula Debnar claims that Archidamus "genuinely tries to help [the Plataeans] reconcile the conflicting demands of their oaths to the Greeks and to the Athenians."[35] Felix Wasserman argues that Archidamus "tries to settle the matter of [Plataea's] loyalty to Athens through an arrangement without resorting to violence."[36] James Morrison notes that "Archidamus shows his skills as a negotiator by avoiding the appearance of forcing the Plataeans into accepting or rejecting a narrow range of demands."[37] According to Pelling, Archidamus "astutely tries to negotiate a settlement; and the Plataeans are clearly tempted."[38] Badian, despite his regret that the debate between Archidamus and the Plataeans has been "surprisingly neglected," does not discuss the details of Archidamus' proposal at all.[39] Scholars are reluctant to address the specifics of the proposal.[40] Those specifies, however, reveal that Archidamus' proposal is revolutionary and surely meant to seem impossible and insincere.

According to Thucydides, Archidamus, when in Attica, did not believe that the Athenians could possibly follow Pericles' plan. This makes his suggestion of a similar plan to an enemy people suspect at best. Furthermore, Archidamus' proposal is far more complicated than that of Pericles, involving careful accounting of land, trees, and possessions, and the unlikely payment of stipends during wartime. The Plataeans, paid by the Lacedaemonians, are to "depart away wherever you wish" (μεταχωρήσατε ὅποι βούλεσθε, 2.72.3). This command is "stated as if it were a kind of freedom" but in fact it leaves the Plataeans with few

34 Gomme, 1956a, *s.v.*, 2.72.3.

35 Debnar 2000, 101. Neither Ruston nor Hornblower comments on Archidamus' proposal.

36 Wasserman 1953, 198.

37 Morrison 2006a, 55. Morrison's reference to appearances suggests that he does not find Archidamus' offer wholly workable or sincere, but Morrison does not discuss it further.

38 Pelling 1991, 130.

39 Badian 1993, 109 and 111.

40 Bauslaugh (1991, 129), for example, in his study of "the concept of neutrality in Classical Greece," fails to describe, much less discuss the details of, what he calls an "offer to hold the city-state in trust until the conclusion of the war."

real options.[41] Archidamus makes no suggestion about where the Plataeans should go. The logical possibility is Athens, given Plataea's history, but by what means of communication and organization could the Lacedaemonians pay the Plataeans a stipend during the war if they moved to Athens or any Athenian territory?[42] And why, if they wanted the Plataeans to remain neutral, would they allow them to move there in any case? Would they be required not to serve in the fleet? Would that be certified in some way?

Are the Plataeans expected instead to move as a group to Lacedaemon or some Peloponnesian-controlled territory?[43] If they did not move as a group, finding the eligible Plataeans in order to pay them their stipends would be a difficult and time-consuming business. If they did move as a group, on the other hand, would the Spartans really expect no help from them for their war effort in exchange for whatever territory they gave them? Furthermore, if the Plataeans were willing to move as a group to Lacedaemonian territory, why would they not simply remain at Plataea and side with the Lacedaemonians? Finally, if the plan is for the Plataeans to move as a group to Lacedaemonian-controlled territory, why does Archidamus not mention it, but instead suggest, with his vague "depart away wherever you wish," that no place is on offer for the Plataeans in Lacedaemon or elsewhere under Spartan influence?

Archidamus' proposal, as presented by Thucydides, is radical and wholly unworkable. Archidamus makes it in part because it provides the pretense, when the Plataeans refuse, that the Plataeans are being unreasonable, and so mitigates the impiety of the Spartans' attack. Thucydides notes that it was "at the precise moment" of the Plataeans' refusal of his second offer that Archidamus turned to invoke "all the Gods and Heroes who hold the land of Plataea" to be his witness that "since these men here first broke the common oath, we came against

[41] Foster 2001, 30.

[42] Debnar (2000, 99) agrees that Archidamus leaves the Plataeans free to go to Athens but does not discuss the logistical difficulties inherent in such a move. Foster (2001, 30), by contrast, sees that "the Plataeans have nowhere to go but Athens" and that "once in Athens and on the Athenian side, it is unlikely that they would ever see their city again."

[43] The Lacedaemonians had settled the Aeginetans expelled from their island by the Athenians at Thyria (2.27).

this land not unjustly." Archidamus specifically mentions in his prayer that "although we offered many reasonable proposals, we met no success" (2.74.2). Archidamus' remarkable, unworkable proposal is made for display only, and its terms are impossible.[44] The Plataeans' apparent willingness to uproot themselves and accept it merely emphasizes how Athenian they are. To some extent, this again calls into question the Athenians' exceptionalism. But unlike the synoecizing Chalcidians, because of the close connection between Plataea and Athens, the Athenian-ness of the Plataeans reflects back on the Athenians and makes them seem all the more powerful and extraordinary.

The Plataeans' Athenian-ness comes, in part, from their old, close connection to Athens. Plataea, an Athenian ally surrounded by pro-Spartan Boeotians, is presumably part of the "other land" that Pericles boasted could make up for the loss of all of Attica, and the Plataeans had often acted like Athenians before. They alone fought with the Athenians at Marathon in the Persian wars.[45] In the later "defense" speech the Plataeans gave before their Spartan judges at the surrender of their city in 427, the Plataeans reminded the Spartans that in the wars against the Mede, "they alone of the Boeotians joined in the attack for the liberation of Greece" (3.54.3). The Plataeans did not act like Boeotians. They acted, in fact, like Athenians. The Plataeans also reminded the Spartans that "although we are mainlanders, we fought in the naval battle at Artemesium" (3.54.4). The mainlanders "became nautical" and acted like the almost-islander Athenians.

Furthermore, in that same speech, the Plataeans explained their behavior to the Spartans by noting that Athens "helped us against Thebes when you shrank back, and to betray them was no longer honorable . . . but it was reasonable to follow their commands readily" (3.55.3). The Plataeans added that this was especially the case "when one had had

[44] Cf. Kagan (1974, 105): The Plataeans' refusal was "the answer, no doubt, that Archidamus expected. He was now free to proclaim, calling the gods and heroes to witness, that the Plataeans, not the Spartans, were guilty of wrongdoing."

[45] Hdt. 6.111, 113. Ominous for the Plataeans' hopes to be allowed to act Athenian is the fact that in their speech at Sparta, the Athenians claimed that "we alone braved the danger of the Barbarian first at Marathon" (1.73.4). Walters (1981b, 1981a) argues that the Athenians' inflated claim is consistent with Attic funerary tradition.

good treatment and at one's own request had attached oneself to them as allies and shared citizenship with them" (3.55.3).[46] The Plataeans claim to be allies and fellow citizens with the Athenians.[47]

The Thebans offer an even more interesting explanation for the Plataeans' behavior, however. In the "prosecution" speech they gave at the Plataeans' show trial before the Spartans in 427, the Thebans repeat and so reinforce the Plataeans' claim about their Athenian citizenship: "you say that it was to punish us that you became allies and citizens of Athens" (3.63.2). They do so, however, only in order to turn that identification into an accusation, and the Thebans have a broader point to make, in any case. The Thebans also repeat the Plataeans' claims regarding the Persian wars, remarking, "when the Barbarian came against Greece they say that only they of the Boeotians did not medize" (φασὶ μόνοι Βοιωτῶν οὐ μηδίσαι, 3.62.1). They use the verb "to medize" here, which was coined during the Persian wars to describe the actions of the Greek states (like Thebes) that did not resist the Persians but joined their cause. The Thebans reject the supposed point of honor that the Plataeans did not medize by claiming that "we say that they didn't medize only for the reason that the Athenians did not" (ἡμεῖς δὲ μηδίσαι μὲν αὐτοὺς οὔ φαμεν διότι οὐδ᾽ Ἀθηναίους, 3.62.2). The Plataeans' resistance to Persia does not count, according to the Thebans, because they were simply doing whatever the Athenians did; they were simply acting Athenian. The Thebans make this point explicit and use it as a condemnation in the next clause: "and following on the same idea, later in turn when the Athenians came against the Greeks, they alone of the Boeotians atticized" (τῇ μέντοι αὐτῇ ἰδέᾳ ὕστερον ἰόντων Ἀθηναίων ἐπὶ τοὺς Ἕλληνας μόνους αὖ Βοιωτῶν ἀττικίσαι, 3.62.2).[48]

[46] This must refer to the events described by Herodotus (6.108.6), who reports that "the Plataeans gave themselves to the Athenians." This event is generally dated to 519 B.C. or (less likely) 509. See Gomme 1956a, *s.v.* 3.68.5.

[47] The Plataeans' claim to citizenship is problematic. After the fall of Plataea in 427, a grant of citizenship was made to the survivors that would not have been required had all Plataeans already held citizenship (cf. Osborne 1981, D1 on Plataea). It is possible that they received a kind of "honorary" citizenship in the sixth century, however. See Amit 1973, 75–78. Cf. MacDowell 1985, 319.

[48] Parry (1981, 190) notes that the Thebans "show how the values of words change with historical changes. What was once called [*medizein*] is now of no

The Thebans coin the new words "to atticize" and "atticism" to describe "acting like Athens" and accuse the Plataeans of being the prime examples of atticizers.

The Thebans use their striking neologisms "to atticize" and "atticism" in order "to make Athens equivalent, as the enslaver of Greece, to Persia in 480 B.C."[49] The word "impl[ies] the same senses of betrayal and criminality."[50] Not only one state medized in the Persian wars. The Thebans' coinage of a verb equivalent to "medize" to describe the Plataeans' betrayal, therefore, suggests that although the Plataeans are, perhaps, the most offensive "atticizers," they are not the only men susceptible to the corruption. Indeed, Thucydides reports that the Thebans later also accused the Thespians of atticism (4.133.1), and the Chians accused a certain faction in their city of "atticism" (8.38.3).[51]

"Atticism" was a useful slogan for the Thebans because "by the parallelism with medism" it represented "the felt immensity of the Athenian threat and the perceived limitlessness of Athenian ambitions."[52] Just as Pericles saw an Athens that could spread to cover half the world, not just the world occupied by Athens' allies but "still more if you want," the Thebans fear an Athens without bounds – an Athens that has made an Athens out of a Boeotian city and will, they charge, make

importance, but [*atticizein*] is enough to damn the Plataeans." Cf. Macleod (1977, 240): "these rhetorical procedures vividly illustrate again how only present interests count in war. . . ."

49 Macleod 1977, 240. The Thebans' rhetoric equates the Athenians with the Persians, and in their speech the Thebans claim that by siding with them the Plataeans betrayed "all the Hellenes." Their rhetoric suggests that just as the Epidamnians pushed out of their city were no longer really Epidamnians, so too the Athenians (and the Plataeans) were no longer really Hellenes.

50 Cogan 1981b, 15.

51 Hornblower (1991, *s.v.* 3.62.2) objects to McLeod's description of "atticize" as a "neologism" on the ground that it is "subsequently used in an unrhetorical section of narrative . . . in a way which suggests it was in ordinary use" (referring to 4.133.1). But the subsequent appearance of the term in a nonrhetorical section merely proves that the Spartan side recognized a good propaganda slogan when they heard one and quickly took up the term with enthusiasm. Cf. Cogan 1981b, 16. Atticism could be a real crime. See *IG* II^2 33 (and Pleket 1963, 75) for a list of Thasians who were expelled from Thasos "on a charge of atticism."

52 Cogan 1981a, 69.

Athenses of others.[53] Once "atticism" was coined, according to Cogan, "the enemy was now the Athenian manner of life, its ideas (these two elements strikingly represented in the institution of democracy) and the fear that those ideas composed a system that was incorrigibly expansionist (even subversive)." Although "Athens is a city one may fight," as Cogan explains, "to Athens' opponents atticism was an ideology that *other* cities might believe or with which they might be 'infected'."[54] Thus the Athenian-ness of Plataea does not diminish Athens' perceived power by undercutting its exceptionalism; instead, it shows the immense force of this city that could remake others in its image.

Curiously, although the Periclean Athens would certainly celebrate the idea of an Athens that might spread across the globe, the Athenians refused to let the Plataeans act like Athenians when they agreed to follow Archidamus' absurd suggestion. Instead, the Athenians drew a sharp line between Athenians and Plataeans. The envoys who went to Athens in 429 to get the Athenians' agreement to Archidamus' lease of Plataea returned with this response: "the Athenians say that in the past, men of Plataea, since they became allies in no way did they ever allow you to be wronged nor will they overlook it now but will help according to their power, and they command you by the oaths your fathers swore to commit no act against the alliance" (2.73. 3). In the Athenian view, the Plataeans are not practically Athenians; they have no share in Athenian citizenship, as the Plataeans will later claim (3.55.3), but are simply allies for the Athenians to command. Furthermore, the Plataean suggestion that they might give up their land in Boeotia and move to Athens is construed as an "act against the alliance." And so it

[53] Debnar (2001, 140–41) argues that "by needlessly repeating the Plataeans' claim to Athenian citizenship (3.55.3) and leaving it unchallenged, the Thebans draw attention to the assertion and even lend it credibility." She calls this evidence of Theban "carelessness" and (139) describes as a "dangerous lack of tact" that the Thebans imply that even at the battle of Plataea, the Plataeans were "mere lackeys of the Athenians." On the contrary, these are deliberate elements of Thebes' accusation against Plataea and Athens. Athens has turned Plataea, which as a Boeotian city ought to be its enemy and ought to have followed Sparta during the Persian War, into a mirror of itself which automatically does whatever Athens does.

[54] Cogan 1981a, 72.

would be, for if the Plataeans gave up their land and moved to Athens, they might well seem less like allies and more like Athenians. This the Athenians are disposed to avoid. The Athenian response insists on a sharp distinction between Athenians and Plataeans.

The Athenian decision is puzzling. As Gomme notes, it is hard to see why the Athenians wished Plataea to resist to the end: "strategy dictated that they could not themselves send effective help.... If they might not defend their own land with their hoplites, still less could they march further afield and risk all to defend Plataea."[55] Nevertheless, the Athenians refused to let the Plataeans act Athenian and move to Athens. The explanation for their puzzling decision probably lies in the Athenians' sense of themselves. Thucydides has so far shown that the Athenians have a vision of their city that extends far beyond Athens. Here he shows his reader that they nevertheless cling tightly to their own uniqueness and will not accept anyone else as Athenian.

The Athenians insist on a strong distinction between Athenians and others, whereas the Plataeans and Thebans show more flexibility. The story of Plataea thus reveals a tension between two different visions of the nonterritorial city. The Thebans and Plataeans see that Athens is more than Attica. In their eyes, however, not just territory but also men are transformed. Plataea, the island of almost Athens in Boeotia, holds "atticizers" who think (and want to act) like Athenians. The Athenians, by contrast, although they see their city as potentially spreading across the seas, nevertheless, in 429, maintain a strict separation between Athenians and others. As Thucydides traces the theme of the city and the Athenians' relation to their homeland, however, he will demonstrate that over time, the Athenians relax their exclusive ideas about who counts as Athenian.

Interestingly, just as the Athenians keep a sharp distinction between Athenians and Plataeans, so, too, does Thucydides. When the Plataeans ultimately surrendered their city to the Spartans in 427, they sparred

[55] Gomme, 1956a, *s.v.* 2.72.3. Kagan (1974, 105) finds the decision so puzzling that he claims that "we may be sure that the Athenians gave no such answer while Pericles was in control. The response must reflect the momentary ascendancy of the war party...."

with the Thebans in the speeches we have already discussed. At the conclusion of this "trial," the Spartan judges repeated the question they had posed at the beginning of the proceedings and asked their Plataean prisoners if they had done anything to help Sparta and her allies in the present war. "As each man replied 'No,'" Thucydides writes, "leading them out they killed them and they made no exception. Of the Plataeans they killed no fewer than two hundred, of the Athenians twenty-five who suffered the siege with them. The women, they enslaved" (3.68.2). Thucydides goes on briefly to report that the Spartans gave the use of the *polis* of Plataea itself for one year to political refugees from Megara and to some remaining members of the Plataean pro-Spartan party. But afterwards the Spartans razed the city to the ground "to its very foundation" and Plataea ceased to exist (3.68.3). "And thus ended matters concerning Plataea in the 93rd year since they became allies of Athens," writes Thucydides (3.68.5).

In their speech the Plataeans claimed that they "shared citizenship" with the Athenians, but in his final remarks on Plataea, Thucydides says nothing about any grant of even provisional or honorary citizenship to the Plataeans at the time of their alliance with Athens ninety-three years earlier. Thus Thucydides keeps Plataeans and Athenians as separate groups, united only by alliance. In his summary, Thucydides could have cited the years that Plataea had existed (as the representatives of Melos do for their city) or the years since the great battle at their city during the Persian wars, but instead, he "calls attention to its long-standing alliance with Athens" and so "to the Athenians' ineffectiveness in aiding Plataea," which again makes a strong contrast between the two groups. The Plataeans remain allies, not Athenians, however much they might atticize.[56]

Thucydides also fails to note here that after the destruction of Plataea, the Plataeans who earlier had escaped to Athens were awarded Athenian citizenship. Hornblower argues that Thucydides kept his account of the Plataeans "deliberately incomplete" on this point to further emphasize

[56] Connor 1984, 92, n. 30. Hornblower (1991, *s.v.* 3.68.5) agrees that Thucydides is "stressing in an oblique but effective fashion how little use that long-standing alliance was to the Plataeans." Macleod (1977, 231) calls it a "dry and devastating comment."

the uselessness of the Plataeans' alliance with Athens.[57] Thucydides' silence on this point, however, also keeps the atticizing Plataeans and the real Athenians separate. If it followed the terms of other citizenship grants, the decree in honor of the surviving Plataeans proclaimed that "the Plataeans are to be Athenians."[58] But Thucydides is silent about this decree, and in his text the Plataeans undergo no such transformation. Thucydides' implication is that despite their evident desire and the Thebans' description of them as "atticizers," the Plataeans cannot be turned into Athenians. They cannot find in Athens what they had in their own *polis*. The subtle effect is to undercut Periclean and Athenian notions of the transferability of the *polis*. What matters, Thucydides insists, is not the Plataeans' ideology or their new citizenship, but the destruction of their real *polis*.

Indeed, the focus of Thucydides' Plataean story is on loss, not transformation. Thucydides' decision not to mention the surviving Plataeans' new citizenship gives an impression of the utter destruction of Plataea – the physical city of which Thucydides tells us was destroyed "to its foundation." Thucydides fails to remind his readers that the Plataean women and children were in Athens (where they had been transported before the beginning of the siege) or that 212 Plataeans had reached Athens the prior year after their daring escape. Mention of these points would have given some sense that Plataea, even separated from Plataean land, could still exist. The atticizing Plataeans might well be expected to believe in such Athenian-style city transformations. But Thucydides reports, instead, that their city was razed "to its very foundation."

Thucydides' use of the phrase "to its foundation" (ἐς ἔδαφος, 3.68.3) is probably meant to stress the enormity and irreversible nature of this event. Thucydides uses "foundation" only two other times, and both are in evocative settings. The first is at 1.10.2 when Thucydides speculates on how an observer, "after much time had passed," would judge the

[57] Thucydides was reluctant, according to Hornblower (1991, *s.v.* 3.68.5) to "take away from the emotional power of his ending by recounting the hospitality and improved status accorded to the Plataeans at Athens after 427." See also Hornblower 1987, 35.

[58] Osborne (1982, 14) proposes just this language for the first provision of the decree in honor of the Plataeans, citing the decree in honor of the Samians (his D4, Meiggs-Lewis 1968, n. 94).

power of Lacedaemon if the polis were deserted "and only the temples and foundations of buildings were left" (εἰ . . . λειφθείη δὲ τά τε ἱερὰ καὶ τῆς κατασκευῆς τὰ ἐδάφη). The image of the silent "foundations" far in the future surely implies that no Lacedaemonians are left to inhabit them. Thucydides' use of the phrase "to its foundation" at Plataea similarly implies the utter destruction of Plataea and the Plataeans.[59] Thucydides' other use of "to its foundation" (ἐς ἔδαφος) closely matches its force in the Plataean episode. When Thucydides reports that the Megarians recaptured the (Megarian) Long Walls from the Athenians, he explains that they "razed them to their foundations" (κατέσκαψαν ἑλόντες ἐς ἔδαφος, 4.109.1). Here Thucydides combines "to its foundation" with the verb *kataskapto*, which Connor has demonstrated has a technical sense.[60] It indicates the destruction of a house, building, or city as a punishment that "connotes the extirpation of the individual and his immediate kin from society."[61] Because the verb is etymologically related to *skapto* ("to dig"), Connor argues that "we should probably imagine the actual removal of some or all of the foundation of the house."[62]

It seems possible that Thucydides' use of "to its foundation" at Plataea carries with it some of the force of *kataskapto* and so implies the utter destruction of Plataea now and forever. If "to its foundation" here does

59 Foster (2001, 47) stresses how "Thucydides details the Spartans' consumption of every bit of Plataea's remaining material culture. . . . The land is alienated, the people are dead or gone, the stones have been reused for new buildings, the last metal has been melted away."

60 Thucydides uses the verb only 4 times (4.109; 5.63.2; 6.7.2; 8.92.10). Connor (1985, 97) contends that the infrequency of its appearance in Thucydides' text argues that he used it technically.

61 Connor 1985, 86.

62 Connor 1985, 85. Thucydides' combining of *kataskapto* at Megara with "to its foundation" makes sense because *kataskapto* implies destruction to the very foundation. But whom were the Megarians punishing? Connor notes that both Plutarch (*Lys.* 15) and Xenophon (2.2.23) use the verb *kataskapto* to describe the razing of Athens' Long Walls at the end of the war. As he describes it (97), "the event becomes an informal Freedom Festival, celebrating the liberation of Greece from Athenian rule. . . ." So the Megarians would seem to be celebrating their liberation from the threat of Athenian domination and extirpating the evidence of the "treachery" of the Megarians who had joined with Athens.

imply a *kataskaphe*, the Thebans' action also underscores their sense of Plataea's betrayal and treachery. They celebrate the destruction of the city as a "freedom day" for Boeotia, freed of its Athenian interloper. Thus Thucydides' notice that the Thebans destroyed Plataea "to its foundation," together with his refusal to mention the surviving Plataeans, both reinforces the Theban charge of treason and betrayal against them and presents the destruction of Plataea as complete, with no sense that the surviving Plataeans have somehow been transformed into Athenians. The final chapter in Plataea's story underscores the separation Thucydides keeps between Athenians and Plataeans and demonstrates Thucydides' focus on loss, not transformation, in his story of this surrogate Athens.

In the summer of 421, the Athenians captured the city of Scione, a small *polis* on the Chalcidice peninsula that had revolted from Athens (see Map 1). They killed all the men of military age and made slaves of the women and children. Thucydides tells us that the Athenians gave the land to the Plataeans (5.32). Because this detail is unnecessary to his account of the course of the war, it is fair to ask what purpose it serves Thucydides to recount it.[63] Thucydides fails again here to mention that these Plataeans had had the privilege of some degree of Athenian citizenship in Athens since the destruction of their Boeotian *polis*. Thus the impression he gives is that the Plataeans have been mere refugees wandering without a *polis* in the years since they lost their city. Whatever their connection to Athens, and however much they were "atticizers," they had not integrated into the city of Athens. The Plataean-Athenians had not "become Athenians." They remained apart and wanted to be a separate *polis*. Now the Plataeans could have this, though in a land far from home. The Plataeans had been willing to leave behind their very own *polis* and move to Athens but were thwarted by Athens. Now, with their real city irretrievably lost, they marched out to Scione to try, as much as possible, to reconstitute their *polis* there. If Pericles was right, and Attica was, for the Athenians, worth no more

[63] Pelling (2000, 61, n. 2) thinks that the event shows the "emblematic qualities of Plataea": "The Athenians treated their disloyal allies at Scione in a way which matched the Spartan treatment of Plataea, then gave their territory to the surviving Plataeans (Thuc. 5.32.1). They were making a point."

than "a little garden or bauble of wealth" (2.62.3) and the loss of all Attica could be erased by possession of the watery half of the world, then the Plataeans, in losing their Plataea in Boeotia, had lost little. They should be able to remake themselves in this new city. Thucydides leaves it up to his readers to decide whether they will be able to do so, but those who deem the Plataeans' burden a heavy one will find in the story of Plataea a worrisome paradigm for Athens. The pathos and focus on loss in Thucydides' account of Plataea's story counsel that the Athenians' decision to separate their city from their ancestral homeland may cost them dearly. Nevertheless, there is no hint in the text that the Athenians saw this danger.

THE ATHENIANS' "OWN LAND" IS THE EMPIRE AND THE SEA

In the years following Pericles' death, Thucydides never presents the Athenians as tempted to defend Attica or choose it over the sea-city Pericles showed them. Instead, the successors of Pericles follow his vision of the city, and this is the vision of the city that Athens' enemies increasingly recognize. The Thebans at Plataea revealed their fear of an Athens that could "infect" others and make them atticize. Even the Spartans, who clung for so long to the hope that invasion of Attica would win them the war, eventually recognized the true extent (and focus) of the city they were fighting, as the campaigns of Brasidas in Thrace demonstrate.

In the wake of the unexpected Athenian victory at Pylos in 425, during which the Athenians fortified a headland in the southwest Peloponnesus and captured 292 Lacedaemonians, including 120 full Spartan citizens (4.38), the Spartans decided to send Brasidas and 1,700 hoplites to Thrace to induce and support revolts among Athens' allies. The reasoning Thucydides gives for the campaign shows that the Spartans had come to see that Athens existed not so much in Attica as in the empire. Indeed, according to Thucydides, the Spartans see an equivalence between their own land and the allied territory of Athens, not between their own land and Attica. Thucydides writes that "now that the Athenians were attacking the Peloponnesus, and not least their own land (οὐχ ἥκιστα τῇ ἐκείνων γῇ), the Spartans hoped to divert them especially if they should hurt them back equally by sending an army against their allies" (εἰ ἀντιπαραλυποῖεν πέμψαντες ἐπὶ τοὺς ξυμμάχους αὐτῶν στρατιάν, 4.80.1).

Thucydides' wording makes an emphatic connection between the Spartans "own land" and the Athenians' acquired territory abroad through the verb *antiparalupo*, translated here as "to hurt back equally." This seems to be a word that Thucydides coined for this very occasion; it occurs only here in Thucydides, and there is no evidence of its use by any other Greek writer.[64] Other compound verbs beginning with *antipara* give a sense of its meaning. *Antiparaballo* means to place side by side so as to compare or contrast. *Antiparatassomai* means to stand in array against. *Antiparecho* means to furnish or supply in turn. *Antipareimi* means to march on opposite sides of a river. Thus such words have a sense of reciprocity and comparison.

The Spartans want to retaliate against the Athenians for having attacked the Spartans' "own land." Thucydides' invention of a verb for this situation suggests that he was particularly concerned about the relationship he was describing. The verb he coined equates the blow the Spartans' received with that which they hoped to inflict and effectively suggests that the "own land" of Athens was not Attica but (in this case) Chalcidice and Thrace.[65]

We learn what the Athenians think of as their "own land" from their response to the revolt of Scione. To the Athenians, nothing but geography matters, but the geography that matters is not Attica but the sea. Thucydides even shows the Athenians mischaracterizing geography in their zeal to connect their "own land" with the sea and to increase

64 According to Classen and Steup (1900, *s.v.* 4.80.1), of forty-one ἀντὶ-compounds that occur only once in Thucydides, nine occur nowhere else in Greek literature.

65 The Spartans' comment is, of course, ironic, because Messenia, the territory that the Athenians had attacked when they fortified Pylos, was not, strictly speaking, the Spartans' "own land." It belonged (at least originally) to the Messenians, whom the Spartans had conquered in their various "Messenian wars" in the seventh and sixth centuries. As Thucydides notes, when the Athenians garrisoned Pylos, the Messenians from Naupaktus sent their best men "as if to their fatherland (for Pylos is part of the former 'Messenia')" (4.41.2).

the sea's reach. Thucydides also demonstrates that the Athenians have a particular interest in islands, which foreshadows both the Melian and Sicilian campaigns.

Brasidas' campaign in Thrace was directed at Athens' colonies and allies in the Chalcidice peninsula (see Map 1). He first induced the city of Acanthus to revolt from Athens, and then in the winter of 424/3, in his greatest coup, he persuaded the Athenian colony of Amphipolis to surrender to him. Soon after, he captured the city of Torone. These losses led the Athenians to make an armistice for one year in the spring of 423. It was during these negotiations that the people of Scione chose (disastrously) to revolt from Athens. Scione lay on the southern tip of the peninsula of Pallene, the southernmost finger of the three-pronged Chalcidice peninsula. It thus lay southeast of the synoecized city of Olynthus, although it did not share in the creation of that "big city." It was cut off from the mainland and from Olynthus by the Athenian occupation of Potidaea, which lay at the isthmus linking the Pallene peninsula to the rest of the Chalcidice. Thus Scione was particularly vulnerable to Athenian attack from the sea and had little hope of help coming to it by land. Indeed, Brasidas himself was forced to come to Scione secretly by boat at night to encourage the Scionians in their revolt. Thucydides represents Brasidas as praising the Scionians in his speech specifically for being brave (or foolhardy?) enough to ignore their geography because "although they were nothing other than islanders (ὄντες οὐδὲν ἄλλο ἢ νησιῶται), they had advanced towards freedom of their own accord . . ." (4.120.3).[66]

Thucydides is clearly very interested in this point, for he otherwise tells us very little of the specifics of what Brasidas said at Scione. Although he includes in his *History* a full speech for Brasidas at Acanthus (4.85–87), with regard to Scione, Thucydides is content to note merely that Brasidas "said the things that he said at Acanthus and Torone" (4.120.3) and adds only a few points tailored to Scione.[67] The first of the Scione-specific points in Brasidas' praise of the Scionians is

[66] As Bosworth (1993, 37, n. 37) notes, this "fatally echoes and inverts the Athenian declaration at Melos (5.97)" that Athens must control all islanders.

[67] Hornblower (1996, 81) describes this technique as the "'periodically adjusted manifesto' by which I mean the way Brasidas' original Acanthus speech is used as an assumed basis for what he says subsequently."

their decision to ignore their position as "nothing other than islanders" and come forward on their own to seize their freedom. This was a sign, Brasidas went on, that on other occasions, too, "they would courageously endure anything else however severe, and that if he were to arrange things as he thought right, he would consider them truly the most loyal friends of the Lacedaemonians and honor them with respect to all other things" (4.120.3).[68] Everything Brasidas said at Scione that was directed specifically to the Scionians (or at least all that Thucydides reports) was predicated on their decision to revolt, although they were "nothing other than islanders."

Importantly, Thucydides reveals that Brasidas thought that the Scionians' geography would determine Athenian resolve against them. After first leaving a small garrison in the city, Brasidas later brought a larger force over to the town because "he thought that the Athenians would come to the rescue of Scione, as if to an island (ὡς ἐς νῆσον), and he wanted to anticipate them" (4.121.2). Brasidas calls the Scionians "nothing other than islanders," using a rhetorical device, "nothing other than" (οὐδὲν ἄλλο ἤ), with the purpose of "flagging up something *not* 'purely' or 'literally' so, but, at most, tantamount to being so."[69] Brasidas also predicts that the Athenians will come against Scione "*as if* to an island." He thus recognizes that Scione is not, in fact, an island, and that the Scionians are not actually islanders. He nevertheless suggests that the Scionians' position as almost-islanders will determine the Athenians' reaction to their revolt. By failing to mention anything else in Scione's relationship to Athens as a determining factor, Brasidas implies that the Athenians base their reactions to revolting cities in their empire on the connection of those cities to the sea.

Brasidas' prediction is surprising, but correct. Indeed, when Thucydides' Athenians judge the Scionians' connection to the sea, they exaggerate its extent. Thucydides reports that when the Athenians heard of the revolt, they "wanted to send out an army as soon as possible because they were angry that now even the islanders saw fit to revolt

68 There is bitterly ironic because, just as the Scionians are not really islanders, so, too, they will not be considered the "most loyal friends of Sparta." Rather, as Hornblower (1996, *s.v.* 4.120.3) notes, Sparta will casually abandon them after the Peace of Nicias of 421.

69 Whitehead 2001, 605.

from them" (εἰ καὶ οἱ ἐν ταῖς νήσοις ἤδη ὄντες ἀξιοῦσι σφῶν ἀφίστασθαι, 4.122.5). Hornblower calls this sentence "startling," as indeed it is.[70] Thucydides does not have the Athenians call the Scionians *like*, or "nothing other than" islanders; the Athenians describe the people of Scione as "those in the islands." Gomme attempted to explain the shock of the sentence away by suggesting readings such as "they are really only *like* islanders" or "they who were now islanders after the capture of Potidaea."[71] We should, however, like Hornblower, accept the sentence as it stands, especially given the preparation from the speech of Brasidas.

Thucydides' phrasing shows the Athenians mischaracterizing geography and exaggerating Scione's connection to the sea. Scione was not an island, but neither was Athens. Regardless, Pericles had urged the Athenians to "think as nearly like" islanders as possible. The Athenian response to Scione shows that the Athenians, having redefined their own geographical reality, were prepared to redefine that of others. Furthermore, the flexibility of their geographical vision helps to reveal the true extent of their "own land" in their eyes. The anger experienced by the Athenians because an island (that was not an island) had revolted from them suggests that they felt particular ownership over islands (and coastal places that the Athenians could imagine were islands), perhaps even those not in alliance with Athens. Scione may not have been an island, but it clearly lay in the part of the world that, according to Pericles, belonged to Athens. The Athenian anger toward Scione seems to grow naturally from Pericles' pronouncement that the Athenians rule half the world. Athens' response to Scione shows that virtually no coastal site is safe and prepares readers for the campaigns against Melos and Sicily. If Scione is an island, then why should real islands be allowed to stand outside the Athenian Empire – especially if the Athenians are, as Pericles said, absolute masters of the sea?

Not everyone accepted this division of the world and agreed that everything tied to the sea was Athenian, however. Thucydides shows that the city of Amphipolis, in particular, rejected this view of Athens. In their speech at Plataea, the Thebans condemned the Plataeans for being "atticizers" and revealed a worldview in which the boundary

[70] Hornblower 1996, *s.v.* 4.121.2.

[71] Gomme 1956b, *s.v.* 4.122.5.

between Athens and other cities was broken down. Amphipolis, however, demonstrates that "atticism" has its defense.

Amphipolis was a colony founded by the Athenians at the mouth of the river Strymon in Macedonia "with Hagnon as founder" in 437/6 (4.102; see Map 1). Thucydides tells his readers that Amphipolis was the third attempt to colonize the place. During Brasidas' Thracian campaign, Amphipolis surrendered to him when he proclaimed moderate terms. In 422, Cleon brought an army against Amphipolis but failed to retake the city for Athens, and in the fighting, both he and Brasidas died.

Thucydides reports that when they learned that Brasidas had died preventing the recapture of their city by Athens, the Amphipolitans voted him elaborate honors and in doing so rewrote the history of their own city. The Amphipolitans buried Brasidas in their agora; they gave him sacrifice as a hero and honored him with games and annual offerings. Furthermore, they "attributed the colony to him as founder" (τὴν ἀποικίαν ὡς οἰκιστῇ προσέθεσαν, 5.11.1). Hagnon the Athenian, the real founder of the colony, the man who had even given the colony its name (4.102), suffered a consequent *damnatio memoriae* or repudiation of memory: "They tore down all the Hagnonian buildings, obliterating anything that might remain as a reminder of his founding, believing that Brasidas had been their savior" (5.11.1).

Thucydides' decision at Amphipolis to devote "a whole 18-line chapter to 'introduce' a single city . . . is unparalleled in Thucydides' whole work."[72] Furthermore, Thucydides "underscores the importance of the region by noting all the attempts to found the colony."[73] Thucydides takes special care to highlight the time and toil required for the Athenians to finally establish their colony at Amphipolis. Hagnon's eventual success was a "triumph, given the series of earlier disasters and Hedonian resistance."[74] Yet the Amphipolitans wiped out this triumph in an instant by an act of imagination and reinvention. Thucydides' focus on the difficult birth and history of Hagnonian Amphipolis serves to emphasize the speed of the transformative power of the Amphipolitans' redefinition of their city.

72 Hornblower 1996, *s.v.* 4.102.1.

73 Kallet-Marx 1993, 173.

74 Hornblower, 1996, *s.v.* 4.102.3.

In his last speech, Pericles claimed that Athens ruled not just its present empire and allies but the whole sea. The Athenians' response to Scione shows them exaggerating the reach of the sea and suggests that they judge all that is on the sea to be theirs. Here, however, the coastal Amphipolitans, a colony of Athens, defy Athenian truth and insist that they are no part of Athens, despite being a coastal city founded by Athens. The Amphipolitans' action mimics Pericles' redefinition of Athens but directly challenges his worldview. They deny both their founding from Athens, and that their position near the sea leaves them in Athens' power. The Amphipolitans demonstrate, in a sense, the defense to "atticism." If Thebes had claimed that Athens could make Athenses of places unrelated to it, the Amphipolitans here assert that even places founded by Athens can throw off "atticism." The Amphipolitans were never proved wrong in this revision of their history or in their insistence that everything on or near the sea does not belong to Athens. Although, under the terms of the Peace of Nicias of 421, the Lacedaemonians were supposed to hand the city back to Athens, they did not do so, and coastal, Brasidas-founded Amphipolis remained outside Athenian control (5.35).[75]

Although the Athenians never recaptured coastal Amphipolis and never forced that part of the sea-girt world back into their vision of Athens, Thucydides soon confirms that Athens and others specifically equated Athens with the sea. In 420, during the uneasy Peace of Nicias, the Athenians made an alliance with three Peloponnesian states, Argos, Elis, and Mantinea, on terms that included the following: "No one under arms is to pass for a hostile purpose through the parties' own territory or that of the allies whom each controls nor by sea unless all the cities – Athens, Argos, Mantinea, and Elis – vote to allow the transit" (ὅπλα δὲ μὴ ἐᾶν ἔχοντας διιέναι ἐπὶ πολέμῳ διὰ τῆς γῆς τῆς σφετέρας αὐτῶν καὶ τῶν ξυμμάχων ὧν ἄρχουσιν ἕκαστοι, μηδὲ κατὰ θάλασσαν, ἢν μὴ ψηφισαμένων τῶν πόλεων ἁπασῶν τὴν δίοδον εἶναι, 5.47.5).[76]

75 Athens made two further attempts to recapture the city but failed each time (5.7, 5.9). It was, of course, because of his failure to prevent the capture of Amphipolis that Thucydides was exiled from Athens (5.26).

76 We have a fragment of the official Athenian copy of this treaty (*IG* I³ 83 = *IG* I² 86 = Tod 1946, n. 72. See also Cohen 1956). The inclusion of this treaty and

In the summer of 419, war broke out between Argos and its neighbor Epidaurus, and the Argives, with some Athenian assistance, invaded and laid waste the territory of Epidaurus. After ravaging the land, the Argives went home, trusting in an Athenian blockade of the peninsular city to keep Spartan and other help from coming to Epidaurus (5.53–55). To the Argives' extreme annoyance, however, it turned out that during the following winter, the Spartans were able to elude the Athenian blockade and introduce a garrison of 300 men to Epidaurus.

The Argives therefore went in complaint to the Athenians and chastised them as follows: "although it had been written in the treaty not to allow hostile forces to pass through the territory of each of them, the Athenians had allowed them to sail past by sea" (Ἀργεῖοι δ' ἐλθόντες παρ' Ἀθηναίους ἐπεκάλουν ὅτι γεγραμμένον ἐν ταῖς σπονδαῖς διὰ τῆς ἑαυτῶν ἑκάστους μὴ ἐᾶν πολεμίους διιέναι ἐάσειαν κατὰ θάλασσαν παραπλεῦσαι, 5.56.2).[77] The reason Thucydides provides for the Argives' irritation is startling. Thucydides specifically says that the Argives complained that the Athenians had allowed the Spartan force to pass by sea (κατὰ θάλασσαν παραπλεῦσαι). However, Thucydides indicates that instead of pointing to the portion of the treaty that uses this very term to cover passage "by sea" (μηδὲ κατὰ θάλασσαν) the Argives quoted in their complaint the clause in the treaty that specified that states must not allow hostile armies to pass through their "territory." The treaty makes a clear distinction between passage through land (διὰ τῆς γῆς) and passage by sea (κατὰ θάλασσαν), but the Argives' complaint merges these two categories of land and sea. The Argives employ a definition of Athenian territory that includes, indeed equals, the sea. In their eyes, Athens' territory, its land, is the sea. In his commentary on this passage, Antony Andrewes argued

> the Argive complaint cannot mean that the Athenians were seriously expected to prevent any and every passage by sea . . . only passage through waters that might

other documents in book 5 (and book 8) is one element that leads Hornblower (1987, 139) and others to think book 5 is "unfinished and therefore presumably late in execution."

[77] The Greek does not use the word "territory" here, but the definite article that appears in the passage clearly refers back to territory. The reference to land is explicit in the portion of the treaty cited by the Argives in their complaint.

reasonably be reckoned Athenian. By the Athenian occupation of Aegina (and Methone) this part of the Saronic Gulf could certainly be so reckoned.[78]

Andrewes tries to limit the novelty of the passage by focusing on what parts of the sea the Argives might reasonably expect the Athenians to control, but he ignores the Argives' striking reference to territory. Their very terminology suggests that Athens' land is the sea. It implies that Athens wholly controls the sea and can be held accountable for any movement on any part of it. Despite Andrewes' attempts at easy explanation, the passage is meant to be surprising. Moreover, this passage directs the reader back to Pericles' claim that the Athenians were absolute masters of all the sea, for the Argives here echo Pericles' boast and follow its reasoning.[79] Indeed, even in his first speech, Pericles told the Athenians that they must "abandon our land" in order to "safeguard the sea and the city." Pericles' Athenian city has no land. The only "territory" it has is the sea, and this is exactly what Thucydides' Argives see.

According to Thucydides, the Athenians agree. In Thucydides' presentation, the Athenians do not correct the Argives. Thucydides thus indicates that the Athenians accepted the Argive view of their territory. Furthermore, this view is entirely consistent with the worldview the Athenians displayed in their response to the revolt of Scione. The Athenians were unconcerned with geographical reality in regard to Scione. They saw a peninsula as an island, and it was the Scionians' status as islanders – that is, their connection to the sea – that was responsible for the Athenians' particular rage against them. This suggests that the Athenians viewed the sea as theirs, just as Pericles had argued it was and prepares for the Argive (and Athenian) judgment that the sea is their "territory."

It is instructive to compare the Athenian worldview as demonstrated at Scione and in the Argive treaty complaint with that evidenced by the Athenian tribute reassessment of 425/4.[80] This "ambitious new assessment" included "many cities not otherwise known to have paid

[78] Andrewes in Gomme et al. 1970, *s.v.* 5.56.2. Steup (Classen and Steup 1912, *loc. cit.*), argues similarly, noting that the ancients preferred to hug the coast. Surely, therefore, the Spartan general was hugging the coast and, because of Athenian control of Aegina and the Methone peninsula, in "Athenian waters."

[79] Classen (in Classen and Steup 1912, *loc. cit.*) saw a reference to Pericles' boast in the Argives' complaint. I think he is right.

[80] *IG* I^3 71 = Meiggs and Lewis 1988, n. 69; Tod 1946, n. 66.

tribute for many years before and still others which are not known to have paid at all."[81] The editors of the tribute lists dubbed this "an unrealistic assessment which contained names of cities from whom Athens could scarcely expect payments," and they concluded that "many [cities] were included for their propaganda value . . . long after they had ceased to belong to the Athenian empire."[82] The reassessment of 425/4, according to Seaman, lists cities "within the actual or *potential* sphere of influence of the Athenian empire."[83] In the 430s, the number of cities on the tribute lists "never exceeded 175." In 425, by contrast, it was "no less than 380."[84] The Athenians who drew up the reassessment of 425/4 clearly had an extensive idea of the reach of their city. The actual connection to Athens (in past tribute or even membership in the Delian League) of these 380 cities does not matter. Rather, taught by Pericles, the Athenians judge half the world to belong to them by right. Thucydides' Athenians judge that the sea and all it touches is theirs.

THE *NAUKRATORES* CLAIM THEIR HALF OF THE WORLD

The worldview on display in Pericles' last speech, in the Athenians' response to the revolt of Scione, in the treaty dispute with Argos, and in the tribute reassessment of 425/4 leads logically to aggressive expansive campaigns like that against the island of Melos. The notorious attack on Melos is no aberration, but a logical step in Athens' assertion of its rule of the sea. The Athenians turned their attention to Melos, a "neutral" island in the Cyclades, in 416 (see Map 1). In his introduction to the campaign, Thucydides makes clear that it was the Athenians' worldview equating Athenian power with the sea that led to the attack, because Melos, Thucydides tells us, was unwilling to submit to Athens "like the rest of the islanders" (ὥσπερ οἱ ἄλλοι νησιῶται, 5.84.2). Thucydides' phrasing claims that all other islands were already in Athens' control and presents the Melos campaign as an attempt to round up the one

[81] Seaman 1997, 402.

[82] Meritt, Wade-Gery, and McGregor (1939–1953), Vol. III, 196, 345.

[83] Seaman 1997, 404. Cf. Eberhardt (1959, 303): "the tributary budget prepared [in 425/4] lacked a real foundation in particular points."

[84] Seaman 1997, 404, n. 74.

outlier.[85] Thucydides has carefully prepared us for such a campaign. An Athens that sees a peninsula as an island and is enraged at its revolt because of this (false) geography could be expected to try to bring into its orbit an actual island, as could an Athens whose allies think the sea is its territory.

Thucydides takes care to show that the mindset that leads Athens to Melos in 416 is nothing new. Ten years earlier, in 426, the Athenians sent sixty ships and two thousand hoplites to Melos under the command of Nicias because the Athenians "wanted to bring over to their side the Melians who were islanders and yet unwilling to become their subjects or to enter into their alliance" (ὄντας νησιώτας καὶ οὐκ ἐθέλοντας ὑπακούειν οὐδὲ ἐς τὸ αὑτῶν ξυμμαχικὸν ἰέναι, 3.91.2). The verbal echoes between the two explanations Thucydides gives about Athenian intentions against Melos underscore the consistency of their worldview. In 426, as in 416, it is specifically the Melians' status as *islanders* that leads the Athenians to attack them because, as the Athenians explicitly remark in the so-called Melian Dialogue, Athens rules the sea. I disagree, therefore, with Parry's claim that Thucydides includes the Melian Dialogue "for purely dramatic purposes, to show the turn the Athenian intellect had finally taken, and to prepare for the Sicilian Expedition which directly follows."[86] Although the Melian campaign surely prepares for the Sicilian Expedition, there is no "turn" in evidence. On the contrary, Thucydides shows us that the thinking of 416 leads back to 426 and back to Pericles.[87]

[85] As Hornblower (1991, *s.v.* 1.144.1) notes, the attack on Melos "does look like an attempt to round off the Aegean empire." Thucydides remarks at the beginning of the war that "all the islands to the east bounded by the Peloponnesus and Crete except for Melos and Thera" were allied to Athens (2.9.4). Thera paid tribute as early as 430/29. Cf. Amit 1968, 218, n. 6.

[86] Parry 1981, 194.

[87] Cf. Macleod (1974, 399): "the motive, and so the political character of Athens' action, is the same in both [attacks]." Cogan (1981b, 4–5) also insists that the Melian debate is not meant to serve as a "moral demonstration" of the increasing violence of the Athenians: "the so-called low point of Athenian brutality (Melos) is antedated by an identical slaughter at Scione six years before (5.32.1). Cf. Orwin (1994, 111), who notes that "in denying the primacy of justice over interest, [the Athenian] envoys merely restate the argument of the Athenian envoys at Sparta and . . . the implicit view of Pericles himself."

Before they attacked the island, the Athenians addressed the Melian council to see if they could persuade them to surrender voluntarily. Thucydides presents the discussion in a point–counterpoint debate between "the Melians" and "the Athenians." In these failed negotiations, the Melians try desperately to argue that they do not, in fact, belong to Athens. They hope to deny any connection to Athens, as Amphipolis had done. For example, at one point, the unnamed Athenian representatives argue that Athens must subdue Melos because "your hatred does not harm us so much as your friendship displays weakness to our subjects – as hatred displays strength" (5.95). The Melians respond by asking, "do your subjects judge fair play thus, that they lump together people who are wholly unconnected with you and those who are for the most part your own colonists or rebels who were subdued?" (σκοποῦσι δ' ὑμῶν οὕτως οἱ ὑπήκοοι τὸ εἰκός, ὥστε τούς τε μὴ προσήκοντας καὶ ὅσοι ἄποικοι ὄντες οἱ πολλοὶ καὶ ἀποστάντες τινὲς κεχείρωνται ἐς τὸ αὐτὸ τιθέασιν; 5.96). The Melians claim that they are "unconnected" (μὴ προσήκοντας) to Athens. Those "connected" to Athens, in their eyes, are colonists sent out from Athens or member states of the Delian League. However, as Thucydides has repeatedly shown, Athenians do not recognize such strict boundaries between what is theirs and what is not. An earlier use of the term "connected to" reminds us of this. In his Funeral Oration, when he revealed his idealized vision of an insubstantial city that ranged over the entire world, Pericles claimed that the whole earth was the grave of brave Athenians. "Not only the inscription on the *stelai* in their home land (ἐν τῇ οἰκείᾳ) marks it," according to Pericles. Rather, there exists a memorial "even in land that is unconnected to them" (ἀλλὰ καὶ ἐν τῇ μὴ προσηκούσῃ ἄγραφος μνήμη, 2.43.3). This passage strongly suggests that just as the Athenians recognize no home territory, so, too, no land is unconnected to Athens. It predicts that the Melians' claim that they are "unconnected" to Athens will fail.

And so it does. The Athenians reply to the Melians' question of whether the Athenians' subjects make no distinction between "people who are wholly unconnected with you and those who are for the most part your own colonists or rebels who were subdued" as follows:

> They think that neither group falls short in a judgment of what is right but that the one group [i.e., those now, at least, unconnected to Athens] escapes because

of their power and that we do not attack them because of fear. So that apart from ruling more through your overthrow we would produce security for ourselves especially if you who are islanders (and weaker ones than others) should not get the better of us who are masters of the sea (ἄλλως τε καὶ νησιῶται ναυκρατόρων καὶ ἀσθενέστεροι ἑτέρων ὄντες εἰ μὴ περιγένοισθε, 5.97).

The Athenians claim that their subjects see no distinction between the two groups except one of power. In their eyes, those "unconnected" to Athens are simply those states Athens has not yet conquered because of fear.[88] But the Athenians reveal that Athens has a special focus on the Melians because they are islanders and the Athenians (as they now describe themselves for the first time) are "masters of the sea" (ναυκρατόρες, literally "masters by ship").[89] The Athenians' new term for themselves echoes Pericles' last speech when he revealed to the Athenians that they were absolute masters of half of the world (γῆς καὶ θαλάσσης, τοῦ ἑτέρου ὑμᾶς παντὸς κυριωτάτους ὄντας, 2.62.2). Pericles did not use the new term that appears in the Melian dialogue, but he did use a combination of words that means the same thing – "masters of the sea." Pericles tells the Athenians that of one whole part of the world they were "absolute masters" (κυριωτάτους).

According to the *naukratores* at Melos, "being connected" to Athens does not need to involve colonizing ventures or treaty obligations. There need be no historical, political, or ethnic tie between Athens and another state to "connect" it to Athens. For the Athenians, all that matters is that the Melians are islanders. The Melians' geography (despite – rather, *because* of the gap of water) "connects" them to Athens. As an island, surrounded by sea, they already are (or at least should be) Athens. The

[88] The Athenians' logic implies that the bond between Athens and the states Melos would judge as "connected" to Athens rests only on force as well. Amphipolis has already shown that even Athenian colonies do not necessarily see any natural connection between themselves and Athens and may resist such a tie if they have the power.

[89] This term does not appear before this point in Thucydides' text and occurs only two other times, once later in this dialogue (5.109) and once in Alcibiades' speech urging the Athenians to undertake the Sicilian Expedition (6.18.5). With this word Thucydides links the policy decision of the Melian campaign with that of the disastrous Sicilian Expedition.

echo of Pericles' last speech in the Athenians' new term for themselves, *naukratores*, and the agreement between Pericles and the Athenians at Melos that no land is "unconnected" to Athens traces the aggressive Athenian policy at Melos back to Pericles. The echo shows that the campaign against Melos is not the result of the new policies of Pericles' deficient successors, but rather the product of a consistent worldview that locates Athens not in Attica but on the sea and all it touches.

Scholars, then, look in vain for a specific precipitating "reason" for the Athenians' attack on Melos. Andrewes, for example, argues that because of the presence of fifteen hundred allied island hoplites in Athens' forces, the expedition was not a "mere monstrosity of aggression, but something with which already subject islanders could sympathise." Andrewes concludes that there was "a case, perhaps even a plausible case, for Athens' attack on Melos" that Thucydides knew but excluded from his text.[90] Others argue that the Athenian attack was precipitated either by Melian contributions to the Spartan war fund or because the island was tributary to Athens and in revolt (based on its presence in the propaganda tribute reassessment of 425/4).[91] However, as Seaman has convincingly shown, the Melian contributions to the Spartan War Fund were most probably made by Melian survivors of the massacre of 416 and therefore are not evidence of earlier Melian help for Sparta that might have precipitated the attack.[92] Furthermore, the presence of Melos in the Athenian tribute reassessment of 425/4 says nothing about Melos' actual tributary

90 Andrewes 1960, 1–2. Macleod (1974, 400) cautions that even if there may have been reasons why islanders might have supported the expedition, "Athens was well able to coerce them, even if they were unwilling."

91 The presence of Melos in the Athenian reassessment of 425/4 led Treu (1953 and 1954; followed by Raubitschek 1963) to argue that Melos was tributary and revolting in 416. The Melians appear on the Spartan war fund list twice (*IG* V 1, 1+ = *SEG* 39,370). Adcock (1932, 4f) dated the Melian contributions to 427 and argued that they precipitated the Athenian attack on the island in 426. See Loomis (1992, 56–76) for a discussion.

92 Seaman 1997, 396ff. Seaman argues that there is no reason to believe that the Athenians killed *all* adult men on Melos. According to Xenophon (*HG* 2.2.9) and Plutarch (*Lys.* 14.3) Lysander restored the Melians to their island, so some must have survived. Seaman concludes that the Spartans likely resettled the surviving Melians somewhere in Spartan-controlled territory after the Athenian capture of their island. Cf. Bleckmann 1993.

status but speaks only to Athenian imaginings about the world and their control of it. Thus the only factor that precipitates the Athenian attack is probably just what Thucydides has the Athenians proclaim in the dialogue: Melos is an island and Athens controls the sea.[93]

Interestingly enough, the Melians were not able to hear the argument the Athenians were making or understand the definition of the city on which it was based. In their response, the Melians again try to make a distinction between themselves and their "unconnected" country and some territory more connected to Athens. The Melians hope that the Spartans will come to their aid on Melos itself, or, failing this, they predict that the Spartans "will turn against your own land (ἐς τὴν γὴν ὑμῶν) and against the remainder of your allies that Brasidas did not approach. So, your trouble will not be over a country which is unconnected to you but rather over your more home-like alliance and land" (οὐ περὶ τῆς μὴ προσηκούσης μᾶλλον ἢ τῆς οἰκειοτέρας ξυμμαχίδος τε καὶ γῆς ὁ πόνος ὑμῖν ἔσται, 5.110.2).

When Thucydides represents the Spartans as planning to "hurt the Athenians back equally" for attacks in the Peloponnesus with the northern campaigns of Brasidas, he shows that the Spartans recognized an equivalence between their "own territory" and the Athenians' empire (4.80.1). The Melians' position here is more ambiguous. On one hand, their first wish for what will sway the Athenians is the traditional invasion of Attica. They tell the Athenians they hope that the Spartans will invade "your own land." On the other hand, they immediately widen their view to include "the remainder of your allies that Brasidas did not approach," and in their last sentence, the Melians link into one thought the Athenians' "more home-like alliance and land" (τῆς οἰκειοτέρας ξυμμαχίδος τε καὶ γῆς), suggesting that despite their desire for an invasion of Attica, the Melians do see that for the Athenians, Acharnae is no more "home-like" than Scione.

[93] Curiously, Seaman (1997, 414, n. 108) assumes that the Athenians must have used "actual arguments" that Thucydides does not give us. So, too, Meiggs (1972, 389) supposes that the Athenians might have argued that the Melians "were enjoying all the benefits derived from Athenian thalassocracy without contributing to the cost." But why must we assume that the Athenians used arguments different from those Thucydides gives us, especially if we accept that the motivation was indeed what he presents: a desire to round off the Aegean empire as a show of strength?

The Melians' use of the adjective "more home-like; more your own" (*oikeioteras*) is an ironic verbal echo of the earlier passages that emphatically deny that the Athenians feel such home attachment, including the Corinthians' claim that the Athenians "consider themselves to have been robbed of their household property" (1.70.7) if they do not get some new thing they want; Pericles' claim in the Funeral Oration that "it is our luck to enjoy the goods from here with no more homegrown and familiar a pleasure than the goods of other men" (2.38.2); his exhortation that the Athenians must "abandon our land and our houses"; his admission that he "would urge you to go out yourselves and lay waste your houses and your land" (1.143.5); and his rebuke that the Athenians are foolish to think that "houses and land" are "important things to be stripped of" (2.62.3). Houses and home are not touchstones to the Athenians. However, although the Melians see that the Athenians do not divide the world into home territory and the rest (meaning Attica vs. all else), they assume that the Athenians see some distinction between their home territory of Attica together with the allied territory of the empire and the rest of the world – that which the Melians would say is "unconnected" to Athens. What the Melians manifestly fail (or refuse) to see is that the only division of the world that the Athenians follow is that articulated by Pericles in his last speech: land and sea. The only important factor in deciding whether Melos belongs to Athens is that they are islanders and Athens is master of the sea. The whole sea is the city, so that Melos has at least as much "to do with them" as Attica does.

The Melian campaign (and the Sicilian Expedition to follow) are often taken as examples of clear divergence from Periclean policy. John Finley remarks that "the conquest of the island [Melos] represents the very kind of extension of Athenian naval power that Pericles feared even to suggest."[94] Gomme argues that "Pericles would have condemned the Sicilian Expedition."[95] Although Hornblower believes that both the Melian and Sicilian campaigns were "not strictly contrary to Periclean strategy" because Athens "was not at open war with Sparta," the use of "strictly" shows that Hornblower thinks that both campaigns represent strong divergences from sound Periclean policy.[96]

[94] J. Finley 1938/1967, 38, n. 56.

[95] Gomme 1945, *s.v.* 1.144.1.

[96] Hornblower 1991, *s.v.* 1.144.1

Hornblower's reference to "open war" shows that he is judging the Melian and Sicilian campaigns against the "Periclean policy" articulated by Thucydides in the *Epitaph* and by Pericles in his first speech, in which a key element is the injunction not to "add to the *arche* during the war" (ἀρχὴν μὴ ἐπικτωμένους ἐν τῷ πολέμῳ, Thucydides, 2.65.7; ἀρχήν τε μὴ ἐπικτᾶσθαι ἅμα πολεμοῦντες, Pericles 1.144.1).[97] Such a prohibition assumes that the Athenian *arche* consists of the states under immediate Athenian domination at a given time. In Pericles' last speech, however, he specifically rejected that notion, telling the Athenians that they were wrong to "think that they hold their *arche* only over their allies" (τῶν ξυμμάχων μόνων ἄρχειν). Athens' *arche*, that is, does *not* include only those states from which it collects tribute, or which it now controls. Rather, according to Pericles, the Athenians *are* "masters of the watery half of the world, both as much as you now hold and still more if you wish" (τοῦ ἑτέρου ὑμάς παντὸς κυριωτάτους ὄντας, ἐφ' ὅσον τε νῦν νέμεσθε καὶ ἢν ἐπὶ πλέον βουληθῆτε, 2.62.2). Pericles recognizes that within their *arche* there exists a division between what the Athenians now "hold" and the rest, but by denying that the Athenians hold their *arche* over only their allies, he strongly implies that the Athenians hold *arche* over the whole of that which he calls them "absolute masters." According to this view, the campaign against Melos is not an attempt to *add* to the Athenians' *arche*, for Melos exists in the part of the world over which the Athenians already hold their *arche*. Athens is merely asserting a more direct control over Melos because, as the Athenians say, it was "unwilling to submit to Athens like the rest of the islanders." Thus the Melos campaign does not diverge from Pericles' policy; on the contrary, it follows the vision articulated in Pericles' last speech exactly.[98]

[97] Thucydides, of course, argues that the Peace of Nicias was a false peace and that the whole period from 431 to 404 was a single war (5.26). In any case, my argument is that the Athenian vision on display at Melos is inconsistent with *any* discussion of "additions" to the *arche* that does not recognize that the *arche* has become the sea and everything it touches.

[98] This is not to say that Pericles would necessarily have countenanced an attack on Melos if he were alive in 416. I mean only to stress that far from clearly diverging from Pericles' policy, the Athenian position on Melos shows striking connections to it. Cf. L. Strauss (1964, 192): "While Pericles might never have said what the Athenians said on Melos and while he might not have regarded

Furthermore, far from seeing their attack as a reckless, acquisitive adventure liable to put the city at risk, the Athenians at Melos think their attack is cautious and protective. The Athenians argue that in addition to "ruling more through your overthrow," the conquest of Melos "would produce security for ourselves" (5.97). Lisa Kallet has called the Melian campaign a "costly demonstration" and argued that a central theme of Thucydides' text here and in his account of the Sicilian campaign is the Athenians' "ostentatious display of their wealth and the implication that this display is a substitute for the exercise of real power."[99] She emphasizes that the reasons the Athenians give for their actions "have primarily to do with how their power *looks* to other Greeks."[100] The Athenians say that onlookers think that they hold back from attacking others (especially islands) because of fear, and that their failure to attack Melos makes them look weak. According to their reasoning, attacking and conquering Melos will increase their stature and thus their actual power and security because their power will have been seen.

Kallet suggests that the Athenians are foolish to reason in this way and to focus so much on the display and perception of power, but Thucydides has already demonstrated that states do judge strength by such means. They watch what people do – and especially what they fail

the Athenians' action against Melos as expedient, his political principle did not differ from that of those Athenians." Palmer (1992, 64–74) traces certain connections between the Melian dialogue and earlier Athenian and Periclean thought. The Athenian representatives at Melos are, famously, anonymous. Some have suggested that this is because the Melian dialogue he reports is invented (cf. de Romilly 1947/1963, 274; Grundy 1948, 436; M. Finley 1954, 615 and 1985, 13; Hudson-Williams 1950, 167, Parry 1981, 194). I decline to believe Thucydides was capable of such wholesale invention. If we accept that something like the Melian Dialogue occurred, one reason why Thucydides did not name the Athenians as individuals may be because he wanted to indicate that the policy at Melos was a general Athenian policy. It did not belong to an Alcibiades (as Plutarch reports) or to anyone else. It was Athenian policy in general and Athenian thinking that led to the campaign. Cf. Cornford (1907, 187): "it was not [Alcibiades], but Athens, that was mad and blinded with the thirst of gain. . . ." Gribble (2006, 450) argues that "the anonymity of the participants in the debate suggest[s] the way the Melians are in the grip of impersonal forces beyond their control."

99 Kallet 2001, 20–21.

100 Kallet 2001, 17.

to do – and assess their might accordingly. A failure to act and to display power (even when not strictly necessary to a military objective) can lead to tangible losses. For example, in the summer of 424, the Athenians were holding the Long Walls of Megara at the port of Nisaea in the hope of finally taking the main upper city as well when Brasidas suddenly appeared on the scene. As Thucydides recounts, Brasidas recognized that Greek *perception* of events was just as important as actual military strength. Brasidas (and the Peloponnesians) remained quiet and waited for the Athenians to attack. He knew that the Megarians "were looking on to see which side would get the victory," and Brasidas reasoned that if he showed himself willing to fight, while not taking the risk of actually bringing it on himself, "the victory would rightly be given to them without the struggle." If they had not appeared ready for battle, however, Brasidas realized that "there would have been no chance for them, but certainly they would have been stripped of the city *as if bested*." His unwillingness to fight would have appeared the same to the Megarians as a loss in battle. Brasidas saw that he must look ready to fight, but he hoped that the Athenians might "not to be willing to fight so that the object for which [he] came might be achieved without a fight" (4.73.1–3).

Brasidas' reasoning focuses intently on what the Megarians will think about what they see happening (and not happening) before their city, and all went according to his hopes. The Athenians drew up for battle but "kept quiet themselves" when Brasidas did not attack; they then eventually withdrew. Soon afterwards, the Megarians opened the gates to Brasidas "as the victor, the Athenians being no longer willing to fight" (τῷ μὲν Βρασίδᾳ . . . ὡς ἐπικρατήσαντι καὶ τῶν Ἀθηναίων οὐκέτι ἐθελησάντων μάχεσθαι, 4.73.4). In a perceptive analysis of this passage, Rood remarks, "the Athenians lose a battle that never takes place; they are not even presented as aware that they have lost one." Brasidas, by contrast, is "above all . . . aware of the importance of being seen."[101] He knows that his display of power may well win him the city.

Thucydides soon shows, furthermore, that the Athenians' display of weakness at Megara, and people's perceptions of the Athenians' loss

[101] Rood 1998b, 66.

of this "battle that never takes place," have important consequences. In his Thracian campaign, Brasidas uses the Athenians' inactivity at Megara to induce the cities of the Chalcidice to revolt. At Acanthus, Brasidas explains that "when I went in aid to Nisaea with the very army I now have, the Athenians were not willing to join with me though they were more numerous, so that it is not likely that they will send out on ships a force against you equal to that army in Nisaea" (4.85.7), and Thucydides specifically remarks that Brasidas' claims about Megara helped to convince the Chalcidians. They decided to revolt from Athens not only because they based their decision "more on uncertain wishing than on secure foresight," but also because Brasidas made "enticing but untrue claims – that at Nisaea the Athenians were unwilling to face him and his single army" (4.108.4–5). The clever Brasidas uses the plain of Megara as a "'didactic arena' . . . for the wider Greek world."[102]

Thucydides makes it clear that Brasidas' claims were inflated and that the Chalcidians were no judges of Athens' strength; their "deception about the power of the Athenians" was, he tells us, "as great as that power was later evident" (4.108.5). Yet Brasidas' false claims helped him to induce the cities of the Chalcidice to revolt, and the lessons that people took from the "didactic arena" of Megara (even if false) led to real difficulties for Athens in the north and costly losses (like that of Amphipolis) that the Athenians, by 416, had yet to resolve. The Athenians' response to Scione's revolt showed that they made a special claim to (even non-island) islands. Since Pericles, the Athenians claimed to rule the sea. The Argives, at least, judged the sea to be the Athenians' territory. Such an ally might well think that Athens fails to subdue a non-Athenian island in its own territory only because of fear and weakness, as would anyone who accepted the Periclean view of Athens. In the "didactic arena," a neutral Melos might well lead to revolts. Therefore, it is not mere foolishness for the Athenians to argue that subduing Melos would display their power and "produce security for ourselves" (5.97).[103]

[102] Rood 1998b, 66.

[103] Cf. Wassermann (1964, 293): "In a world where power alone counts, respect for neutrality would be regarded not as an act of voluntary restraint, but as a sign of weakness."

In the *Epitaph*, Thucydides wrote that Pericles predicted victory for Athens "if they kept quiet and took care of the navy, if they did not add to the *arche* during the course of the war and if they did not take risks with the city." However, Pericles actually warned the Athenians to "safeguard the sea and the city," and in his last speech he told the Athenians their *arche* consisted of the sea itself. The *naukratores* at Melos seem to believe, as Pericles told them, that they rule the sea and ought to control all islands in it. Pericles' formulation of "sea and city" blurs the boundaries between them, just as the Athenians on Melos blur (indeed, deny) the boundaries between land connected (and unconnected) to them. All that matters is the connection to the sea. In their eyes, Melos ought to be theirs already, so that bringing it into the rightful control of Athens is more defensive than reckless. By capturing it, these Athenians safeguard the sea/city they recognize.

WILL HOME-CONFUSION LEAD TO HOME-WAR?

The Athenians believe that their position is manifestly stronger than that of the Melians and that if the Melians would simply face facts rather than chasing dreams, they would see this. In their very first address to the Melians, the Athenians say, "if you have met with us in order to calculate your suspicions about the future (ὑπονοίας τῶν μελλόντων λογιούμενοι) or for any other reason than to take counsel concerning the salvation of your city on the basis of present circumstances and the situation you can see (ἐκ τῶν παρόντων καὶ ὧν ὁρᾶτε), we can stop. But if for this, we can speak" (5.87). They later urge the Melians to consult based on "the possibilities (τὰ δυνατά) derived from what each side truly thinks" (5.89). When the Melians ultimately refuse to give in to them, the Athenians complain that the Melians "alone . . . judge things to come to be more clear than what you can see and in your wishful thinking gaze at things unseen as if they have already occurred" (μόνοι . . . τὰ μὲν μέλλοντα τῶν ὁρωμένων σαφέστερα κρίνετε, τὰ δὲ ἀφανῆ τῷ βούλεσθαι ὡς γιγνόμενα ἤδη θεᾶσθε, 5.113.). The Athenians thus deftly wield the theme of the near and the far against the Melians and condemn the foolishness of their inability or unwillingness to judge their situation on the actual facts at hand.

The Melians fail, in particular, to properly judge *syngeneia* ("kinship") and "the hold it exerted on others." Whereas the Athenians are Ionians, the Melians are Dorians and thus ethnically related to the Spartans. The Melians argue that the *syngeneia* "that binds Melos to Sparta should help insure that Sparta will take action" (5.108.1).[104] It will make the Melians seem "more trustworthy." The Athenians, however, have already noted that "of men we know, the Lacedaemonians make it most evident that they consider the pleasant virtuous and the expedient just" (5.105.4). They respond to the Melians' trust in *syngeneia* by remarking that the Lacedaemonians will look not to the "good will" of the Melians but to their own strength "from a practical standpoint." The Athenians correctly predict that "it is not likely that they will cross over to an island when we are *naukratores*" (5.109). The Athenians claim that questions of expediency and practicality will trump any ties of *syngeneia* between Sparta and Melos.[105]

By the time of the attack on Melos, the trial of the Plataeans had already demonstrated (both to the wider Greek world and to Thucydides' reader) that ties of *philia* between states had lost their power.[106] *Philia* describes that "continuum of attachment that extends in a stable system of relationships from the self to one's immediate family and friends and then outwards to one's *polis* and one's race." It involves also "shared hostility or *echthra*."[107] In their defense speech, the Plataeans appealed to the Spartan dead from the battle of Plataea not to allow "their best friends" to be handed over to the Thebans, "their worst enemies." Thucydides makes the contrast emphatic with the immediate juxtaposition of the words "worst enemies" and "best friends" (μηδὲ τοῖς ἐχθίστοις φίλτατοι ὄντες παραδοθῆναι, 3.59.2). Nevertheless, "the Spartan living consult their present interests on the principle of shifting *philia*" and condemn the Plataeans.[108] The Spartans' new "friends," the

104 Crane 1996, 151.

105 Cf. Wilson 1989, 149: "In the Melian dialogue . . . the ideal of race is again unmasked as unreliable."

106 Cf. Morrison (2000, 129) who argues that by now, "the reader has already learned" that "decisions are based on considerations of advantage, not elevated sentiments or a rosy picture of the past."

107 Wilson 1989, 147.

108 Wilson 1989, 149.

Thebans, were "useful" to them for the present war (3.68.4), and that trumped their old ties of *philia* with the Plataeans from the old war. The dilution of the power of *philia* at Plataea strongly suggests that *syngeneia*, too, may have lost its strength in interstate relations.

Indeed, the Athenians' very explanation at Melos of what "connects" them to states reveals that they have no regard for *philia* or *syngeneia* in their judgment. The Melians divide the world into states "wholly unconnected" to Athens and states "who are for the most part your own colonists or rebels who were subdued" (5.96). The Melians think that what connects a state to Athens is a shared history, as metropolis and colony (which would likely involve also at least some ethnic connection) or shared membership in the Delian league. Yet the Athenians do not limit themselves in this way. What "connects" a state to Athens is the sea and nothing else. Neither *philia*, nor history, nor *syngeneia* figures in their thinking.

The Syracusan general Hermocrates saw this clearly. When he tried to rally Sicily against the first Athenian campaign there in 427, he argued that no one should think that "the Chalcidian element is safe because of Ionian kinship [with the Athenians]" (τὸ δὲ Χαλκιδικὸν τῇ Ἰάδι ξυγγενείᾳ ἀσφαλές, 4.61.2). This was because "it is not against races that they attack . . . but aiming at the good things of Sicily" (4.61.3). Just like the Athenians at Melos, Hermocrates argues that the Athenians do not use *syngeneia* or *philia* to judge where they should expand and whom they should support or attack. *Syngeneia* has no importance to them. The Athenian Euphemus later argues that this kind of thinking is, in fact, particularly appropriate to Athens. "To a man who is a tyrant or to a city ruling an empire," he explains, "nothing is illogical that is expedient nor home-like (οἰκεῖον) that is not trustworthy (μὴ πιστόν)" (6.85). The Melians believed that the *syngeneia* they shared with the Spartans would make them seem "more trustworthy" (πιστότεροι) and would induce the Spartans to help them (5.108.1). Euphemus emphatically insists here that a tyrant or a tyrant city judges trustworthiness by some standard wholly separate from blood and ethnic connections. Furthermore, only those who are trustworthy according to that standard are really kin. Kinship, which would seem an immutable characteristic, is dependent on some other factor. According to Pericles, preserving the empire meant giving up the houses and land of Attica. According to

Euphemos, holding onto an empire means judging the "homelike; the familiar" not by *philia* or *syngeneia* but by some other standard entirely.

This evidence of the declining hold of *philia* and *syngeneia* in interstate relationships shows that the Athenians see the world more clearly than do the Melians.[109] Furthermore, as the Athenians predict, the Spartans do not honor their bonds of *philia* and *syngeneia* with Melos and do not come to their aid. The Melians are, therefore, eventually forced to surrender to the Athenians who, as Thucydides reports in one sentence, "killed as many of the men of military age that they captured; the children and women they enslaved. They themselves colonized the territory, sending out later five hundred colonists" (5.116.4). Thus the history that follows the dialogue also seems to prove the foolishness of the Melians.[110] At the same time, it seems to demonstrate the clear thinking of the Athenians, the correctness of their assessment that they are *naukratores*, and the power of their sea-city.

The dialogue is not quite so straightforward as this, however. The Athenians present the Melians' refusal to deliberate based on the present circumstances and possibilities instead of on hope for the future as the depth of foolishness. Yet, as Macleod remarks, the "domineering method of the Athenians . . . reveals . . . a weakness of their own. Their refusal to look into the future is far removed from the foresight (πρόνοια) which characterizes the Thucydidean statesman."[111] In addition, as Parry remarks, their dismissal of the future includes a "deliberately reckless entrusting of themselves to immediate reality."[112] Furthermore, the

[109] Cf. Morrison (2000, 129): the Athenians provide "a kind of instruction for the Melians that is analogous to what Thucydides teaches the reader of his *History* . . . to the extent that by reading Thucydides' *History* the reader has 'experienced' the war, he or she is now better versed in the ways of the world than the Melians. . . ."

[110] Cf. Palmer (1992, 72–73): "Would not an intelligent, sympathetic friend of the Melians, observing the Melians' predicament, advise them to do precisely what the Athenians advise them to do?"

[111] Macleod 1974, 391.

[112] Parry 1981, 195. Cf. Liebeschuetz (1968, 75): "The Athenians look at the present and can see nothing that will save Melos. They are right. The Melians look to the future. They are right too. Melos is destroyed. But the very next sentence in the history begins the story of the decline of Athens and the justification of the Melians." Cf. Morrison 2000, 137–38.

Athenians' definition of their sea-city knows no bounds. According to the Athenian logic at Melos, virtually any island or coastal site ought to be subdued in order to provide security to Athens' sea-city. Protecting "the sea and the city" is much more complicated than protecting the Athens in Attica and seems to lead inevitably to an endless series of acquisitive campaigns.

Finally, Thucydides gives his reader reason to believe that the state that denies ties of *philia* and *syngeneia* in interstate relations and judges the "home-like" by other standards may suffer for this internally. When Hermocrates warned that the Athenians would not spare the Ionians in Sicily, he argued that their shared danger should forge a new unity among Sicilians. "*Stasis*," he says, "especially destroys cities and Sicily" (4.61.1). Hermocrates urges the Sicilians to think of themselves as "neighbors and inhabitants of a single land surrounded by water and called by one name – Sicilians," instead of identifying themselves as members of individual *poleis* – as, for example, Leontinians or Syracusans. In this way, he says, they will "escape both the Athenians and home war" (4.64.5). Hermocrates uses the word *stasis*, which properly means "conflict within a *polis*," to refer to conflict between Sicilian *poleis*. "Home war" (οἰκεῖος πόλεμος), Hermocrates' other phrase for *stasis*, emphasizes that *stasis* is a war at home, within the *polis*. It underscores that Hermocrates is transferring to interstate politics the language of *stasis* within a city.[113] In Hermocrates' formulation, the Sicilians' failure to recognize their Sicilian unity is equivalent to the failure of citizens within a *polis* in *stasis* to recognize their affinity and unity.[114]

Thucydides analyzes the nature of *stasis* when he describes the faction fighting in Corcyra in 427. According to Thucydides, *stasis* occurs in a *polis* when other bonds supersede and destroy those of *philia* and *syngeneia*. For example, Thucydides says that the Corcyrans killed "of their own those seeming to be enemies" (σφῶν αὐτῶν τοὺς ἐχθροὺς δοκοῦντας εἶναι ἐφόνευον, 3.81.4). A man's "own" ought to include the members of his close, and then extended, family, and ultimately his whole *polis* community. The *philia* that binds that group assumes a concomitant

[113] Cf. Loraux 1997/2002, 39.

[114] Price (2001) argues that Thucydides conceived of the Peloponnesian War itself as a kind of *stasis* within the Greek people.

"shared hostility or *echthra*."[115] In *stasis*, however, those who should share *echthra* instead feel it toward each other because *stasis* destroys the ties that bind even the closest men. In the slaughter in Corcyra, for example, Thucydides tells us that "every kind of death occurred and, as is customary in such situations, there was nothing that did not happen and still worse. Fathers killed sons. . . ." (3.81.5).[116] Even the ties of *philia* within the *oikos* were violated. Indeed, Thucydides explains that "kinship became more foreign than party tie" (καὶ μὴν καὶ τὸ ξυγγενὲς τοῦ ἑταιρικοῦ ἀλλοτριώτερον ἐγένετο, 3.82.6). It is for this reason that *stasis* is termed "home war" because in *stasis* those within the *polis* and even within the home, who ought to be *philoi*, become enemies.

Hermocrates applies this pattern of intra-*polis* war to inter-*polis* conflict in Sicily. His extrapolation from the smaller canvas to the larger encourages the reader to wonder if an equivalence runs in the opposite direction as well. Will a state that denies ties of *syngeneia* and *philia* in interstate relations come to deny them *within* the *polis* and so suffer *stasis*? Will Athens, in particular, which, in interstate relations "judges the home-like as those who are trustworthy" on some criteria other than kinship come to judge the "home-like" this way within the *polis* as well? An Athenian echo in Thucydides' description of the *stasis* in Corcyra argues that it will. At an early stage in the Corcyran *stasis*, the Corcyran democrats were afraid that fifty-three Peloponnesian ships under Alcidas and Brasidas, which were making threatening feints in the area, would sail against the city (3.77–80). The *demos*, therefore, held negotiations with their defeated oligarchic opponents who had taken refuge in the temple of Hera and urged them to join with them "so that the city might be saved" (ὅπως σωθήσεται ἡ πόλις). Using this argument, the *demos* was able to persuade some of these oligarchs to "go on board ship" to fight the Peloponnesians (τινας αὐτῶν ἔπεισαν ἐς τὰς ναῦς ἐσβῆναι, 3.80.1).[117] Soon, however, news that sixty Athenian ships were coming

[115] Wilson 1989, 147.

[116] As Loraux (1997/2002, 39) notes, this is the image of *stasis* for Thucydides: he "would have liked to condense all its horror in the murder of a son by his father."

[117] The Corcyrans briefly "hate with one spirit," in the words of the choral song of the *Erinyes* in the *Oresteia*. Loraux (1991, 37) notes that this is one way to stress the unity of a city.

to aid the democrats caused the Peloponnesians to withdraw. With the threat gone, the Corcyran democrats returned the ships to port, "and all those whom they had persuaded to go on board ship they killed as they disembarked" (ἐκ τῶν νεῶν ὅσους ἔπεισαν ἐσβῆναι ἐκβιβάζοντες ἀπεχρῶντο, 3.81.2).

Not once but twice Thucydides uses "to go on board ship" – the "catch-phrase" of 480 – to describe the Corcyran factioneers. Earlier in the text, in a highly favorable context, this phrase signaled the Athenians' astonishing and powerful ability to reimagine their *polis*; here it describes a ruse used against fellow citizens in a *stasis*-ridden city that cannot agree on the nature of the *polis*. Rood calls this echo a "perversion of the spirit of 480."[118] Not quite. Rather, with this echo Thucydides hints that the "spirit of 480" holds within it the "spirit of 411" and the "spirit of 403" – the spirit, that is, of the *stasis* that will soon come to Athens.[119] In 480, the Athenians radically transformed their *polis* into the sea-borne city we see at Melos. The creation of that city, however, required the abandonment of home and houses. It caused the Athenians to judge the "home-like" anew. The Athenians at Melos judge "connection" to Athens not by *philia* or *syngeneia* or history but merely by power and attachment to the sea. The Athenian echo at Corcyra hints that just as Athens disregards ties of *philia* and ignores boundaries between home and foreign in its empire, soon it will fail to recognize the ties of blood and *philia* within the city: The city that denies its homeland will, in part because of this, soon suffer home war. Thus, when the Melians hope that soon, with Spartan help, the Athenians' "trouble will not be over a country which is unconnected to you but rather over your more home-like alliance and land," their words contain an ironic hint of trouble in the very homeland the Athenians deny: *stasis* in Attica.[120]

[118] Rood 1999, 152.

[119] With only one exception, Thucydides reserves the phrase "to go on board ship" for the Athenians and Corcyrans. In the one exception (4.25), Thucydides uses the phrase for the Syracusans, who, of course, he judged to be "most like the Athenians in character" (8.96.5). The phrase, then, seems to be used for Athenians and people like Athenians and so hints that the Athenians are (or will be) like the Corcyrans.

[120] Cf. Greenwood 2006, 86.

In the Melian dialogue, the Athenians repeatedly deploy the theme of the near and the far against the Melians. The Melians seem foolishly unable to comprehend their real danger and think their ties of *syngeneia* with Sparta are strong enough to save them. However, the Melians (and the dialogue) actively redeploy the *topos* against the Athenians. When they complain (and the Athenians agree) that the Athenians make no distinction between their colonies and subject allies and "people who are wholly unconnected to you," the dialogue suggests that the Athenians completely ignore ties of *syngeneia* and *philia* and see no distinction between here and there, between home and away.[121] The Melians' "near and far" misjudgments about present and future, hope and fact, lead quickly to their disastrous defeat and death. Thus far, the Athenians' "near and far" (mis)judgments about home and foreign seem not to have harmed them. But the emphatic juxtaposition of the two peoples and their misjudgments in this dialogue suggest that this may not last.[122] One further parallel between the Melian Dialogue and the Funeral Oration confirms this. We recall that just as the Melians foolishly "gaze at the indistinct as if it has already happened," so Pericles urged the Athenians to "gaze" in erotic fascination at his vision of

[121] Young (1968, 120, n. 18) notes the irony of the Athenians' use of the *topos* of the near and the far in the Melian Dialogue because of its application to the Athenians' behavior in the Sicilian Expedition, but he does not note the irony within the Melian Dialogue itself.

[122] Thucydides includes a nod forward to Athens' fall in this dialogue. The Melians argue that the Athenians ought not to disregard considerations of justice in case they are ever overthrown. Many scholars have seen here a reference to the debate that occurred after Athens' defeat when, according to Xenophon, the Athenians "thought that they would suffer the sort of things they made the Melians, colonists of the Lacedaemonians, suffer (*HG* 2.2.3). Liebeschuetz (1968, 76) argues that this future "justifies" the Melians. Orwin (1994, 101, n. 8) objects that Xenophon "cannot sustain conclusions as to how Thucydides would have presented the debate following the defeat of Athens." Furthermore, Athens' actions at Melos were *not* decisive. The Spartans decided not to destroy Athens in order to keep it as a counterweight against Corinth and Thebes. Nevertheless, if Xenophon's reports are true, no reader after the end of the war could hear this prophecy of the Melians without thinking of Athens' fall. This foreshadowing powerfully links Athens' ultimate defeat with the aggressive, expansive policy used at Melos and the definition of the city it presumes.

the city – a city that focused not on Attica and the land and houses there, but on the sea itself.[123] This echo suggests that the Athenians are as deluded as the Melians.[124] Indeed, when Thucydides turns from Melos to immediately begin his account of the Sicilian Expedition, he shows that the Athenians' refusal to recognize any boundary between their and others' territory contributed to their decision to take on the campaign. Second, Thucydides demonstrates that the Athenians add a Melian-type misjudgment about present and future, hope and fact to their "near and far" misjudgments about home and away. This combination then leads them to disaster.

Thucydides' narrative from Pericles' death through the Melian campaign shows the Athenians following a flexible vision of Athens that at its most expansive imagines a city at sea, or rather, a city coextensive with the sea, ruling all islands and coastal territories. Especially in the newly coined term for themselves as *naukratores* – "masters of the sea" – the Athenians link their expansive, aggressive policy at Melos to Pericles' ambitious last speech and his articulation of an Athens in control of half the world, where the sea and rule of the sea mattered far more than Attica. As we move into the Sicilian narrative, we see this flexible, sea-focused vision of Athens repeatedly working *against* the Athenians, confusing political debate, fueling their enemies abroad, and ultimately, exacerbating civil strife at home.

[123] Crane (1996, 245–6) stresses the use of "gaze" in each passage, but to a different purpose.

[124] Thus, although I approve of Perry's (1937, 427) comment that in the Melian Dialogue, "the folly of the Melians' rather than the cruelty of the Athenians is the chief subject of contemplation," I would argue that in addition to the folly of the Melians, Thucydides means for us to recognize the increasing folly of the Athenians.

3 The City Sets Sail

ATHENS DECIDES TO INVADE SICILY

The Melos campaign is the "prelude" to Sicily.[1] The Athenian position articulated at Melos – that no island should be out of the control of the *naukratores* – argues that Sicily, that greatest of Greek islands, should belong to Athens as well. Thucydides implies the connection between Melos and Sicily with the speed of his narrative. After he notes the end of Melos – "of the Melians they killed as many of the men of military age that they captured; the children and the women they enslaved. They themselves colonized the territory, sending out later five hundred colonists" (5.116) – Thucydides turns immediately to Sicily: "during the same winter the Athenians wanted to sail to Sicily again with a greater force than the one with Laches and Eurymedon and to subdue it if they could . . ." (6.1.1).[2] As with Melos, Thucydides takes care to note that the Sicilian Expedition does not represent some new aberration in Athenian policy making; Thucydides' reference to the expeditions of Laches in 427 (3.86) and Eurymedon in 425 (4.2) remind readers that the Athenians had long had their eyes on Sicily.[3]

[1] Wasserman 1947, 30. Cf. Kallet, 2001, 19.

[2] Whether the modern book divisions of the *History* go back to Thucydides remains under debate. The division into eight books was not the only system known to the scholiasts Dover (1965, xvii), and Hemmerdinger (1948) and Canfora (1970, 1–53; 2006, 14, 23) have argued for a division into single-year rolls. Without a book division between books 5 and 6, Melos and Sicily would seem even more connected.

[3] Thucydides has conflated two expeditions into one. An expedition under Laches and Charoiades went out in 427 with twenty ships (3.86.1). In 425, Eurymedon

Thucydides' reference to the campaign of Eurymedon and his claim that the Athenians now planned to subjugate the island serve to give a sense of the mood in Athens on the eve of the Sicilian Expedition. When the generals of this earlier expedition returned to Athens, the Athenians exiled two of them, Pythodorus and Sophocles, and fined Eurymedon "because, although it had been possible for them to subdue Sicily, they were suborned by bribes and withdrew" (4.65.3). Thucydides explains the decision as follows:

> So powerfully did they feel their present good fortune that they expected that nothing would withstand them, that they would achieve both the practicable and the impracticable just the same, whether with a great force or an inferior one (μεγάλῃ τε ὁμοίως καὶ ἐνδεεστέρᾳ παρασκευῇ). The reason was their shocking success in most things, which lent strength to their hope (4.65.4).[4]

The Athenians here sound very much like the Melians, whom the Athenians condemned, because "in your wishful thinking you gaze at things unseen as if they have already occurred" (5.113).

Almost immediately Thucydides confirms the hint that the Athenians will not deliberate wisely about Sicily. Ambassadors from the Sicilian *polis* of Egesta had come to Athens to urge the Athenians to help them in their war with the Sicilian cities of Selinus and Syracuse. The Egestans promised that they themselves "would provide sufficient money for the war" (6.6.2), so the Athenians sent envoys to Sicily to check on the availability of the money. On the basis of the envoys' positive report, the Athenians voted to send sixty ships to Sicily under Alcibiades, Nicias, and Laches (6.8.2). However, Thucydides tells his reader that what the Athenians heard from the Egestans and their own envoys was

and Sophocles were sent with an additional forty ships (4.2.2). The total number of ships is the same that the Athenians originally propose to send in 415 (6.8.2).

4 Particularly because Thucydides takes care to show that the Athenians' force for Sicily was *not* as great as they seemed to believe (see below), was no greater (at least initially) than the expeditions of Laches and Eurymedon or the expedition of Pericles to Epidaurus, and was special mostly in display, this passage, with its reference to the Athenians' belief that the size of their force did not matter, seems especially pointed toward the Sicilian Expedition. As Allison (1989, 79) remarks, "this crucial passage at 4.65 helps to create the mood of the first chapters in Book 6."

"attractive but untrue particularly concerning the money, that there was a great deal available in the temples and the treasury" (6.8.2).

The Athenians themselves do not discover this until they get to Sicily. Thus Thucydides indulges here in a temporal dislocation by anticipating the Athenians' later discovery that "the rest of the money the Egestans promised was not there" (6.46.1).[5] At the time of its discovery by the Athenians, Thucydides describes the ingenious ruse whereby the Egestans convinced the Athenians of their enormous wealth by dazzling them with the constant display of the same borrowed gold and silver cups and bowls at a series of banquets (6.46.3). Thucydides tells his reader the truth about the money during the debate about whether to send the expedition, however, in order to make the Athenians seem foolish and credulous in their decision making.[6] Thucydides emphasizes this with his language. The "attractive but untrue" (ἐπαγωγὰ καὶ οὐκ ἀληθῆ) words the Athenians believe recall the "enticing but untrue" (ἐφολκὰ καὶ οὐ τὰ ὄντα) words of Brasidas that encouraged the Chalcidians to revolt (4.108.5).[7] In the narrator intervention at that point, Thucydides condemns the Chalcidians because they were "judging more on uncertain wishes than on secure foresight, as men are accustomed to entrust what they desire to unexamined hope and to deny with peremptory logic whatever they do not want." When Thucydides begins his narrative of Sicily by noting that the Athenians were deceived by speeches that were "attractive but untrue," he signals to his readers that the Athenians are reasoning as poorly as the Chalcidians.

In our discussion of the Melian Dialogue, we noted that although the Melians were condemned because they confused hope and reality, present and future, the Melians and Thucydides redeployed the theme of the near and the far against the Athenians because they failed to distinguish between home and abroad – between land that belonged to them and

[5] See Gribble (1998, 50) for a discussion of such narrator interventions, which compare "story (or chronicle time) with the time of narration."

[6] Cf. Kallet (2001, 31): the Athenians "are easily fooled by false indicators of power, like showy wealth."

[7] Bosworth (1993, 36) points out that Thucydides comes "closest . . . in his own right to echoing the language of the Melian Dialogue" when he criticizes the cities who "swallowed Brasidas' propaganda." He notes (36, n. 34), but does not discuss, the parallel to the Sicilian Expedition.

land that did not. At Melos, of course, the Athenians suffer no harm. This echo of the disastrously muddled thinking of the Chalcidians, however, hints, as we begin the account of the Sicilian Expedition, that there is danger ahead for the Athenians. Indeed, Thucydides' account of the debate about the expedition shows that it is the combination of a (Melian or Chalcidian) confusion of hope and fact and the (uniquely Athenian) confusion between home and abroad that leads them to disaster.

Thucydides does not give his reader any of the speeches that led to the initial decision to sail to Sicily. Instead, he recounts two speeches made four days later at an assembly held "to discuss how to equip the ships as quickly as possible and to vote for the generals anything they wanted for the expedition" (6.8.3). At that assembly, the general Nicias "came forward to speak with the desire to turn the Athenians from their plan." Nicias, Thucydides reports, "thought the *polis* had not deliberated well, but, on a slight pretext that looked sound, was aiming at the whole of Sicily – a large undertaking" (6.8.4). Because Thucydides has already told the reader that the Athenians' hopes for money in Sicily were vain, the narrative itself conspires to give Nicias's ultimately futile attempt to change the Athenians' decision great weight. Nicias serves here as a kind of Herodotean "tragic warner," taking on a role akin to that of Artabanus, who tried in vain to dissuade Xerxes from invading Greece.[8]

Nicias's very first words make powerful links to the Melian Dialogue and the theme of the near and the far. Nicias urges his fellow citizens "to save what they have and not risk what is ready to hand for what is invisible and off in the future" (τά τε ὑπάρχοντα σῴζειν παραινοίην καὶ μὴ τοῖς ἑτοίμοις περὶ τῶν ἀφανῶν καὶ μελλόντων κινδυνεύειν, 6.9.3), just as the Athenians scolded the Melians because they "judge things to come (τὰ μὲν μέλλοντα) to be more clear than what they can see" and "gaze at things unseen (τὰ δὲ ἀφανῆ) as if they have already

[8] Marinatos (1980, 305–10) points out certain structural correlations between Nicias's and Artabanus's speeches. She builds on the work of Cornford (1907, 190–220) and Hunter (1973, 131–32, 179). For readers familiar with Herodotus, the similarity between Nicias and Artabanus invites comparison between the Sicilian Expedition and the Persian wars. As Cornford (1907, 201) notes, Thucydides "turned against Athens the tremendous moral which his countrymen delighted to read in the *Persians* of Aeschylus and the *History* of Herodotus."

occurred" (5.113).[9] Furthermore, Nicias defies the set purpose of the assembly, which was called to discuss the details of the fitting out of the expedition, and implores the Athenians to reconsider whether they should send the ships and take on "with so short a discussion over things so great, persuaded by foreigners, a war that is unconnected to us" (μὴ οὕτω βραχείᾳ βουλῇ περὶ μεγάλων πραγμάτων ἀνδράσιν ἀλλοφύλοις πειθομένους πόλεμον οὐ προσήκοντα, 6.9.1). Here Nicias echoes not the Athenians of the Melian Dialogue but the Melians who twice insisted that they "were unconnected" to Athens (μὴ προσήκοντας 5.96; 5.110.2) and hoped that Brasidas would invade the Athenians' remaining allies so that the source of the Athenians' troubles would be their "more home-like alliance and land" not a country that is "unconnected" to Athens (5.110.2). The Sicilian Expedition, in Nicias's presentation, would fulfill the Melians' prediction, bringing adversity to the Athenians because of a land and a war "unconnected" to them.[10] The Athenian envoys at Melos, however, denied that any island could be "unconnected" to them as long as they were *naukratores* (5.97). In suggesting that Sicily is "unconnected" to Athens, therefore, Nicias begins his speech with a very un-Athenian argument that is not likely to sway men eager to hear "enticing but untrue things."[11] However, in suggesting a limit to Athenian claims (which the reader knows the Athenians will overstep) the warner Nicias recalls Herodotus' presentation of the Persian expedition of Xerxes as a campaign that transgressed physical boundaries by bridging the Hellespont, digging a canal through Mount Athos, and trying to conquer a land the Persians regarded as "entirely separate" (1.4).[12] Nicias thus facilitates Thucydides' increasingly overt

[9] Cf. Stahl (1973, 72): "Nicias very much uses the same language which the Athenians use in the Melian Dialogue." Kitto (1966, 335) calls it "no distant echo of what Thucydides gave to 'the Athenians' in Melos." Cf. Young (1968, 120, n. 18).

[10] Greenwood (2006, 86) remarks that it is "possible" to interpret the Melians' reference to a war "unconnected" to Athens as "an allusion to Sicily. . . ." She does not note the specific verbal echo in Nicias's speech, however, which makes the allusion virtually certain.

[11] Tompkins (1972, 194) also points out that Nicias has a "tendency to admit concessions that weaken his argument."

[12] Cf. Cornford (1907, 204).

presentation of the Athenians as the new Persians and contributes to Thucydides' suggestion that the Athenians' inability to distinguish between home and away, between the native and the foreign, will be part of their downfall.

Nicias repeatedly emphasizes the divide and the distance between Athens and Sicily. The Athenians will be following the arguments of "foreigners" (6.9.1); he tells the Athenians that they will be "leaving many enemies here even while they desire to sail over there and lead others back here" and so emphasizes that Sicily is in a realm apart (6.10.1). He reinforces this by noting that even if they conquered the Sicilians, they would "hardly be able to rule them because they are many and far away" (6.11.1). Nicias implores the older men in the audience not to become "mad lovers of the far away" (δυσέρωτας . . . τῶν ἀπόντων, 6.13.1) and to vote that the Sicilians "keeping the same present boundaries with us" are to be left alone to enjoy their own goods (6.13.1). But Athenians, by their very nature, have never left anyone alone, and Athenians who enjoy the goods of others with as "homegrown a pleasure" as their own (2.38.2) are not likely to leave the Sicilians to enjoy theirs in peace. Nicias's arguments, in short, are *not* appropriate to his audience. This is evident especially in a striking metaphor Nicias employs: "It is necessary to consider all these things, and it is no time to run risks *when the city is still at sea* or to grasp after another *arche* before we have secured the one we already have" (ὥστε χρὴ σκοπεῖν τινὰ αὐτὰ καὶ μὴ μετεώρῳ τε ⟨τῇ⟩ πόλει ἀξιοῦν κινδυνεύειν καὶ ἀρχῆς ἄλλης ὀρέγεσθαι πρὶν ἣν ἔχομεν βεβαιωσώμεθα, 6.10.5).

Nicias says that the city is still *at sea*. The word he uses, *meteoros*, means, first, raised off the ground. It refers to things on the surface, such as prominent eyes or shallow breaths. Meaning "in mid-air," it can represent astronomical phenomena. Metaphorically, it can describe something that is uncertain, unsettled, buoyed up or in suspense. This last meaning is the reading that the standard Greek-English lexicon gives to this very passage.[13]

[13] Liddell, Scott and Jones, *s.v.* μετέωρος III. "metaph. of the mind, *buoyed up, in suspense*." Bétant (1843–1847) agrees, glossing Nicias's phrase to indicate things whose "foundations are not secure."

Kenneth Dover reads the phrase as "probably 'in a delicate position,'" and that is surely part of what we should understand the word to convey in Nicias's speech.[14] But *meteoros* can also be used to describe a ship on the high seas, and Thucydides uses it nine times in this sense: The Corinthians see the Corcyran ships "at sea and sailing towards them" (μετεώρους τε καὶ ἐπὶ σφᾶς πλεούσας, 1.48.2); the Corinthians "drew up their ships on the open sea but remained quiet" (παραταξάμενοι μετεώρους ἡσύχαζον, 1.52.2). A merchant ship anchors in open water (ὁρμοῦσα μετέωρος, 2.91.3); Paches is relieved because he did not catch Alcidas in mid-ocean (ἐπειδὴ οὐ μετεώροις περιέτυχεν, 3.33.3); the Athenians fall on the Lacedaemonian ships "at sea and in formation" (τὰς μὲν πλείους καὶ μετεώρους ἤδη τῶν νεῶν καὶ ἀντιπρῴρους, 4.14.1). Because of the lack of space for mooring during their siege at Pylos, while some crews ate a meal on shore, "the other ships anchored at sea" (αἱ δὲ μετέωροι ὥρμουν, 4.26.3). Off Peiraion, although they gathered the rest and anchored, the Peloponnesians "lost one ship on the sea" (καὶ μίαν μὲν ναῦν ἀπολλύασι μετέωρον οἱ Πελοποννήσιοι, 8.10.3); Astyochus sailed quickly for Samos "in case he could catch the ships on the high sea" (εἴ πως περιλάβοι που μετεώρους τὰς ναῦς, 8.42.1). Thucydides can even use the word in this sense for men: At the awful climax of the battle in the harbor at Syracuse, "as many men as had not been captured on the sea" (ὅσοι μὴ μετέωροι ἑάλωσαν) fell into the camp (7.71.6). This last passage shows that Thucydides does not use *meteoros* only for ships even when it means "at sea."

Thucydides uses *meteoros* most often (fifteen times) to designate position on land, especially to refer to the higher ground that soldiers hope to seize in battle.[15] He is not fond of using *meteoros* to describe things "in suspense." Indeed, he employs it only once in this sense, to describe the agitated state of Greece on the eve of war: "the rest of Hellas was unsettled as the first states clashed" (ἥ τε ἄλλη Ἑλλὰς ἅπασα μετέωρος ἦν, 2.8.1). When it does not describe position on land, *meteoros* in Thucydides' work, usually means "at sea."

[14] Dover in Gomme et al. 1970, *loc. cit.*

[15] 2.77.3; 3.72.3; 3.89.2; 4.35.4; 4.36.2; 3.44.2; 3.46.2; 3.57.2; 3.112.3; 3.124.3; 3.128.2; 3.128.3; 4.32.3; 5.6.3; 7.82.3, according to Bétant.

Thucydides' own usage and the venerable image of the "ship of state" encourage us to hear the sounds of the sea when Nicias speaks of the *meteoros polis* and to read it as "when the city is at sea." The image of the ship of state goes back at least to Alcaeus, who uses it in an extended metaphor about the confused political situation in Mytilene: "I fail to understand the direction [*stasis*] of the winds: one wave rolls in from this side, another from that, and we in the middle are carried along in company with our great black ship, much distressed in the great storm."[16] Alcaeus repeats the image in another fragment: "this wave in turn comes (like?) the previous one, and it will give us much trouble to bale out when it enters the ship's. . . . Let us strengthen (the ship's sides) as quickly as possible, and let us race into a secure harbor."[17] Alcaeus uses the image so much that he irritated Heraclitus, who complained that "the islander overdoes the seafaring in his allegories, and he compares most of the troubles which assail him because of the tyrants to storms on the high seas."[18] As Robin Nisbet and Margaret Hubbard remark, "anybody who had enjoyed a rhetorical education must have known about the figure [of the ship of state]."[19] The image was very popular for Athenian poets[20] and politicians as far back as Solon.[21] The image of

[16] Frag. 208 Campbell 1982 (trans. Campbell).

[17] Frag. 6 Campbell 1982 (trans. Campbell).

[18] *Homeric Allegories* 5.9; (Buffière 1962).

[19] Nisbet and Hubbard 1970, 180. The popularity of the image – especially in times of crisis for the state – is indicated by Silk's (1974, 123) argument that the very word for political strife, *stasis*, seems itself to be a metaphorical use of a concept from navigation. *Stasis* means both the "lie of the winds" and "political 'faction,' a usage that was doubtless as topical in seventh-century Aeolic as in all later Greek." See also Page (1955, 187, note to *stasis* in his passage Z2): "the meaning may be either 'the strife of the winds' . . . or 'the quarter in which the wind lies." The very word *stasis*, that is, may presume the ship of state.

[20] Pelling 2000, 16. For example, at *Wasps* 29, Sosias relates that his dream was "momentous, it's all about the whole ship of state" (trans. Henderson). The scholiast to this line remarks, "the poets are always comparing cities to ships" (Koster 1978). Sophocles uses the figure at the beginning of the *Oedipus Tyrannus* (22f): "King, you yourself have seen our city reeling like a wreck already; it can scarcely lift its prow out of the depths, out of the bloody surf." (Trans. Grene in Grene and Lattimore 1991). There are many other examples.

[21] Plutarch (*Solon* 14.6) reports that Solon received the following oracle from Delphi: "Sit in the middle of the ship, steering straight; you have many

the ship of state is particularly apt for Athenians, of course, who "went on board ship" to fight on behalf of their *polis* at Salamis and for whom, because their "real" *polis* was occupied by the Persians, their ships were the only *polis*. As Herodotus reports, to the taunts of Adeimantus that he was an a-*polis* or "cityless" man, Themistocles said "that he had a city and a land greater than theirs so long as he had two hundred ships filled up with men" (Hdt. 8.61). Both Nicias's and Thucydides' audiences, that is, are primed to read the *meteoros polis* as a "city at sea." This is, furthermore, how the scholiast understood the words. He explains Nicias's phrase as "when our city is not safely anchored" (τῆς πόλεως ἡμῶν οὐκ ἐν τῷ ἀσφαλεῖ ὁρμούσης).[22]

Nicias's image of the city on the eve of the Sicilian Expedition, then, is of a ship at sea, running for harbor from the dangers of the ocean. He urges the citizens to ground the ship of state safely, secure the empire they have, and not seek any more. Nicias thus sets up a clear contrast between this "new empire" and the old and insists that seeking the new will endanger the old. But just as his argument that Sicily is "unconnected" to Athens is unlikely to persuade the grasping Athenians, Nicias's central metaphorical image is ill chosen for his audience. The Athenians were encouraged by Pericles to see the sea not as danger, but as security. "Safeguard the sea and the city," Pericles said (1.143.5); a city at sea is precisely what Pericles' vision of Athens imagined. Pericles told the Athenians that they ruled all the sea, and the Athenians at Melos confirm that they believe they are *naukratores* (5.97).[23] The treaty with Argos, Elis, and Mantinea of 420, furthermore, indicates that the Athenians and at least some of their allies view the sea as the Athenians' "territory" (5.56.2). In this model of the world, the land is no safer

helpers in Athens" (trans. Fontenrose: Oracle n. Q67, Fontenrose; n. 15, Parke-Wormell).

[22] Hude 1927, *s.v.* 6.10.4. The scholiast goes on to state that Thucydides transfers the words "from boats not yet anchored." Spratt (1905, *loc. cit.*) read the phrase as "proleptic," with Nicias urging the Athenians "not to risk our state on the high seas." This is unnecessary. We can just as easily read the naval metaphor as a reference to the present city. S. Lattimore (1998, *loc. cit*) translates the phrase as "to take chances with a city in mid-voyage."

[23] It is not, therefore, a question of adding a "new" *arche* to the old, for Sicily exists in that part of the world that the Athenians already rule.

than the sea. On the contrary, the land – not the sea – is the foreign (and hence dangerous) element. In this model, a *meteoros polis* should run *from*, not to, harbor. That such thinking persisted throughout the Sicilian Expedition is evidenced by an anecdote that Thucydides reports from the final great battle in the harbor at Syracuse. If an Athenian general saw any ship slacking in the fight, he would call out to the captain of the ship and ask "whether they were retreating because they considered the extremely hostile land more homelike now than the sea, which through no small effort they had made their own" (ἠρώτων, οἱ μὲν Ἀθηναῖοι εἰ τὴν πολεμιωτάτην γῆν οἰκειοτέραν ἤδη τῆς οὐ δι' ὀλίγου πόνου κεκτημένης θαλάσσης ἡγούμενοι ὑποχωροῦσιν, 7.70.8). This confirms that for the Athenians, the sea is judged their own and seems "more home-like" and safer than the land. An image of the "city at sea," the *meteoros polis*, thus, is not likely to scare Nicias's audience to caution.

Thucydides' inclusion of the image, however, shows that the Athenians' conception of their city as a city at sea helped lead them to disaster in Sicily. This becomes clear in the two speeches that follow Nicias's attempt to dissuade the Athenians from their plan. First, Alcibiades, in response to Nicias's warnings, urged the expedition on in part by arguing that "our ships will provide the security either to remain, if things go well, or to depart, for we shall be *naukratores* over all the Sicilians" (ναυκράτορες γὰρ ἐσόμεθα καὶ ξυμπάντων Σικελιωτῶν, 6.18.5). Alcibiades counters Nicias's words of caution by denying any danger in the voyage for the city at sea. He uses the word *naukratores* to argue that the Athenians will be safe in Sicily. In the Melian Dialogue, the Athenians' status as *naukratores* was part of the argument that combined safety with conquest: "apart from ruling more through your overthrow we would produce security for ourselves especially if you who are islanders (and weaker ones than others) should not get the better of us who are *naukratores*" (5.97). The echo suggests that the Sicilian Expedition was fueled by the same insistence that no land is "unconnected" to Athens if it is connected to the sea and that Athens rules the sea.[24]

[24] Rood (1998b, 176–77, n. 67) need not be so hesitant when he argues that "perhaps the need to conquer *islands* expressed by the Athenians in the Melian Dialogue (V 97, 99) is pertinent."

Nicias then goes on to merge the *meteoros polis* with the expedition in a crucial second speech. The warnings from his first speech failed to counter the exhortations of Alcibiades, and the Athenians "were much more eager than before to make the campaign" (6.19.2). Although, according to Thucydides, Nicias "recognized that he would not any longer be able to dissuade them with the same arguments," he nevertheless came forward to speak again, and his words were instrumental to the decision. Nicias's hope was that he might be able to change their minds with the size of the force "if he made his requirements great" (6.19.2). Therefore he told the Athenians that they had to take a large army of hoplites to Sicily as well as archers and slingers to defend against the Syracusan cavalry. They had to have a decided superiority of ships to bring in supplies more easily and had to bring grain with them, both wheat and barley, and bakers from the mills. He summarized the situation for the Athenians with this image:

> We must consider ourselves to be going to found a city among foreign and hostile people (πόλιν τε νομίσαι χρὴ ἐν ἀλλοφύλοις καὶ πολεμίοις οἰκιοῦντας ἰέναι); as such we must control the countryside straightaway on the first day we occupy it or recognize that if we fail everything and everywhere will be hostile (6.23.2).

With these words Nicias imagines the Sicilian expedition as a floating city. To be sure, Nicias merely urges his fellow citizens to "consider themselves" to be going to found a city in Sicily. But the image he has chosen has at its heart the idea of a people abandoning their present city and putting their population, their goods, their sacred objects, and their officials – in short, everything that makes up their city – onto their ships. With this image, he imagines the Sicilian Expedition as a city at sea – the very thing that, he had used in his earlier speech as an image to scare the Athenians into voting against the campaign. The *meteoros polis*, which Nicias had originally urged the Athenians to ground in order to secure the old empire, now has a new destination. Nicias's image in this second speech imagines the *meteoros polis* landing in Sicily.[25]

[25] L. Strauss (1964, 226) spoke of "Athens in Sicily," and saw how connected this vision was to Pericles' vision of the city. He did not, however, trace this city imagery elsewhere in the text.

Harry Avery drew attention to what he called the "colonization" theme in the Sicilian narrative. He argued that with this theme, Thucydides

> wished to imply that the Athenian expedition of 415–413 was of such a magnitude that it was tantamount to a large scale effort at colonization. The force that was sent out was large enough . . . to be considered a city in its own right. Therefore the Athenians in sending out the expedition were in effect implanting a new city in Sicily. . . . [26]

Later, however, Avery goes beyond the argument that Thucydides was suggesting that the expedition was *like* a colony when he says that "the idea that this was a colony is never overtly stated, partly because the expedition failed and partly because this aspect of the expedition was probably never part of the official plan or one of the stated goals."[27] Avery implies that at least for some Athenians, an unofficial plan or unstated goal of the expedition was the founding of an actual Athenian colony in Sicily.[28]

We need not be so literal here, however, and suppose that we have found Thucydides hinting at a secret Athenian policy. Nicias's presentation of the expedition as a city is merely the continuation of the theme that we have been tracing, for Nicias's vision is the culmination of Pericles' ideal of the city.[29] Nicias's image conjures a real city at sea – that which Pericles could only approximate – a city dependent only on the sea and wholly divorced from the land. Yet even in his own speech Nicias indicates the vulnerability of such a city. Nicias focuses much of his talk of preparation on supplies and argues that the Syracusans' main superiority to the Athenians is in cavalry and "using homegrown and not imported grain" (σίτῳ οἰκείῳ καὶ οὐκ ἐπακτῷ χρῶνται, 6.20.4).[30] For Pericles, imports were a sign of strength (2.38.2). For Nicias, the need

[26] Avery 1973, 8.

[27] Avery 1973, 8–9.

[28] Avery (1973, 9, n. 1) cites Green (1970, 131) as an earlier exponent of this idea.

[29] Longo (1975, 94 and n. 26), although he does not connect the "polis-theme" to Pericles, agrees that it should not be reduced to an idea of colonization.

[30] Hermocrates identifies supplies as the reason that there have been few long expeditions (6.33). Thucydides himself points out in the *Archaeology* that the army the Greeks led to Troy was small because they did not have the money to bring great stores of supplies (1.11). Nicias's focus on supplies is another point

to import is the greatest weakness of the city at sea he has conjured. Later, too, when the Spartans fortify Decelea and the Athenians lose control of their own countryside, imports will be a mark not of strength but of weakness. Thucydides reports that "the city needed every single thing to be imported," and it became "instead of a city . . . a fortress" (τῶν τε πάντων ὁμοίως ἐπακτῶν ἐδεῖτο ἡ πόλις, καὶ ἀντὶ τοῦ πόλις εἶναι φρούριον κατέστη, 7.28.1). It becomes evident that cities may need homegrown goods.

Nicias's city is the ultimate abandonment of Attica, and Nicias's city at sea is – from the first – symbolically in opposition to the real city of Athens in Attica. One of the causes of the Peloponnesian War is the dispute over the conflicting interests of colonies and their mother cities played out between the cities of Epidamnus, Corcyra, and Corinth. When Nicias urges the Athenians to consider themselves to be founding a city in Sicily, therefore, the reader has cause to wonder to which city the soldiers of this city-expedition will give their ultimate loyalty – to Athens or to this idea of a city in Sicily. Nicias's new city foretells *stasis* for Athens.

Thucydides shows that Nicias's image of the expedition as a city had the opposite of his intended effect. Far from dissuading the Athenians from their plan, Nicias's image of the city at sea bred a foolish overconfidence. When Nicias completed his second speech, with its exaggerated estimates of what the expedition would require, Thucydides notes that "it seemed to the Athenians that he had advised them well and that now there would be great security for the expedition." Indeed, the Athenians were so sure of victory that, Thucydides tells us, "a passion fell on all of them alike to sail out" (καὶ ἔρως ἐνέπεσε τοῖς πᾶσιν ὁμοίως ἐκπλεῦσαι, 6.24.3). Like Artabanus, the Athenians' tragic warner did the opposite of what he originally intended and (albeit inadvertently) encouraged the Athenians to sail.[31] Furthermore, Nicias's image encouraged the

that links him with Artabanus, who argued that Xerxes' expedition would have great difficulty with supplies.

[31] Cf. "the opposite occurred for him" (6.24.2). Marinatos (1980) does not make this comparison between Nicias and Artabanus, partly, perhaps, because she believes Thucydides presents Nicias at the end "as a heroic man" (309). Thucydides may well do this at 7.85.1, but Thucydides' portrait of Nicias includes a number of blemishes, not the smallest of which is his trying for a second time (after the failure of the same tactics in the Pylos debate) to avoid a given event

Athenians to prefer the far-off city he conjured in Sicily to the one in Athens. Thucydides emphasizes this immediately when he completes his thought:

> a passion fell on all of them alike to sail out, the older men thinking that they would either subjugate the places against which they sailed or that a great force would not be overthrown by anything, the younger men because of a desire for the sight and spectacle of the far off and all in high hopes that they would survive (6.24.3).

Thucydides thus shows the Athenians becoming "mad lovers of the far away" – the very thing Nicias had warned them about (and then inspired them to become).

Thucydides uses phrases that dramatically wield the theme of the near and the far against the Athenians.[32] Because of his emphasis on *eros*, it is impossible not to hear an echo here of the story of Coronis, who "hungered for things remote" (ἤρατο τῶν ἀπέοντων, Pindar Pythian 3.20).[33] Thucydides' words also evoke Aeschylus' Clytemnestra, who pretended to hope that "no lust seize on these men to violate what they must not" (*Ag.* 341–2).[34] They are a dramatic statement of the folly of the Sicilian Expedition.[35]

by urging it on the assembly. Cf. Kallet (2001, 152). As Rood (1998b, 167) notes, unlike other tragic warners, "Nicias contributes to the fulfillment of his own predictions" (citing Cogan 1981a, 279, n. 18). For example, Nicias's image of the expedition as a city enticed his audience on. Thus Kitto (1966, 335), is too limited when he says that the problem is merely that "the Athenians preferred to listen to Alcibiades." They listened to Nicias's description of the city at sea as well.

32 Hornblower (2004, 73), who insists that "we must not treat speeches by the Athenians at Melos, by Nicias in 415, or by anyone else, as a statement by the authorial Thucydides," calls this passage "the closest the authorial Thucydides gets to combining hope and desire censoriously."

33 Trans. F. Nisetich. Cornford (1907, 206) goes so far as to say that Nicias is "quoting" from Pindar's story. Cf. Rood 1998b, 177, and n. 68, Kitto 1966, 327, and Young 1968, Appendix 1.

34 Trans. Lattimore in Grene and Lattimore 1959. Cf. Connor (1984, 167, n. 22) who agrees with Cornford's (1907, 214) judgment that "must not Thucydides have intended this dark allusion which so terribly fits the sequel?" Cf. also Rood 1998b, 177, and n. 68.

35 This should not be taken to mean that I am unaware that Thucydides in other places indicates that the Sicilian Expedition could have succeeded. Although

Thucydides' triple use of *eros* in his account of the decision to send the expedition to Sicily is striking and contributes to his presentation (in the narrative as a whole) of the Sicilian Expedition as a city opposed to the real city of Athens and a danger to it. It also connects the confusion about what Athens is – and the *stasis* that grew from that confusion – back to Pericles. Thucydides' text links the people of Athens with *eros* once before Nicias's speech – in Pericles' Funeral Oration, in which Pericles famously and impressively told the Athenians "it is necessary that you, gazing every day at the power of the city as it really is, become its lovers" (τὴν τῆς πόλεως δύναμιν καθ' ἡμέραν ἔργῳ θεωμένους καὶ ἐραστὰς γιγνομένους αὐτῆς, 2.43.1). The *eros* that the Athenians felt for the Sicilian campaign and the city at sea Nicias conjured for it would seem to identify them as fickle lovers, quick to turn their enthusiasm from the Athens they knew to Nicias's imagined city in Sicily. The beloved city Pericles showed them was neglected, and the Sicilian city they now loved was a danger to Pericles' Athens.

On another important level, however, the Athenians had not shifted their allegiance when they felt a passion for the Sicilian campaign. The *eros* that Thucydides says they felt for Sicily may help to define the love object that Pericles meant to show them. Pericles urged the Athenians to fix their eyes on the power of Athens as it really was and to become its lovers. Pericles insists that in this love, the Athenians must look beyond surfaces to the real (ἔργῳ) power of Athens. Thus we can conclude that in Pericles' view, some Athenians did not understand this power (or the city) clearly or know what exactly to love. This idea forcefully recalls Pericles' last speech, in which he explicitly revealed to the Athenians his new vision of the actual power of the city. Pericles' remarked in that speech that "you think that you hold your *arche* only over your allies, but I tell you that of the two useful parts that the world is divided into,

Thucydides says that the expedition was a "mistake" in 2.65.11, as Westlake (1958) shows, the rest of the passage implies that if *other* mistakes had been avoided, that first mistake might yet have succeeded. For example, Gylippus almost did not reach Syracuse in time, and Thucydides remarks, "The Syracusans came this close to danger" (7.2.4). Palmer (1992, 139, n. 7) points out that here Thucydides "repeat[s] exactly (and uniquely) the words he used to describe the hairsbreadth escape of the Mytileneans. . . ." Nevertheless, that the expedition *might* have succeeded does not somehow disprove that in his presentation of the decision to send the expedition, Thucydides paints it as madness.

land and sea, you are complete masters over all of the latter, both as much as you now hold and still more if you wish" (2.62.2). This serves as a gloss on the Funeral Oration, revealing the kind of Athens Pericles wanted the Athenians to love. Thus when the Athenians fell in love with the Sicilian Expedition, which Nicias had urged them to think of as a city at sea, they were, in fact, indulging Pericles' invitation to love.[36] They had seen the power of the city as Pericles imagined it and loved it.[37]

Thucydides charges that the new love was destructive, however, because the narrative brands the city at sea, the Sicilian city, as a rival and a danger to the Athens in Attica. Thucydides underscores the opposition between the two cities when he describes the effect of the Athenians' passion for the campaign on the crucial decision about whether to go to Sicily. Even after Nicias's second speech, there were some in Athens who opposed the campaign, but the high pitch of Nicias's rhetoric and the passions it roused in the majority silenced them. Thucydides notes that "because of the excessive enthusiasm" of the majority, those who remained opposed to the expedition kept quiet because "they were afraid that they might appear to be ill-disposed to the city if they voted against it" (δεδιὼς μὴ ἀντιχειροτονῶν κακόνους δόξειεν εἶναι τῇ πόλει ἡσυχίαν ἦγεν, 6.24.4). Once Nicias urged the Athenians to imagine the expedition itself as a city, no reference to the "city" is straightforward. Thus it is unclear exactly what city Thucydides means his reader to understand in his comment. Does he mean that the men who wished to vote against the creation of the city-expedition might appear ill-disposed to the city in Attica or the imagined new foundation in Sicily? Thucydides' remark here cleverly demonstrates that the assembled Athenians do not have the same city. Thucydides' presentation

36 Cf. L. Strauss (1964, 226), who argues that "the *eros* of the Athenian for Sicily is the peak of his *eros* for his city." Palmer (1992, 105) asks, "does not the Athenians' Periclean *eros* for their city give birth to their *eros* for Sicily?"

37 Balot (2001 170) claims that here "Pericles' civic *eros* has been transformed into a destructive urge to acquire more." Similarly, Monoson (1994, 276, n. 81) claims that the love the Athenians "exhibit for the expedition is not the restrained, honorable love that Pericles refers to but a furious, raging eros." I think, on the contrary, that the Sicilian *eros* simply demonstrates most graphically the nature of Periclean *eros*. Cf. Foster 2001, 205, n. 26.

of this debate, then, presages both the disaster in Sicily to come and the *stasis* to follow.[38]

THE CITY-FLEET DEPARTS

The Athenians, of course, did decide to send the expedition to Sicily and placed Alcibiades, Nicias, and Lamachus in command of a force of no fewer than one hundred triremes and five thousand Athenian and allied hoplites (6.25.2). Thucydides provides a powerful description of the sailing of this floating city and the reactions it caused in the people of Athens and in the Greek world in general. On the day of departure, he writes, "the Athenians themselves and any of their allies who were present went down to the Piraeus at dawn on the day appointed and filled up the ships to put out to sea. Virtually the whole rest of the population in the city, both of citizens and foreigners, went down with them." (6.30.1–2). Later he remarks that "to the rest of the Greeks it seemed more like a display of power and wealth than a military expedition against enemies" (Καὶ ἐς τοὺς ἄλλους Ἕλληνας ἐπίδειξιν μᾶλλον εἰκασθῆναι τῆς δυνάμεως καὶ ἐξουσίας ἢ ἐπὶ πολεμίους παρασκευήν, 6.31.4).

As Connor noted, "symbolically, the city itself, not an Athenian expedition, moves against Syracuse."[39] Thucydides emphasizes that the entire population of Athens went down to the waterfront to see the troops off. Then, by making it clear that to outsiders the expedition seemed to represent Athens' power itself, Thucydides suggests an equation

38 The references Thucydides makes in his archaeology of Sicily to the Cyclopes and Lastrygonians (6.2.1) and to the settlements made in Sicily after the war by Trojan refugees "invite" a comparison between the Sicilian Expedition and the Trojan War, according to Luginbill (1999, 197). The troubles Odysseus and Agamemnon faced when they returned home from Troy reinforce the sense this passage gives that after the war, *stasis* will come to the city that sent the armada. See Rood (1998a) for a discussion of epic resonances and allusions in Thucydides' presentation of the Sicilian campaign.

39 Connor 1984, 176, n. 46. Longo (1975, 87–88) underscores Thucydides' interest in the "totality" of the defeat in Sicily and how the equation of the expedition with a city furthers that symbolism.

between Athens and the expedition. His word choice here also confirms that Nicias's floating city, which the Athenians now loved, was the same as the love object Pericles urged on the Athenians. Thucydides says the city at sea appeared to be a display of the power (τῆς δυνάμεως) of Athens, and Pericles bid the Athenians fix their eyes on the power (τὴν τῆς πόλεως δύναμιν) of Athens and become her (or its) lovers.

Yet at the same time Thucydides does not allow the reader to forget the conflict between the city-expedition and the other city of Athens in Attica. In the very next sentence, he notes, "if someone calculated the outlay from the city, both that of the state and the private expenses of those serving . . . it would be found that in all many talents were being taken out of the city" (πολλὰ ἂν τάλαντα ηὑρέθη ἐκ τῆς πόλεως τὰ πάντα ἐξαγόμενα, 6.31.5). Here, despite Nicias's presentation of the expedition itself as a city, Thucydides paints an image of the departure of the fleet that focuses on removal. As Kallet remarks, "the vocabulary makes as vivid as possible the removal of vast wealth from the *polis*."[40] Thucydides' wording also gives a primacy to the city in Attica over the city-expedition. It is the Attic city, not the city at sea, that Thucydides here pointedly calls the city. Thucydides uses words that show that alongside the city-expedition there remained the physical city of Athens and demonstrates that Nicias's city-expedition was a dangerous drain on the land-bound city in Attica.

Thucydides places great emphasis on the wastefulness of the gaudy display in the fleet that dazzled the spectators, and throughout his description he foreshadows the failure to come.[41] For example, Thucydides tells us that the crowd, initially disheartened by the imminent departure of loved ones, "on account of the number of each of the things that they saw, cheered up at the sight" (διὰ τὸ πλῆθος ἑκάστων ὧν ἑώρων, τῇ ὄψει ἀνεθάρσουν, 6.31.1). Because Thucydides himself gives us only two specific numbers for the fleet, he leaves the impression that the spectators could not have judged the size of the fleet accurately. He underscores that the spectators took heart merely at the *look* of things. Thucydides calls the force the "first" force to be "most extravagant and splendid of those up to that time" (παρασκευὴ γὰρ αὕτη

[40] Kallet 2001, 61.

[41] Cf. Jordan (2000) and Kallet (2001, 48–66).

πρώτη ... πολυτελεστάτη δὴ καὶ εὐπρεπεστάτη τῶν ἐς ἐκεῖνον τὸν χρόνον ἐγένετο, 6.31.1).[42] He carefully calls this force the most splendid and extravagant; it was not the most formidable. He underscores this point with the comparison that follows immediately: "in the number of ships and hoplites the one against Epidaurus under Pericles and the same one against Potidaea under Hagnon was not less" (6.31.2). Thucydides' "first," furthermore, although on one level comparing the fleet to all prior fleets ("up to that time"), serves on another level to remind us that this force was only the first of two sent to Sicily. This first one was, in fact, inadequate, and had to be reinforced later. The "first" sits uneasily with Thucydides' superlatives, but this ill-fitting "first" looks forward to Thucydides' description of this fleet's departure from Corcyra: "so great was the first force that sailed over for the war" (6.44.1). Calling the fleet the first underscores its inadequacy (by reference to the need for a second) and so foreshadows the failure of the expedition.[43]

Kallet also remarks on Thucydides' emphasis on competition.[44] Thucydides reports that the soldiers "competed" (ἀμιλληθέν, 6.31.3) to see who looked the best. Then, using a noun of the same root, he says that the captains held a race (ἅμιλλα, 6.32.2) to Aegina. As Rood notes, this is the very word that Herodotus used to describe the contest that the Persian fleet held at Abydos before sailing for Greece (7.44).[45]

[42] Thucydides seems to conflate two thoughts: "this was the *first* force to. . . ." and "this force was the *most*. . . ."

[43] Cf. Allison 1989, 91–92. S. Lattimore (1998, 321, n. on 6.31) is wrong to argue that "the sense is certainly not 'the first expedition'. . . . Thucydides would never have undercut this set-piece by alluding to the future relief force." That is exactly what Thucydides is doing. Hornblower (2004, 336), in dissent, wonders "why a display of power should somehow be thought inconsistent with the possession of power?" But the curious use of numbers, the comparison to the earlier fleets, and the reference to this fleet as the "first" all combine to indicate that although the fleet "appeared" powerful, it was not all that it seemed to the spectators.

[44] Kallet 2001, 54. Cf. Jordan (2000) and Rood (1999). See now Hornblower (2004, 327–53) who argues (329) that "the Sicilian books are a depiction of an *agon* or struggle of the kind celebrated by Pindar" and that "the departure of the Sicilian Expedition is . . . strongly Pindaric in the sense that it recalls the start of that other epic sea-voyage, the quest of Jason and the Argonauts."

[45] Rood 1999, 153.

Rood comments that for the Athenians, like the Persians, "the brilliant display of the present is overshadowed by the destruction that awaits." As the Athenians' fleet sets out, Thucydides compares it with that of the Persians.[46] Connor notes that in attacking Sicily, Athens "move[s] chronologically backward to confront its own past. The analogy between the Persian invasion and the Athenian attack on Syracuse . . . involves a recapitulation of a crucial episode in the history of the city, with a reversal of Athens' role."[47]

The sense is that the Athenians are repeating their abandonment of Attica in the Persian wars but in a way that will lead not to victory, growth, and empire but to defeat and devastation. Thucydides underscores this point in his comparison between this fleet and that of Pericles against Epidaurus. In numbers of ships, that earlier one was not inferior. The difference was that it set out "for a short voyage" (ἐπί τε βραχεῖ πλῷ, 6.31.3). By contrast, throughout his description of the departure of the Sicilian fleet, Thucydides emphasizes the length of the journey in emotive passages that resonate with the theme of the near and the far. The relatives of the soldiers accompanied them to the Piraeus, "going with hope and with lamentations at the same time, hope that they would acquire something, lamentations at the thought of whether they would ever see them again, taking to heart how long a voyage from their own territory the voyage was" (καὶ μετ᾽ ἐλπίδος τε ἅμα ἰόντες καὶ ὀλοφυρμῶν, τὰ μὲν ὡς κτήσοιντο, τοὺς δ᾽ εἴ ποτε ὄψοιντο, ἐνθυμούμενοι ὅσον πλοῦν ἐκ τῆς σφετέρας ἀπεστέλλοντο, 6.30.2). And Thucydides ends his description of the fleet by noting that

> the expedition became no less famous for the wonder of its daring and for the splendor of its display than for its military superiority over those against whom it was sent and because it was the greatest voyage from home ever attempted, with the greatest hope for the future in contrast to the present circumstances (καὶ ὅτι μέγιστος ἤδη διάπλους ἀπὸ τῆς οἰκείας καὶ ἐπὶ μεγίστῃ ἐλπίδι τῶν μελλόντων πρὸς τὰ ὑπάρχοντα ἐπεχειρήθη, 6.31.6).

Thucydides does not call the expedition the "greatest force" (because he has already shown that earlier expeditions were at least as big) but the

[46] Foster (2001, 209) points out that "the strategy is even more emphatic in Thucydides than in Herodotus" because "Xerxes' fleet really is big."

[47] Connor 1984, 176.

"greatest voyage" and focuses on the magnitude of the hope that led the Athenians on. What is impressive is that the Athenians were daring enough to go so far from home. The clear implication is that a closer tie to home would have kept them safer.

The mention of Pericles in Thucydides' description of the departure of the fleet, together with Nicias's advice in his second speech that the Athenians must think of themselves as going to found a city in Sicily, raises further worries. Nicias's image must bring to mind Pericles' judgment, when he spoke of it as a possible Spartan tactic, of the difficulty of building fortifications in enemy territory. "It is hard even in peacetime," Pericles told the Athenians on the eve of the war, "to construct a rival city" (τὴν μὲν γὰρ χαλεπὸν καὶ ἐν εἰρήνῃ πόλιν ἀντίπαλον κατασκευάσασθαι, 1.142.3). Any reader who remembers Pericles' warning must worry about the Athenians' chances for success in planting their floating city in Sicily.[48]

Scholars who discuss this passage interpret Thucydides' reference to Pericles in his fleet departure scene as a critique of present policy and judgment. Borimir Jordan, for example, argues that the comparison between the Sicilian fleet and the fleet sent against Epidaurus and Potidaea is meant to emphasize that although the Athenians thought the fleet they were sending to Sicily was "the extraordinary double expedition by land and sea that Nicias had warned was necessary," it was, in fact, merely a "beauteous but conventional force."[49] Stahl, for his part, focuses on the disparity in cavalry between the two expeditions. Nicias had been especially concerned about Syracusan cavalry and worried about getting Athenian horses to Sicily, but when Thucydides compares the

[48] Rawlings (1981, 142–43) makes a strong argument that Thucydides meant deliberately to link Pericles' speech with Nicias's image. Rawlings (143) points out that the Athenian expedition in Sicily is "precisely the strategy that Pericles says the Spartans might bring to Attica."

[49] Jordan 2000, 69. He also suggests that Thucydides meant to indicate that in contrast to Athens on the eve of the Sicilian Expedition, the Athenians under Pericles mounted fleets commensurate with their aims and were willing to spend the sums required for their ambitions. A comparison with Potidaea and Samos reveals the "startling insufficiency" of the sums devoted to the Sicilian Expedition. But see below for the full import of the comparisons Thucydides is making.

Sicilian fleet with that of Pericles and Hagnon, "he mentions, also, their three-hundred horse, but he cannot mention any horse for the present expedition." Stahl judges this "comment through silence?" and shows how it contributes to Thucydides' description of the fleet as a "scene of splendor doomed to be destroyed."[50]

However, Thucydides' comparison does not only criticize the Sicilian expedition. Thucydides' reference to Pericles' expedition to Epidaurus in this passage is his only reference to Pericles after the *Epitaph*. Were his desire only to criticize the size or the composition of the Sicilian fleet, he could have compared it simply to "the fleet of the expedition against Potidaea under Hagnon." There would have been no need to specify that this same fleet had two separate missions in the summer of 430, one under Hagnon and an earlier one under Pericles. Including Pericles' raid on Epidaurus does not help readers assess the size of the Sicilian fleet, and so Thucydides' mention of Pericles here seems a deliberate choice to invite reflection on Pericles himself. It urges readers to reevaluate Pericles' policy at a crucial turning point in the war.

When urging the Athenians to war, Pericles claimed that "if they invade our country by land, we will sail against theirs" (1.143.4). Pericles' expedition to Epidaurus represents just such an Athenian raid on Peloponnesian territory. Pericles went on to claim that "it will not be a similar thing for some portion of the Peloponnesus to be cut off and the whole of Attica. For they will not be able to lay hold of other territory without fighting for it, but we have plenty of land both in the islands and on the mainland" (1.143.4). Pericles argued that raids against the Peloponnesus would be much more devastating to the Peloponnesians than the loss of all Attica would be to Athens because "we have plenty of land." But sea-born raids did not have the devastating effect that Pericles expected. Indeed, the raid of which Thucydides chooses to remind his readers was wholly ineffective according to Thucydides. As H. T. Wade-Gery remarked, "Pericles' huge effort against Epidaurus (6.31.2; motive, cf. 5.53) is recorded as a minor futility."[51] Donald Kagan quotes in full Thucydides' account of the results of the expedition (2.56) "in all its flatness":

[50] Stahl 1973, 66 and 72–74. Quotations from 73–74.

[51] Wade-Gery 1961, 904.

When they arrived at Epidaurus in the Peloponnesus they ravaged most of the land. And when they made an attack on the city they arrived at the hope of taking it, but they were not successful. Leaving Epidaurus they ravaged the land of Troezen, Halieis and Hermione, which are all on the coast of the Peloponnesus. From there they sailed to Prasiae, a coastal town of Laconia; they ravaged its land, took the town, and sacked it. When they had done this they returned home.[52]

In his only reference to Pericles after the *Epitaph*, Thucydides chooses to remind his readers of *this* campaign. H. D. Westlake has argued that Pericles' sea-borne raids were designed to inflict "so much economic distress that . . . the Peloponnesian League would have no heart to continue the war."[53] He judges that they could have eventually "undermined" the very structure of the Peloponnesian League and "hasten[ed] the attainment of [Pericles'] defensive aims."[54] But of course Pericles' sea-borne raids did no such thing, as is evident from the continued state of war sixteen years after Pericles' speech and fifteen years after his expedition to Epidaurus.

Hornblower reminds us that Thucydides "postpone[s]" until this point his "candid authorial acknowledgement of the huge scale of the Athenian attack on Epidaurus." He argues that Thucydides has thereby "masked Athenian aggression (or rather Athenian failure to stick to the Periclean defensive strategy) by a narrative device."[55] Yet Thucydides' purpose cannot be to "mask" the nature of the attack on Epidaurus. Had that been Thucydides' goal, he simply would have continued his silence. Thucydides was under no compulsion to mention Pericles' raid on Epidaurus.[56] That he does so suggests, on the contrary, that his purpose is not to mask but to emphasize that even with Pericles present, Athenian policy was not simply defensive. Pericles had, after all, made reference to just such raids in his first speech. Thucydides' mention

[52] Kagan 1974, 72.

[53] Westlake 1945, 84.

[54] Westlake 1945, 82–83. Kagan (1974, 76) describes the "great rewards" that success in devastating the territory of coastal Peloponnesians or, especially, sacking Epidaurus would have brought. See Brunt (1965, 271) for a dissenting view.

[55] Hornblower 1994, 146.

[56] Cf. Rood 1998b, 125: "but why revert to the earlier expedition at all, let alone in so emphatic a way?"

of Pericles here, furthermore, is decidedly negative. Reference to one of Pericles' ineffective raids so many years after Pericles argued they would be decisive in the war undercuts Pericles' wisdom and foresight. In addition, Thucydides' reference to Pericles at this critical moment also links his policy to the mad voyage now beginning. Raids on the Peloponnesus – even raids of this surprising size – were not devastating; what was devastating – but to the Athenians – was the suggestion that Attica was nothing and that other land would serve as well. Pericles' boast that Athens ruled the sea and his exhortation to the Athenians to abandon their land and their houses encouraged the longing for the far-off that fuels this "longest voyage from home ever attempted" (6.31.6). Pericles helped to sever the tie to home that might have kept the Athenians away from Sicily.[57]

Thucydides' narrative does not allay the foreboding that imbues his description of the fleet. After his account of the departure of the fleet, Thucydides moves the scene to Syracuse. There the Syracusan demagogue Athenagoras casts further doubt on the prospects of the Athenian expedition in a speech at Syracuse, using words that directly challenge Nicias's hopes for the new city-expedition. Athenagoras argued, first, that the reports of the coming Athenian invasion were probably false, because "it is not likely that they would leave behind the Peloponnesians and the war there which they have not securely ended and come willingly after another war no less great" (6.36.4). He also listed the reasons why the Syracusans should feel confident of victory if, against all expectation, it turned out that the rumors were true: Syracuse was, of necessity, larger than the invading force; the Athenians would have no cavalry with them; they would not have as many hoplites, because they would have to transport them by sea; furthermore, the journey alone would be taxing enough. Athenagoras summarized the situation with this powerful image: "Even if they came with a city as great as Syracuse and, having planted it on our borders, made war from it, they would scarcely seem to me to avoid being utterly destroyed" (παρὰ τοσοῦτον γιγνώσκω, μόλις ἄν μοι δοκοῦσιν, εἰ πόλιν ἑτέραν τοσαύτην

[57] I do not agree, therefore, with Rood (1998b, 125) that "Thucydides' contrast suggests that the Sicilian expedition is the one which infringes Periclean policy." Thucydides' comparison shows how Periclean the Sicilian expedition is.

ὅσαι Συράκουσαί εἰσιν ἔλθοιεν ἔχοντες καὶ ὅμορον οἰκίσαντες τὸν πόλεμον ποιοῖντο, οὐκ ἂν παντάπασι διαφθαρῆναι, 6.37.2).

This is a remarkable passage. First, Athenagoras, whose name means something like "Athenian speaker," makes the same kind of assessment of the strengths and weaknesses of the combatants in which the speakers at the beginning of the Archidamian war engaged.[58] His confidence in victory echoes Pericles' confidence then. Furthermore, he displays a prescience similar to that Thucydides gives to Pericles in his first speech to the Athenians. Athenagoras has, of course, no way of knowing that Nicias urged the Athenians to imagine the expedition as a city in his speech in Athens. That Athenagoras picks up Nicias's image mimics Pericles' apparent (but faulty) omniscience when he seems to answer the strategic points made by the Corinthians and Archidamus at Sparta. Also like Pericles, Athenagoras denies the force of his enemy's ideas. Athenagoras's foreknowledge gives his judgment special weight. Even the grandest dreams of the Athenians are known and refuted by the enemy. The "Athenian speaker" assesses Athenian rhetorical reconstructions of the army as a city and declares that redefinition alone will not suffice – will, indeed, be dangerous.

THE CITY-FLEET GROUNDS IN SICILY

After the Athenian city-expedition arrived in Sicily in 415, its enemies continued Athenagoras' work in undercutting it. The Athenians failed to make an immediate attack on Syracuse, as the Syracusans had expected and feared (and as Alcibiades had urged), and the delay raised the Syracusans' confidence with every passing day. In fact, according to Thucydides, the Syracusans urged their generals to lead them out against the Athenians to draw them into battle. The Syracusan cavalry was particularly eager, Thucydides says, and contemptuous of the Athenians.[59]

58 Yunis (1996, 111) implies that Thucydides made up not just his speech, but Athenagoras himself in order (116), with Pericles, to "represent two poles – demagogue and political leader." Yunis does not, however, specifically list Athenagoras' speech as one he thinks Thucydides wholly made up (62, n. 9)

59 That Thucydides singles out the taunts of the cavalry is particularly ironic because Nicias was especially concerned about the Syracusans' cavalry. However,

On reconnaissance missions, the cavalry repeatedly rode up to the Athenians and hurled insulting remarks at them. Of these jibes, Thucydides chooses to report only one. Making mocking reference to the ostensible purpose of the expedition, the cavalry asked the Athenians "whether they themselves had not really come to live with them (the Syracusans) in a foreign land rather than to resettle the people of Leontini in their homeland" (ἐφύβριζον ἄλλα τε καὶ εἰ ξυνοικήσοντες σφίσιν αὐτοὶ μᾶλλον ἥκοιεν ἐν τῇ ἀλλοτρίᾳ ἢ Λεοντίνους ἐς τὴν οἰκείαν κατοικιοῦντες, 6.63.3).

With their suggestion that the Athenians have come to the foreign land of Sicily in order to live there, the Syracusans take up Nicias's suggestion that the expedition really represents a city in transit, but they turn the city theme on its head to make it an image of cowardice and theft. The implication is that the Athenians, having fled from their troubles in their own land, now plan to steal the land of someone else. The Syracusans' remark, in its reference to the Leontinians' "homeland" (οἰκείαν), is based on the understanding that people have essential connections to particular parcels of land (even if their enemies sometimes try to or do push them off).[60] But the Syracusan cavalry clearly see that this does not apply to the Athenians, because they suggest that the Athenians have little connection to their "homeland" and have voluntarily left it in order to take up someone else's. The cavalry correctly judge that the Athenians do not make proper distinctions between what is "homelike" and what is not. The Athenians have abandoned their own homes, and therefore "foreign" land, which ought to be off-limits, is not.

The Syracusans' remark, in its suggestion that the Athenians' may try to take some Sicilian land for their own, makes explicit the abandonment of Attica and the original city of Athens that is implicit in

as Stahl (1973, 66) notes, when Thucydides lists the force going to Sicily, he mentions only "one horse transport carrying thirty horses" (6.43). "Author's irony by no-comment method?" wonders Stahl. Cf. L. Strauss 1964, 201. As Stahl (1973, 69) remarks, the cavalry are "devastating" in the later stages of the campaign (6.32.2, 6.33, 6.62.3). Longo (1975, 91) notes the "ironic" nature of the cavalry remark but does not discuss it in any detail.

60 Note that the Syracusans deploy the typically Thucydidean use of "homeland" to refer to "*polis*-land," not to the home of an individual family. Cf. Crane 1996, 145.

Nicias's vision of the city at sea. At the same time, their remark raises an echo, but a subversive one, of the proud actions of Athens during the Persian wars. During that conflict, in order to get the Peloponnesians to stay and fight the Persians at Salamis, Herodotus says that Themistocles threatened to take the entire Athenian fleet, and indeed the entire Athenian city, off to Siris in Italy (8.62). Of course, Themistocles did not do so. If he abandoned Attica and Athens itself, it was only temporarily and with the intention of regaining it. Here the Syracusans are made to raise the question of what kind of abandonment lay behind Nicias's image of the expedition as a city and, indeed, what kind of abandonment has lurked behind Pericles' vision all along. That Thucydides is particularly interested in raising these questions is clear from the way he constructs his narrative. Although Thucydides indicates that the cavalry said other insulting things, only this comment on the city theme was important enough, in Thucydides' eyes, to merit mention. Thucydides does, however, take care, to note that other insults were hurled – thus alerting the reader to his judgment that it was this one that mattered.

The source of the taunt is also important, for the Athenians' weakness in cavalry soon led them to retreat to Catana (6.71). Ultimately the Athenians set out to wall off the city of Syracuse in order to besiege it into surrender. But despite great effort, the Athenians were not able to complete a circuit wall around Syracuse. In 414, after a year of fruitless attempts to wall in the Syracusan city, Nicias wrote a letter to Athens in which he described the dire predicament of the Athenians. He reported that because of the large number of the enemy and the presence of a Spartan general on the scene, the Athenians had failed to prevent the Syracusans from building a counter wall to their own siege wall. There was, therefore, no longer any hope of the Athenians blockading Syracuse. The result, according to Nicias, was that "it has turned out that we who supposed we were besieging others are ourselves suffering the same thing on land at least (ξυμβέβηκε τε πολιορκεῖν δοκοῦντας ἡμᾶς ἄλλους αὐτοὺς μᾶλλον, ὅσα γε κατὰ γῆν, τοῦτο πάσχειν), for we cannot go out far in to the country because of their cavalry" (7.11.4). Nicias's city at sea was grounded on land, and Nicias likens the army, walled up behind defensive fortifications, to a city under siege. The city in Sicily, like the city in Attica, huddled behind its walls, dependent on its navy, which, as the reader knows, would ultimately be defeated as well.

Given the events of the narrative so far, Nicias's image of the army as a besieged city is full of foreboding. One of the first actions of the war was the Athenian blockade of Potidaea, which ended with Thucydides' dramatic picture of the men and women of Potidaea walking out of their city, each with one or two garments, to whatever haven they could find (2.70.4). Then came the siege of Plataea, which ended also in defeat, with the Plataeans eventually moving to Scione, itself reduced by the Athenians through siege. To this list we may add Melos and Mytilene, each taken by siege. In Thucydides, besieged cities fall. The added irony, of course, is that the Athenians had a powerful reputation on the offensive side of a siege – a reputation to which Nicias alluded when he remarked that the Athenians "supposed we were besieging others." As Thucydides tells us in the *Pentekontaetia*, the Spartans called in the Athenians to help with their siege of Mount Ithome because "the Athenians were known to be good at siege warfare" (1.102.2). There are many ironic reversals in the Sicilian campaign. Being "good at siege warfare" is only one of a number of characteristics that Sicily revealed the Athenians had lost.

If the Athenians found it difficult to build a *polis antipalos* or "rival city" in Sicily, the Peloponnesians did not find the same difficulty in Attica. In 413, the Peloponnesians determined that the Athenians had broken the peace of Nicias when they aided Argos against the Spartans (6.105) and so, at the very beginning of spring, they invaded Attica under King Agis, the son of King Archidamus, who had led the initial invasions of Attica at the beginning of the war some eighteen years earlier. This time, however, instead of merely ravaging agricultural land, destroying farm buildings, and then retreating, the Peloponnesians built a fort at the village of Decelea about thirteen or fourteen miles from the city center in the northeast region of Attica (See Map 3). Thucydides does not say that the Spartans found it difficult to do so and gives no hint that the Athenians made any attempt to stop the Spartans. Thus the Spartans disprove Pericles' confident assessment that it is hard to build a fortification in enemy territory (1.142.3). The Athenians fulfilled Pericles' prediction, but the Spartans succeeded beyond his expectation.

In telling his story of the renewal of the war in Athens, Thucydides interweaves his narrative of events in Sicily with events in Attica, inviting comparisons between the two. Indeed, the two situations become increasingly similar. In his letter home to Athens in the previous winter of 414, Nicias said of the city-army in Sicily that "we who supposed we were besieging others are ourselves suffering the same thing at least on land" (7.11.4). In like manner, the city in Attica became besieged by the Spartans' fortification. With Decelea fortified, the Athenian countryside was constantly in danger; it was no longer really in Athenian control.

The fortification of Decelea was, in some sense, the full realization of Pericles' vision of the city and the full revelation of its flaws. Pericles had insisted that "neither their fortification-building nor their navy is worth worrying about" (1.142.2). He had, in that same first speech, told the Athenians that "if they invade our country by land, we will sail against theirs, and it will not be a similar thing for some portion of the Peloponnesus to be cut off and the whole of Attica" (1.143.4). In his discussion of the Decelean fortification, Thucydides is careful to show that Pericles was wrong. The entire passage undercuts Pericles' insistence that only the sea and the "city" mattered and, indeed, that the "city" could successfully be divorced from the land of Attica, as Pericles had urged.

Thucydides devotes two long and powerful paragraphs to a description of the effects on Athens of the fortification of Decelea. He begins them by stating that the fortification "greatly harmed Athens":

> by the ruin of wealth and the destruction of the population it particularly damaged affairs. For formerly the invasions were short and they did not prevent the Athenians from enjoying and using their land the rest of the time. Now, however, the Lacedaemonians were sitting there all the time and sometimes attacking them with greater forces and at other times ravaging the countryside with the regular garrison and making plundering raids out of its need. And when Agis the king of the Lacedaemonians was there, who took the war very seriously, the Athenians were greatly harmed. They were robbed of their whole countryside and more than 20,000 slaves had run away, most of whom were skilled workers. And all their sheep and draft animals were lost. . . . and the shipment of necessities from Euboea, which formerly had gone more quickly overland from Oropos through Decelea, became a great expense going by sea and Sounion (7.27.3–7.28.1).

Thucydides sums up his discussion with this image: "The city needed every single thing to be imported and instead of a city it became a fortress" (τῶν τε πάντων ὁμοίως ἐπακτῶν ἐδεῖτο ἡ πόλις, καὶ ἀντὶ τοῦ πόλις εἶναι φρούριον κατέστη, 7.28.1). Pericles had urged the

Athenian population to move within the walls of the *asty*-Piraeus corridor, to depend on the empire and the navy, and to look on that as the city. Thucydides reveals the reality and the weakness of Pericles' vision: The city became a fortress and the empire and navy could not supply it without difficulty. Pericles, in the Funeral Oration, boasted about the city's imports as evidence of its power and delights (and revealed the Athenian inability to distinguish the homegrown from the foreign) when he crowed "because of the greatness of the city everything from every land comes in to us and it is our luck to enjoy the goods from here with no more homegrown and familiar a pleasure than the goods of other men" (2.38.2). Here we see his city, having severed its connection to the land, reduced to a complete reliance on imports. They cannot get the "goods from here" because they were "robbed of their whole countryside" (τῆς τε γὰρ χώρας ἁπάσης ἐστέρηντο, 7.27.5). Athens is deprived even of its own resources.

Thucydides' narrative encourages comparison with Pericles' vision as it looks back to the beginning of the war. The invasion of 413, for example, was led by Agis, the son of King Archidamus, who had led the first invasions of Attica some eighteen years earlier. The irony is palpable: Archidamus, in his speech to the Spartans cautioning against the war, had warned that the Spartans must not think that the war would be over immediately if they devastated Athenian land. "I fear," he said, "that it is more likely that we shall leave the war to our sons" (1.81.6). Here we see his son still fighting the same war, just as Archidamus predicted.[61] We should contrast this prescience with the forecast of Pericles, who derisively suggested that the Peloponnesians would be undone "if, as is likely, the war is lengthier for them than they expect" (1.141.5). Archidamus' son's invasion eighteen years after Pericles' speech shows that it was not only for the Spartans, but for the Athenians and Pericles as well, that the war turned out to be much longer, and quite different, than expected.[62]

Thucydides himself more explicitly encourages his readers to make a comparison with Pericles' vision when, in this same passage about the

[61] Cf. Rawlings 1981, 47.

[62] Cf. Connor (1984, 51): "[T]he reader knows it is not just 'for them' that the war turns out to be longer than expected."

Decelean fortification, he turns to a discussion of attitudes at the beginning of the war. This is a passage with "startling temporal shifts."[63] Thucydides begins with a reference to the Athenians' "passion for victory" (φιλονικίαν):

> Standing guard in relays on the battlements by day, and all of them except the cavalry by night, some out under arms, and others on the wall, summer and winter long, they were distressed. And it especially oppressed them that they had two wars at the same time. And they had got themselves into such a passion for victory that no one hearing about it before it happened would have believed it – that when they themselves were being besieged by a fortification of the Peloponnesians they did not evacuate Sicily but besieged Syracuse in the same way instead, a city in itself no less than that of the Athenians. In doing so they made the unexpectedness of their power and daring so great – since at the beginning of the war, although some thought the Athenians would survive one or two or three years, no one thought they would last longer than that if the Peloponnesians invaded their land or that they would come to Sicily in the seventeenth year after the first invasion already worn out in all ways by the war and would take on besides another war no less than the older one from the Peloponnesians (7.28.2–3).

This passage, on one hand, is a testament to the remarkable resilience of Athens and is, in one sense, a validation of Pericles' confidence at the beginning of the war. Surely Thucydides' remarks on the unexpected resilience of the Athenians are meant to make readers think of Pericles. When they read "no one thought they would last longer than that," his readers, as it were, respond, "but Pericles did."[64] On the other hand, the text requires a second "but" – "but Pericles, even though he saw that Athens could last longer than two or three years, never envisioned this, and may not have had a strategy to deal with it." Indeed, the whole tenor of the passage is one of madness.[65] How could the Athenians, exhausted as they were from the war, think that they could "take on

[63] Rood 1998b, 125.

[64] Rood (1998b, 126) argues that we hear of this perception only now because "the disregard for the effects of Decelea was its most striking falsification."

[65] Rood (1998b, 126) argues that "by reaching back into the past and looking ahead, Thucydides could portray Athens' will to resist as splendid yet imprudent" and concludes that "the ambivalent response to Athens that the *History* as a whole encourages is here encapsulated."

another war no less than the older one" and capture Syracuse? What led to this "unexpectedness of their power and daring"? Is it not, at least in part, that they had been told – and believed – that they were "complete masters" of half the world, "both as much as you now hold and still more if you wish"?

There is another charge against Pericles here as well. The passage on the effects of Decelea and the Athenians' obstinate resolution is designed to reveal the Athenians' muddled thinking and confused priorities – priorities learned from Pericles. Thucydides' digression on the fortification of Decelea and its effect on Athenian finances is meant, in part, to explain why Athens sent back to Thrace thirteen hundred peltasts who were supposed to sail with reinforcements going to Sicily under the general Demosthenes. The Thracians arrived too late for the voyage, and the Athenians returned them to Thrace, Thucydides tells us, because "it appeared too expensive (πολυτελὲς ἐφαίνετο) to keep them for the war coming from Decelea" (7.27.2). The mention of Decelea as an explanation for the Thracians' return prompts Thucydides to explain what was occuring at Decelea, and he segues into the passage quoted above.

The passage about the Thracian mercenaries and the Athenians' response to their "two wars" is "charged, narratively speaking."[66] Thucydides says carefully that it "appeared" extravagant to use the Thracians in Attica, leaving it open whether it really would have been. There is, as Kallet stresses, "considerable irony" in this comment because of its echo of the wasteful, extravagant display of the departure of the fleet to Sicily, with its elaborate decorations and contests (6.31.1): "[H]ere, if the Athenians had decided to use the Thracians in Attica, the cost incurred would have been justifiable, given the seriousness of the Spartan presence in Decelea. To continue to fight the war in Sicily was extravagant; to deal with the Spartans at home was essential."[67] The passage suggests that the Athenians lost the ability to prioritize. But if they did, they learned what Pericles taught: to devalue their land. Pericles bid the Athenians to imagine they were islanders, to imagine their city as an island. He told them that their houses and cultivated land were no more

66 Kallet 2001, 125.
67 Kallet 2001, 125.

to be valued than "a little garden or bauble of wealth" (2.62.3). He told them that Attica was a superfluous extravagance and claimed that "it will not be a similar thing for some portion of the Peloponnesus to be cut off and the whole of Attica" (1.143.4). The Athenians believed him. The result was that the Athenians' city became "a fortress," and the Athenians did not even know enough to focus on turning it back into a city.[68]

THE REMAINING CITY AND THE GREAT NAME OF ATHENS FALLS

Meanwhile, the Athenians in Sicily were also facing increasing difficulties. In the same summer of 413 that saw the fortification of Decelea in Attica, the forces in Sicily, which had already been frustrated on land in their attempts to wall in Syracuse, also suffered defeat at sea. Indeed, one of the most powerful themes of the Sicilian Expedition is the stripping from the Athenians of their naval superiority. As it turns out, the Athenians were not, as Pericles boasted, supreme masters of the watery part of the world, nor was naval skill as difficult to learn as Pericles had suggested. In his first speech to the Athenians, Pericles had remarked that their enemy "will not easily gain expert status on the sea. Not even you who have been practicing ever since the Persian wars have completely accomplished that" (1.142.6–7). The Sicilian campaign reveals that the Syracusans were, apparently, faster learners than the Athenians. Indeed, Hermocrates, the Syracusan leader, encouraged the Syracusans to attempt a naval battle with the Athenians with an argument that appropriated Athenian success in the Persian wars and again casts the

[68] The consequences for the rest of Greece of Athens' confused priorities (and of the war itself) are summarized in Thucydides' account of the massacre that the rejected Thracian mercenaries perpetrated on the tiny unwalled village of Mycalessos on their way home from Athens. As Palmer (1989; 1992, 115) writes, "Thucydides impress[es] upon us how barbarism was making inroads into the heart of the Greek world" as a result of the war. Orwin (1994, 135–36) sees an analogy between Mycalessos and "the old way of life at Athens," the "last vestiges" of which "have now fallen victim to the Spartan occupation of Decelea. See also Kallet 2001, 121ff.

Athenians in the role of the Persians. "The Athenians did not have a hereditary and everlasting skill at sea," he said. "Rather, they were even more mainlanders than the Syracusans and only became sailors when they were compelled to by the Medes" (7.21.3). Here, the brave and astonishing deed that earlier in the work served as an example of the unique and daring Athenian character is produced as encouraging evidence for the Athenians' enemies that both daring and seamanship are not the exclusive prerogatives of Athenians. Anyone can acquire this skill.[69]

Hermocrates also, of course, directly challenges Pericles' definition of the Athenians. Central to Pericles' vision for victory was the invincible nature of islanders. "If we were islanders, who would be harder to catch?" he asked, urging his Athenians to "think as nearly like this as possible" (1.143.5). Hermocrates, years later, replies that despite what they may think and hope, the Athenians are still just mainlanders underneath a nautical veneer – indeed "even more mainlanders than the Syracusans" (ἠπειρώτας μᾶλλον τῶν Συρακοσίων ὄντας). Events soon proved Hermocrates right. In a battle in the great harbor of Syracuse in 413 (7.37–41), the Athenians were defeated by the Syracusans, who then "had the secure expectation that they were far stronger at sea" (7.41.4).

Hermocrates' mention of the Athenians' acquisition of naval skill in the Persian wars fits with Thucydides' thematic comparison of the Athenians to their former enemies, the Persians. Hermocrates himself implicitly compared the two when he argued that the Athenians' campaign was an opportunity for the Sicilians to win glory because, "in this very way, when the Mede failed quite unexpectedly, these Athenians themselves were glorified on account of the fame they acquired because he had come against Athens; and it is not unlikely that the same thing will happen to us" (6.33.6). The Persian parallel has importance for the city theme. The Athenians at Sparta presented their decision to abandon Attica, to become a city of sailors in order to fight the Persians, as the defining moment for their city. In Sicily the Athenians seem to lose

[69] Cf. L. Strauss (1964, 206): "the spirit of initiative, daring and inventiveness by which the Athenians hitherto excelled has left them and now animates their enemies; the Athenians have become Spartans and the Athenians' enemies have become Athenians." See also Connor 1984, 190–91.

their defining qualities. They are no more a city of sailors than are the Syracusans, and their ability to redefine the city is not their salvation but their destruction.

Soon after the great battle in the harbor, the reinforcements that Nicias had requested in his letter home arrived from Athens under the command of the generals Demosthenes and Eurymedon. At this crisis point, the new general Demosthenes speaks explicitly in a way that values Attica and the Attic city over the conceptualized city in Sicily. Upon his arrival, Demosthenes determined to attack the heights above Syracuse, called Epipolae. There, one of the Syracusan counter walls frustrating the Athenian attempt to blockade the city was especially vulnerable. Unfortunately, the attack was a complete rout, and the Athenian generals met afterward to discuss their difficult situation. Demosthenes argued for a quick retreat while they had naval superiority because of the newly arrived ships. The logic Thucydides tells us Demosthenes used is striking: "It was better for the city," he said, "for them to make war against those who were building fortifications in their own land than against the Syracusans who were no longer easy to conquer" (καὶ τῇ πόλει ὠφελιμώτερον ἔφη εἶναι πρὸς τοὺς ἐν τῇ χώρᾳ σφῶν ἐπιτειχίζοντας τὸν πόλεμον ποιεῖσθαι ἢ Συρακοσίους, οὓς οὐκέτι ῥᾴδιον εἶναι χειρώσασθαι, 7.47.4). Especially after Nicias's repeated characterizations of the army in Sicily as a city, Demosthenes' judgment about what is better for "the city" is deliberate and pointed. For Demosthenes, there was only one city and no doubt about the relative values of Attica and Sicily. The Athenians, he said, should fight "in" and, implicitly, for "their own land." The Athenians, according to Demosthenes, should pry their eyes away from their far-off Sicilian love and focus again on their traditional city. Attica belonged to them; Sicily did not. And, he implied, in direct contradiction to Pericles, Attica and the city there could not be replaced by imperial conquests. Of the "two wars" that Thucydides mentions in 7.28, that is, Demosthenes urged the Athenians to focus on the one in Attica. Ironically, Demosthenes here echoes Nicias's own earlier arguments against the expedition.[70]

70 Cf. Palmer (1992, 107): "Demosthenes . . . appears to be thinking only of the public interest at this crucial juncture, and whose arguments is he echoing [compare 7.47.3–4 with 6.9.3, 6.10.1, 6.11.1, and 6.12.1]?"

Nicias, however, although he agreed that "their affairs were in a bad way," was reluctant to withdraw the expedition, in part because of his apprehension about how this decision would be perceived at home, so the Athenians subsequently suffered a second momentous defeat in the great harbor of Syracuse despite the advantage in numbers they had as a result of the recent naval reinforcements (7.51–55). The Syracusans then decided to try to capture the entire Athenian force and so blocked up the mouth of the harbor (7.59.2). With this action, the fleet became, as it were, besieged – just like a city walled in by the enemy. The battle that ensued when the Athenians tried to force their way out, furthermore, curiously transformed sea into land. The Athenians put everyone they could find on their ships and so manned 110 ships with rowers and marines but also archers and javelin throwers (7.60–4-5). This necessarily changed the Athenians' tactics. As Nicias tells his men in a speech before the battle, "in addition many archers and javelin-men will go on board and a crowd of men which we would not employ if we were fighting a sea-battle on the open sea because the weighing down of the ships would hinder our skill; but they will be a benefit to us in the land battle we are compelled to fight here from our ships" (7.62.2). In Syracuse, therefore, the long-held Athenian plan of avoiding land battles and depending on their naval superiority was of no avail.

Nicias's harangue to his fighters before the final battle in the harbor, in addition to revealing the tactical oddities of the coming battle, further demonstrates the contrast between Nicias's and Demosthenes' priorities and understanding of the city. Demosthenes had earlier urged that it was best for "the city" for the Athenians to fight "in their own land" (7.47.3–4), demonstrating that the only city that existed for him was the one in Attica. Nicias, on the other hand, takes an entirely different position. In his speech to the troops, he conceptualizes the army as a city in a particularly dangerous way and again reveals his failure to focus his, or the army's, loyalty on the city in Attica. In fact, Nicias suggests that the army has detached itself from Athens. He reminds the Athenians in his audience that

> you did not leave behind other ships in the ship-sheds like these here or a class of hoplites and if anything other than winning occurs for us, your enemies here will immediately sail there and those of us remaining there will be unable to ward off those there and those coming against them (7.64.1).

In his contrast between "here" and "there," and especially in his talk of the danger to Athens and "those of us remaining there," Nicias seems to imbue the city in Attica with supreme importance. Yet his subsequent comments show that it is actually "here" and his city-army in Sicily that remain Nicias's focus.

Nicias tells the men "since we are in the same contest for both groups, take heart, if you ever have, and consider, each and every one of you, that those of you who will now be on the ships are, for the Athenians, the infantry and the ships and the remaining city and the great name of Athens" (7.64.2). This is symbolic of the magnitude of the Athenians' eventual defeat, of course, but Nicias's comment also makes the conflict of loyalties and interests in Sicily all the more severe. Although it may represent the "great name of Athens" (τὸ μέγα ὄνομα τῶν Ἀθηνῶν), the army in Sicily was not "the only remaining city" (ἡ ὑπόλοιπος πόλις). Athens itself still stood. This force in Sicily was not the last remaining hope of the Athenian people, as that of Themistocles had been. As Thucydides reminds his reader in the *Epitaph*, "after they had failed in Sicily . . . they nevertheless held out for eight years . . . and they did not give in until, falling afoul of each other in their private disagreements, they were overthrown" (2.65.11).[71] The loss in Sicily was not the end. Yet just like the Athenians who hoped to send the Thracian peltasts to Sicily but found the expense of them too dear for the defense of Attica, here we see Nicias explicitly investing his city in Sicily with greater importance than it ought to have – at the expense of the city in Attica.

This is evident from the very beginning of his speech, when Nicias warns that for the Athenians and their allies, no less than for the enemy, "the coming contest, equally common to all, will be over salvation and fatherland" (ὁ μὲν ἀγὼν ὁ μέλλων ὁμοίως κοινὸς ἅπασιν ἔσται περί τε σωτηρίας καὶ πατρίδος, 7.61.1). Nicias goes on to explain that only if they win will it be possible for each of them "to see his home *polis* wherever it is" (τὴν ὑπάρχουσάν που οἰκείαν πόλιν ἐπιδεῖν, 7.61.1), and so he seems ultimately to focus on a return to Athens in

[71] The manuscripts read three years, but this dating does not conform to the length of the war, so most scholars judge that the "three" should be changed to "eight." Connor (1979, 269ff), on the other hand, argues that the passage is corrupt and "any figure – three, five, eight or ten – is otiose."

Attica. Nevertheless, Nicias's comment that the Athenian army will fight "for their fatherland" is powerful, and "a reversal of the usual topos that only those invaded are fighting in defense of their country."[72] The comment continues the symbolic equation of the expedition with a city and supports the Syracusan cavalry's charge that the Athenians were coming to take up a new homeland in Sicily.

Just before the beginning of the battle, Nicias reinforces the sense that the Athenian army is fighting for its fatherland right there in Sicily. Fearing that what he had said so far was inadequate, Nicias called forward each of the trierarchs and addressed him by his patronymic, his own name, and his tribe name. He urged them not to betray themselves or their ancestors, reminded them of the freedom of their country, and said "all the other things as well which men in so great a time of crisis would not mention if they were on their guard against seeming to speak in an old-fashioned way, above all platitudes about women and children and ancestral gods" (καὶ ὑπὲρ ἁπάντων παραπλήσια ἔς τε γυναῖκας καὶ παῖδας καὶ θεοὺς πατρῴους προφερόμενα, 7.69.2).[73] The references to women, children, and ancestral gods are appropriate to an army fighting "for salvation and fatherland" in their own country where rape, slavery, the burning of temples, and utter destruction will follow a loss; they are not appropriate to an invading army of men far away from home. Such references, do, however, further the symbolic equation of the expedition with a city.

It is interesting that Nicias's Sicilian city includes both Athenians and foreigners. Rood notes Periclean echoes in Nicias's speech to his forces and argues that "by having the foreigners in the fleet share in

[72] Rood 1998b, 196.

[73] Lateiner (1985, 203–5) argues that Thucydides "faults Nicias here," and Cagnazzi (1986, 493) claims that Thucydides makes his observation "with distaste," but Rood (1998b, 195) is probably right that "the generalizing remarks . . . suggest that most men would speak as Nicias does." Lateiner (205) describes how Nicias "retreats to an earlier political world, in which . . . appeals relying on wives, children and gods of the fathers worked." This is consistent with the way Thucydides crafts the Sicilian Expedition as a replaying of the Persian wars and reinforces the echo in Nicias's remarks of the *Persians* and the past war when the Athenian city and its women, children, and ancestral gods really were in danger.

this Periclean conception, Nicias tries to make the whole force homogeneous – an image of Athens."[74] Nicias knows that his force is not really homogeneous, however; he recognizes that each man has "his own home *polis* wherever it is," and he directs different remarks to the Athenians and to the foreigners in his army. But even his remarks that single out the foreigners elide them with Athenians. He claims that the sailors in the fleet were "considered during the whole time as Athenians even though you were not, admired throughout Hellas because of your knowledge of our speech and your imitation of our customs, you shared no less in our empire, as far as benefiting from the fearsomeness towards our subjects and not suffering harm" (7.63.3). Nicias claims that the foreigners serving with the Athenians were the whole time regarded as Athenians. Here, Nicias acknowledges the worldview of the Thebans, who would surely charge these foreign sailors with atticism, and confirms that Athens' enemies see no real distinction between Athenians and foreign allies. Importantly, Nicias makes the same claim in his speech. It is not only the Athenians in the fleet but all those "who will be on the ships" whom he calls "the remaining city and the great name of Athens." Both Athenians and foreigners make up the city in Sicily. When the Athenians set up their city on Samos, Thucydides is even more explicit in demonstrating that the city comprised both "real" Athenians and atticizers.

Nicias's exhortation to his trierarchs to remember their "women, children and ancestral gods," recalls the messenger speech from Aeschylus's *Persians* 402–5: "A great concerted cry we heard: 'O Greek Sons, advance! Free your fathers' land, Free your sons, your wives, the sanctuaries of paternal gods, the sepulchers of ancestors."[75] This echo furthers Thucydides' presentation of the Sicilian campaign as a reversal of the Persian wars but also focuses our attention on the difference between the two situations. At Salamis, the Athenians freed their fatherland, children, wives, and ancestral gods because they "went on board ship" and faced the danger. Their ability to redefine the city allowed them to reclaim their actual homeland. In Sicily, by contrast, the redefinition of the expedition as the Athenian city endangers the

[74] Rood 1998b, 193.

[75] Trans. S. Bernadete in Grene and Lattimore 1959. Cf. Rood 1998b, 195.

city in Attica by dividing loyalties and causing the men of the city-army to invest too much importance in the imagined city at the expense of the one in Attica. The implication is that the Athenians are in danger of losing their home *polis* because of a failure to recognize where it is.

Despite Nicias's rhetorical excess, his men did not prevail. As the infantry watched from the shore, the Athenian navy was once again defeated by the Syracusans. Thucydides gives a telling detail of the battle that is full of irony. He says that if an Athenian naval general saw any ship slacking in the fight, he would call out to the captain of the ship and ask "whether they were retreating because they considered the extremely hostile land more homelike now than the sea which through no small effort they had made their own" (ἠρώτων, οἱ μὲν Ἀθηναῖοι εἰ τὴν πολεμιωτάτην γῆν οἰκειοτέραν ἤδη τῆς οὐ δι' ὀλίγου πόνου κεκτημένης θαλάσσης ἡγούμενοι ὑποχωροῦσιν, 7.70.8). Thucydides' generals accuse the captains of witlessly thinking the land is "more homelike" (οἰκειοτέραν). They contrast the falsely "homelike" land with the sea, which they describe as "owned" by the Athenians. The comments of the generals raise the question of what the Athenians value and what belongs to them: land or sea, Attica or empire.

The comment echoes earlier statements about the Athenians' "home" attachments in an interesting way. Thucydides' narrative so far has shown that the Athenians do not define their "homeland" as Attica but rather, according to Pericles' last vision of the city, that they view all the sea and all islands and coastal territory as theirs. Thus the claim of the generals that the Athenians had "made the sea their own" echoes Pericles' boast in his last speech that the Athenians were masters of half of the world, as well as the Athenians' claim at Melos, and Alcibiades' claim on the eve of the expedition, that the Athenians were *naukratores* (2.62.2; 5.96, 6.18.5). But the comment of the generals suggests that the Athenians' flexible definition of what is "home" may actually work against them in this case, especially because the certainties the Athenians have long believed no longer exist. The generals, like Pericles, contrast land and sea and insist that it is the sea that belongs to the Athenians. The land only appears to be "homelike." Yet Nicias had already characterized this battle as a land battle, and the sea around Syracuse, at least, was far from being the Athenians' own. Furthermore, Nicias's conception of the army as a city, and the Athenians' flexibility in what land they considered their "homeland," encouraged just what the generals feared – a hope, on the part of the Athenians, to find some safety (even a home?) on land far from home, with little thought left of that other city in Attica. In this passage we see the Athenian men fulfilling the taunt of the Syracusan cavalry, who asked whether they had really "come to join with them in colonizing a foreign land" (6.63.3).

FEW OUT OF MANY RETURNED HOME

After the Syracusans defeated the Athenians in the final battle in the great harbor and the Athenians were not able to force their way out by sea, the generals resolved on a land retreat (7.73). It is not clear to where, exactly, they expected to retreat, or how (or indeed if) they hoped ever to return to Athens, if they abandoned their fleet. The suggestion is that the army now really meant to settle down as a city in Sicily, permanently separated from Athens. The hint that the Athenians planned to stay in Sicily is taken up by what Thucydides says Hermocrates feared at this point. After the last battle, Hermocrates suspected that the Athenians meant to retreat by land, and "he thought that it would be a terrible thing if so great an army, retreating by land and settling down somewhere in Sicily, should wish to make war against them again" (νομίσας δεινὸν εἶναι εἰ τοσαύτη στρατιὰ κατὰ γῆν ὑποχωρήσασα καὶ καθεζομένη ποι τῆς Σικελίας βουλήσεται αὖθις σφίσι τὸν πόλεμον ποιεῖσθαι, 7.73.1). The use of the word "settle" here suggests permanence and implies that the city at sea might permanently ground itself in Sicily.

Thucydides himself explicitly and dramatically revisits the theme of the army as a city when he describes the preparations for the army's withdrawal. He paints a pitiful picture of the soldiers abandoning the sick and dying and leaving the dead unburied as they fled to an uncertain future (7.75.1–4). In the midst of his description, he includes this image: "they were like nothing other than a city, reduced by siege, in flight – and not a small city; for of the whole crowd not less than forty thousand men marched out" (οὐδὲν γὰρ ἄλλο ἢ πόλει ἐκπεπολιορκημένῃ ἐῴκεσαν ὑποφευγούσῃ, καὶ ταύτῃ οὐ σμικρᾷ· μυριάδες γὰρ τοῦ ξύμπαντος ὄχλου οὐκ ἐλάσσους τεσσάρων ἅμα ἐπορεύοντο, 7.75.5). This rounds out the fate of the city that Nicias urged the Athenians to imagine themselves sending to Sicily. Nicias revealed in his letter home to Athens that that city-army, despite its hopes, was besieged (7.11.4), and here we see the final act as the population of the city, reduced by siege, fled in despair.

When Nicias falsely claimed that the battle was "over salvation and fatherland" and urged his trierarchs to remember their "women, children and ancestral gods," he evoked in his men just the image of the destruction of a defeated city that Thucydides alludes to here. This "emotionally charged and dramatically heightened passage" belongs to a tradition of such passages on the capture of cities that goes back to Homer.[76] The passage foreshadows the fall of Athens in Attica and so configures Athens as one in "a succession of mortal cities," but because the passage focuses on the destruction of the city-army in Sicily, it also reinforces the notion that the "fatherland" Nicias spoke of was in Sicily, not Attica.[77]

Nicias saw the discouragement of his pitiful troops as they prepared to march out, and so went along the ranks and tried to comfort and encourage them (7.76.1). His remarks reveal his overvaluation of the city in Sicily and show that his confused priorities lead to a final (and real) abandonment of the city in Attica:

> Consider that you yourselves are a city straightaway wherever you settle down (λογίζεσθε δὲ ὅτι αὐτοί τε πόλις εὐθύς ἐστε ὅποι ἂν καθέζησθε) and that no other city of those in Sicily could easily meet your attack or could root you out once you had settled yourselves somewhere. With regard to the march, you yourselves must take care that it is safe and well-ordered with each one of you thinking nothing other than that in whatever spot he is forced to fight, if he wins, this he will hold as both fatherland and fortress (τοῦτο καὶ πατρίδα καὶ τεῖχος κρατήσας ἕξειν, 7.77.4–5).

[76] Paul 1982, 146–47. Cf. Hornblower 2004, 344.

[77] See Rood (1998a no pagination) on the "idea of a succession of mortal cities." See Palmer (1992, 20) for "allusions to Athens as the new Troy" in Pericles' first speech.

Nicias's image is not merely a metaphor employed to inspire confidence in the army because of its size, but represents the final abandonment of Attica and the city there, for Nicias actually suggests finding not just a fortress (τεῖχος) in this alien land, but actually a fatherland (πατρίδα). When Nicias said before the battle that the contest was "over salvation and fatherland," he at least made the suggestion that what he really meant was that, for the Athenians, it was over the chance to see one's fatherland again by return to the "home *polis*" (οἰκείαν πόλιν, 7.61.1). Here, however, Nicias says explicitly that wherever the men "settle" in Sicily will be their "fatherland." Alcibiades had originally urged the Sicilian campaign partly on the grounds that the Sicilians would be quick to retreat to other lands if things went badly for them because the Sicilians had no regard for "their own home fatherland" (περὶ οἰκείας πατρίδος, 6.17.3).[78] The *strategoi* during the battle feared that the Athenians found the land more "homelike" than the sea, and here it is the Athenians who think of abandoning their "home *polis*" in the hope of finding another fatherland in Sicily.[79]

Nicias concluded his speech with the thought that "men are the city, not walls or ships empty of men" (ἄνδρες γὰρ πόλις, καὶ οὐ τείχη οὐδὲ νῆες ἀνδρῶν κεναί, 7.77.7). Connor calls the phrase "men are the city" an "apparent cliché," but argues that "in their context the words become part of a powerful thematic progression in the work" that transforms the expedition "from a mighty fleet leading out a city . . . to a collection of individual and vulnerable human beings." Connor judges that the theme inverts "the calculus of power in the archaeology with its emphasis on the physical and quantitative bases of power, especially walls and ships. In the last ironic analysis all depends on men, not on material resources."[80] Kallet, too, emphasizes "the contrast between Nicias's definition of the polis and the Periclean version presented in

[78] Of course, Thucydides judges that the Syracusans were most similar in character to the Athenians (8.96.5). That similarity is, perhaps, represented in Alcibiades' remark.

[79] There is, of course, great irony in the suggestion that one could find a "fatherland" far from one's fathers and the "sanctuaries of paternal gods" and "sepulchers of ancestors" that urge the Greeks on in the *Persians* (402–5). See, e.g., Longo (1975, 97).

[80] Connor 1984, 202–3.

the Funeral Oration, in which the polis is an abstraction, an entity that makes men worthy as citizens, not the reverse." Nicias, she says, "inverts the Periclean vision."[81] But there is not only inversion here. The idea that "men are the city" may be an old and venerable motif, but what the Athenians, and the Athenians alone, did with this idea is entirely new. The ability of the Athenian men in the Persian wars still to conceive of themselves as the city of Athens when they had lost the physical city (and its material resources) was what saved them. Both the Athenians and the Corinthians emphasized in their speeches before the war the radical, daring (and decidedly not clichéd) thinking and (most importantly) action of the Athenians at Salamis. To be able really to believe that "men are the city" and to act on that thought was the defining moment for Athens. The inclusion of this event in Athenian and Corinthian prewar calculations of the power on both sides shows that, at least since that defining moment at Salamis, for the Athenians there has always been more than just the "physical and quantitative bases of power," as Connor writes.[82]

Furthermore, the narrative's repeated characterization of the men Nicias speaks to as a city also makes his comment fresh. The (apparent) cliché, that is, serves to highlight the singular nature of this use. The men Nicias speaks to are numerous enough to constitute a city; they are far enough away from home to wonder if they could ever return to their real city, and they have heard for years that their city has nothing to do with Attica but is instead an abstraction focused on the sea and maritime conquests. These men, that is, are primed to hear Nicias's words not as a stock bromide but as a serious explanation of what constitutes the city – in part because of Pericles' redefinition of an existing city. Pericles' purpose was to give the Athenians a conception of themselves that would allow their power to range beyond the city in Attica. But the result was that the Athenians began to think that any group of them, detached from a city that still existed, could be the city. Nicias's "cliché," therefore, flirts with both *stasis* and dissolution. Indeed, Nicias's comment foreshadows the *stasis* to come when the Athenian factioneers on Samos put Nicias's claim that the "men are the city" into actual

[81] Kallet 2001, 162.
[82] Connor 1984, 202–3.

practice and constitute themselves as a city on Samos. Nicias's claim that "men are the city," furthermore, dangerously supports the plan of his men to "settle" in a new fatherland somewhere in Sicily.[83]

Thucydides underscores that the Athenians will fail even in this misguided endeavor, however. When Nicias said the men would find a fatherland and fortress wherever they "settle down," he used the same word (καθέζομαι) that Thucydides had used earlier to describe Hermocrates' planning against just this possibility. Hermocrates thought that it would be a terrible thing if so large an army, having "settled" someplace in Sicily (καθεζομένη ποι τῆς Σικελίας, 7.73.1), should make war against them. Thus Hermocrates tried to get the magistrates of Syracuse to set up roadblocks and garrison the passes. When he was unable to persuade them to do so, on his own initiative, he had messengers ride up to the Athenian camp, pretending to be friendly to the Athenians, to warn soldiers to tell Nicias not to lead the army away during the night, because the Syracusans were guarding the roads. The Athenians believed the false story, and the generals put off their retreat not only for the night after the last sea battle, but for another whole day (7.73.1–74.1). In the meantime, Thucydides tells us, the Syracusans "marching out with the cavalry blocked off the roads throughout the countryside leading to where the Athenians were likely to go and guarded the fords of the streams and rivers and stationed themselves to meet and stop the army wherever it seemed best" (7.74.2). When Nicias urges his troops to consider that they will find a fortress and a fatherland wherever they "settle down," the reader knows that Hermocrates has taken care that this city-army will not settle down again anywhere. Thucydides describes the Athenians marching out of their camp, with each man carrying with him "whatever he could that was useful" (7.75.5). This description brings to mind the other departure from a city reduced by siege that Thucydides took care to describe, that of Potidaea (2.70.3–4). There the men and women marched out, each carrying one or two garments, but they at least could

[83] Mossé (1963, 292), by contrast, remarks that despite the equation Thucydides makes between the army in Sicily and a city (e.g., at 7.75.5), "in reality, however, Athens and the allied cities remained intact," and he cites 7.77.7 as proof that "the goal of all the men was to see their native land again, to return home."

hope to find a haven in friendly Olynthus. The Athenians were not to be so lucky.

The Athenians advanced about four and a half miles that first day, but their progress over the next few days was severely compromised by the precautions the Syracusans had taken against them. Finally Demosthenes and Nicias decided to try to lead their men away from a camp they had made in a plain. But in the dark and confusion, the army was divided, and the group under Nicias got far ahead of Demosthenes. The next day the Syracusans and their allies met with Demosthenes' half of the army and attacked it throughout the day. Toward the end of the day, Demosthenes surrendered his army to them. On the following day the Syracusans tried to get Nicias to surrender, but his terms were not acceptable, so they surrounded and attacked his army as they had Demosthenes'. On the next day they slaughtered a large part of his army as the men rushed to quench their thirst in the river Assinarus. Nicias eventually surrendered to stop the slaughter, so the whole Athenian army was killed or captured.

The great battle in the harbor of Syracuse "inevitably evokes the Battle of Salamis – the decisive naval engagement of the Persian invasion, fought in narrow quarters, and resulting in a victory that brought special glory to Athens."[84] But in Syracuse "the Athenian role is, of course, now totally reversed, since the victors of Salamis have become the defeated of Syracuse."[85] Thucydides makes deliberate comparisons between Salamis and Syracuse. For example, the destruction of the fleets of the Persians and the Athenians are "captured in mirror-scenes" in Herodotus and Thucydides.[86] Rood compares Herodotus' account of Xerxes' shifting emotions as he watched the battle of Salamis (Hdt. 8.88, 90) with Thucydides' description of the Athenians on land straining to follow the fight in the harbor (7.71). Even the Syracusans' decision to try to stop the withdrawal of the Athenians is an echo of the Persian wars. After the battle of Salamis, despite Themistocles' encouragement, the Greeks failed to sail to the Hellespont to destroy Xerxes' bridges and cut off the retreat of his army (Hdt. 9.108–110). Hermocrates, on the

[84] Connor 1984, 197. Cf. Rood 1999, 159ff.
[85] Connor 1984, 197.
[86] Rood 1999, 153.

other hand, succeeded where the Greeks failed: "the new Themistocles achieves what has hitherto seemed unlikely or impossible – the actual capture of the invading force."[87]

Kallet has emphasized a curious detail in Thucydides' account of the desperate march for safety of the Athenian army that puts a last ironic touch on the characterization of the army in Sicily as a city and serves as a climax to Thucydides' presentation of the Sicilian Expedition as a reversal of the Persian wars.[88] After being surrounded, Demosthenes agreed to surrender his army to the Syracusans, according to Thucydides, on the terms that "no one was to be put to death either by violence, imprisonment, or by deprivation of absolutely necessary nourishment" (7.82.2). When Thucydides describes the surrender itself, however, he adds a vivid detail: "and all together six thousand surrendered themselves and they laid down all the silver that they had, throwing it into upturned shields, and filled up four shields" (7.82.3).[89]

Kallet argues that Thucydides' inclusion of this detail when he has not mentioned any agreement about money in the terms of surrender suggests that he has a special interest in it. In Kallet's reading, Thucydides' point is ironic, intending to contrast the "many talents" carried out by the city-fleet to Sicily (6.31) and the attendant extravagance and display with the "paltry amount" of four shields'-worth of silver collected from six thousand men.[90] Kallet demonstrates that each shield would probably have contained between two and a half and three talents. Thus the total amount taken from the men would be about ten to twelve talents – not a particularly large sum when contrasted with "the extravagance and expectations" with which the fleet set out. Kallet concludes, "thus by choosing to plant a visual image of money before

[87] Connor 1984, 198. L. Straus (1964, 226) argues that in a way, "Athens' defeat is her triumph: her enemies have to become in a manner Athenians in order to defeat her."

[88] Kallet 2001, 172–76.

[89] Foster (2001, 236) notes that Thucydides "finished off the materials of the Sicilian Expedition in the same manner as he finished off the materials of the city of Plataea, accounting for every last thing and making sure the reader knows that every element has been consumed."

[90] Kallet 2001, 175.

the reader at the devastating end of the expedition, Thucydides reminds us of the destruction of the city's financial resources."[91]

Kallet's interpretation is compelling, but the force of Thucydides' image is even greater than she suggests. Kallet explains the value of a shield's-worth of silver for her modern readers but assumes – and indeed, her reading requires – that ancient readers would immediately recognize the visual image of four shields' worth of silver as a (relatively) "paltry amount." But from what context would ancient readers derive such knowledge? At least in Athens they would know the look of a talent of silver from the yearly procession of tribute in the theatre of Dionysus at the beginning of the tragic festival of the Greater Dionysia.

In his speech "On the Peace," the fourth-century Athenian orator Isocrates catalogued what he saw as the arrogance of imperial Athens:

> So accurately did they discover how men are most hated that they voted to divide up the annually incoming silver tribute talent by talent and to bring it into the orchestra, when the theatre was full, at the festival of Dionysus (82).

Isocrates says specifically that the money was divided up and paraded about talent by talent (κατὰ τάλαντον). As Antony Raubitschek noted, "the money was divided into talents when it was carried into the theatre so that the spectators could easily estimate the total value of the display."[92] Thus, as Simon Goldhill argues, "the display was not just a piece of pomp and splendor. . . . Rather, it was a demonstration before the city and its many international visitors of the power of the *polis* of Athens, its role as a force in the Greek world. It was a public display of the success in military and political terms of the city."[93]

Readers familiar with this display of the tribute talent by talent (as Thucydides' Athenian readers and all the foreigners who witnessed

[91] Kallet 2001, 175. The image of the coins makes the destruction of the city's finances obvious, for the silver coins that were heaped up in the shields in Sicily were some of the last silver coins minted by Athens for years. As Seltman (1955, 137) notes, once Decelea was fortified, offering a safe haven, "the miners deserted in such numbers that operations shrank speedily and at last the silver ceased to be worked altogether." Those four mounds of fine Attic silver tetradrachms paid out to the Sicilian masters were some of the last of their kind.

[92] Raubitschek (1941, 358), citing Rogers (1910, 76).

[93] Goldhill, 1990, 102.

the procession at the Dionysia would be[94]) would have a rough idea of the volume of a talent of silver and so could estimate the worth of Thucydides' four shields-full of silver.[95] And for a reader familiar with this display, Thucydides' striking visual image of the paltry worth of Demosthenes' army would likely call this far grander demonstration of power to mind. Thus the comparison that Thucydides intends by this visual detail is probably not only between the wealth that went out with the fleet in 6.31, and the sad sum that remains, but also between that sum and the vast wealth collected each year by the central imperial city of Athens. This would then call to mind the resources Athens *could* have spent in Sicily and reinforce Kallet's argument that Thucydides intends throughout the Sicilian books to chastise Athens for its churlishness with resources for the Sicilian campaign.

Yet the irony goes even deeper. Thucydides' image of the four shields heaped with silver makes an implicit and ironic link to the collection and display of the allies' tribute to Athens. But in Sicily the situation is reversed.[96] In Sicily it is the Athenians who pay. Given the text's repeated equation of the army in Sicily to a city, most recently when Thucydides himself described the defeated army as similar to a "city reduced by siege" (7.75.5), the scene of the payment of these four shields' worth of silver serves as a symbolic tribute payment to the Syracusans by the defeated army-city. This completes the transformation of the Athenians underscored by Thucydides' evocation of the Persian wars in his account of the Sicilian campaign. It was the Athenians' victory in the Persian wars and their willingness to follow up that victory, with, for example, the siege of Sestos (1.89) that led to their *arche* and put most of the Aegean

[94] Of course the Greater Dionysia was open to foreigners, and Goldhill (1990, 103–4) speaks of a "specific awareness of the connection of the Great Dionysia, the ceremony of bringing in tribute in the presence of the *xenoi*, with the city on display."

[95] For the idea that the tribute was paid and/or displayed in bags and jars like hydriae, Raubitshek (1941, 358–59), citing Meritt et al. (1939–1953, Vol. I, 123, fig. 178; Cf. Meritt 1937, fig. 1), points to a stele of a decree of Athenian tribute (*IG* I³ 68) that carries a fragmentary crowning relief showing two hydriai and what Raubitschek takes to be "several money bags" "which presumably contained the tribute brought to Athens by the allies." See now Lawton (1995, 81, n. 1).

[96] As Rood notes (1999, 163), "Syracuse reverses Salamis."

into tributary status below them. Throughout the Sicilian campaign, however, Thucydides links the Athenians to the invader Persians, and, at the end, the result is not Athens receiving tribute but a pseudo, rival Athens, utterly defeated, like a city reduced by siege, paying it.

The shields in which the city-army's money was collected would probably have had another resonance as well. Isocrates includes more than the display of tribute in his list of the arrogant extravagances of imperial Athens. Right after mentioning the display of tribute "talent by talent," he says that "they also led into the theatre the sons of those men who had died in the war." Aeschines describes the ceremony thus:

> when the city had better customs and followed better leaders, the herald would come forward and place before you the orphans whose fathers had died in battle, young men clad in the panoply of war; and he would utter that proclamation so honorable and so incentive to valor: "These young men, whose fathers showed themselves brave men and died in war, have been supported by the state until they have come of age; and now, clad thus in full armor by their fellow citizens, they are sent out with the prayers of the city, to go each his way" *Against Ctesiphon*, 3.154)[97]

Pericles himself makes mention of the practice in the Funeral Oration (2.46.1).

The shields in which the defeated Sicilian city-army placed its tribute might well recall, for readers thinking of the tribute display in Athens, the procession of war orphans and the shields and war panoply in which the orphans paraded,[98] because the defeat of the (now) subject and tribute-paying city-army would create many more such orphans. As Thucydides says, "few out of many returned home" (καὶ ὀλίγοι ἀπὸ πολλῶν ἐπ' οἴκου ἀπενόστησαν, 7.87.6). Thus the resonance back to the tribute display at the Greater Dionysia underscores the loss in Sicily not only in financial, but also in human terms.[99]

[97] Trans. Adams 1919. See Stroud (1971, 288ff) for a discussion of the Athenians' public support of war orphans. The support may go back to Solon and is attested as extant already in the period of 478–462 (*Ath. Pol.* 24.3).

[98] See Goldhill (1990, 105–14) for a description of the practice.

[99] Connor (1984, 208, n. 55) argues that "few out of many" is a final reference back to the Persian wars because it "evokes Darius' ghost in Aeschylus's *Persians* 800, who refers to the survivors of the expedition against Greece as 'few from many' (παῦροί τε πολλῶν)."

Thucydides' comment that "few out of many returned home" is his final statement on Sicily. All that follows in book 7 is the summary line, "these events happened concerning Sicily" (7.87.6). Thucydides' remark serves as the climax to a "pathos intervention," in which Thucydides explains that "this Hellenic event turned out to be the greatest in this war and, as it seems to me, of Hellenic events of which we have heard, most splendid for the victors and most unfortunate for those destroyed" (ξυνέβη τε ἔργον τοῦτο [Ἑλληνικὸν] τῶν κατὰ τὸν πόλεμον τόνδε μέγιστον γενέσθαι, δοκεῖν δ᾽ ἔμοιγε καὶ ὧν ἀκοῇ Ἑλληνικῶν ἴσμεν, καὶ τοῖς τε κρατήσασι λαμπρότατον καὶ τοῖς διαφθαρεῖσι δυστυχέστατον, 7.87.5). As David Gribble remarks, "There is a sense in which all previous climaxes of pathos have been leading up to it."[100] In this climax Thucydides remarks that the Athenians were "utterly defeated in every way . . . in, as the saying is, 'total destruction'" (κατὰ πάντα γὰρ πάντως νικηθέντες . . . πανωλεθρίᾳ δὴ τὸ λεγόμενον, 7.87.6). Thucydides' use of "total destruction" may be an allusion to Herodotus (2.120.5), who says that the gods were "laying plans that, as the Trojans perished in total destruction (πανωλεθρίῃ), they might make this thing manifest to all the world: that for great wrongdoings, great also are the punishments from the gods."[101] If so, with it Thucydides further links the greatness of his theme to both the Persian and the Trojan Wars.[102] With his characterization of the destruction of the fleet-city as "total," Thucydides also links the utter destruction of the city-army in Sicily to the fate of the other destroyed cities of his

[100] Gribble 1998, 52. As Fowler (1989, 91) notes, this is "as clear a closure as one could imagine," including "a formal statement of closure, and generalizing comment in the form of a 'backward look'" and also "unqualified assertion" which, as Smith (1968, 183) explains, indicates that "a point has been reached beyond which nothing further can or will be said."

[101] Strasburger (1958, 39, n. 3), Marinatos Kopf and Rawlings (1978), and Connor (1984, 208, n. 57) explore the possibility that Thucydides intends to suggest a similar divine element to the Athenians' punishment. Rood (1998a) is rightly skeptical.

[102] Cf. Rood (1998a) and also S. Lattimore (1998, 407, *s.v.* 7.87). Mackie (1996, 113) remarks that "by recalling [Herodotus' description of Troy], Thucydides manages to link the destruction of the Athenian forces to that of Troy (and indeed to the Persian expedition)."

work – to Plataea, "razed to its foundation" (3.68.3), to Scione, and to Melos.[103]

Thucydides' final report that "few out of many returned home" also resonates with the city theme and, in devastating brevity, repudiates the city in Sicily. Thucydides writes here with the greatest art and greatest care.[104] That few "returned home" (ἐπ' οἴκου ἀπενόστησαν) underscores that the men of Sicily had real homes that were not in Sicily. Thucydides thereby criticizes the imaginary cities conjured for the Sicilian expedition, the Athenians' fascination for foreign lands in preference to home, and indeed, the Athenians' failure to recognize where their "homeland" truly lay.[105]

Thucydides' emphasis throughout on the Athenians' peculiar ideas of home and homeland makes any reference to "home" important, but especially so in his final comment on a disastrous expedition that saw so many Athenians, who had "yearned for the far off," dying on an expedition that was "the longest voyage from home" (6.31.6). The import

[103] The echo of Troy's destruction gives a final reinforcement to Thucydides' equation of the army in Sicily with a city. Cf. Longo 1975, 103, n. 5. With it, Thucydides also places the city-army in Sicily in the succession of mortal cities that his evocation of Troy implies. Interestingly, with this word, Thucydides also contrasts the fate of the Sicilian city with the final fate of Athens, which was *not* utterly destroyed.

[104] Connor (1984, 208), for example, describes the "contrasting patterns of alliteration" Thucydides uses: "'p' sounds for words indicating much and many and 'o' sounds for negatives and words indicating annihilation . . . until the two extremes merge in a cascade of phrases that combine the two elements and fuse the two alliterative systems."

[105] Thucydides' words here call to mind his account of the failure of the Athenians' adventure in Egypt from which, also, only "few out of many" survived (ὀλίγοι ἀπὸ πολλῶν . . . ἐσώθησαν, 1.110.1). The attempt to conquer Egypt during the *Pentekontaetia* represents, until Sicily, the furthest extent of Athenian ambitions. As Bruell (1981, 26–27) remarks, "as one reads through the [*Pentekontaetia*] as a whole, one finds it increasingly difficult to account for the remarkable range and extent of Athenian expansionist activity . . . by recourse to a concern for the city's safety alone." Egypt, that is, undercuts the Athenians' claims that they were "compelled" to take up their empire out of fear, and shows that glory and advantage were, perhaps, more powerful motivators. The nod to the attempt on Egypt at the end of the Sicilian narrative is perhaps meant to indicate, again, that the impulses that led the Athenians to Sicily are nothing new.

of the phrase is suggested also by the Homeric allusion in the verb "returned home" (ὑπενόστησαν), which "perhaps suggests the sufferings and *nostoi* or 'Returns' from Troy."[106] The "Homeric resonance" no doubt "evokes the emotive force that the idea of *nostos* has in epic: the bitterness of separation from home, the longing for the day of return, the *nostimon emar*, and the joy when that day arrives."[107] Thucydides' use of the phrase, however, has an important difference from Homer's. This verb occurs six times in Homer (four times in the *Iliad* and twice in the *Odyssey*).[108] Homer uses it with the adverb ἄψ meaning "backwards, back again" but feels no need to specify further where the "return" would have gone. Thucydides, by contrast, has used the Homeric verb but added the essentially redundant "homewards" (ἐπ' οἴκου). Thucydides adds the redundant "home" to underscore that the Athenians have lost their return in part by confusing where their home and city lay.

The men of the expedition, as the generals feared, may have hoped to find Sicilian land "homelike." Nicias likened the army to a city from the beginning and urged the men in defeat to believe that they could find a fortress and a fatherland in Sicily. But Demosthenes was right to try to focus the Athenians' attentions on the one city in "their own land." In the end, Thucydides implies here, the men's home and so, too, their city, was in Attica, not Sicily.

[106] Hornblower 1987, 116. Cf. Allison 1997, 512ff.
[107] Rood 1998a.
[108] Cf. Allison 1997, 513: *Il.* 1.60, 8.499, 12.115, 17.406; *Od.* 13.6, 24.471.

4 The Oligarchic City[1]

ALCIBIADES AND THE ATHENIANS REDEFINE THE CITY

After the sustained artistry of the Sicilian books, most readers find what follows anticlimactic at best.[2] This is partly because book 8 is unfinished.[3] Further difficulties are that "the historian had to find a

[1] A version of portions of this chapter appeared in an article in *The Journal for Hellenic Studies* (Taylor 2002). I am grateful to the Society for the Promotion of Hellenic Studies for permission to use that work here.

[2] Cf. J. Finley (1963, 246–47): "Had Thucydides lived to complete his work, he would no doubt have risen to a final climax."

[3] Although L. Strauss (1964, 227, n. 89), Wettergreen (1980, 104–7), Konishi (1987, 5–6), Forde (1989, 171, n. 53), Palmer (1982b, 833; 1992, 139, n. 2), and Munn (2000, 325) have all suggested that the text we have ends where Thucydides wished it to end, most scholars agree that the text is unfinished. Andrewes (in Gomme et al. 1981, 369ff) documents the many peculiarities that have led scholars to argue that book 8 is incomplete and unpolished. More recently, scholars have begun to suggest that the differences between book 8 and the rest of the work may be deliberate. Cf. Macleod (1983a, 141): "its more tentative and less dramatic style may indicate not so much that [Thucydides] had not thought through his material, as that he was seeking new ways of presenting it, and felt he had a different kind of material to present." Gribble (1998, 66) remarks that "the greater fragmentation of book 8 and the increased use of the narratorial voice to mediate between focalisations on relatively unimportant points seems to me more likely to represent a conscious decision for a different type of narrative than evidence of a first draft." Dewald (2005, 144–45) has recently demonstrated "profound structural similarities between the Sicilian books and book viii that indicate . . . that the last five years of the narrative of the *History* are formed on comparable narrative principles."

way of beginning again after so triumphantly concluding his work,"[4] and that the symbolism of the Sicilian disaster, which equated the expedition with a city, means that "the destruction of the expedition is thus emotionally the destruction of Athens itself, and the virtual end of the war."[5] Yet Thucydides warns his reader early on that it is not defeat by any enemy (either Syracusan or Spartan) that destroyed Athens, but *stasis*: "they did not give in," he tells us in the *Epitaph*, "until falling afoul of each other in their private disagreements they were overthrown" (2.65.12). And in his so-called second preface, Thucydides defines the end of his story as the point when "the Lacedaemonians and their allies put an end to the empire of the Athenians and occupied the Long Walls and the Piraeus" (5.26). Thus, despite the emotional high (or low) point of the Sicilian defeat, the reader knows that the Sicilian Expedition was not the end of the war or of Athens. Readers know also that eventually Athens succumbed to *stasis* – to violent disagreement about conflicting ideas of the city.

So far we have been tracing ideas of the city of Athens that have not involved political affiliation and have not (directly, at least) threatened the democratic city in Attica. Many of these ideas have addressed the geographical dimension of the polis, exploring how much the city needs to be grounded in the territory of Attica. Pericles had an expansive idea of the city that abandoned Attica for a city centered on the ships and the empire. In his last speech, Pericles focused great attention on the sea itself. In Sicily, we saw hints of an Athens unmoored from its traditional supports, in the imagery of the expedition as a city itself.[6] The Athenians in Sicily had so freed themselves from any ties to Attica that they could imagine settling in Sicily and finding a city and a "fatherland" there. These Athenians redefined the city in a way that severed it from its traditional home territory; they would seem to have believed that Attica and its land and houses are not essential to Athens. Athens, to be Athens, need not be in Attica.

For Erbse (1989, 66), book 8 is "a masterpiece" and in ways "equivalent if not superior to the best parts of the first seven books."

[4] Macleod 1983a, 141.

[5] Connor 1984, 210.

[6] Thompson (2001, 25) remarks that Thucydides "leaves Athens exposed as the *polis* which cuts off its own moorings."

After the Sicilian Expedition, some Athenians redefined the city to reject another traditional element of Athens – its democracy. Oligarchic conspirators argued, and the people accepted, that Athens, to be Athens, need not be democratic. Modern commentators on book 8 have wrongly stressed the violence and terror in Thucydides' account of events as an explanation of Athens' shift to oligarchy in 411. In truth, Thucydides' presentation of the oligarchic coup in 411 shows that many Athenians in Athens at this time accepted oligarchy quite easily; they judged that democracy was not essential to Athens. Even an oligarchic city could be "the city."

Other Athenians elsewhere, however, disagreed. The Athenians on Samos eventually came to define democracy as *the* essential element of the city, more important even than the men or the walls, buildings, and land in Attica. During the Epidamnian civil war, the men pushed out of the city soon lost the title to the name "Epidamnian" and became simply "the exiles" (1.25.1, 2). The Samian Athenians reject such logic because they reject the importance of the physical location of the city and insist instead on the supreme importance of political affiliation. Pushed out of the city by the war, the men of the fleet reject the idea that the men in Attica have any claim to being the city if they have rejected democracy. Consequently, the Samian Athenians define themselves as the real city and go so far as to propose attacking the false Athens (and the false Athenians) in Attica. Thucydides' presentation of these events is designed to make readers judge the competing claims to being "the city" of these rival Athenses.

A speech Alcibiades gave in Sparta foreshadows the questions on which Thucydides' account of the coup and countercoup of 411 focuses.[7] Alcibiades had fled from his command in Sicily in order to avoid almost certain conviction by a hostile Athenian court on trumped-up charges of having profaned the Mysteries (6.61).[8] He was sentenced to death in abstentia and, while in exile from Athens, fled to Sparta. As an Athenian

[7] This speech is one of the most controversial in the *History*. Yunis (1996, 62, n. 9) lists Alcibiades' speech at Sparta as one of those speeches we should suspect "was never delivered in any form." On the other hand, Forde (1989, 78, n. 9) thinks both of Alcibiades' speeches are authentic.

[8] Alcibiades was accused of participating in irregular and offensive celebrations of the Mysteries of Demeter and Kore carried out in private homes (6.28.2–3).

in Sparta, there to aid the enemy against his own city, Alcibiades apparently felt some need to defend his actions. He insisted that the Spartans really had no cause to think badly of him at all on the following grounds:

> I do not focus my love of the city where I am wronged but where I acted as a citizen in security. Nor do I consider myself now to be proceeding against a fatherland that still exists but rather I consider myself to be recovering one that no longer exists. And the true lover of his city is not the one who does not attack his city when he has lost it unjustly, but the one who, because of his longing, attempts to recover it in any way possible (6.92.4).

Alcibiades, we see, is no traitor. Indeed, in his eyes, treason is impossible, for a man's city is only his city as long as it values and rewards him properly. Once it ceases to do that, it is no longer his city, and a man is entitled to take any action against it to compel it to treat him as he thinks right and thus become his city again – just as he might act against any enemy. In fact, Alcibiades is a patriot because he loves his city – his idea of his city, in which he has the full rights he believes he deserves – so much that he will "attempt to recover it in any way possible." Alcibiades' argument that a man is free – indeed almost compelled – to attack his city "in order to recover it" once it has failed to honor or reward him as he sees fit is a primer for faction fighting that is based upon a dangerous cooption of the ability to conceptualize the city.

Alcibiades here echoes the description the Athenian ambassadors in Sparta before the war gave of Athens' daring actions in the Persian wars. According to the ambassadors, when the Athenians went on board their ships to fight the Persians at Salamis, "we, rising up from a city that no longer existed (ἀπό τε τῆς οὐκ οὔσης ἔτι ὁρμώμενοι), and taking the risk on behalf of a city of which there was only little hope of it existing (καὶ ὑπὲρ τῆς ἐν βραχείᾳ ἐλπίδι οὔσης κινδυνεύοντες), joined together in saving both you and ourselves" (1.74.3). So, Alcibiades claims, he too is fighting to *recover* a fatherland that no longer exists (μᾶλλον τὴν οὐκ οὖσαν ἀνακτᾶσθαι). The grave difference between Alcibiades' comment and that of the Athenian ambassadors, however, is that at Salamis, Athens truly had been abandoned. It did not exist any longer as Athens, because it had been ceded to the Persians. The Athens that Alcibiades claims no longer exists, on the other hand, still remains in Attica, inhabited by (so they would think) Athenians. As Debnar comments, "by asserting that his recovery of his country will restore it politically, [Alcibiades] implies that it is not the Athenians, but he himself who makes the city."[9] But this is the position of any factioneer. He claims the right to define the city according to the characteristics he chooses no matter what other (in his eyes former) members of the city might think.

At Epidamnus, only the Epidamnians in the city and not the exiles retained the name of "the Epidamnians." According to Alcibiades, however, it is he, the exile, who claims to define (perhaps even to be) the city (despite what those so-called Athenians in Athens might think). The issues – as they will be also in Thucydides' account of the introduction and defeat of oligarchy in Athens – are geography and political affiliation and the underlying question of what defines the essential characteristics of the city. Alcibiades and the Samian Athenians reject the primacy of geography, or, to put it another way, they reject the primacy of Attica over other territories that might be the city.

In the next two chapters we will be examining two interrelated and surprising elements in Thucydides' account of the *stasis* of 411. First, in Thucydides' presentation, no one either in Athens or on Samos initially cares much about democracy. Indeed, Thucydides stresses how little resistance the Athenians made to oligarchy. Furthermore, of the Athenians discussed, those in Attica cared about democracy least. Thucydides' presentation of the rise of the Four Hundred in Athens is consistently unfavorable to the democrats. He paints them as weak, passive, and little attached to their democracy. In their passivity (and weak connection to democracy), the Athenians in Athens do not look like traditional Athenians. Second, as we will see in chapter 5, when they eventually return to democracy, the Athenians in Samos abuse the men in Attica for abandoning democracy and claim that in doing so, they are no longer really Athenian. Because they privilege political affiliation above all else, the Samian Athenians claim that their community on Samos is the real Athens, not that oligarchic city in Attica. The narrative, that is, continues to raise the question of the ultimate definition of the city. Must

[9] Debnar 2001, 212. Cf. Palmer (1982a, 1992, 99): "Alcibiades consistently acts in his relations with the Athenians, the Spartans, and the Persians as though he were himself a city."

the Athens in Attica be Athens or, if other characteristics are privileged, can Samos be Athens?

The Athenians in Attica lose their right to be Athens, according to the men in Samos, because of their oligarchic sympathies and their weak attachment to democracy. However, of the coup in Athens, Thucydides says outright that

> it was a difficult matter, in approximately the hundredth year after the tyrants were deposed, to put an end to the liberty of the Athenian *demos*, a people which was not only not subject to anyone but which also for over half this time was itself accustomed to rule others (8.68.4).

Thucydides' use of the words "put an end to their liberty" (ἐλευθερίας παῦσαι) suggests an oppressive takeover much against the will of the majority of the Athenian people, and this is how his narrative is usually understood. Moses Finley, for example, claims that Thucydides' text shows that the Four Hundred came to power in "a classic mixture of terror and propaganda."[10] However, although revolution, terror, and propaganda have their place in Thucydides, his narrative gives a much more nuanced picture of the rise of oligarchy than is usually recognized. In fact, Thucydides takes great care to charge the Athenian people themselves with a large share of responsibility for the oligarchy. Some embraced it outright for the sake of money. Others accepted it with only a token reluctance. Thucydides shows few, if any, resisting oligarchy and defending the traditional regime. Despite Thucydides' explicit statement, his text demonstrates that it was not, in fact, particularly "difficult" to end the democracy in Athens.

Thucydides' statement about the "difficulty" of introducing oligarchy in Athens is curious because, as we shall see, his narrative shows that it wasn't actually very difficult at all. It is curious for another reason as well. When Thucydides writes (ironically, as the narrative shows) that it was difficult to put an end to the Athenians' liberty, he seems to equate "freedom" with democracy. Chapter 8.68 begins with Peisander, whom

[10] M. Finley 1971, 4. He is echoed by Kagan (1987, 145) who reads Thucydides' account as a "coup by means of terror, force and deceit." Andrewes (in Gomme et al. 1981, 255) speaks of a "genuinely revolutionary coup." Price (2001, 310) mentions "violence, threats and deception."

Thucydides describes as "in general the most zealous open proponent of doing away with the democracy" (ξυγκαταλύσας τὸν δῆμον). After a survey of the abilities of Peisander's co-conspirators in oligarchy, the chapter ends with Thucydides' comment about putting an end to the liberty of the Athenian people. Thucydides thus seems to equate the end of democracy with the end of the Athenians' freedom. This is surprising because such a use of "freedom" is inconsistent with his usage of the word elsewhere; ἐλευθερία generally means a state's freedom from outside control in Thucydides. A strain of political discourse equates "freedom" with democracy, of course,[11] but that is the rhetoric of factioneers and not a judgment that a supporter of moderate oligarchy would agree with. Yet, difficult as commentators have found it to ascertain the nuances of Thucydides' own political leanings, he hardly seems a rabid democrat.[12] Thucydides, then, includes in his account of the narrative of the coup of 411 an authorial statement that not only misrepresents the difficulty of the oligarchic "coup" but also uncharacteristically uses *stasis* rhetoric that suggests democracy is essential to the free city.

This curious comment highlights elements of particular interest in the story of the introduction of oligarchy: First, it points out how easy it actually was to end democracy in Athens, and second, it asks how important democracy really was (and how important it ought to be) to the idea of Athens. As we will see in chapter 5, the Athenians on Samos come to believe democracy is essential (more essential, certainly, than mere geography) and so define themselves as Athens. On the other hand, democracy had much less importance, Thucydides insists, among the Athenians in Athens (and, at first, even among those on Samos). Thucydides' emphasis on how little attached to democracy the Athenians in Athens were is important because it undercuts the Samian

[11] See, e.g., Aristotle *Pol.* 1291b, 35–36: "for assuming that freedom [ἐλευθερία] is chiefly found in a democracy, as some persons suppose, and also equality, this would be so most fully when to the fullest extent all alike share equally in the government." (trans. Rackham 1932) or the "Old Oligarch" ([Xen] *Ath. Pol.*) 1.8: "For the people do not want a good government under which they themselves are slaves; they want to be free and to rule (ἐλεύθερος εἶναι καὶ ἄρχειν, trans. Bowersock 1968).

[12] Ober (1998) has recently located Thucydides among elite dissenters from democracy.

Athenians' argument that democracy is essential to Athens. This is an easier argument to put forth if most Athenians were terrified by violence and propaganda into voting for oligarchy. It is much harder to make if they put up little resistance in defense of their ancestral constitution. As Thucydides shows us there was little resistance; the introduction of oligarchy was *not* difficult.

"THE CROWD WAS UPSET FOR THE MOMENT"

The story begins, fittingly enough, with that great patriot Alcibiades. Having lost his Spartan refuge, Alcibiades had fled to Tissaphernes, the Persian *satrap*, or provincial governor, of the coastal region of Asia minor. Soon, however, Alcibiades' position with Tissaphernes grew precarious and he wanted to return to Athens – but not to the Athens that had condemned and exiled him in abstentia. Alcibiades' goal, as he told his earlier collaborators the Spartans, was to "recover a fatherland that no longer exists" (6.92.4). For Alcibiades to return to Athens, however, Athens had to change. Therefore he sent messages to the Athenians with the fleet on Samos and told them that "he was willing to return home, to provide Tissaphernes as a friend to them and to live with them as a fellow-citizen if it was in an oligarchy and not in the base democracy that had exiled him" (ἐπ᾽ ὀλιγαρχίᾳ βούλεται καὶ οὐ πονηρίᾳ οὐδὲ δημοκρατίᾳ τῇ αὐτὸν ἐκβαλούσῃ κατελθών, 8.47.2).

Alcibiades made his proposal to "the most powerful men" in the fleet, with instructions to make it known to "the best men," and it was the trierarchs and the "most powerful men" that Thucydides says then set themselves to destroying the democracy (8.47.2). But the movement was not for long confined to the upper classes or the elite, who might be thought to be naturally sympathetic to oligarchy. After various individuals went to discuss matters with Alcibiades and formed a party from "the right people" (τοὺς ἐπιτηδείους), they "openly said to the multitude that the king would be their friend and would provide funds for the war if Alcibiades were brought back from exile and they were no longer governed by a democracy" (ἐς τοὺς πολλοὺς φανερῶς ἔλεγον ὅτι βασιλεὺς σφίσι φίλος ἔσοιτο καὶ χρήματα παρέξοι Ἀλκιβιάδου τε κατελθόντος καὶ μὴ δημοκρατουμένων, 8.48.2). In Thucydides' presentation there is no propaganda or deceit. Those supporting the proposal explained it openly to the masses. Thucydides soon reiterates the point, noting that "those working for the oligarchy considered Alcibiades' proposals among themselves and the majority of their band after they had communicated them to the crowd of troops" (ἐπειδὴ τῷ πλήθει ἐκοίνωσαν, 8.48.3).

The movement to oligarchy begins as no hidden plot. There is neither "terror" nor "propaganda" in this first act of the rise of the oligarchy of the Four Hundred; the initial conspirators of Thucydides' text present the proposal to the troops without duplicity. The leaders of the movement do not specifically mention oligarchy, but they show no hesitation in informing the men that the end of the democracy is a precondition of their scheme (8.48.2).[13] Thucydides depicts no tiptoeing around the real issue. Rather than indicating that fraud was involved, Thucydides emphasizes the openness of the oligarchic leaders' initial appeal to the troops. Thucydides' narrative suggests, quite simply, that the leaders of the movement expected no difficulty from the men. His text soon confirms that they were right.

Consider how the masses react to the plan: "As for the crowd, even if it was upset for the moment at what was being done, because of the satisfying hope of pay from the king, it calmed down" (καὶ ὁ μὲν ὄχλος, εἰ καί τι παραυτίκα ἤχθετο τοῖς πρασσομένοις, διὰ τὸ εὔπορον τῆς ἐλπίδος τοῦ παρὰ βασιλέως μισθοῦ ἡσύχαζεν, 8.48.3). Of this passage, Connor comments that it encourages "something close to disdain of democracy."[14] Whether Thucydides meant to encourage disdain of a constitutional system in his readers or not, he surely meant them

[13] Kagan (1987, 121), citing McCoy (1970), points out that "there was no use of the word *oligarchy*" in the presentation to the troops. He thus suggests that deceit did have a role to play in the plan, and that the leaders of the movement could not have expected Athenian sailors, the backbone of democracy, to accept an openly oligarchic proposal. But Thucydides' narrative does not support Kagan's reading. It is true that the word oligarchy itself is not used in front of the troops, but it is hardly more delicate to say (as they did) that "Alcibiades will bring us money from the king if we are not ruled by a democracy" than to say that "Alcibiades will bring us money from the king if we are ruled by an oligarchy."

[14] Connor 1984, 227.

to be struck by the feelings of the men of the fleet. As Thucydides presents them, these Athenians have little love for the rights and privileges of democracy, because their heads have been turned by the sound of money. These men do not equate democracy with freedom. Kagan charges that Thucydides' explanation here is "tendentious." These men, he writes, "had stronger motives than greed for being willing to consider even unwelcome proposals late in 412 and to think such unthinkable thoughts as were being proposed to them. The salvation of their city was at issue."[15] This is perfectly true. After the failure of the Sicilian Expedition and the revolt of much of the empire, the Athenians were in desperate need of money to fund the war they deemed crucial to Athens' existence. But Kagan's defense of the men only highlights how differently Thucydides draws the picture. In Thucydides' text, Kagan's "unthinkable thoughts" are quite easily thought; the men are upset "for the moment" (παραυτίκα) only. As Kagan himself points out, Thucydides' men seem motivated by simple greed. [16]

Thucydides deliberately crafts the episode to emphasize the men's love for money and suggest that they have little love for anything else. No one opposes the oligarchic proposals for longer than a "moment." The crowd of sailors were upset only for the moment, because they were reassured by the prospect of money from the king. The implication is that this mass of men cares little about ideology, office holding, or voting rights in the assembly – they care only about pay. If they are to receive that money for serving democratic offices or for military duty in the service of a prosperous democracy, that is well and good, but if the coffers of the democracy have gone empty, these men are perfectly happy to receive their pay from the Persian king through the middle man of an oligarchic Athens. They have been away from home for a long time and can expect to be away from home for even longer. What do they care, practically, about democracy, the franchise, payment for office holding, et cetera, as long as they can get their pay for serving in the fleet? Thucydides implies that the war has made democracy superfluous

[15] Kagan 1987, 121.

[16] Kallet (2001, 263) writes of this crowd, "as Thucydides portrays it, their desire for money outweighed their fear of the potential for damage and danger within the polis if Alcibiades were restored." Cf. Greenwood (2006, 94): "the crews are prepared to 'sell out' on democracy."

for these men. This overturns the traditional association between naval power and democracy. As Gomme noted about the Long Walls, their creation of an Athens "dependent on the sea" signaled in Athens "the permanent domination of the democracy."[17] Yet these sailors do not seem to follow the calculus that Athens' dependence on their labor on the ships means that they deserve a great say in Athens' governance. Naval powers, it seems, do not have to be democracies.

This passage also undercuts the connection between democracy and Athens. Thucydides' text, of course, closely links democracy with Athens and suggests in a number of places that during the course of the war, Athens tended (whether intentionally or not) to export its system to its allies. In his Funeral Oration, for example, Pericles proudly called Athens' democratic system of government a "model" for its neighbors (παράδειγμα δὲ μᾶλλον αὐτοὶ ὄντες τισὶν ἢ μιμούμενοι ἑτέρους, 2.37.1). When Thucydides discusses the courses of *stasis* throughout the war, he describes how the Peloponnesians and the Athenians extended their influence around the Greek world by each supporting factioneers of their own political persuasion in various civil conflicts (3.82.1). Diodotus, in the Mytilene debate, claimed that in all cities the democratic element was friendly to Athens and urged a course on the Athenians that would not alienate the democrats of the Greek world (3.47). When the Thebans coined the term "atticize" in the trial of the Plataeans, they surely had in mind the idea that Athens was trying (at Plataea and elsewhere) to export its peculiar government and way of life. As Cogan wrote, "'Atticism' was an ideology that *other* cities might believe."[18] Thespiae lost its walls because it atticized, and the democrat Tydeus in Chios was killed on a charge of atticism (8.38.3). It is, then, extremely interesting that the sailors of the city that was so associated with democracy that it seemed able to "infect" other states with the same political position should themselves so easily contemplate switching sides. Far from causing others to atticize, these Athenian sailors themselves will no longer atticize. The Thebans' coinage of "atticize" and "atticism" implies an essential connection between Athens and democracy. The Athenian sailors' reaction to the oligarchic proposals severs that connection. If

[17] Gomme 1945, *s.v.* 1.107.4.
[18] Cogan 1981a, 72. Italics Cogan.

democracy is essential to Athens, the war has destroyed that Athens, or at least these men no longer see the connection.

The ease and speed with which, according to Thucydides, the men of the fleet accept the oligarchic proposals is impressive – impressive enough to cause some commentators to write it out of their narratives. Andrewes, for example, misrepresents the situation, writing that "Alcibiades' proposals were put to the men of the fleet, who disliked the prospect of oligarchy but did not mutiny."[19] Andrewes does not describe Thucydides' men, however; the men Thucydides pictures might well mutiny over back pay, but not over changes to the democracy. [20]

Commentators write out the fleet's easy acceptance of oligarchy because of its implication for all of Athens. Kagan, for example, argues that the oligarchic movement's beginning on Samos rather than in Athens is "evidence of the powerful general support for the traditional full democracy. . . ."[21] On the contrary, the "crowd" (ὁ μὲν ὄχλος), the sailors in the fleet, will have been mostly *thetes*, members of the lowest property class in Athens. As such, they would be likely to be disenfranchised by any oligarchy.[22] They should vigorously defend the democracy if they perceive it to hold many benefits for them. That these lower-class sailors accept oligarchy so easily suggests that they see no such benefits and hints that Athenians of higher status, who might expect both to

[19] Andrewes, 1992, 471. So Shipley (1987, 123) claims that the men "reluctantly accepted the establishment of an oligarchy in Athens," but Thucydides shows little reluctance among them.

[20] McCoy (1973, 80) ignores the role of the sailors altogether. In his narrative, "influential" men go to Alcibiades to confer with him. Then a "conspiracy (*xynomosia*) of 'suitable' persons" met "in private" to study Alcibiades' proposals, and "the conspirators" vote to send Peisander to Athens. McCoy does not mention that in Thucydides, the ringleaders spoke of their plans "openly" (8.47.2), so "conspiracy" and "conspirators" and meetings "in private" are allowed to imply that the masses were kept in the dark.

[21] Kagan 1987, 112. He makes this claim partly because he believes that the critical core supporters of the movement on Samos were upper-class men of hoplite status. However, this reading is not supported by the text. See Taylor 2002, n. 23. See also Amit 1962, 173–74.

[22] The *thetes* were probably denied the franchise even in the moderate oligarchy of the Five Thousand instituted after the fall of the Four Hundred. See Rhodes 1972.

retain their civic rights and gain more political power in an oligarchy, would accept that system even more easily. Thucydides emphasizes how easily the sailors abandon democracy and so raises doubts in his readers about the commitment to democracy of the rest of the Athenians. The movement's beginnings on Samos are a powerful sign of the lack of support for democracy in Athens. As Thucydides' narrative shows, once the conspirators widened their plot, the oligarchs encountered no more difficulty with the Athenians in Attica than with those on Samos.

Once the sailors on Samos were committed to oligarchy, the next step was to bring Athens itself over to oligarchy, for the aim of Alcibiades was not merely to lead the fleet but to "recover a fatherland that no longer existed" (6.92.4) and lead in Athens. Thus the generals on Samos began to plot how to effect the political change in Athens. Only the general Phrynichus was skeptical of Alcibiades' motives, his influence with Tissaphernes, and the practicality of the plans, so he counseled against the plot. Furthermore, he urged the Athenians to consider that "for the Athenians this above all must be guarded against – that they not devolve into *stasis*" (περιοπτέον εἶναι τοῦτο μάλιστα, ὅπως μὴ στασιάσωσιν, 8.48.4). As Thucydides shows, Phrynichus' reading of Alcibiades turned out to be entirely correct. Thus, like Nicias earlier in the work, Phrynichus serves as a warner figure who alone can see what is coming. Only he of the Athenians on Samos argued against the proposed faction fighting, and he alone appears as something resembling a statesman. His opposition to *stasis* suggests that he has a loyalty to an Athens beyond Alcibiades' petty concerns about his own position there and beyond even the question of its political constitution. It is a supreme irony, then, that when the Athenians ignored his advice and prepared to send Peisander and others to Athens to negotiate for the recall of Alcibiades and the overthrow of the democracy, Phrynichus was ready to betray his city in a shockingly direct way. Afraid that Alcibiades would, in fact, be recalled to Athens and fearful that he would face retaliation for speaking against the idea, Phrynichus sent a message to the Spartans warning that Alcibiades was plotting against them to make Tissaphernes help the Athenians (8.50). When this letter was revealed to Alcibiades and, through him, to the forces on Samos, Phrynichus then wrote to the Spartans and gave them detailed instructions on how to attack and destroy the Athenian forces on Samos. Thus the one man who originally spoke against the destruction of the Athenian democracy and faction fighting of any sort was revealed as no less self-serving than that "patriot for himself," Alcibiades.[23]

This narrative raises the question of whether any Athenians still subordinated themselves and their concerns to their city. This had once been one of their conspicuous traits. The Corinthians at Sparta, for example, warned the Peloponnesians about their enemy and said of the Athenians that "they use their bodies for their city's sake as if they were not their own" (1.70.6). And Pericles in the Funeral Oration made a radically new presentation of, in Clifford Orwin's words, "the centrality to human life of citizenship in a city now conceived as primary, over and against both the family and piety."[24] Phrynichus' switch from being the only statesman to argue against *stasis* to being willing to hand his city over to the enemy raises the question of whether any Athenians recognized the primacy of their city anymore or whether all, like Alcibiades, recognized only a city that especially benefited themselves.[25]

THE PEOPLE IN ATHENS DO NOT RESIST

Thucydides' presentation of the response in Athens to the oligarchic machinations does not calm the readers' worries. Thucydides consistently paints the Athenians as apathetic and weak, little devoted to democratic Athens and as greedy and self-serving as Phrynichus or Alcibiades. After the fleet at Samos accepted the switch to oligarchy, the leaders of the movement sent Peisander with an embassy to Athens to present the plan to the citizen body in an assembly (8.53–54). Thucydides takes a little more than a paragraph to describe the Athenians' reaction to Peisander's proposal up to the point when they "gave in"

[23] The quoted phrase is from the title of Pouncey's (1980) chapter on Alcibiades. There is symbolism in Phrynichus' letter. Steiner (1994, 227) notes that "writing is a symbol used by the sources to identify both the mythical and historical opponents of Athenian democracy" (citing Loraux 1981/1986, 184–85).

[24] Orwin (1994, 15, n. 1), citing Edmunds 1975, 44–70.

[25] Cf. Palmer (1989, 372–73): "Book 8 presents a picture of Athenian domestic politics in which the 'Alcibiadean' understanding of patriotism . . . rules supreme."

and voted to send ten men to negotiate the matter with Alcibiades and Tissaphernes. This paragraph is crucial to our understanding of the introduction of oligarchy in Athens. Many commentators find in it elements of deceit and Athenian resistance that are not, in fact, present. Especially because we must see this absence, it is necessary that we examine the passage (almost) in full. Here is Thucydides' account:

The ambassadors of the Athenians sent out with Peisander from Samos arrived in Athens and made speeches to the people, summarizing the major points and particularly that if they recalled Alcibiades from exile and did not live under the same kind of democracy it would be possible for them to have the king as an ally and to overcome the Peloponnesians. When many people spoke out in opposition concerning democracy . . . Peisander, coming forward in the face of a great deal of opposition and indignation, led aside each one of the men opposing the plan. He asked each if he had any hope for the salvation of the city if someone does not persuade the king to switch sides to them, since the Peloponnesians have no fewer ships ready for action at sea than they do and have more cities allied to them and have the king and Tissaphernes providing them funds, but none existed for themselves. And when those questioned said "No," then he said straight out to them that "This is not possible for us unless we administer the *polis* more sensibly and put the offices more into the hands of the few so that the king will trust us, and do not deliberate more about the government now than about our salvation (for it will also be possible later for us to change it if something does not please us) and unless we recall Alcibiades who alone of men now is able to effect all this." The people at first did not receive the proposal concerning oligarchy well but after being clearly instructed by Peisander that there was no other salvation, being afraid and also buoyed up by the hope that it would be altered, they gave in (8.53–54.1).

For some commentators, the particular words Peisander used in this assembly free the Athenians from responsibility for the switch to oligarchy. The Athenian majority, they contend, did not understand that Peisander was proposing an oligarchy. For example, Thucydides says that Peisander told the assembly that "they could have the king as an ally and win the war against the Peloponnesians if they recalled Alcibiades from exile and did not live under the same kind of democracy" (Ἀλκιβιάδην καταγαγοῦσι καὶ μὴ τὸν αὐτὸν τρόπον δημοκρατουμένοις). Later, Peisander told the people that aid from the king was impossible "unless we administer the *polis* more sensibly and put the offices more into the hands of a few" (εἰ μὴ πολιτεύσομεν τε σωφρονέστερον καὶ ἐς ὀλίγους μᾶλλον τὰς ἀρχὰς ποιήσομεν). The argument is that Thucydides represents Peisander here as guilty of deliberate fraud because he attempted to hide that what he hoped to institute was an oligarchy.[26]

This reading privileges Peisander's first statement, when he says the democracy must not be "of the same kind" and so implies that the state will still in some way be a democracy, over his second, when he says the Athenians must administer the *polis* "more sensibly" and "put the offices more into the hands of the few." But despite Peisander's implication about the continued existence of the democracy, and even despite his careful qualifier that the Athenians would put offices only "more" and not wholly into the hands of the few, even the dimmest of Athenians must have heard the roots of oligarchy (*oligarchia*) in the phrase "put the offices (*tas archas*) more into the hands of the few" (*es oligous*). To give only the few the power to rule is, after all, the definition of oligarchy. Kagan, however, mutes this clause when he says of Peisander's second statement about sensible government and putting the offices more into the hands of the few that "the second clause appeared to explain the first in a way that made the project seem even less threatening. The implication was that the democracy would remain the same in all respects, except that there would be a limitation on office holding."[27] Kagan puts his faith in, and argues that the Athenians believed without question, Peisander's implication that the democracy would remain in some form. Furthermore, Kagan specifies that except for the limitation on office holding, "the democracy would remain the same in all respects."[28] Peisander, of course, was deliberately vague about how much "the same" the government would stay.

[26] Lintott (1982, 136), for example, says that Peisander used "vague and soothing phrases." Price (2001, 306) speaks of "euphemism." Kagan (1987, 131–32), building on his contention that the initial appeal to the troops on Samos had suppressed the use of the word "oligarchy," claims that here, "the terms used to describe the change in mode of government were even less alarming than before." Cf. McCoy 1973, 82.

[27] Kagan 1987, 133.

[28] Andrewes (in Gomme et al. 1981, *s.v.* 8.53.3) agrees, claiming that Peisander "suggests a system in which the assembly would retain its powers and existing membership." Westlake (1989, 185) goes even further, asserting that Peisander "conveyed the impression that the proposed constitution would not involve any fundamental change."

Peisander, in fact, does not say most of what commentators claim for him, nor is it likely that the majority of Athenians had faith that it really lay behind his words. In fact, after Thucydides says that Peisander told the Athenians they could have Alcibiades and the king as an ally if they "did not live under the same kind of democracy," he notes that "many people spoke out in opposition concerning democracy" (ἀντιλεγόντων δὲ πολλῶν καὶ ἄλλων περὶ τῆς δημοκρατίας). This strongly implies that the Athenians knew perfectly well that what was at stake was "the democracy." Given the paucity of information that Thucydides' Peisander provides about his plan, only the most credulous listener, and one none too careful with his constitution, would vote for the proposal based on faith that "the democracy would remain the same in all respects." At the very least, someone might have asked how much "more" into the hands of the few the offices would be placed. Thus, even if the popular reading were credible, Thucydides' text would brand the Athenians as none too bright and far from vigilant in defense of their democracy.

Thucydides' narrative, however, specifically denies that the Athenians were confused about the substance of Peisander's proposal. First, Thucydides says that Peisander "spoke straight out" (σαφῶς ἔλεγεν) when he told the Athenians that they had to "put the offices more into the hands of the few" (8.53.3). Thucydides' phrase (σαφῶς ἔλεγεν) means "spoke clearly, plainly, distinctly, accurately." Thus, rather than emphasizing any deceit in Peisander's presentation, Thucydides leads readers to believe that Peisander was straightforward in describing his plan. Furthermore, Thucydides himself labels this proposal oligarchic. After his description of the assembly, Thucydides says that "the people at first did not receive the proposal concerning oligarchy well" (ὁ δὲ δῆμος τὸ μὲν πρῶτον ἀκούων χαλεπῶς ἔφερε τὸ περὶ τῆς ὀλιγαρχίας). Especially because of Thucydides' explicit statement that Peisander spoke clearly to the people, I read these words to mean that the people responded poorly at first to a proposal that they perceived to be about oligarchy.[29]

[29] Andrewes agrees (in Gomme et al. 1981, *s.v.* 8.54.1) that "Thucydides thought that they understood what was at issue." Price (2001, 307) concurs: "The public understood the meaning of [have a democratic government in] 'a different manner' and did not take it well." Kagan (1987, 133), however, believes that the majority of Athenians were befuddled about the oligarchic nature

Nevertheless, persuaded by Peisander's arguments, they eventually gave in.

The Athenians in Athens, then, although more reluctantly than those on Samos, ultimately voted to accept Peisander's proposal knowing full well that they were voting for oligarchy – not the limited oligarchy they eventually got, of course, but oligarchy nevertheless. They were not deceived. How, then, does Thucydides say Peisander persuaded the Athenians to abandon their one hundred year old democracy? How difficult a job did Peisander have?

It was certainly not as easy a sell as it was on Samos. The Athenians were reluctant. Thucydides mentions their opposition three times and says it was great.[30] He says that "Peisander came forward "in the face of a great deal of opposition and indignation" (πρὸς πολλὴν ἀντιλογίαν καὶ σχετλιασμὸν). The Athenians did not embrace Peisander's proposal but only "gave in" (ἐνέδωκεν) to what he argued was the inevitable. But as we shall see, Thucydides nevertheless insists that it was not really all that hard to get the Athenians to abandon their democracy.

Consider the reasons why the Athenians gave in, according to Thucydides. First, Peisander said that the Athenians could return their constitution to its present form later, if they wanted. Thucydides has already shown that Peisander had no expectation that the Athenians would be able to do this, so Peisander is clearly guilty of deceit here. Nevertheless, Thucydides tells us explicitly that the Athenians believed him. Andrewes correctly characterizes this as "surprising innocence when we remember their usual suspicion about tyranny and oligarchy. . . ."[31] So Thucydides includes a detail that shows the Athenians to have been remarkably naive.

In addition, Thucydides says that the Athenians gave in because of their fears and because they were clearly taught by Peisander that there

of Peisander's expressed intentions. Thucydides, according to Kagan, "must be referring to those listeners who understood what lay behind the ambiguity of [being governed] 'more sensibly' but surely not to the majority, for the assembly as a whole accepted Peisander's arguments." That is, the fact that the majority accepted Peisander's proposal proves that the majority did not understand his meaning. Rather, they understood it and simply did not care that much

30 8.53.2 (bis), 8.54.1.

31 Andrewes in Gomme et al. 1981, *s.v.* 8.53.3.

was no other way out. Subsequent events, however, when the Athenians retrieved their position without Persian aid, demonstrate that there was another way out, that Peisander was wrong, and that the people were too quick to believe that they had been well taught. There is more than a little irony in Thucydides' comment that the Athenians gave in only after they were "clearly instructed by Peisander."

Thucydides has also shaped his description of the assembly to characterize the Athenians as easy converts to oligarchy. For example, Thucydides explains the Athenians' decision in one quick sentence (8.54.1). When he says the Athenians "at first" received Peisander's proposal about oligarchy badly, the momentum of the sentence is already hurtling toward their acceptance. The effect is to diminish the weight of their opposition, to make it seem short-lived and weak. Furthermore, just as at Samos, Thucydides silences the voices of those opposed to oligarchy. He says the opposition was great, but he does not show this to the reader. He gives no impassioned defense of the existing order; no one argues that the democracy can still win the war without Alcibiades and without Persian aid. Indeed, Thucydides gives Peisander's opponents no names and virtually no words. Only Peisander gets to declaim. All the opposition can muster is a muttered "No" to his question about whether there is any other salvation for them.[32] But, as Andrewes notes, "Athenian demagogues were not usually so easy to silence." Thucydides has made Peisander's opponents seem lifeless and weak. Despite Thucydides' words about opposition, the passage makes it seem that in Athens, as on Samos, there are no committed democrats at all.[33]

[32] McCoy (1973, 81) claims that Peisander "took the objectors aside one by one" and (n. 11) spoke "privately" with them. He thus furthers his claim of secrecy in the oligarchs' dealings. McCoy presumably bases his claim on Thucydides' report that Peisander "led forward each one of his objectors." But as Andrewes (in Gomme et al. 1981, *s.v.* 8.53.2) notes, this means "'calls them forward' individually . . . and questions them, much as a speaker in a lawcourt may interrogate his opponent during his speech (eg. Pl. *Apol.* 24cff)." It is no indication of secrecy.

[33] Andrewes (in Gomme et al. 1981, *s.v.* 8.53.2) recognizes that "the scene has been dramatized" but denies that Thucydides was the playwright, because (373) he believes that parts of book 8 consist of Thucydides' transcriptions of his informants' reports in his own "characteristically complex style" but from their point of view, not his own. In Andrewes' opinion (*s.v.* 8.53.2), Peisander's

There is a final argument in Peisander's presentation to the assembly that may have swayed even committed democrats to accept oligarchy, however. Peisander said that the Athenians needed to take care not to "deliberate more about the government now than about our salvation" (καὶ μὴ περὶ πολιτείας τὸ πλέον βουλεύσομεν ἐν τῷ παρόντι ἢ περὶ σωτηρίας, 8.53.3). Here Peisander gets to the heart of a man's relation to and definition of his city. At Sparta, Alcibiades had claimed that if his city did not treat him right or grant him proper benefits or glory, a man could, indeed should, attack it to return it to a form that would do so and that he could then recognize as his own. Here Peisander seems to speak on a higher plane. He distinguishes the city from its political persuasion, suggesting that there is an existence, a definition to the city, that transcends political identification. He would seem to argue that Athens is not by nature democratic; democracy is not essential to Athens. This means that Athens can still be Athens even if its government is oligarchic and, most importantly, that men who are staunch supporters of democracy should nevertheless acquiesce to an oligarchic regime if therein lies the survival of the city. They should not oppose a plan for survival just because the city that survives is not democratic.[34]

A reader's response to this argument is necessarily complex. On one hand, if followed it would end factional warfare in a city. Second, this is the very argument that the Athenians themselves used on Melos. They insisted again and again that the Melians must focus on nothing

tour de force in the assembly represents a provisional account written from the point of view of an oligarchic extremist exile who "relished describing to Thucydides how Peisander had routed the demagogues." Andrewes recognizes the antidemocratic tenor of the passage but attributes it to an unspecified oligarchic informant whom Thucydides has mindlessly parroted. This strikes me as unlikely. I agree that book 8 is unfinished, but that does not mean that all of it is unpolished and provisional, nor do I think the hypothesis that book 8 is incomplete somehow negates Thucydides' presentation and characterization of the Athenians. The tenor of this passage is consistent with Thucydides' characterization of the Athenians on Samos and elsewhere in the book and we should, therefore, reclaim this passage as Thucydides' own work. For Erbse (1989, 14), this scene is "in no way provisional; it is masterly."

34 This is, in fact, the argument that Kagan (1987, 121) uses to explain away the acceptance of oligarchy by the fleet.

but their city's salvation (5.87, 91.2, 101, 105.4, 111.2, using the same word for salvation employed here). Freedom and honor (and, presumably, political affiliation) must be secondary.

On the other hand, Peisander's argument is linked intimately with his deliberately deceitful (although not ultimately incorrect) argument that the Athenians can change their constitution back to a democracy later if they want to. This must taint his argument about the salvation of the city. Furthermore, Peisander's reasoning makes an ominous echo back to the model factioneers on Corcyra. There Thucydides tells us that when the democrats feared that the Peloponnesians would take advantage of their internal confusion to sail against the city or make some other bold attack, they entered into negotiations with the oligarchs "so that the city might be saved" (ὅπως σωθήσεται ἡ πόλις, 3.80.1), just as Peisander urged the Athenians to take counsel for their salvation (περὶ σωτηρίας). The similar situations and the use of words of similar root encourage readers of Athens' *stasis* to look to Corcyra for help in evaluating Peisander's argument. The Corcyran democrats succeeded in persuading some oligarchs to fight with them, and they all went "on board ship" to fight their foreign enemies. Thucydides' use of that Athenian catch-phrase further encourages a comparison with Athens and Peisander.

On Corcyra, we recall, as soon as the danger from the enemy was past, the Corcyran democrats slaughtered the men they had persuaded to "save" the city with them and thus revealed that with the external threat neutralized, they shared no vision of the city with their internal oligarchic enemies. This echo seems to brand Peisander's argument about a transcendent city whose survival is of the highest importance a crafty lie.

Should, then, the Athenians in assembly have cried out in response to Peisander, "No. Athens, my Athens, is a democracy, and the survival of the city under any other system would be just the form with no substance. To keep Athens a democracy, to keep my city, as I understand it, alive, I will fight you"? Or is that not the position of Alcibiades? Thucydides does not answer these questions here, but they are integral to his work. When Peisander says the Athenians must think of the survival of the city, not its constitutional form, Thucydides' text, which has focused throughout on the changing definition of Athens in the war, urges readers to ask, "the survival of whose city?"

At the same time, Thucydides' text urges the reader to wonder at these Athenians, for Thucydides' entire description of Peisander's first visit to Athens paints an unfavorable portrait of the Athenian democrats. They "give in" to their fears and to arguments soon shown to be false, and so sacrifice their constitution to their salvation too easily and before it is necessary. They credulously believe soothing but disingenuous promises that they can easily undo what they are doing. Finally, they mount no direct defense of their democracy; no one at the crucial assembly has a quotable word to say in its favor.[35] This characterization of the Athenians in Athens dovetails with that of the men on Samos, who cared not about democracy but only about their pay. Neither group, according to Thucydides, made Peisander's work very difficult, and neither group was very careful of its liberty, if liberty equals democracy.[36]

THE ASSEMBLY DOES NOT RESIST

The characterization of the *demos* as (at best) weak supporters of democracy continues as Thucydides moves into his account of the oligarchic conspirators' next steps. In this phase of the coup of 411, the oligarchs used violence and intimidation against the Athenians. It is clear, therefore, that they expected and met resistance to their plans. However, Thucydides' presentation shows that the oligarchs did not face as

[35] Although she does not see its role in Thucydides' (unfavorable) characterization of the democrats, Cagnetta (1980, 255) notes the absence in book 8 of debate on the change in constitution from the democratic point of view.

[36] This is not to say, of course, that Thucydides is not critical of the oligarchs as well. Nor do I mean to suggest that the Athenians enthusiastically embraced Peisander's secret plan for the extremely limited oligarchy of the Four Hundred. But commentators have consistently exaggerated the element of deceit required to get the Athenians to vote for oligarchy and have underplayed the role in the switch to oligarchy of the Athenians themselves. Furthermore, commentators have not recognized sufficiently the negative elements of Thucydides' characterization of the Athenian *demos*.

much (or as staunch) opposition as one would expect from Thucydides' authorial comment on the "difficulty" of ending democracy in Athens and his suggestion there that democracy equals liberty.

For example, after the crucial assembly, the Athenians voted that Peisander and ten others should sail out to Tissaphernes and Alcibiades and make with them whatever arrangements seemed best (8.54.2). Peisander also, according to Thucydides, "approached all the secret clubs which already existed in the *polis* for court cases and elections, and encouraged them to unite and plan in common to overthrow the democracy" (8.54.4). Peisander then sailed out on the embassy to Tissaphernes. When he returned to Athens later that spring, Peisander found out that "most everything had already been done by the conspirators" (8.65.1) Among other things, some young men "secretly killed a certain Androcles, a particular leader of the *demos* and one who had taken a leading role in the banishment of Alcibiades" (8.65.2). They killed him, according to Thucydides, "for both reasons, both because of his demagoguery and also believing that they would please Alcibiades since he was returning and would make Tissaphernes their friend" (8.65.2). Along with Androcles, they killed "certain other unsympathetic individuals in the same way, secretly" (ἄλλους τινὰς ἀνεπιτηδείους τῷ αὐτῷ τρόπῳ κρύφα ἀνήλωσαν, 8.65.2).[37]

Thucydides here recounts the first known political murders in Athens since the assassination of Ephialtes. After a brief description of the oligarchs' propaganda (to which we shall return shortly), he describes the effect these murders had on the mass of Athenians. The common view is that in his description Thucydides indicates that the Athenian people were so terrified by these events that they were unable to oppose an oligarchic movement that, apart from this campaign of violence, the great mass of them would have fought vigorously. Commentators find here the first element of Finley's "classic mixture of terror and propaganda" that they argue explains away the Athenians' acceptance

[37] The word I have translated as "unsympathetic" is, literally, "unsuitable." Loraux (1986, 121–23) traces the use of this word in book 8 and shows how Thucydides here and elsewhere deliberately imitates a *stasis* language that employs "vague words (which are) open to all the combinations and all the re-orderings to which an accommodating signifier can lend itself." This argues, again, that book 8 is not some provisional draft but is composed with artistry.

of oligarchy.[38] Yet Thucydides' account is more nuanced than this. The oligarchs did engage in a calculated campaign of political intimidation that terrified Athenians. However, Thucydides' text strongly suggests that many Athenians supported the oligarchy without compulsion. In short, Thucydides tells us that it is not political intimidation alone that accounts for the Athenians' move to oligarchy.

For example, Thucydides inserts in the very heart of his account of the so-called terror campaign an indication that the oligarchs felt little need of terror tactics. Right after he mentions the murder of Androcles and the others and before he goes on to describe the atmosphere this engendered in Athens, Thucydides notes that "a proposal was made beforehand by them that no one but men in the armed forces were to receive pay and that no more than five thousand were to have a share in the government" (λόγος τε ἐκ τοῦ φανεροῦ προείργαστο αὐτοῖς ὡς οὔτε μισθοφορητέον εἴη ἄλλους ἢ τοὺς στρατευομένους οὔτε μεθεκτέον τῶν πραγμάτων πλέοσιν ἢ πεντακισχιλίοις, 8.65.3). Scholars disagree over whether "to have a share in government" refers only to the right to stand for and hold office or if it includes even the basic democratic right to vote in the assembly.[39] Here the phrase most likely refers to the right to vote in the assembly because the other element of the proposal, the abolition of all but military pay, already effectively limits the right to hold office to those men who can afford to serve without pay. The limitation of either right to only five thousand men, however, would clearly move Athens away from democracy and toward oligarchy. Thucydides brands this proposal propaganda; he calls it a "pretence directed at the masses" (εὐπρεπὲς πρὸς τοὺς πλείους, 8.66.1) and says that the revolutionaries really intended to take over the city themselves in a much more narrow oligarchy. Thucydides nevertheless makes it clear that the conspirators put this false program out for public consumption. One designs propaganda, of course, to be appealing to the target audience; one pretends to give the people what they want. The oligarchic conspirators did not openly advocate their plan of putting

[38] M. Finley 1971, 4. Kagan (1987, 143), for example, speaks of a "calculated policy of terror that would weaken the opposition and open the way for the overthrow of democracy."

[39] See above, n. 22.

power into the hands of only Four Hundred men. We may conclude, therefore, that they doubted that this would be widely popular. We may also conclude, however, that they judged that the abolition of pay for offices and the limitation of rule to only five thousand men would not be too offensive to the mass of Athenians. The Athenians, again, seem unconcerned with democracy and none too careful of their liberty if liberty equals democracy.

Even Thucydides' long account of the effect of the political murders on the Athenians in which modern commentators have seen a terror campaign has elements in it that undercut the view that most Athenians vigorously opposed oligarchy and would have fought against it had they not been so terrified. For example, although Thucydides says that the council and assembly still met, he says that the people "made no resolutions that were not approved by the conspirators; rather the speakers were from this group and the things that were going to be said were scrutinized by them beforehand. And no one of the rest of the people spoke in opposition because they were afraid. . . . " (8.66.1–2). This passage seems to oppose "the conspirators" to "the people" and so allows the interpretation that the majority of the people were locked in conflict with the conspirators. On the other hand, the conspirators' easy dominance of the people urges one to ask how great a proportion of the people were in fact among the "conspirators" and supported the oligarchic machinations. Thucydides, in fact, reports that "the people were afraid and saw that the conspiracy was large" (δεδιὼς καὶ ὁρῶν πολὺ τὸ ξυνεστηκός), explicitly leading the reader to suspect that the oligarchic movement had wide support. This very report, that is, begins to subvert the interpretation that the great mass of the people would have opposed "the conspirators" if it were not for the terror. It hints that there was little opposition not only because of terror but also because of weak support for democracy.

Thucydides' choices of what to include in his account corroborate this hint. As is the case in his description of Peisander's persuasive triumph in the assembly when the Athenians voiced no opposition to Peisander's initial proposal about oligarchy, Thucydides depicts no Athenian resistance here. Thucydides could have described someone who spoke out against oligarchy and was killed for it so that the reader might focus on the Athenians' tragic but heroic resistance. Instead he emphasizes that the Athenians were uncharacteristically passive in the face of intimidation. He chooses to remark that no one even tried to investigate the murders or take action against those suspected of the crimes; instead, "the people kept quiet and were so panic-stricken that even if they had kept silent, they considered it a benefit if they didn't suffer some violence" (ἡσυχίαν εἶχεν ὁ δῆμος καὶ κατάπληξιν τοιαύτην ὥστε κέρδος ὁ μὴ πάσχων τι βίαιον, εἰ καὶ σιγῴη, ἐνόμιζεν, 8.66.2). The parallel to the people's reaction to Peisander's first proposal is instructive. Thucydides' Athenians mustered no great opposition to oligarchy at that time and were upset only "at first," when no terror yet existed to excuse them. The passage about the so-called terror charges that passivity continued to infect the Athenians even as the revolution gained momentum.

Thucydides' text not only brands the Athenians passive and unconcerned with democracy; it also insinuates that they are cowards. That it contradicts itself in doing so only underscores its commitment to a negative portrayal of the Athenians. Although Thucydides had earlier indicated that the conspiracy was widespread, he later implies that the people were cowardly when he suggests that the conspiracy was actually rather small. The Athenians were ignorant, Thucydides tells us, of the true size of the conspiracy. The Athenians' ignorance of each other left them unable to discover the truth and so, in the face of this ignorance, they terrified themselves into believing that the conspiracy was greater than it really was (8.66.4–5). In his account of the "terror," then, Thucydides shows that if the Athenians were scared, it was at least partly because they terrified themselves into silence. With a little courage and a little investigation, the Athenians might have realized that they could defeat the conspiracy. The suggestion is that the Athenians' lack of opposition may have been due not only to the oligarchs' campaign of terror, but also to their own cowardice.

The effect of the last part of Thucydides' account of the mood in Athens most powerfully undercuts the notion that the Athenians failed to oppose the oligarchy only because of violent intimidation and deceit. Thucydides ends his account by pointing out that the democrats were quick to believe that even members of their own party were in on the plot. He then confirms that the people were right, "for men were in on it whom no one would ever have thought would turn to oligarchy.

And these men caused the greatest lack of trust in the masses and were particularly helpful to the security of the few since they solidified the *demos'* suspicion of itself" (ἐνῆσαν γὰρ καὶ οὓς οὐκ ἄν ποτέ τις ᾤετο ἐς ὀλιγαρχίαν τραπέσθαι· καὶ τὸ ἄπιστον οὗτοι μέγιστον πρὸς τοὺς πολλοὺς ἐποίησαν καὶ πλεῖστα ἐς τὴν τῶν ὀλίγων ἀσφάλειαν ὠφέλησαν, βέβαιον τὴν ἀπιστίαν τῷ δήμῳ πρὸς ἑαυτὸν καταστήσαντες, 8.66.5).

This point, of course, buttresses the charge that support for the oligarchy was actually quite widespread and directly challenges the preferred modern account that the Athenians were terrified and deceived into accepting an oligarchy, for Thucydides does not say that anyone believed these men had been terrified into supporting the oligarchy or were deceived about its oligarchic intentions. On the contrary, they seem to have joined of their own free will. This image of formerly staunch democrats now willing and knowledgeable members of the oligarchic party, which serves as the climax of Thucydides' account of the so-called terror campaign, undercuts that very account because it does not indicate that a valiant Athenian *demos* was forced by violence and lies to acquiesce only very reluctantly to oligarchy. A campaign of violence clearly occurred: The oligarchic conspirators committed political murders to intimidate their opponents, and some Athenians were afraid. But this is not all that Thucydides has to say. Other Athenians, it is quite clear, simply supported oligarchy or did not much care either way, and nobody made the job of the oligarchic conspirators very difficult.

The secret plan of the core oligarchic conspirators was, of course, to replace the democratic council and assembly with the group known as the Four Hundred, and the oligarchs had never breathed a word of this to the general public. The Athenians had accepted in principle a move to an oligarchy as early as Peisander's first visit to Athens, but he had never indicated that he meant to place the government into the hands of so few men. In this the core conspirators are, of course, guilty of deception, and we can assume that they were silent about their ultimate plans because they judged most Athenians would not support such a narrow oligarchy. The reader might then expect the Athenians to put up some resistance to the installation of this very limited oligarchy if, as the common view has it, they accepted a moderate oligarchy only under the duress of the war or were initially confused even about

Peisander's moderate proposals. In Thucydides' account, however, the Athenians make no move in opposition even when the conspirators finally openly propose the government of the Four Hundred. They raise neither whisper nor finger in defense of their " liberty," and this is not due to any oligarchic deception. Nor is this passivity and disinterest due to terror or intimidation, despite modern commentators' attempts to find force in this part of Thucydides' narrative. In short, Thucydides' narrative of the actual installation of the Four Hundred continues his negative characterization of the Athenians as essentially passive, weak, and unconcerned with preserving their democratic "freedoms."

The conspirators began the final stage of their coup by calling an assembly at which they proposed the creation of a committee of ten men who would bring proposals on government to the people at a subsequent assembly. That second crucial assembly was held, Thucydides tells us, at Colonus, "where there was a shrine of Poseidon about ten stades from the city" (8.67.2). There the committee of ten moved that any Athenian should be able to propose whatever he liked; that is, the laws against illegal bills were suspended. With this effected, the revolution was on: Peisander proposed that office holding and salaries under the present constitution should end, that five presidents should choose one hundred men, each of whom would choose three others, and that "these Four Hundred men, entering the council-house, should govern with full powers in whatever way they think best and should convene the Five Thousand whenever it seems good" (8.67.3).

Thucydides makes no mention of terror tactics or overt intimidation at either the preliminary meeting or the second meeting at Colonus. Thucydides' description of the meetings closely follows his chapters describing the campaign of violence that at least partly cowed the people into silence, but he does not mention any intimidation in his description of the assemblies at which the Athenians actually voted the Four Hundred into power. He does not claim that any member of the assembly felt any fear or acted in fear; nor does he allude in any way to terror. His point, therefore, does not seem to be to charge that the Athenians' actions at the Colonus assembly should be understood primarily as the actions of a terrified people. Indeed, as Thucydides tells us, all the Colonus meeting did at first was allow any Athenian to propose whatever he wanted, and this makes the assembly seem rather benign. Kagan remarks that "the provision inviting any Athenian to make any proposal he liked suggests an atmosphere of freedom of speech totally at odds with the menacing and tightly controlled mood at Colonus."[40] Thucydides does not, however, describe any such mood. Thus he avoids a ready opportunity to ascribe the Athenians' actions to intimidation and allows the reader the conclusion that some Athenians voted for oligarchy because they wanted oligarchy. Thucydides' failure to describe coercion at the Colonus meeting does not erase his account of the political murders in Athens or mean that some Athenians were not terrified, but it does indicate that intimidation is not the only reason the Athenians voted for the Four Hundred.

Recoiling from this conclusion, however, many modern commentators manage to find threat, menace, and manipulation in these events, particularly in the location of the second meeting at Colonus. But none of the arguments for why Colonus might be intimidating is convincing.[41] Commentators who believe in a staunchly democratic Athenian *demos* are forced to find intimidation in the choice of Colonus as a meeting spot because Thucydides' account of the assemblies at which the Athenians

[40] Kagan 1987, 148.

[41] Some argue, for example, that because Colonus was outside the walls and so vulnerable to enemy attack, only hoplites, men with arms and men more inclined to oligarchy, would be present (Cf. Hignett 1952, 275) or that this would allow an armed guard to be present ostensibly to protect from enemy attack but in reality in order to intimidate the people. But as Andrewes (in Gomme et al 1981, *s.v.* 8.67.2) notes, this is unlikely. Kagan (1987, 147) nevertheless claims that "just moving . . . to an unusual and unfamiliar place would have been unsettling . . . and would make it easier for Peisander and his collaborators to dominate the scene." He fails to explain why. Colonus, only one mile from the city, is likely to have been very unsettling to many. Lang (1948, 280) agrees that the choice of Colonus was "a subtly terroristic move," but fails to explain exactly how. Steiner (1994, 223) suggests that the move was made merely "to discourage the market loafer from attending." "How better," she asks, "to draw a more conservative or naïve audience than to relocate outside the Pnyx?" But again, if merely discouraging the "market loafer" allows oligarchy to flourish, democracy is not well rooted in Athens. Despite the ingenuity of these commentators, the decision not to assemble on the Pnyx probably had nothing to do with terror or intimidation. It is likely that the Pnyx was simply too closely associated with democracy. See Taylor 2002, 104–5.

voted the Four Hundred into power is otherwise completely free of any mention of coercion.

Compulsion and terror do not explain the Athenians' vote. According to Thucydides, they considered Peisander's proposal about the Four Hundred in an open assembly free from threats or intimidation. If he had wanted to describe things differently, he could have.

In fact, Thucydides' presentation of the Athenians' response to Peisander's proposal underscores his interest in stressing how little resistance the Athenians mounted to the oligarchy. He does it, once again, with silence. Thucydides simply says that "after it ratified these measures, with no one saying anything in opposition, the assembly was dissolved" (ἐπειδὴ ἡ ἐκκλησία οὐδενὸς ἀντειπόντος, ἀλλὰ κυρώσασα ταῦτα διελύθη, 8.69.1). Kagan supplies the description that Thucydides omits: "the constitutional change had been imposed on a terrified, confused, and leaderless assembly."[42] Thucydides, however, has none of this. His assembly barely appears in the passage as subject or object, much less as the beneficiary of three adjectives excusing it from what it had done. Of the assembly, Thucydides notes only that it ratified the proposal and that "no one said anything in opposition." If the Athenians' vote for oligarchy is to be explained by reference only to terror and confusion, as many would have it, Thucydides has done much to conceal it.[43] Indeed, we should recognize the implications of Thucydides' reticence. None of the Athenians at Colonus had anything to say in defense of democracy as they voted for oligarchy.

THE COUNCIL DOES NOT RESIST

Thucydides' account of the expulsion of the democratic council by the Four Hundred and that group's takeover of the council-house is even more revealing of the weak support for democracy in Athens. Thucydides begins by setting the scene: Because of the state of emergency due to the

[42] Kagan 1987, 156. Cf. McCoy (1973, 88) who claims that the assembly was "overawed by the threat of force presented by the conspirators."

[43] Price (2001, 311, n. 73) recognizes "the shocking abnormality of an Assembly, in which vociferous opposition would have been normal, essentially disempowering itself without any debate or resistance."

presence of the enemy at Decelea, "all the Athenians were always either on the walls or at their posts" (8.69.1). The conspirators, therefore, "on that day allowed those who were not in the know to depart as they were accustomed to do," but they told their own party to wait about quietly a little distance from the arms, "and if anyone stood in the way of what was being done to take up the weapons and not allow it" (8.69.2). Thucydides also notes that certain Andrians, Teneans, Aeginitans, and three hundred Carystians who had come for this purpose were given the same instructions. When all were in their places, the Four Hundred, with daggers concealed under their cloaks, together with their 120 young toughs went into the council-house (8.69.3).

Thucydides' description of the plans of the Four Hundred is elaborate. The large buildup leads readers to expect some response from the council commensurate with the preparations of the Four Hundred and Thucydides' expense of words. What Thucydides provides, however, is a quick denouement showing that the Four Hundred's fear of armed resistance was ill-founded:

> They came upon the members of the council chosen by lot who were in the council chamber and told them to take their pay and depart. They themselves had with them the money for the whole rest of their term and they gave it to them as they went out. When the council, saying nothing in opposition, withdrew in this way, and the rest of the citizens took no counter action, but kept quiet, the Four Hundred came into the council chamber (8.69.4–70.1).

Commentators, again, tend to stress violence in their analysis of this event.[44] It is true that the conspirators were prepared to use violence. As Thucydides tells us, they carried hidden daggers and had a force of hundreds of men to back them up, but this is not the whole story. We must note that no violence actually occurred. Thucydides makes no reference to threats or fear in the actual confrontation between the Four Hundred and the council. Thucydides' councilors do not suffer any violence, nor do they react to threats or show any fear. They do not cower in dread, prevented from standing their ground in defense of democracy only because of fear for their lives. Thucydides could have drawn the picture thus, but he did not. In his text, the councilors, told to take

[44] Lintott (1982, 139), for example, says that the conspirators removed the democratic council "by force straight away after the Colonus meeting."

their pay and go. Thucydides is brutally concise on this point, saying that the Four Hundred themselves gave the money to the councilors as they were going out of the chamber (αὐτοὶ καὶ ἐξιοῦσιν ἐδίδοσαν). The image, then, is of the councilors meekly and silently filing out of the council chamber, yielding democracy to the Four Hundred as they clutch their pay in their hands. The Four Hundred were ready and willing to use force, but, as Thucydides makes quite clear, there was no need.[45] What quieted this group, he suggests, were not daggers but money. The abundance of Thucydides' description of the preparations of the Four Hundred to counter resistance makes its absence that much more obvious. The surprising contrast emphasizes that the council and people did nothing to resist the final and crucial step in the overthrow of the democratic structure. Jonathan Price compares the terror in Athens to the *stasis* model of Corcyra.[46] If we do so, however, we should note the difference in the level of violence in Athens and Corcyra. In Corcyra the oligarchs, in order to prevent the island from being "enslaved" to

[45] Many commentators believe that the Four Hundred feared active violent resistance. They have some difficulty working with Thucydides' text, however, because it is not clear that the replacement of the democratic council took place right after the Colonus meeting. That the expulsion took place right after Colonus is almost essential if one believes the Four Hundred feared active opposition, for the council could serve as a locus of resistance. See Hignett 1952, 276 and Lintott 1982, 139. Thucydides' text, however, makes the Four Hundred "on that day" tell their followers to stand around by the arms and also tells them "to allow those who were not in on the secret to go home as usual." As Andrewes (in Gomme et al. 1981, *s.v.* 8.69.1–2) rightly notes, the "going home" mentioned here does not seem to refer to citizens leaving the assembly but rather to their leaving "the place where the arms are." Thus it seems to refer to men leaving from a regular daily parade under arms, and Thucydides seems to place a parade under arms – not the assembly at Colonus – right before the Four Hundred move to the Council house. As Andrewes notes (in Gomme et al. 1981, *s.v.* 8.69.2), this seems "curiously rash." The alternative, of course, is to suppose that the Council house was taken over on a later day. Of this possibility, Andrewes (in Gomme et al. 1981, *s.v.* 8.69.2) remarks that "by the day after Colonus [the Four Hundred] would have a clearer idea whether trouble was likely, and it was not impossible that they took precautions on this day which were not strictly necessary." Thucydides' text, of course, makes abundantly clear what Andrewes will only hint at most delicately. The Four Hundred took precautions on that day that were well beyond what was required.

[46] Price 2001, 308–10.

Athens, killed sixty democrats, including a number of the members of the council, before the city devolved into widespread fighting (3.70–71). In Athens the oligarchs paid the councilors, and the councilors quietly made way for them, "saying nothing in opposition" (οὐδὲν ἀντειποῦσα).[47]

The text proclaims that all this council really cared about was the money due them for the rest of their term.[48] This, of course, rounds out a characterization of Athenians that began with the crowd on Samos, who, in Thucydides' description, were upset only for the moment at the loss of their democracy but were cheered at the happy prospect of money from the Persian king. At the beginning of Thucydides' story about the rise of the Four Hundred and at its end, what moves the Athenians is money. In addition, Thucydides records no audible resistance from the *demos*. Indeed, he underscores their passive silence by repetition. The assembly dissolved itself "with no one saying anything in opposition (οὐδενὸς ἀντειπόντος, 8.69.1) and the council "withdrew," we are told, "saying nothing in opposition" (οὐδὲν ἀντειποῦσα, 8.70.1). Thucydides uses the same phrase to drive home the Athenians' silence. In fact, Thucydides' democratic Athenians barely speak in his whole account of the rise of the Four Hundred. They say almost nothing when Peisander first proposes oligarchy in his initial visit to Athens; they have no objection to make at the meeting preliminary to Colonus; and they ratify Peisander's proposal at Colonus "with no one saying anything in opposition." With the council, Peisander and company seem to have anticipated the one objection these men might have made by paying them off. Thus the councilors withdrew without a word. This is a far cry from the Athenians at the Spartan congress before the war, who so overwhelmed the Spartan ephor Sthenelaidas with words that he

[47] Price (2001, 316) recognizes but does not discuss that there was in Athens "no reign of terror." Mossé (1973, 23) notes that the council "had twice been the passive instrument of oligarchic revolution," but he does not discuss the events to which he refers.

[48] If the dating of Aristotle's *Ath. Pol.* 32.1 is correct, we are talking about pay for a month. See Andrewes in Gomme et al. 1981, *s.v.* 8.69.4. The Four Hundred's emphasis on the pay due the councilors contains powerful symbolism, of course. It proclaims the men unfit to rule; only men who require no pay from the government will have a share in the government of the new Athens.

objected "I do not understand these long speeches of the Athenians" (1.86.1). Furthermore, the rest of the citizens are again wholly passive. They "took no counter-action, but kept quiet" (καὶ οἱ ἄλλοι πολῖται οὐδὲν ἐνεωτέριζον, ἀλλ' ἡσύχαζον, 8.70.1). As it turns out, it was not all that difficult to deprive the Athenians of their liberty.

And so we return to the passage with which we began: "it was a difficult matter, in approximately the hundredth year after the tyrants were deposed, to put an end to the liberty of the Athenian *demos*" (8.68.4). As we have seen, Thucydides' narrative contradicts this statement. He depicts Athenians both on Samos and in Athens who care more for money than democratic institutions. He records no voice speaking in favor of democracy. He shows no active resistance to the oligarchic conspiracy but instead depicts a passive Athens. He indicates that support for the oligarchy was widespread and had even infiltrated democratic strongholds. Finally, although he details the oligarchs' violence, his text does not attribute the Athenians' acceptance of oligarchy to terror alone. Why, then, does Thucydides say the oligarchs' task was so difficult?

Connor claims Thucydides' comment "recalls the pathos statements that sometimes accompany moments of loss and suffering in the *Histories*."[49] Perhaps. More likely, Thucydides writes with piquant irony. The context certainly suggests as much. Thucydides makes his statement during his account of the Colonus meeting. Chapter 67 ends with Peisander's proposal to create the Four Hundred. Then, instead of recounting the Athenians' response to the proposal, Thucydides segues in chapter 68 into a long digression on the remarkable abilities of the other three main conspirators – Antiphon, Phrynichus, and Theramenes. The enumeration of the powers of these men is necessary, according to Thucydides, to quiet the surprise of the reader that the enterprise succeeded although it was so daunting. The comment in question follows, and Thucydides returns immediately to his main narrative to describe the Athenians' response to Peisander's proposals. The entire passage runs thus:

it was a difficult matter, in approximately the hundredth year after the tyrants were deposed, to put an end to the liberty of the Athenian *demos*, a people which was not only not subject to anyone but which also for over half this time was itself

[49] Connor 1984, 225.

accustomed to rule others. After it ratified these measures, with no one saying anything in opposition, the assembly was dissolved, and right afterwards they led the Four Hundred into the council house in the following way (8.68.4).

Thucydides' placement of these two sentences is significant. They directly contradict each other, and I believe Thucydides expects us to notice this. I agree with Nietzsche that Thucydides "needs to be turned over line by line, and his hidden thoughts read as clearly as his words: there are few poets so rich in hidden thoughts. "[50] Thucydides' description of the dissolution of the assembly "with no one saying anything in opposition" is calculated immediately to undercut his statement that the enterprise was especially difficult. The contrast highlights the question of the Athenians' responsibility for their own "enslavement." The juxtaposition is deliberately "subversive," meant to make readers think carefully and well about the narrative and their own biases and expectations.[51]

Thucydides' comment about the difficulty of depriving the Athenians of their liberty might be what Thucydides' democratic readers would expect. It is certainly what some modern commentators want to believe. Yet Thucydides' narrative defies this expectation and belief. It was not, after all, very difficult to end democracy in Athens. Thucydides' unusual equation in this passage between the end of democracy and loss of liberty heightens the drama of the passage. It also further suggests that he writes with irony about both the Athenians and democracy

[50] Nietzsche, "*What I Owe to the Ancients*," 2 in *Twilight of the Idols* (trans. Lange).

[51] Hornblower identifies a somewhat similar "subversive" effect earlier in the text. In his first speech, Pericles strongly suggests that Athens will not need to raise new funds to fight the war. "Surpluses sustain wars," he tells the Athenians, "not violent tax increases" (αἱ βίαιοι ἐσφοραὶ, 1.141.5). Only a few years after Pericles' confident speech, however, Thucydides notes that to fund the siege of Mytilene, the Athenians "then for the first time raised a property tax of two hundred talents" (πρῶτον ἐσφορὰν, 3.19). Thucydides here uses the same word for taxation that Pericles employed in his speech, encouraging the reader to make the connection and the critique. As Hornblower remarks (1991, *s.v.* 1.141.5), "the combination of the two passages is subversive: Pericles' financial foresight, praised at 2.65, was not, even on the evidence of Thucydides' own text, perfect."

itself.[52] If democracy does equal liberty, then ending a city's democracy (and liberty) should be difficult. Peisander's task was not difficult, however. This encourages readers not only to wonder if the Athenians themselves made an equation between democracy and liberty, but also to question the validity of the equation itself. The narrative of the coup of 411 suggests, that is, that the Athenians in Athens believed neither that democracy equaled liberty nor that democracy was essential to their city.

Yet perhaps those men are not Athenians and their city not Athens. Thucydides' statement that it was difficult to deprive the Athenian people of their (democratic) liberty is false only if we insist that the men in Athens are the Athenian people and their city in Attica Athens. Thucydides' text hints at a different calculation, however. If democracy is essential to Athens, at least, Thucydides' text suggests that the real Athens and the real Athenians (if they exist at all) are on Samos. For it was the men on Samos who first resisted the Four Hundred and the men on Samos who first reembraced democracy. For them, democracy is essential, and democracy is the main criterion of Athenian-ness. Because of their (re)commitment to democracy, the men on Samos will suggest that it is they who are the real Athenians and their community the real city.

[52] That Thucydides does not overtly signal his ironic intent means nothing. Tompkins (1993, 105) notes that although "Greek literature has numerous devices available for qualifying or undercutting an adjective . . . by and large Thucydides avoids these, preferring the most rigorous sort of irony, which lacks any verbal signal and so forces readers to engage in interpretation on their own, that is, to look for secondary meanings behind the bald statement. . . ."

5 The City on Samos

THE CITY IN ATHENS WAS QUIET

We saw in the previous chapter that the Four Hundred had a relatively easy time turning Athens to oligarchy, notwithstanding Thucydides' explicit comment to the contrary. As Thucydides continues his narrative to cover the fall of the oligarchy, he shows that the real difficulty that the Four Hundred faced in ending the liberty of the Athenian people came first from the Samians, then from the Athenians on Samos, and only late from the men in Athens. The effect is to reinforce the impression that the Athenians (and especially the Attic Athenians) do not really care about democracy. Moreover, when the Samian Athenians finally do focus on democracy, they consider abandoning the Athens in Attica altogether as they constitute themselves a (democratic) city on Samos. Although many commentators find the men on Samos sympathetic, Thucydides' presentation of them is far from favorable. Thucydides focuses on the destructiveness of their factioneers' zeal and on the danger of a portion of the city insisting that it alone is qualified to judge what the city should be. His narrative underscores the benefits of political compromise and implies that compromise and reconciliation are only possible for Athens around the image of the traditional city in Attica.

The Four Hundred had very little to fear from the men in Athens, as Thucydides' description of the council's meek withdrawal "saying nothing in opposition" (οὐδὲν ἀντειποῦσα, 8.70.1) demonstrates. Thucydides forcefully confirms this impression in the very next paragraph, which reveals again how quiet and passive the men in Athens were in the face of oligarchy. The oligarchic leaders hoped to take speedy advantage of what they thought was their position of strength and so treated with King Agis for an end to the war (8.70.2). King Agis had a different (but, as we learn, incorrect) analysis of the situation, however. Thucydides presents this to his readers in a fascinating passage that underscores that the Four Hundred were in no danger from the men in Athens, who were "quiet" in the face of oligarchic revolution:

Agis thought that the city was not quiet and that the demos would not so quickly hand over its ancient liberty. Because he also calculated that if they saw a large army of his, they would not keep quiet,[1] and, furthermore, because he did not believe that they were no longer in turmoil at present, he answered nothing encouraging to those coming from the Four Hundred. Instead, he sent for a large army from the Peloponnesus. Not much later, using the garrison from Decelea together with the men recently arrived from the Peloponnesus, he himself marched right up to the walls of the Athenians. He expected that they would be more likely to yield on his terms because they were thrown into turmoil or that he would not fail from capturing the Long Walls without a blow because they would be deserted on account of the disturbance likely to occur both inside and outside (8.71.1).[2]

Most editors think this passage corrupt, especially because of the repetition of the two infinitives of "keep quiet" (ἡσυχάζω) in the beginning of the paragraph. Commentators, therefore, generally counsel deletion of one of the two references to "quiet."[3] Raymond Weil, however, retained

[1] Reading ἡσυχάσειν.

[2] I translate a combination of the texts of Weil (1972) and Maurer (1995).

[3] Dobree (1874, *loc. cit.*), for example, deleted the whole phrase "the city was not quiet" at the beginning of the passage. Most editors followed him. Andrewes (in Gomme et al. 1981, *s.v.* 8.71.1), however, found "more attraction" in Goodhart's proposal to keep the first reference to the city's quiet but to change the *second* reference to quiet ("they would not keep quiet") to "they would rise up." Classen (reported in Classen and Steup, 1922), by contrast, reverses Goodhart's proposal; he suggests keeping the second reference to quiet while excising the first (in favor of a phrase like "were still in *stasis*"). Most recently, Maurer (1995, 157–58) accepts Dobree's deletion of the first infinitive and the first reference to the city's quiet. Andrewes, however, thought the "trouble . . . more diffused" than could be fixed by mere deletion of one of the infinitives. He thought it "possible that [Thucydides] made several attempts to put this sentence into the form he wanted" and that the "editor" who is assumed to have collected and preserved Thucydides' work after his death "kept too much from his various

both infinitives relating to "quiet" because "the extraordinary, dramatic circumstances in which the Athenians find themselves exact a systematic analysis as clear as it is possible and demonstrate that this analysis . . . is reproduced accurately."[4] Hartmut Erbse, too, argued that if Thucydides had something special to say he might well employ "a repetition of ἡσυχάζειν ["keep quiet"] which is to us troubling."[5]

Depending on the text one accepts, Thucydides makes reference here either four or five times to Agis's expectation that the Athenians were in a state of confusion and turmoil: (1) "Agis thought that the city was not quiet," (2) "he calculated that if they saw a large army of his, they would not keep quiet," (3) "he did not believe that they were no longer in turmoil at present," (4) "he expected that they would be more likely to yield on his terms because they were thrown into turmoil," and (5) "he expected that . . . he would not fail from capturing the Long Walls . . . on account of the disturbance likely to occur." But to Agis's surprise, when he brought his large army against Athens, "the Athenians were not in motion in any way with respect to internal affairs" (οἱ Ἀθηναῖοι τὰ μὲν ἔνδοθεν οὐδ᾽ ὁπωστιοῦν ἐκίνησαν, 8.71.2). The city was "quiet" after all. And so Agis retreated to Decelea.

In his comments on this passage, Rood remarks on "the self-control that contradicted Agis's expectations" and how it "aligns" with "earlier displays of Athenian endurance."[6] Rood, that is, reads the city's "quiet" favorably. Being "quiet" was an essential element of Pericles' original war strategy, of course. Thucydides reports in his *Epitaph* of Pericles that Pericles said that the Athenians would win the war "if they kept quiet" (ἡσυχάζοντας), if they took care of the navy, did not add to the empire during the war, and did not take risks with the city (2.65.7).

drafts." Steup (Classen and Steup, 1922, *loc. cit.*) agreed that we have here two Thucydidean versions of a sentence that have been wrongly combined.

[4] Weil (1972), *loc. cit.*, n. 2. Rood (1998b, 276, n. 77) calls this "a good point" but accepts Dobree's deletion nevertheless.

[5] Erbse 1989, 18.

[6] Rood (1998b, 276), citing 1.105.4, 3.16.1. Rood is unusual in discussing the content of the text in question. Although editors have expended great amounts of energy trying to determine the correct text of the passage, the passage has received almost no attention from commentators attempting to determine what place the information it conveys has in Thucydides' narrative.

Furthermore, the Athenians' ability to keep quiet had once before frustrated a Spartan king hoping for *stasis* in Athens. When Agis's father, Archidamus, first invaded Attica, Thucydides explained that he expected that his ravaging of the land would either force the Athenians to come out against him in battle or would provoke the Athenians to *stasis*. His expectations, however, were unrealized. Although the city "was in a state of every kind of excitement" (2.21.3), Pericles "kept the city under guard and as much quiet as he was able" (καὶ δι' ἡσυχίας μάλιστα ὅσον ἐδύνατο εἶχεν, 2.22.1). Because the Athenians remained quiet, Archidamus' hopes were thwarted. This (apparent) parallel might seem to support Rood's reading. However, attention to the context Thucydides gives to the Athenians' inaction in 411 demonstrates that Thucydides' emphasis on the Athenians' surprising quiet at this time underscores again how little concerned with democracy the men in Athens are.

Agis thought the Athenians would not be "quiet" and would be in disarray because, Thucydides tells us, he "thought that the *demos* would not so quickly surrender their ancient liberty" (οὐδ' εὐθὺς οὕτω τὸν δῆμον τὴν παλαιὰν ἐλευθερίαν παραδώσειν). In Thucydides' representation, Agis equates being quiet with quickly surrendering liberty. The "quiet" the Athenians show Agis, therefore, is not "self-control." It continues Thucydides' presentation of the weak defense of liberty and democracy put up by these Athenians, and it stresses their lukewarm commitment to democracy. Thucydides again makes clear that these quiet Athenians will be no trouble to the Four Hundred.

The passage, furthermore, has an antidemocratic tone. Thucydides' statement that Agis "thought that the *demos* would not so quickly surrender their ancient liberty" by remaining "quiet" in the face of oligarchy echoes Thucydides' own ironic editorial comment that "it was a difficult matter to put an end to the liberty of the Athenian *demos*" (8.68.4). According to Thucydides, Agis, just like Thucydides himself, equates liberty with democracy. The apparent equation of "liberty" and democracy is strange enough in Thucydides' comment. It is stranger still coming from a Spartan king who is unlikely to have thought that a state must be democratic to be free. Nevertheless, both Thucydides and (so he tells us) Agis use an extreme *stasis* logic that equates liberty with democracy. Furthermore, at the same time, Thucydides emphasizes that the course of events disproved this *stasis* logic. If democracy equals liberty, then the Athenians, who invented democracy, should have put up a vigorous fight to defend it against the oligarchic revolution. However, Thucydides' narrative shows that they did not fight for it when the Four Hundred came to power. Here again, we see them surprisingly (in the eyes of Agis) putting up no fight for it. The Athenians' weak commitment to democracy, that is, strongly implies that democracy does not equal liberty and further implies that democracy is not essential to Athens.[7]

On the other hand, the Athenians' quiet is very un-Athenian. During their speech at the debate at Sparta, the Corinthians remarked that someone would speak correctly if he summed up the Athenians by saying that "they have been constituted by nature neither to have quiet (ἡσυχίαν) themselves nor to allow it to others" (1.70.9). But in 411, despite Agis's expectation that they "would not keep quiet," Thucydides tells us that "the Athenians were not in motion in any way with regard to internal affairs" (8.71.2). Thucydides has already underscored the "quiet" of the Athenians by emphatic repetition of forms of both the noun and verb for "quiet" in his narrative of the rise to power of the Four Hundred. The crowd of sailors on Samos, "even if it was upset for the moment . . . because of the satisfying hope of pay from the king, kept quiet" (ἡσύχαζεν, 8.48.3). In Athens, no one investigated the oligarchs' crimes or took action against them. Instead, "the people kept quiet" (ἡσυχίαν εἶχεν ὁ δῆμος, 8.66.2). When the councilors meekly took their pay and withdrew before the Four Hundred, "the rest of the citizens took no counter-action, but kept quiet" (οἱ ἄλλοι πολῖται οὐδὲν ἐνεωτέριζον, ἀλλ' ἡσύχαζον, 8.70.1). Now again, Thucydides emphasizes the quiet of the men in Athens when he says that Agis thought that the city was not quiet, that the *demos* would not be quiet if it saw a large army of

[7] Bearzot (2006a, 53) is incorrect to argue that this passage shows that Thucydides is not ironic in his earlier comment on democracy and liberty because he offers here "a similar evaluation again." Bearzot writes as if a repetition confirms Thucydides' first comment. But Thucydides does not repeat himself because this second comment is not his; it represents (so he claims) Agis's thoughts. And Agis's thoughts represent, quite surprisingly, the viewpoint of a democratic factioneer. More importantly, the surrounding narrative proves Agis's evaluation wrong, just as the narrative around Thucydides' earlier statement proved it wrong.

his, or both (no one suggests excising both references to quiet).[8] The echo of the Corinthians' original characterization of the Athenians underscores how uncharacteristic such quiet is for Athenians. The Athenians in Athens, at least, are not acting like Athenians.

These un-Athenian Athenians offer another way of answering the conundrum posed by Agis's disappointed expectation that the Athenian *demos* "would not so quickly surrender their ancient liberty" and Thucydides' ironic claim that "it was a difficult matter to put an end to the liberty of the Athenian *demos*" (8.68.4). Perhaps, instead of using events in Athens to show that democracy is not equal to liberty and so not essential to Athens, we should conclude that the men in Athens are not Athenians and their oligarchic city is not Athens. This seems strange until we realize that the men on Samos come to just this conclusion. The reborn democratic factioneers on Samos claim that they are the true Athenians and the true Athens. It is their zeal (which Thucydides ultimately condemns) that threatens the Four Hundred.[9]

Thucydides confirms that the un-Athenian Athenians in Athens will be no trouble to the Four Hundred right after his discussion of Agis's thwarted foray against Athens. After Agis withdrew to Decelea, the Four Hundred made further overtures to him, which he treated with more respect. On his advice, the Four Hundred sent representatives to Sparta to negotiate a settlement to the war (8.71.3). They also sent representatives to Samos to tell the men there soothing things about events in Athens because, Thucydides tells us, "they feared the very thing that happened, that the naval masses would not themselves be willing to remain in the oligarchical system and that with the trouble starting from there, the navy might banish them" (δείσαντες μή, ὅπερ ἐγένετο, ναυτικὸς ὄχλος οὔτ᾽ αὐτὸς μένειν ἐν τῷ ὀλιγαρχικῷ κόσμῳ ἐθέλῃ, σφῦς τε μὴ ἐκεῖθεν ἀρξαμένου τοῦ κακοῦ μεταστήσωσιν, 8.72.2). Here Thucydides tells the reader not only of the fears of the Four Hundred, but in a proleptic comment ("the very thing that happened"),

8 If we were to judge the passage to represent two different versions of the sentence (as do Andrewes and Steup), it would be easy to argue that one of the two infinitives of "keep quiet" belongs to each.

9 Thucydides does not agree that the Samian Athenians are the true Athenians. His narrative, however, leads the reader along this path to the viewpoint of the Samian democratic factioneers.

he jumps ahead of the time of his narrative to confirm that those fears were justified.[10] Danger to the oligarchy came, he tells us, not from Athens or from any active Athenians there (about whom, the passage leads us to understand, the Four Hundred had no fears) but from Samos.

Because they anticipated problems from the men on Samos, the Four Hundred sent ambassadors with two arguments to give the men there. First, the ambassadors were to claim that the government in Athens was one of Five Thousand, not Four Hundred, men. This point was meant to limit the apparent change in the government. A government of Four Hundred was narrowly oligarchic, but a government of Five Thousand might strike some as quite democratic.[11] Second, the ambassadors should explain to the men on Samos that "the oligarchy had not been set up to do any harm to the city or the citizens but for the salvation of the entire state" (ἀλλ' ἐπὶ σωτηρίᾳ τῶν ξυμπάντων πραγμάτων, 8.72.1). This point mirrors Peisander's argument in the assembly in Athens at which the Athenians took the first step toward oligarchy. Peisander said there that it had come to a question not of the constitution but the salvation of Athens (8.53.3). The argument only works, however, if one accepts that the city has not, in fact, been irreparably harmed by the change of constitution. An ideological purist would argue that the city has not been saved at all. The Four Hundred find such ideological purists on Samos. Whether these men would, indeed, save the city or destroy it is one of the questions Thucydides' text asks.

THE SAMIANS RETURN THE FLEET TO DEMOCRACY

The Four Hundred were right to fear danger from Samos, as both Thucydides' proleptic comment ("the very thing that happened," 8.72.2)

[10] Rood (1998b, 274–75) discusses the complex technique of Thucydides' two "parallel narratives" describing first the introduction of oligarchy and then its dissolution. Delebecque (1965, 53) argued that the large number of prolepses in book 8 resulted from Thucydides' recognition that he was not going to be able to finish his work. More likely, however, it comes from the complex nature of the narrative.

[11] See, for example, Rhodes (1972, 121): "as [Thucydides] himself reminds us, 'democracy' could mean different things to different men."

and the surprising speed of Thucydides' text underlines. Right after Thucydides reports the fears of the Four Hundred and their decision "immediately after their government was established" (8.72.2) to send ambassadors "to reassure the army" (8.72.1), Thucydides reports that "there was already on Samos a revolutionary movement regarding the oligarchy" (ἐν γὰρ τῇ Σάμῳ ἐνεωτερίζετο ἤδη τὰ περὶ τὴν ὀλιγαρχίαν, 8.73.1). Thucydides emphasizes that the men on Samos quickly came to the "revolutionary movement" that those in Athens could not muster.

It is significant that at the beginning of his narrative of the return of Athens to democracy, Thucydides locates the revolutionary movement "on Samos" and not among the Athenians. This highlights what the narrative reveals, that although the Athenian fleet was quick to accept oligarchy, it is Samians and not Athenians who take the initiative in defending democracy and bringing the Athenians of the fleet back to democracy. Thucydides is explicit about these points. At the very beginning of the coup narrative, Thucydides took care to note that it was "the forces of the Athenians on Samos" who joined with Alcibiades in making the initial moves toward oligarchy in the fleet (οἱ ἐν τῇ Σάμῳ Ἀθηναίων στρατιῶται, 8.47.2). He then almost immediately repeats that it was "the trierarchs of the Athenians on Samos" (οἱ ἐν τῇ Σάμῳ τριήραρχοί τε τῶν Ἀθηναίων, 8.47.2) and the leading men who set themselves to destroying the democracy. Andrewes calls Thucydides' repetition of "on Samos" and "of the Athenians" "at least untidy."[12] On the contrary, I think Thucydides' repetition is deliberate and meant to underscore both that so much of the Athenian force was "on Samos" (a point the newly made democrats on Samos stress later) and that the move to oligarchy began among "the Athenians." The repetition also stresses the contrast with the return to democracy. The "revolutionary movement regarding the oligarchy" occurred "on Samos" but not "among the Athenians" (8.73.1). The Athenians have very little to do with it and play a conspicuously and curiously minor role in Thucydides' narrative of the "new things" on Samos.

This portion of book 8 is one of the most complex sections of Thucydides' narrative, in which he employs new techniques in order to

[12] In Gomme et al. 1981, *s.v.* 8.47.2.

address events occurring simultaneously in different areas. Thucydides uses flashbacks, cross-references, and proleptic comments to convey this complex material. For example, right after Thucydides describes the decision of the Four Hundred to send ambassadors to Samos to reassure the army (8.72), he switches the narrative back to Samos. Because Thucydides has been concentrating on Peisander and Athens for the last eight sections, the reader has heard nothing of recent events on Samos. In his last report about Samos, Thucydides related the decision to send Peisander to Athens on the trip that ended in the Colonus meeting (8.64.1), and he mentioned a plan to try to instigate the overthrow of democracy in the *polis* of Samos (8.63.3). Thus when Thucydides shifts his narrative back to Samos after the installation of the Four Hundred in Athens, he needs to explain events in Samos since Peisander's departure for Athens in a way that allows readers to see how the two narrative strands connect. He tells the story of events in Samos in an extended flashback and binds his two narratives with cross-references.

When Thucydides shifts his focus back to Samos, he notes that "there was already on Samos a revolutionary movement regarding the oligarchy" and remarks that "the following events occurred at about the same time that the Four Hundred were conspiring together" (ξυνέβη τοιάδε γενέσθαι ὑπ' αὐτὸν τὸν χρόνον τοῦτον ὅνπερ οἱ τετρακόσιοι ξυνίσταντο, 8.73.1). As Rood observes, this cross-reference is "required for the correlations between events to be understood."[13] Thucydides uses the cross-reference so readers can see the temporal relation between the two stories – that, for example, things on Samos had already moved away from oligarchy by the time the Four Hundred were planning to send their conciliatory envoys there. The cross-reference, however, also highlights how unexpectedly the narrative proceeds and how small a role the Athenians have in it.

Thucydides remarks that "there was already on Samos a revolutionary movement regarding the oligarchy." This cross-reference relates back to Thucydides' report that the Four Hundred sent out ambassadors "to reassure the army" (παραμυθησομένους τὸ στρατόπεδον, 8.72.1) because they feared that discontent with oligarchy among the men in the "naval crowd" (ναυτικὸς ὄχλος) would lead to the end of their

[13] Rood 1998b, 273, n. 68.

own government. The cross-reference also refers to Thucydides' proleptic comment that what the Four Hundred feared occurred (8.72.2). The cross-reference, that is, primes readers to expect an account of a change back to democracy among the Athenians (the "army," the "naval crowd") on Samos. Thucydides' reference to there being "already a revolutionary movement regarding the oligarchy" also suggests that what Thucydides will give is an account of the Athenians' return to democracy. The "already" (ἤδη) shows that the plans of the Four Hundred to reassure the "army" and the "naval crowd" were too late, suggesting that the "revolution" in question occurred among them. Furthermore, the very idea of a "revolutionary movement" (ἐνεωτερίζετο) also suggests the Athenians, because it was only the Athenians on Samos who had embraced oligarchy and thus only the Athenians who could experience a "revolutionary movement regarding the oligarchy." The focus would seem to be on Athenians, and readers would reasonably expect that what will follow is an account of the return to democracy among the men of the fleet. But the cross-reference is misaligned. Thucydides primes his reader to expect an account of the Athenians' "revolution" against oligarchy, but what he offers instead is a story about the Samians and Samos. The peculiar nature of Thucydides' presentation of these events has not received the attention it deserves.[14]

Because we must, once again, recognize an absence, it is necessary to quote the relevant passage in full. Thucydides begins by going back in time to the plot to return Samos to oligarchy that he reported in 8.63.3:

> The Samians who had earlier risen up against the men of rank and influence and constituted the democratic element changed round again (μεταβαλλόμενοι αὖθις) under the influence of Peisander and the Athenian conspirators on Samos. There were about three hundred Samian conspirators and they were planning to attack the others since they were democrats. The conspirators killed a certain Athenian called Hyperbolas, a wretched character who had been ostracized not because of any fear of his power or reputation, but because of his wickedness and the shame he brought to the city. They killed him in concert with Charminos, one of the generals, and some

[14] As Lateiner notes (1998, no pagination), "Book VIII has never received the literary analysis that its unmined riches demand. Analyst critics cheerfully washed their hands of its literary issues after pointing out the compositional problems (early, late, finished, unrevised?)."

of the Athenians on their side, giving a proof of their trustworthiness to them. And the conspirators did other such things with these Athenians and set themselves to attack the Samian people. But when the people got wind of it they told the generals Leon and Diomedon what was about to happen. (Because they were honored by the *demos*, Leon and Diomedon did not willingly accept the oligarchy.) The Samian people also told Thrasybulus the trierarch and Thrasylus the hoplite and others who always seemed to them to oppose the conspirators. The people asked the Athenians not to look on while they [the Samian people] were destroyed and Samos, through which alone the Athenians' empire had survived until now, was alienated from the Athenians. (καὶ οὐκ ἠξίουν περιιδεῖν αὐτοὺς σφᾶς τε διαφθαρέντας καὶ Σάμον Ἀθηναίοις ἀλλοτριωθεῖσαν, δι' ἣν μόνον [μέχρι νῦν] ἡ ἀρχὴ αὐτοῖς ἐς τοῦτο ξυνέμεινεν, 8.73.1–4).

Thucydides' focus throughout this account is on the Samians. The story begins with the Samian *demos* getting wind of an oligarchical plot against the democracy in their own city. Samians are the initial actors and speakers, and their focus is Samos. Furthermore, it is the Samians (and not the Athenians) who first reveal a staunchly democratic view of Athens.

The Samian *demos*, Thucydides tells us, asked the Athenians Leon, Diomedon, Thrasybulus, and Thrasylus "not to look on while they [the Samian people] were destroyed and Samos, through which alone the Athenians' empire had survived until now, was alienated from the Athenians." The Samians' appeal for their own preservation makes sense, because the oligarchic conspirators probably planned to kill certain of their most staunch political opponents.[15] Yet the appeal to prevent Samos from being alienated from Athens is not immediately understandable. The Samians begged the Athenians to prevent an oligarchic coup on Samos, but it is hard to see how such a coup could lead to the alienation of Samos from the Athenians because the Athenian fleet on Samos and Athens itself were at that point oligarchic. An oligarchic coup on Samos would bring the city of Samos more in line with Athens, not alienate it from an oligarchic Athens.

Peisander and his colleagues moved other states to oligarchy at approximately this same time, and Thucydides tells us that "when the cities received moderate government and freedom of action, they went

[15] When the *demos* originally came to power, they killed two hundred oligarchs and exiled four hundred more (8.21).

on to outright liberty," meaning "liberty" from Athens (σωφροσύνην γὰρ λαβοῦσαι αἱ πόλεις καὶ ἄδειαν τῶν πρασσομένων ἐχώρησαν ἐπὶ τὴν ἄντικρυς ἐλευθερίαν, 8.64.5). The result of these other oligarchic coups around the Aegean might suggest that an oligarchic Samos would revolt from Athens (and so be alienated from it), but Thucydides gives no indication that the oligarchic Samians intended to revolt from Athens after they overthrew the Samian democracy. On the contrary, the Samian oligarchs were happily working at murder (among other things) in concert with some of the Athenian generals on Samos to demonstrate their reliability to the Athenians (8.73.3). Furthermore, the presence of the Athenian fleet on Samos distinguished it from the rest of the Aegean and could serve to prevent a revolt. Thucydides does not hint in his narrative of any intention by the Samian oligarchs to revolt.[16] How, then, could an oligarchic coup alienate Samos from oligarchic Athens?

The Samians' fear makes sense only if one conceives of the Athenians and Athens itself as necessarily democratic, so that oligarchy and anything oligarchic must be alien to Athens. This thinking mirrors the equation of democracy and "freedom" in Thucydides' ironic editorial comment and in his account of Agis's analysis of the situation in Athens. It is a bold and partisan vision, however – especially at a time when Athens itself is oligarchic. It is also impressive that this bold vision about the nature of Athens should be articulated first by Samians. The quiet Athenians in Athens do not seem to believe that liberty equals democracy or that Athens, to be Athens, must be democratic. They are sitting still for oligarchy. Even on Samos, it is the Samians who first champion this vision of democratic Athens. The Samians' argument is the reverse of Peisander's argument in the first assembly at Athens. It *is* a question of the constitution, these Samians assert, and it is this insistence that will restore Athens to democracy. How well such insistence cares for the salvation of the city is another question entirely, however.

The story of the return to democracy in the Athenian fleet on Samos begins with Samians, and the reversion to the idea that Athens *must* be a democracy arises first among Samians and in regard to the future of

[16] Cf. Quinn (1981, 20): "at no time is the reader given the slightest inkling that Samos is regarded as a possible source of revolt. . . ."

Samos, not Athens. It is the Samians who articulate a democratic vision of Athens, and it is from the Samians' viewpoint that readers first find democrats again among the Athenians. Thucydides' entire narrative is from the Samians' point of view. They have knowledge of the plot; they have a perception of Leon and Diomedon as only weak supporters of oligarchy and of Thrasybulus and Thrasylus as opponents of oligarchy. They speak, even if only in indirect discourse. The Athenian proto-democrats on Samos, on the other hand, are passive. It is only after being prodded by the Samian democrats that the Athenians began to stir to action.[17] But even then, the only action Thucydides tells us about is in regard to Samos[18]:

> When [Leon, Diomedon, Thrasybulus, and Thrasylus] heard this, they went to each one of the soldiers and bid him not to allow it, and not least to the *Paraloi* [the sailors on the Athenian state ship *Paralos*] who were all free Athenian citizens and always opposed to oligarchy even when it did not exist. Leon and Diomedon left behind certain ships to be a guard for them whenever the fleet should sail out. The result was that when the Three Hundred attacked them, because all these people came to their aid, and especially the men of the *Paralos*, the Samian majority prevailed. They killed thirty of the Three Hundred, and punished three of the ringleaders with exile. However they did not remember any wrongs against the rest and lived as fellow citizens in a democracy for the future. The Samians and the soldiers sent the *Paralos* with Chaireas the son of Archestratos (an Athenian man who had been eager for the revolution) to Athens to report what had happened (ἀπαγγελοῦντα τὰ γεγενημένα, 8.73.5–74.1).

We see here that the Athenians on Samos put up a fight for Samos – behavior they did not display to prevent their own city from becoming oligarchic. When it was a question of oligarchy in Athens, these same Athenians were upset "for the moment only" (8.48.3).

[17] Bearzot (2006b, no pagination) claims that the antidemocratic revolution on Samos was stopped by the "reaction of Democratic Samians, guided by Athenian generals and officials including Thrasybulus." But the Athenians are not guiding the Samians in Thucydides' text. So, too, Buck (1998, 27) overstates when he claims that Thrasybulus and Thrasylus rallied not just "the sailors" but also "the Samian democrats." On the contrary, the Samian democrats rallied the Athenians.

[18] This passage continues immediately from the one quoted above.

Once again, the absences in Thucydides' account are important. There is no clear indication, for example, of what the Samians said to galvanize the Athenians, nor of what the Athenian generals said to the individual men and the sailors on the *Paralos*. We hear no ideological explanation of why they should care about Samos's democracy and have no hint of why the Athenians accepted whatever argument they heard. Indeed, the story is very hard to imagine from the Athenian perspective because Thucydides is so close-mouthed about the Athenians' actions and motivations. This reluctance to explain and to narrate is even more pronounced when we examine Thucydides' account – if one can even call it that – of the return to democracy among the Athenian fleet. Here, too, Thucydides' curious presentation has been overlooked by critics.[19]

Immediately after Thucydides reports the victory of the Samian *demos* over the Samian oligarchs, he says, "the Samians and the soldiers" sent the *Paralos* with Chaireas the son of Archestratos to Athens to report "what had happened" (8.74.1). The Athenians on Samos sent this ship in ignorance of how far the coup had already moved in Athens. They presumably sent the ship in the hope that news of "what had happened" on Samos would prevent a final move to oligarchy in Athens. We must speculate here, however, because Thucydides does not explain the motivation of the mission. Exactly what news the *Paralos* carried is also unclear. Given what Thucydides has explained up to this point in the narrative, the reader must understand that Chaireas and the *Paralos* were sent to Athens to report the failure of the oligarchic coup in the *polis* of Samos because that is all that Thucydides has described. All we have heard is that "the Samian majority prevailed" over the

[19] For example, Price (2001, 312) gives no real discussion of Thucydides' account of the return to democracy on Samos, remarking only that "an aborted oligarchic *coup* in Samos had strengthened the democracy both on the island and in the Athenian fleet, which at first had grudgingly accepted oligarchy in principle but now joined hands with the Samian democrats and affirmed its own identity as a democracy." If anything, the Samian democrats grabbed the Athenians' hands and dragged them along. Mossé (1964, 4) speaks of "the initiative of the resistance" coming not only from the sailors of the Athenian fleet but also from the generals and a trierarch. He does not discuss that the principal "initiative" came from Samians. I suspect that commentators' silence about 8.73 stems in part from unease at the import of the passage: that the Athenians on Samos needed to be prodded by Samians to begin to resist oligarchy.

Three Hundred (8.73.6). The dispatch of the *Paralos* occurs immediately afterwards. However, in his account of the departure of the ship, Thucydides calls its captain, Chaireas, one who "had been eager for the revolution" (μετάστασις). This urges the reader to infer that the Athenian forces on Samos must have themselves experienced a return to democracy because a "revolution" or "change over" does not apply to the situation in the city of Samos, which *prevented* a revolution and so *kept* its democracy. A "revolution" or "change over" better suits the fleet *switching* from oligarchy to democracy. Thus the news of "what had happened" that the *Paralos* carried to Athens probably included word of a return to democracy in the fleet.

Thucydides primed the reader to expect an account of this "change over" when he resumed his narrative in Samos with the introductory cross-reference that "there was already at Samos a revolutionary movement regarding the oligarchy" (8.73.1). Thucydides' introduction makes it all the more striking that he fails to tell the story of this change of attitude. Thucydides never in so many words says that the Athenian fleet reembraced democracy, and he never gives a narrative of the event. Thucydides says that those who heard the appeal of the Samian democrats themselves approached individual soldiers, and the crew of the *Paralos* to urge them "not to allow it" (8.73.5). In context, this must mean simply not to allow the planned *coup* against the Samian *demos*. That *coup* was indeed foiled, and the next thing Thucydides reports is that the Samians and the soldiers sent Chaireas and the *Paralos* to Athens to tell "what had happened." Yet Thucydides himself doesn't tell his reader what happened. He never tells his reader how an appeal to individuals and the crew of one ship to stop a revolution in Samos was transformed into a reversion to democracy throughout the whole fleet.

Did the victory over the Samian oligarchs inspire everyone? Or did Leon and Diomedon, Thrasylus and Thrasybulus and the others have to appeal to their comrades to make them return to democracy? If so, what did they say? We do not know, for Thucydides does not tell us.[20] There is no narrative, no description, no speeches, not even a simple

[20] Note how Buck (1998, 26) is reduced to speculating that "Thrasybulus, as well as others, had presumably been speaking out against oligarchy vigorously. . . ." Buck has no idea what Thrasybulus and Thrasylus said or did because Thucydides does not tell us.

explicit statement that the Athenians had reembraced democracy. Even the one basic, factual statement Thucydides gives is extremely vague and fails to say that anyone supported democracy, only that some came to reject oligarchy: "there was a revolutionary movement regarding the oligarchy" (8.73.1).

The silence among and about the Athenians is astounding. The initial impetus to democracy comes from the Samians, and Thucydides gives the Athenians' return to democracy virtually no space in his narrative. Thucydides' failure to describe what must have been a stirring event severely limits its power in the narrative. The absence of speeches, or even indirect discourse, in the mouths of Leon and Diomedon, Thrasybulus and Thrasylus calling their countrymen back to their ancestral constitution, the missing description of the sailors' recognition of their "true" political nature – in short, the absence of the story – all limit the readers' sense of the Athenians' change of heart.

One might attempt to explain these absences by appeal to the unfinished character of book 8, but that is a confession of utter defeat. It is far better to deal with the book as we have it and wait to consign some passage to the status of disposable first draft until we have determined whether its themes and characterizations conform with the rest of the work.[21] In this case, the themes do conform with the rest of the work, suggesting that the passage ought not to be so readily discarded. Thucydides' curious presentation undercuts the Athenians' return to democracy. This is consistent with Thucydides' characterization of the Athenians throughout the earlier part of book 8 as (at best) weak democrats, from the sailors' quick acceptance of oligarchy on Samos (8.47.3), to the Athenian council's and assembly's silent retreat before the Four Hundred, to the "quiet" of the people and the city in the face of oligarchy (8.70.1, 8.71.1). In Thucydides, even as they return to democracy, no Athenians seem to care much about it.

Thucydides says that Leon and Diomedon, "because they were honored by the *demos* did not willingly accept the oligarchy" (8.73.4). He reports that Thrasybulus and Thrasylus and others "always seemed [to the Samians] to oppose the conspirators" (8.73.4), and later says of

[21] See Connor (1984, 217), who argues against relying on "the conventional explanation that Thucydides died before completing the book and would radically have modified it if he had lived on." Cf. L. Strauss (1964, 227, n. 89).

Thrasybulus and Thrasylus that "these two had been the most prominent leaders of the change" (προειστήκεσαν τῆς μεταβολῆς, 8.75.2). However, the narrative itself never shows this. Thucydides fails to give words in support of democracy to Leon, Diomedon, Thrasylus, or Thrasybulus or to the crew of the *Paralos* either at the time of the introduction of oligarchy to the fleet or at the return of democracy. This exactly parallels Thucydides' silencing of the people in the face of Peisander's speech in the first assembly in Athens (8.53). The effect of this silencing is to lessen the readers' impression that the Athenians (rather than the Samians) have embraced democracy.

The many political flip-flops that Thucydides has taken pains to underline also undercut the readers' impression that anyone's attachment to democracy is serious. The democratic sailors of the Athenian fleet, although upset "for the moment," were quickly reconciled to oligarchy as long as it brought them their pay (8.48.3). The people in Athens received the idea of an oligarchy poorly "at first," but Peisander easily brought them round (8.53.3). Some men in Athens who had been staunch democrats surprised their former fellows by finding a place for themselves among the oligarchs (8.66.5). The Samian oligarchs themselves had once "constituted the *demos*" (ὄντες δῆμος) but had "changed round *again*" (μεταβαλλόμενοι αὖθις, 8.73.2), thus showing that their earlier embrace of democracy was *itself* a switch from an even earlier support for oligarchy.[22] We now hear, elliptically, of a "revolution" and a "change" (μετάστασις and μεταβολή, 8.74.1, 8.75.2) among the Athenians of the fleet. Who is to say that these re-minted Athenian democrats of the fleet would not "change round again" themselves? Democratic Athens, it is quite clear, is not in Attica. Thucydides' presentation of the democratic revolution on Samos causes the reader to wonder if it exists even there or, if it does, whether it belongs among the Athenians or the Samians.

Cogan has discussed the "ideological" phase of the Peloponnesian War and places the start of it, for the Peloponnesians, at the Thebans' speech at Plataea. There, as we saw above, the Thebans accused the Plataeans of "atticism" or of being like the Athenians (3.62.2). As

[22] Cf. Quinn 1981, 21: "the word αὖθις has failed to attract the attention it deserves. This was the second time that the Three Hundred had changed sides. Clearly, therefore, they had originally belonged to the oligarchic class. . . ."

Cogan notes, "atticism" is something that other cities might take up or "with which they might be 'infected'" (to take a Peloponnesian point of view).[23] Thucydides' narrative of the return to democracy on Samos and among the Athenians on Samos certainly suggests that the Samians have succumbed to "atticism." But his presentation of the democratic revolution on Samos causes us to wonder whether the Athenians themselves are still "infected."

THE CITY ON SAMOS ABANDONS ATTICA

Thucydides does eventually describe the words and actions of the Athenians on Samos. When he does so, it becomes clear that the men of the fleet did defiantly lay claim to the title of democratic Athens. To do so, however, they were happy to abandon the Athens in Attica and to redefine themselves as a city. The democratic factioneers, that is, are associated with perhaps the most dramatic revisioning of Athens in the text, and Thucydides' presentation of them is *not* favorable.

The newly made democrats had sent the *Paralos* to Athens to give word of the switch to democracy on Samos in ignorance that the Four Hundred had already taken power there (8.74.1). When the *Paralos* arrived, the Four Hundred immediately took over the ship itself, arrested a few of its crew, and put the rest on another ship on guard duty around Euboea. However, Chaireas, the captain of the *Paralos*, made it back to Samos with an alarmist account of the coup in Athens (8.74.2–3). The first impulse of the democrats on Samos was to attack the pro-oligarchic Athenians in their midst, but cooler heads pointed out that this would be fatal with the enemy fleet close by. Instead, their leaders Thrasylus and Thrasybulus (whom Thucydides only at this point describes as "the most prominent leaders of the change") now "wished clearly to change things on Samos towards democracy" (λαμπρῶς ἤδη ἐς δημοκρατίαν βουλόμενοι μεταστῆσαι τὰ ἐν τῇ Σάμῳ, 8.75.2).

The leaders of the democrats made all the soldiers – especially those who had been oligarchic sympathizers – swear binding oaths that they would all "act democratically, avoid dissension, carry on the war against the Peloponnesians zealously and be the enemies of the

[23] Cogan 1981a, 72.

Four Hundred" (δημοκρατήσεσθαί τε καὶ ὁμονοήσειν καὶ τὸν πρὸς Πελοποννησίους πόλεμον προθύμως διοίσειν καὶ τοῖς τετρακοσίοις πολέμιοί τε ἔσεσθαι, 8.75.2). The last three points are not surprising and are appropriate to the military character of the fleet, but what of swearing to act democratically? How might a fleet or army be or not be democratic? Perhaps by accepting only generals chosen by the regular democratic processes, and not any generals sent out by the Four Hundred. But they would seem to have covered this point when they swore to be the enemies of the Four Hundred and to have no dealings with them. Thus the men of the fleet must mean something different when they swear that they will be democratic. As the narrative shows, the fleet soon took on a character much like a political organization, making appropriate Thrasybulus's and Thrasylus's comment that it was "democratic." In effect, the men on Samos substituted themselves for Athens and set themselves up as the city.

Thucydides' own description underscores this substitution, for he begins to correlate the fleet with the city. He writes that "during this time they were set in rivalry with one side trying to compel the city to be a democracy and the other to compel the army to be an oligarchy" (ἐς φιλονικίαν τε καθέστασαν τὸν χρόνον τοῦτον οἱ μὲν τὴν πόλιν ἀναγκάζοντες δημοκρατεῖσθαι, οἱ δὲ τὸ στρατόπεδον ὀλιγαρχεῖσθαι, 8.76.1). There is here a powerful and deliberate parallelism between army and "city." Far from the army being a subordinate institution of the city, the two are equated in power and intention, and Thucydides gives no clear indication of which is the more legitimate representation of the Athenians.[24] This last point gets to the heart of the matter and to the heart of *stasis*. The Athenians on Samos were confronted with an offensive change of government and responded with actions that suggested that the city-center of Athens, by virtue of changing to oligarchy, was no longer due their loyalty and was, in fact, no longer truly Athens.[25] As Cogan writes, the fleet follow the "principle

[24] Loraux (1991, 45) remarks on "the very widespread tendency in historical writing and in decrees of reconciliation to present *stasis* as the confrontation of two interchangeable halves of the city."

[25] Cf. Price 2001, 313: "The Athenian fleet at Samos was acting and thinking of itself as the legitimately constituted state of Athens, even though the Four Hundred at Athens occupied the site of the *polis* and held nominal legitimacy."

that a city is constituted and recognized not so much by its material existence in a specific physical location as by its ideological position and beliefs."[26]

In response to Athens' failure (in their eyes) to be Athens, the fleet began to act like a city. Immediately after his comment equating city and fleet, Thucydides tells us that the soldiers held an assembly (ἐποίησαν δὲ καὶ ἐκκλησίαν εὐθὺς οἱ στρατιῶται, 8.76.2). They deposed from office the generals and trierarchs who had been elected in Athens and chose new generals and trierarchs from the men present. The men of the fleet took to themselves the duties of the citizen-body of Athens and, as they had sworn, abided, in their political actions, by democratic principles. The men on Samos, in short, replaced the city of Athens.[27]

In this same assembly, speakers stood and made "encouraging speeches" to each other about their situation (8.76.3–7). Commentators often find these men and their rhetoric inspiring and think that Thucydides' presentation of them is wholly favorable. Westlake, for example, chastises Thucydides for his lack of objectivity in book 8 because in his presentation of the Athenian *stasis* of 411, "his attitude is so conspicuously more favorable to the democrats than to the oligarchies [sic]."[28] According to Westlake, in Thucydides' text, "the Athenian troops are seen to have remained as determined as ever to uphold their ancestral democracy at whatever cost to themselves."[29] That is, Westlake sees the Athenians on Samos as selfless in their loyalty to democracy. Connor endorses Westlake's view that Thucydides presents "the democrats at Samos" as "for the most part genuine patriots who were prepared to make sacrifices in order to preserve the security of Athens under democratic government."[30] As we shall see presently, however, the touching

[26] Cogan 1981a, 160–1.

[27] Andrewes (in Gomme et al. 1981, *s.v.* 8.76.2) remarks that the men "regard themselves as having taken over the functions of government." Wettergreen (1980, 102) calls the group "Athens-on-Samos."

[28] Westlake 1989, 191.

[29] Westlake 1989, 188.

[30] Connor 1984, 221. Greenwood (2006, 96) claims that the men on Samos "hold a functional assembly (8.76.2) as opposed to the dysfunctional assemblies in Athens." Price (2001, 314) argues that Thucydides gives his reader "a contrast between a healthy, even 'normal' political process taking place in Samos . . . and

devotion to democracy that these commentators find in the Athenians' speeches barely exists. Furthermore, commentators do not take into account the dangers for Athens in the views expressed by the fleet, and especially in their willingness to abandon the Athens in Attica altogether. What these men are "touchingly" willing to "sacrifice" because of their ideological purity is the city itself. The men of the fleet are "patriots" willing to suffer to bring back into existence a lost city only if Athens is, by nature, democratic. But that is the viewpoint of a factioneer. If this is not the case – if Athens is not necessarily democratic – these "patriots" on Samos are determined to uphold their ancestral democracy not only at whatever cost to themselves, as Westlake says, but also at whatever cost to the city of Athens in Attica.

Consider what the men of the fleet say of Athens. They claim that "there was no reason to lose heart because the city had revolted from them (ὅτι ἡ πόλις αὐτῶν ἀφέστηκεν) for it was the smaller group that was revolting from the larger group who was, besides, more well-provided for in every way" (8.76.3). The men here go beyond Thucydides' own equation of city and fleet (when he said that "one side" was "trying to compel the city to be a democracy and the other to compel the army to be an oligarchy," 8.76.1) to insist that they have priority over the city. They make themselves the whole from which the city has separated itself. Furthermore, the fleet's emphasis on an entirely material calculus is striking.[31] Athens is to be despised, the democrats say, because it lacks resources, money, ships, and good advice. No one has a word to say about Athens' position in their hearts, of their shared attachment to the land where the autochthonous Athenians first arose and where their ancestral graves lie. There is no sense of loss of homeland. These Samian

an unhealthy process in Athens." Forde (1989, 162), for his part, calls this scene "touching" because of the "quiet courage" of the men of the fleet and "their patriotic devotion to a city that in their minds barely exists any more."

[31] In a purely material sense, the democrats may be correct. If it is true that it is a case of "the smaller group . . . revolting from the larger group," that they were "more well-provided for in every way" than Athens and that Athens had "no more money to send," then the fleet is more important and more powerful than the city. But the emphasis is entirely on material concerns. Price (2001, 314) rightly recognizes that "the Athenian self-representation at Samos should not be accepted . . . as blessed with the historian's approval" because "the Athenians' deliberations at Samos rested on a calculation of raw power."

Athenians repeatedly point out the superfluity of Athens itself and deny its importance to the war:

> Since they had the whole fleet, they could compel the other cities which they ruled to pay them money just as well as if they started out from there. For the *polis* which they had – Samos – was not weak and came within a hair's breadth of taking away Athens' control of the sea when they were at war against each other, and they would ward off the enemy from the same place as before. Because they had the ships they were more able to procure supplies than those in the city (8.76.4).

Samos, it turns out, works as well as a base for the war as Athens. In fact, it is a better base for securing supplies. If they lose Athens, they will still be stationed on Samos, just like before. If this is all true, and one's calculus is entirely material, why should there be any focus on the Athens in Attica at all?

The democrats even seem to take on the point of view of the enemies of Athens in their calculations. They remind themselves that "the *polis* they had – Samos – was not weak and came within a hair's breadth of taking away Athens' control of the sea when they were at war against each other." Here, the Athenian democrats take pride and strength from the fact that, as they claim, an enemy of Athens had once nearly taken away Athens' control of the sea. These men, that is, seem to be assimilating to a Samian (rather than an Athenian) point of view.

And these Samian-Athenians are happy to point out that they – like the Samians of old – are now able to take away Athens' control of the sea. The Athenians in Attica are *naukratores* no longer:

> Even earlier it was because of them sitting as guards on Samos that they had controlled the sea route into Piraeus and now they themselves were in the position that if they were not willing to hand the government back over to them, they themselves were more able to keep them off the sea than to be hemmed in by them.

The men are eloquent about the worthlessness of that city in Attica:

> The city was of little or no use to them as far as prevailing over the enemy, and they had lost nothing since those ones had no more money to send (rather the soldiers were supplying themselves) nor good advice, which was the thing that justifies cities' control over armies. But even in this those men in Athens had done wrong since they had abolished the ancestral laws while they themselves were preserving them. And they themselves would try to force the men in Athens to do the same.

So that not even in regard to men who could give them useful advice were they the worse off in themselves (8.76.6).

These men clearly feel no connection to the city in Attica. It has nothing to offer them, and the men are quick at least to imagine severing their ties with it.

The men flirt with abandoning Athens entirely when they argue that because they have the whole fleet, they can compel the cities of the empire to pay tribute just as well as they could if they sailed "from there" (ἐκεῖθεν, 8.76.4) "for," they tell themselves, "the *polis* which they had – Samos – was not weak" (πόλιν τε γὰρ σφίσιν ὑπάρχειν Σάμον οὐκ ἀσθενῆ). The men juxtapose the one city, on Samos, with the other city (although it is not named), and the whole speech argues that the Samian city is the better. To lose Athens would not be to lose much. The fleet's last words of encouragement to themselves make this explicit: "The main thing was that even if they failed at everything, since they had a fleet so large there were many places to retreat where they could find cities and land" (τό τε μέγιστον, ἢν ἁπάντων σφάλλωνται, εἶναι αὐτοῖς τοσοῦτον ἔχουσι ναυτικὸν πολλὰς τὰς ἀποχωρήσεις ἐν αἷς καὶ πόλεις καὶ γῆν εὑρήσουσιν, 8.76.7). One city will do as well as another.

The fleet propose actually to abandon Attica and Athens. They echo the abandonment of Themistocles but in a new and dangerous way. Themistocles urged the Athenians to abandon Attica and Athens in the face of an invading foreign foe. However, according to the account of it the Athenians gave at the Spartan Congress, the abandonment allowed the Athenians, who joined together "with our whole people" in the abandonment, to keep fighting "on behalf of a city that had little hope of existing" (1.74.3). Thus in the Athenians' account, only the abandonment of Attica held out the possibility that the Athens that all the people wanted could exist again through victory at Salamis. The Samian-Athenians' abandonment of Athens, by contrast, entails forever severing one part of the Athenian people from the other. They could be "with our whole people" no longer.[32]

32 Andrewes (in Gomme et al., *s.v.* 8.76.7) remarks that "from the colonial period and earlier, the Greeks were familiar with the idea of making a collective fresh start somewhere else," citing Themistocles' threat before Salamis, but he does not note the difference in the situations, especially that the Samian factioneers' new start would not be "collective."

John Wettergreen claims that the "position of the Athenians on Samos" is "confirmed by the authority of Pericles," citing Pericles' comments on the "unassailable" nature of islanders.[33] This must be wrong if by "confirmed" he means supported as right by Thucydides. It is correct, however, if he means that the Athenians on Samos base their reasoning on a Pericles-like vision of the city, for the fleet's actions and plans represent the culmination of the possibilities inherent in Pericles' redefinition of Athens and abandonment of Attica. By so radically redefining the city, Pericles served as a model to other men who might themselves redefine Athens. Pericles' vision argued, and the fleet accepted, that Athens consists of the fleet, the empire, and some defensible spot. By so disparaging Attica and never mentioning any value in Athens beyond the defensibility of its walls, Pericles left open the possibility that that defensible spot need not be Athens. In this the fleet concur; they have no hesitation in imagining abandoning the existing city altogether and replacing it with another. The fleet propose that they, although only a part of Athens, can go elsewhere and still be Athens. Thus the ability to redefine the city, and the ability to imagine abandoning it, make the faction fighting of 411 all the more divisive. Instead of thinking that they must regain their city, instead of working to arrange some *rapprochement* with the men of the city, the fleet propose to abandon it and them altogether.

The fleet see this possibility as salvation, but we should ask if the fleet do not imagine thereby the end of Athens itself. There are many reasons for concern. First, we have here a return to the restless movement of the period described in the *Archaeology*. Then, we recall, the Athenians were the most rooted and stable, the most free from faction (1.2.6). These new Athenians on Samos, however, embrace faction fighting. They do not wait for an invader to do so, but are happy to push themselves out of their native city in a move destructive to it and perhaps to themselves. Leo Strauss called *stasis* a kind of "rebarbarization."[34] Here we see the Athenians, in *stasis*, reverting to an early restless state with no certain,

[33] Wettergreen 1980, 109, n. 24.

[34] L. Strauss 1964, 156. For Palmer (1982b, 833, n. 13), Thucydides' whole book traces the arc we see here. It is "an account of the terrible decline from the peak of Greek greatness (1.1.1–2), a decline that is marked by the reintroduction of barbarism into the heart of Greek life."

fixed homeland. The fleet's comments throughout, furthermore, threaten to return Athens to a primitive state. For example, the fleet reiterate the power of the navy, but the fleet on Samos threaten to deprive Athens of the use of the sea. They point out that the advance post at Samos was actually essential to securing the sea lanes to Piraeus and that "they themselves were more able to keep the Athenians off the sea than to be hemmed in by them." The Samian-Athenians thus threaten to reverse the course of the history recounted in book 1 and change Athens back into a pre-Themistoclean, non-nautical city. Finally, if the fleet sailed off to a new Athenian future elsewhere, they would leave the Athens in Attica bereft of defense. Without its fleet, it would certainly soon be starved into submission by Sparta, which eventually did happen in 404. Thus these "patriots" encourage themselves with a vision sure to lead to the destruction of their own city – if Athens is their city.

The men of the fleet, then, are not to be approved.[35] They have far too much of their savior Alcibiades in them. At Sparta, Alcibiades claimed that he was not a traitor because the city he was attacking was not his own. The fleet's position is much the same. They are quick to deny that Athens is their city. They feel that they have the right to compel those in Athens to the political system they would prefer, and if they fail in that, they are happy to sever their ties with Athens altogether. They are willing to give up Athens and consign it to destruction or Spartan control in order to preserve the democracy in some reconstituted Athens elsewhere.[36]

The risks to Athens in the fleet's position are grave. Commentators nevertheless often endorse the fleet (and claim that Thucydides does so too) because they perceive the fleet to be devoted to democracy. Westlake calls them "determined . . . to uphold their ancestral democracy at whatever cost to themselves," and Connor describes them as "prepared to make sacrifices in order to preserve the security of Athens under

[35] The later narrative demonstrates that readers should not agree with the Samian-Athenians' claim to be the true Athenians.

[36] Cf. Wettergreen (1980, 103): "Book VIII shows the three normal parts of a city separated by place: the many on Samos, the few in Athens, Alcibiades scurrying between them. . . . All three held to the Alcibiadean opinion: 'My good or Athens' destruction."

democratic government."[37] Yet the Athenians in Thucydides have very little to say about democracy. In fact, Thucydides separates even these Athenians on Samos from the return to democracy: the Samians must prod them on, Thucydides' narrative does not focus on their point of view, and no Athenians explain why they prefer democracy.

The word itself is used, of course. For example, Thucydides reports that Thrasybulus and Thrasylus "wished to clearly change things on Samos towards democracy" (λαμπρῶς ἤδη ἐς δημοκρατίαν βουλόμενοι μεταστῆσαι τὰ ἐν τῇ Σάμῳ), so they made all the soldiers swear to uphold democratic principles (ὥρκωσαν πάντας τοὺς στρατιώτας δημοκρατήσεσθαι, 8.75.2), and Thucydides says that the army tried to force a democracy on the city (οἱ μὲν τὴν πόλιν ἀναγκάζοντες δημοκρατεῖσθαι, 8.76.1). Thucydides also presents the fleet as claiming to preserve "the ancestral laws" (τοὺς πατρίους νόμους) when those in the city were trying to destroy them. But no one explains why one should prefer this system. Despite commentators' assertions that the men on Samos are deeply committed to democracy, when they finally speak, they do not have a word to say about it. No one, for example, echoes Thucydides' ironic editorial comment (or Agis's analysis of the situation in Athens) and equates democracy with liberty. "Liberty" might be something worth endangering one's city for, but no one on Samos suggests that democracy is essential to a man's freedom. Thucydides' ironic comment that does so at the point when the Four Hundred took over the council house in Athens serves to highlight the absence of such arguments among the men of the fleet.[38]

Thucydides' discussion of the reasoning and propaganda of factioneers during his account of the *stasis* in Corcyra should also make us careful and critical of the arguments of the Athenian factioneers on Samos. Of the civil wars that engulfed the Greek world during the war, Thucydides writes, "the leaders in the cities, with a good-sounding

[37] Westlake 1989, 188; Connor 1984, 221.

[38] Loraux (1981/1986, 181) gives a table of some of the terms by which democracy was "defined in some fifth-century Athenian works," including "power of the people, rotation of offices, power of law, political liberty, freedom of speech, individual freedom, political equality, equality of speech, responsibility of magistrates, justice, drawing of lots, misthophoria." All of these are absent from the discussion of the "democrats" on Samos.

slogan on each side – political equality for the majority and aristocratic moderation – made the common good, which they paid court to in words, their prize" (οἱ γὰρ ἐν ταῖς πόλεσι προστάντες μετὰ ὀνόματος ἑκάτεροι εὐπρεποῦς, πλήθους τε ἰσονομίας πολιτικῆς καὶ ἀριστοκρατίας σώφρονος προτιμήσει, τὰ μὲν κοινὰ λόγῳ θεραπεύοντες ἆθλα ἐποιοῦντο, 3.82.8). Thucydides says that the factioneers had pretty arguments to make about why they were fighting, but what they were really fighting about was power. Thucydides' analysis of faction fighting in book 3 is a model to which readers must harken back when Athens begins to devolve into faction fighting. The analysis in book 3 would lead us to understand that behind the Athenian democrats' pretty arguments lies a crude desire for power. What is so striking, then, is that as Thucydides presents them, at least, the Athenian democrats on Samos do not even have the façade of pretty arguments about "liberty" or "political equality for the majority." When the Athenians finally speak in their "encouraging speeches," they are eloquent only about why they can safely abandon Athens, not about the benefits of democracy. Because the narrative has consistently suggested that the Athenians on Samos have little connection to democracy, their use of the word and their oaths to uphold the "democracy" or the "ancestral laws" do little to make their commitment to it seem real or admirable. And without a well-articulated reason why democracy is so important, their willingness to abandon Athens for it is all the more disturbing. So, then, far from being conspicuously more favorable to the democrats than to the oligarchs (as Westlake claims),[39] Thucydides' narrative implies that the men on Samos were quick to attack and abandon their city for no well-understood or well-articulated reason. They are zealous but unthinking.

In addition to pushing them to redefine (and so to abandon) Athens, the zealotry of the Athenians on Samos also seems to encourage them to redefine who was Athenian. As we have seen, the impulse back to democracy on Samos came first from the Samians, not from the Athenians. The Samians were the ultimate "atticizers" and were the first to argue that Athens was naturally democratic. One possible response to the argument that Athens is necessarily democratic is to think that the democratic is necessarily Athenian. If this is true, the Samians would

[39] Westlake 1989, 191.

have a strong claim to being Athenian. Thucydides' narrative of the return to democracy on Samos suggests that the Samians were, indeed, recognized as Athenian.

Immediately after he reports the victory of the Samian *demos* over the Samian oligarchs, Thucydides says that "the Samians and the soldiers" (οἵ τε Σάμιοι κὰι οἱ στρατιῶται) sent the official state ship *Paralos* to Athens to report "what had happened" (8.74.1). There was news to give both about the city of Samos (which had escaped an oligarchic coup) and about the Athenian fleet on Samos (which had returned to democracy), but Thucydides' wording says that the Samians participated in sending the Athenian state ship *Paralos* – an action one would think belonged rightly to Athenians alone. Furthermore, Thucydides says that Thrasybulus and Thrasylus "wished clearly to change things on Samos towards democracy" (8.75.2). Thucydides specifies that the changes toward democracy occurred "on Samos," not "among the Athenians on Samos." Finally, when the fleet swore its oaths to abide by the democratic constitution, avoid dissension, prosecute the war, and oppose the Four Hundred, they did not restrict the oaths to the Athenians present on Samos; "all the Samians of military age swore the same oath" (8.75.3). In fact, Thucydides tells us, "the soldiers shared all their affairs with the Samians including whatever would come of the dangers. . . . " (καὶ τὰ πράγματα πάντα καὶ τὰ ἀποβησόμενα ἐκ τῶν κινδύνων ξυνεκοινώσαντο οἱ στρατιῶται τοῖς Σαμίοις, 8.75.3). Andrewes calls this "a curious expression for an unusual idea; the reference is presumably to prospective success or failure in facing the dangers."[40] But the emphasis in the verb used (ξυνεκοινώσαντο, "they shared," "they made common between them") is on sharing between Athenians and Samians. When Thucydides announces one sentence later that "the soldiers" (οἱ στρατιῶται) held an assembly, his report that the soldiers cooperated with the Samians in everything and planned to share the outcome of the risks being run with them suggests that they may have shared this assembly with the Samians as well. The soldiers took on themselves the right to hold an assembly as the new city of Athens because they were democratic. They denied that the city in Attica was Athens because it was an oligarchy. The men on Samos, therefore, seem

[40] In Gomme et al. 1981, *s.v.* 8.75.3.

to define Athenian-ness by political affiliation. According to that logic, the democratic Samians, who pushed the Athenians to decide that they should be democratic, would seem to have as much claim to the title "Athenian" as the ethnic Athenians themselves.[41]

Thucydides' ironic comment that it was difficult to end the liberty of the Athenian people is inconsistent with his account of the introduction of oligarchy to Athens. The Athenians in Athens accepted oligarchy relatively easily and were uncharacteristically "quiet." The Athenians in Athens, that is, did not act like Athenians. Of all the men described in the *stasis* narrative so far, it was the Samians who were the most committed to democracy, so if democracy is essential to Athens, it was the Samians who were most Athenian. Thucydides' narrative, with its emphasis on the sharing between Athenians and Samians, suggests that the fleet-city on Samos, having split from Athens and the Athenians there, defined its citizen body to include both Athenians and Samians.[42]

This openness provides a strong contrast with Athens' treatment of the Plataeans earlier in the war. The Thebans accused the Plataeans of "atticism," and the Plataeans themselves claimed that in the sixth century, the Athenians had given them a share of their citizenship. The Plataeans, furthermore, were willing to act like Athenians and abandon their land and move to Athens when the Spartans besieged their city. But the Athenians would not let them do so, and so consigned many of them to their deaths at the Spartan show trial. Of those who escaped to Athens, Thucydides fails to report that the Athenians granted them Athenian

[41] Buck (1998, 28) notes that the Samians join in the vote "as if they were honorary Athenians."

[42] Cf. Sordi (2000, 107): "already in 411 Thrasybulus had joined the Samians to the Athenians." We should recall that in 405 B.C., when only the Samians remained loyal to Athens, the restored democracy in Athens, usually so jealous with the privilege, voted Athenian citizenship to all Samians (Meiggs and Lewis, n.94). Was this, in effect, a ratification of the ad hoc arrangements of the Athenian fleet-city on Samos? Sordi adduces also the parallel of Thrasybulus' attempt to grant citizenship to the metics who fought for the restoration of democracy in Athens. Buck (1998, 28) notes that what Thrasybulus attempted at that time is "foreshadow[ed]" by his treatment of the Samians. If Thucydides' text accurately represents the situation on Samos, Thrasybulus may have been led to his new ideas about Athenian citizenship by the contrast between Samian passion for democracy and Athenian passivity.

citizenship (3.68). Instead, he later presents them marching out of Athens to try to reconstitute a *polis* at the site of the destroyed Scione (5.32). Thucydides' emphasis is on the difference between Plataeans and Athenians and on the Athenians' jealous guarding of their Athenian-ness. That seems no longer to be the case. After not just Attica but even the Athens in Attica is abandoned for ideological reasons, traditional ideas of Athenian-ness based on ancestry or residence make far less sense. If the only important factor in defining Athens is democracy, then the only important factor in defining an Athenian is democracy, too.[43]

THE SAMIAN-ATHENIANS ALMOST ATTACK "THEMSELVES"

After the fleet on Samos returned to democracy, there were two rival groups of Athenians, the democrats on Samos and the oligarchs in Athens, and two rival Athenses – the traditional city in Attica and the city on Samos – each of which claimed to be the true city. This part of Thucydides' narrative examines what happens to a city when it is split asunder. It raises important questions about the value or danger of ideological purity (which fired the democrats on Samos) and investigates the claim to being "Athens" that each side made (and the legitimacy of those claims). Thucydides' focus throughout is on political compromise centered on the Athens in Attica.

Most curiously, it was Alcibiades who acted to save the city in Athens from the men of the city on Samos. Whether made up of Athenians or Athenians and Samians, the city on Samos was little inclined to treat with Athens, its traditional *polis*. Despite their return to democracy and Alcibiades' role in the original oligarchic plot, the Samian-Athenians

[43] In 410, after the restoration of the democracy, the Athenians passed a law that decreed that "if anyone overthrows the democracy at Athens or holds office after the democracy has been overthrown, he shall be an enemy of the Athenians and shall be killed with impunity" (Andocides 1.95, trans. Edwards). This decree views political affiliation as more important than actual *syngeneia*. An oligarch or supporter of oligarchy is hereby defined as an "enemy of the Athenians." He cannot logically be part of Athens.

remained fixated on the benefits Alcibiades might bring them because "they thought that their only chance of salvation was if he could move Tissaphernes from the Peloponnesians and over to them" (8.81.1). Thus they voted to recall Alcibiades. When he returned to the democratic fleet, Alcibiades gave a speech in which he exaggerated his power with Tissaphernes and promised to bring the Phoenician fleet to the Athenians (8.81.2–3). The men of the Athenian fleet, proving that, despite their claims, they were no better at good counsel (or judging Alcibiades) than the men of the Attic city, "immediately elected him general with the former ones and handed over to him all their affairs" (8.82.1). Their embrace of Alcibiades calls into further question the strength of the commitment to democracy in the city on Samos as Alcibiades had lately been the champion of oligarchy. The fleet on Samos seem here to be judging Alcibiades more by the value of what he could bring to them than by his ideological credentials. They were very committed to their anger at Athens in Attica, however, as their response to Alcibiades' speech shows.

Alcibiades fired the courage and optimism of the fleet to such a degree that Thucydides tells us that "not one would have traded for anything his present expectation both of salvation and of punishing the Four Hundred, and due to their sudden contempt for their present enemies because of what had been said they were ready to sail against the Piraeus" (8.82.1–2). Alcibiades, however, who knew the truth of the likelihood of their having the Phoenician fleet fighting beside them, was against this proposal. To forestall it and to pretend that there was complete confidence between himself and Tissaphernes, Alcibiades sailed away to him immediately in order to arrange things for the war (8.82.2–3). Thus it was Alcibiades, that "patriot for himself," who initially saved the Attic Athens from an attack by the fleet.[44]

The "patriots" on Samos were not long to be prevented from compelling the city in Attica to their will, however, even if it meant leaving foreign enemies behind them. The ambassadors sent out by the Four Hundred to explain the oligarchy in Athens finally arrived in Samos to placate the troops. They declared, as Thucydides long ago predicted they would, that the change in government had not been intended to

[44] Pouncey (1980, 105) describes Alcibiades in this way.

weaken the state but to save it (8.86.3). They also said that the full proclaimed Five Thousand would have a share in government and that no outrages had been committed against any relatives of the fleet. The men on Samos would have none of it, however, and in their anger proposed again to sail against the Piraeus. Alcibiades, however, for a second time prevented the men from attacking Attica.[45] Thucydides contends that if Alcibiades had not stopped the men on Samos from attacking Attica, "it is absolutely clear that the enemy would have occupied Ionia and the Hellespont immediately" (8.86.4).[46] Thucydides goes on to state his opinion that in preventing such an attack, "it seems that then Alcibiades for the first time and less than no other was a benefit to his city" (καὶ δοκεῖ Ἀλκιβιάδης πρῶτον τότε καὶ οὐδενὸς ἔλασσον τὴν πόλιν ὠφελῆσαι, 8.86.4).[47]

Kagan disputes Thucydides' judgment of Alcibiades' service:

> The possibility always existed that the Four Hundred would betray the city to the enemy as, in fact, they seem to have tried to do. The loss of Athens would surely have been a disaster of greater proportions and one harder to retrieve than the loss of Ionia and of the Hellespont. An attack on the Piraeus, on the other hand, given the serious division within the Four Hundred, might have been quickly successful. A united Athenian force could then have sailed to the Hellespont and fought a naval battle.[48]

[45] Holzapfel (462–64) thought that this passage and 8.82.1–2 were doublets, both written by Thucydides, about a single event. Andrewes (in Gomme et al. 1981, *s.v.* 8.86.4) rejects this view but nevertheless thinks "it remains odd that the second report takes no notice at all of the earlier occasion." Erbse (1989, 19), however, insists that the passages are only "superficially similar" and need no cross-reference.

[46] This passage represents one of Thucydides' "hypotheses." In his study of them, Flory (1988, 47) notes "how noteworthy and how remarkably numerous Thucydides' hypotheses are." Furthermore, they show a "high degree of speculation."

[47] I do not find convincing Ptaszek's (1994) argument that (reading ἐδόκει) this represents Thucydides' description of the judgment of the men of the fleet. Cf. Andrewes (in Gomme et al. 1981, *s.v.* 8.86.4): "there need be no doubt that this is Thucydides' personal judgment." I follow Andrewes (*loc. cit.*) in reading πρῶτον here. As Andrewes notes, "There is no difficulty, *pace* Steup, in the combination of πρῶτον τοτε with οὐδενὸς ἔλασσον: Thucydides is saying both that this was the first occasion, and that the service rendered was extremely valuable."

[48] Kagan 1987, 183.

Kagan's argument is based on the priority of Athens. "The loss of Athens," he says, "would surely have been a disaster of greater proportions . . . than the loss of Ionia and the Hellespont." This, of course, is an entirely different calculus than that of the Athenians and Samians on Samos. In their encouraging speeches to each other, the men on Samos specifically argued that the loss of the city was not to be much bemoaned. "They had lost nothing," they said, "since those ones had no more money to send (rather the soldiers were supplying themselves) nor good advice which was the thing which justifies cities' control over armies" (8.76.6). The loss of Ionia and the Hellespont, however, would destroy their chances of making a city out of Samos, their ships, and their empire. What is particularly interesting in this passage, however, is that Thucydides here seems specifically to endorse the fleet's argument of what constitutes the city. He commends Alcibiades for preventing the loss of Ionia and the Hellespont as if those imperial possessions were, in fact, more important than Athens itself, or at least more important than returning, the Athens in Attica to democracy. Thucydides seems little interested in that.

Thucydides' position is more nuanced than this, however, as the wording of his commendation of Alcibiades shows. He praises Alcibiades for his first and greatest benefit to his city. At a time when Thucydides has made clear that both the men on Samos and the men in Athens claim to be "the city," these words are highly charged. Which city did Alcibiades benefit? Despite seeming to judge the Hellespont and Ionia more important than the Attic Athens, what Thucydides really praises Alcibiades for is preventing the men on Samos from using their ideological purity as an excuse to attack the Attic city. Thucydides describes the loss of Ionia and the Hellespont as an inevitable result of the fleet's desires, but the core of Thucydides' praise of Alcibiades is that "when the Athenians on Samos were set to sail against themselves . . . he prevented them" (ὡρμημένων γὰρ τῶν ἐν Σάμῳ Ἀθηναίων πλεῖν ἐπὶ σφᾶς αὑτούς . . . κωλυτὴς γενέσθαι, 8.86.4). This designation of the men in Athens as "themselves" *vis à vis* the men on Samos is powerful and important, especially given the apparent definition of "themselves" of the men on Samos. The Athenians on Samos, as we have seen, seem ready to include in "themselves" even Samians as long as they are democrats. Such men would not be likely to judge the Athenians in Athens as "themselves" because of their hatred of oligarchy. Thucydides' praise of

Alcibiades rests on his preventing the Athenians on Samos from acting on their ideological enmity and attacking men who Thucydides insists, despite their oligarchy, were, in fact, still "themselves." The emphasis in the passage is strongly on the unity of the two groups.[49]

Alcibiades was no democrat, and his vision of the city mirrored neither the fleet's disdain for the Attic city nor its insistence on democracy. It does echo Thucydides in an important respect, however. Alcibiades gave the assembly's response to the delegates from Athens and told them that although he did not oppose the Five Thousand ruling, they had to dismiss the Four Hundred and institute the council of Five Hundred as before. Thucydides finishes his account of Alcibiades comments as follows:

> in general he bid them to hold out and not to give in to the enemy in any way. While the city was preserved (σῳζομένης τῆς πόλεως), there was great hope that they would come to an agreement with themselves, but once either one of the two was lost, either the one on Samos or them, there would be no one left for anyone to be reconciled with (8.86.7).

When Alcibiades speaks of the city here, he means the Athens in Attica. When Alcibiades says that "while the city was preserved, there was great hope that they would come to an agreement with themselves," the statement follows immediately upon his exhortation to the men in Attica "not to give in to the enemy in any way." This suggests that when he speaks of the *polis* here, he means the traditional city in Attica (which the men in Athens might surrender to the enemy) and that he values this traditional city that the fleet had rejected earlier.

The words Thucydides reports for Alcibiades here strikingly echo Thucydides' own authorial comment in this section of the text. Just as Thucydides praises Alcibiades for preventing the men on Samos

[49] Loraux (1993, 91) remarks that "in narrating civil strife, the tendency among Greek historians is to regularly substitute the reflexive ('themselves') for the reciprocal (*allelous*, 'some/others')." Nevertheless, she calls it "spectacular" that Thucydides says that the fleet is going to attack "themselves." Although in reality the fleet was intending to attack men whom they saw as a separate group, Thucydides' language does not admit this division and simply "erases the other . . . in the same." The emphasis throughout is on "the representation of unity."

from sailing against "themselves" (8.86.4), Alcibiades implies that his primary goal is for them "to come to an agreement with themselves" (πρὸς μὲν γὰρ σφᾶς αὐτοὺς . . . πολλὴν ἐλπίδα εἶναι καὶ ξυμβῆναι). Alcibiades' emphasis would seem to be on reconciling the two groups to each other (or, as he and Thucydides would say, with "themselves").

What this required, however, was political compromise. The men of the fleet recently had sworn solemn oaths to abide by the democratic constitution (8.75.2). Twice they had wanted to sail against Athens to compel it to their democratic will. Yet their spokesman Alcibiades now acquiesces to the rule of the Five Thousand. Alcibiades, therefore, either completely ignored the will of the men of the fleet or he radically changed their minds. Thucydides stresses the command Alcibiades had over the fleet when he writes that "there was not another man in existence who could have held the mob in check at that time" (8.86.5), suggesting that perhaps Alcibiades simply over rode the desires of the fleet. On the other hand, Thucydides implies that Alcibiades persuaded the men, and did not just ignore them, when he explains that "he used his tongue to such effect that he diverted them from the anger that they felt against the delegates on personal grounds" (8.86.5). It would seem, then, that Alcibiades convinced the democrats on Samos to compromise on democratic principle. Because Thucydides praises Alcibiades for his actions ("his first and greatest act of service to his city"), it would seem that Thucydides commends the compromise as well. If this is the case, Thucydides is hardly commending and supporting the men on Samos for being willing, as Westlake described them, "to uphold their ancestral democracy at whatever cost to themselves" or for being prepared, as Connor wrote, "to make sacrifices in order to preserve the security of Athens under democratic government." Rather, Thucydides praises the men on Samos when they are willing to compromise (with "themselves") and not insist on democratic government.[50] Alcibiades, the master of fluid definitions of the city, taught political flexibility to the men of the fleet and urged them to a return to a more traditional definition of the city. He called them back from the argument of the "encouraging speeches" according to which any location, as long as it was democratic, could be their city. Athens, Alcibiades argued, was in Attica even under the rule

[50] Westlake 1989, 188; Connor 1984, 221.

of the Five Thousand. Thucydides' praise of Alcibiades suggests that he agreed.

Even that city in Attica was soon torn by *stasis*, however. The oligarchs in Attica split into two groups, with the more radical in the *asty* and the more moderate based in the Piraeus. Theramenes and the moderate hoplites proclaimed support for a government of Five Thousand and opposed the more narrow oligarchy of the Four Hundred (8.92.10–11), and the next day the hoplites marched to the Theatre of Dionysus in the Piraeus, where they held an assembly (8.93.1). The hoplites of the Piraeus, that is, like the fleet on Samos, took to themselves the functions of a *polis*. There were at this point, then, three Athenses: one in Piraeus, one on Samos, and one in the *asty*. Any member of each, however, claimed that his alone was legitimate. When Thucydides describes the situation in the Attic Athens, a series of echoes of earlier events stresses the danger Athens faced because of the Athenians' ability to redefine the *polis*.

Two of the Attic Athenses almost met in battle when the Athenians in Piraeus decided to march on the Athenians in the *asty*. The appearance of the Peloponnesian fleet, however, prevented any fighting. Thucydides' presentation of the Athenians' response to this crisis is revealing. Thucydides explains that "on the grounds that the war with the enemy was more important than this private war and was not far off but actually coming against their harbor," the Athenians raced "with their whole people" (πανδημεί) to the Piraeus to man the ships and guard the walls. (8.94.3). Using his "catchphrase" from the Persian wars, Thucydides says of the Athenians in 411: "some went on board the ships that were already there and some launched others" (καὶ οἱ μὲν ἐς τὰς παρούσας ναῦς ἐσέβαινον, οἱ δὲ ἄλλας καθεῖλκον, 8.94.3) to try to defend Euboea from the Spartans.

Rood argues that Thucydides' use of the catchphrase "to go on board ship" here is meant to show that these Athenians "are the same Athenians as of old."[51] If Rood means that Thucydides intends to indicate that they are quick, powerful, and successful, the text does not bear him out. Rather, Thucydides' account of the Athenians' failed defense of Euboea presents them as bumbling incompetents, not as the victors of Salamis. These Athenians were bested all around. They were bested in

[51] Rood 1999, 148.

battle, although they were outnumbered by only forty-two to thirty-six ships, in part because they were compelled to fill their ships with men who had never trained together as crews, because their main fleet was at Samos. They were bested in cleverness and planning as well, defeated by the soldiers' desire for dinner and the Euboeans' simple expedient of closing the market. The Spartan commander saw that his men had a meal before they put to sea, but the Athenians in Euboea, when they saw the Spartans coming and tried to man their ships, found that their sailors were far away, scrounging a meal from houses on the outskirts of town because the Euboeans had arranged that no food was for sale. In addition, they were bested in knowledge and analysis. They thought Eretria a friendly city (despite its having refused them food), so many of them were needlessly slaughtered when they chose to flee there. Finally, the importance of Euboea bested them. "Now that Attica was cut off," Thucydides remarks, "Euboea was everything to them" (Εὔβοια γὰρ αὐτοῖς ἀποκεκλῃμένης τῆς Ἀττικῆς πάντα ἦν, 8.95.2).

If Rood means instead that these are "the Athenians of old" because of their easy ability to redefine their city, the narrative supports him, for Thucydides makes allusion to the *stasis* Athens suffered because of this ability even as he uses his "catchphrase." Thucydides claims that the Athenians raced "with their whole people" to the Piraeus to man the ships and guard the walls (8.94.3). Thucydides' claim means, first, that the presence of the enemy had allowed the Athenians in Attica to paper over the divide between the city in the *asty* and the city in the Piraeus. Thucydides' remark that the Athenians were "with their whole people," however, simultaneously directs our attention to their prior division and the fact that they were so recently split (even within Attica) into two cities and two peoples.

On a second level, furthermore, his use of "with their whole people" (πανδημεί) with the "catchphrase of 480" is bitterly ironic. The Athenians who raced to "go on board ship" at the Piraeus might be (temporarily) "with their whole people" *vis-à-vis* the men in Attica, but in 411 (unlike in 480) the Athenians were not really "with their whole people," because their real force lay with the fleet on Samos, among Samians and Athenians who believed that they, and not the men in Athens, were the city. Those Samian-Athenians, moreover, had recently contemplated manning their ships either to attack the city in Attica or to abandon it altogether in favor of their own idea of the city. The Athenians of 411 are "the Athenians of old," then, only in their speed in reimagining and redefining their city.

Rood is right, nevertheless, to direct our attention to the Athenians of old, for this section of the *History* resounds with echoes of earlier events. Thucydides lays before his readers the whole scope of the war. With these echoes, Thucydides implies that the Athenians' ability to redefine their *polis* – and the *stasis* attendant on it – was at least in part responsible for their loss of the war.

The bumbling Athenians of 411 were not able to prevent the revolt of Euboea. Because of this loss, the Athenians were terrified. "When news of the events concerning Euboea came to the Athenians," Thucydides reports, "the greatest panic of all before occurred (ἔκπληξις μεγίστη δὴ τῶν πρὶν παρέστη). For neither the misfortune in Sicily, although it had seemed to be enormous then, nor any other at all terrified them so much" (8.96.1). Here Thucydides seems to contradict what he reported about an aborted Peloponnesian raid on the Piraeus in 428. Although the Peloponnesians did not actually attack the Piraeus at that time, the smoke from the raid they made on Salamis caused the Athenians in the *asty* to think that the Peloponnesians had taken Piraeus. Consequently, according to Thucydides, "a panic broke out smaller than none of the others in the war" (ἔκπληξις ἐγένετο οὐδεμιᾶς τῶν κατὰ τὸν πόλεμον ἐλάσσων, 2.94.1). In book 8, however, Thucydides insists on the magnitude of the emotion in 411.[52] Thucydides takes care to explain why:

> when the army in Samos had revolted, when there were no other ships nor men to go on board them, when they themselves were in *stasis* and it was unclear when

[52] The passage about the aborted raid on the Piraeus in 428 contains a hypothesis by Thucydides about what might have been. Flory (1988, 54) notes that "almost every one of [Thucydides'] hypotheses occurs in a passage where the author says that what did happen was the worst, the biggest, or the greatest event in the war or in human history." This suggests that Thucydides is less interested in actually ranking the panics than in simply marking their magnitude with hyperbole. We thus should not use the contradiction regarding which panic was really the greatest as a guide to whether Thucydides knew of the later raid when he wrote about the first, as Gomme (1956, s.*v.* 2.94.1) and Rusten (1989, *s.v.* 2.94.1) do. See Hornblower (1991, *s.v.* 2.94.1).

they would fight themselves, when so great a disaster had followed in which they had lost their ships and – the main thing – Euboea, which had benefitted them more than Attica, how could they not be despondent? What especially disturbed them and most closely, was if the enemy, since they had won, would have the daring to sail straightaway to the Piraeus, which was now empty of ships and they thought that the Spartans were virtually there already (8.96.2–3).

The Athenians' "panic" over the loss of Euboea, and Thucydides' stress on the absence of ships for defense, leads us further back in time to another "panic" – that over the revolt of Chios (8.15). At that time, "because of their present panic" (ὑπὸ τῆς παρούσης ἐκπλήξεως), the Athenians "immediately" (εὐθὺς) cancelled the penalties on using the thousand-talent reserve fund "for anything other than if the enemy should sail against the city with a fleet and it was necessary to ward them off" (2.24.1). The Athenians then used those funds to man ships to recover Chios (8.15.1–2). Because of this, when the Peloponnesians came with a fleet into waters off the Athenians' coast, caused Euboea to revolt, and seemed likely any minute to sail into the Piraeus, now "empty of ships," the Athenians had no reserve fund of money or ships to defend the Piraeus, the *asty*, or the city in Attica because they had used them on Chios. Thus the danger to Athens in 411 is due in part to the Athenians' failure to focus their defense on the city of Attica. Their choice to use the reserve fund of money and ships on Chios left the Attic city defenseless.[53]

Without downplaying the danger in which the Athenians had put themselves by choosing Chios over Athens, Thucydides nevertheless indicates that on this particular occasion, the lack of ships did not

[53] Of the Athenians' decision, Kallet (2001, 247) remarks that "a rational decision to set aside the money is now canceled because of irrational fear upon learning of the revolt of Chios; this was not a direct threat to Athens itself. The emotional context in which Thucydides embeds the decision suggests criticism of it." By the comparison Thucydides means the reader to note (and to criticize) the city the Athenians chose to protect with this decision. When the Athenians were faced with the "two wars" – in Decelea and in Sicily – the Athenians chose to protect anything but Attica. The make a similar choice with regard to Chios. Kallet asserts that the revolt of Chios "was not a direct threat to Athens itself," but this is not the judgment of the Athenians. They focus on a wider definition of the city of Athens.

matter because of the weakness and timidity of the Athenians' enemy. The Athenians were terrified that the Spartans would follow up their victory at Euboea with a raid on the Piraeus "now empty of ships and they thought that the Spartans were virtually there already." Thucydides specifically hypothesizes that "if they had been more daring," the Spartans "could easily have done this" (ὅπερ ἄν, εἰ τολμηρότεροι ἦσαν, ῥᾳδίως ἂν ἐποίησαν, 8.96.4). The Spartans, however, did not do so. And so, Thucydides tells us,

> the Spartans proved not on this occasion alone, but also on many others that they were the most convenient for the Athenians to fight against. For as the farthest from them in character – the one people being quick, the other slow; the one enterprising, the other timid (οἱ μὲν ὀξεῖς, οἱ δὲ βραδεῖς, καὶ οἱ μὲν ἐπιχειρηταί, οἱ δὲ ἄτολμοι) – they were obliging in general and particularly in the case of a naval power (8.96.5).

Thucydides' judgment echoes the Corinthians' characterization of the Athenians and the Spartans from before the war: the Athenians were "quick both to contrive things and to put them into effect" (ἐπινοῆσαι ὀξεῖς καὶ ἐπιτελέσαι ἔργῳ ἃ ἂν γνῶσιν, 1.70.2); they were "bold beyond their power" (οἱ μὲν καὶ παρὰ δύναμιν τολμηταὶ, 1.70.3). The Spartans, by contrast, were "defending themselves . . . by procrastination" (τῇ μελλήσει ἀμυνόμενοι, 1.69.4); they were "delayers" (μελλητάς, 1.70.4), and the Corinthians begged them to "end your slowness now" (μέχρι μὲν οὖν τοῦδε ὡρίσθω ὑμῶν ἡ βραδυτής, 1.71.4). The coincidence with the characterization from two decades earlier is striking.[54]

Thucydides underlines the unchanging weakness of the Spartans when he states that 411 was not the only occasion when they demonstrated how obliging they were. One of the other occasions was the aborted raid on the Piraeus in 428 that caused the Athenians to "panic" so much. Thucydides emphasizes this point in the explanations he gives for the Spartans' two failures. About the (non)raid of 411 he writes that "if they had been more daring they could easily have done it" (ὅπερ ἄν, εἰ τολμηρότεροι ἦσαν, ῥᾳδίως ἂν ἐποίησαν, 8.96.4).

[54] Kallet (2001, 279) calls Thucydides' "scathing judgment" a "highly compressed version of the Corinthians' fuller portrait of the contrast in book 1 (1.68–71)."

About the (non)raid of 428 he judged that "if they had been willing not to shrink back, it could easily have happened" (ὅπερ ἄν, εἰ ἐβουλήθησαν μὴ κατοκνῆσαι, ῥᾳδίως ἐγένετο, 2.94.1). These two hypothetical sentences of identical shape stress the characteristic weakness of the Spartans throughout the war. At the same time, the weakness of the Spartans paradoxically undermines the Athenians' position. Thucydides stresses how "easy" it would have been for the Spartans to take the Piraeus in 428 or 411 and so shows that if the Athenians had had even slightly more daring enemies, the war might have been over, and lost, in 428.

These two hypotheticals also resonate with Thucydides' final comments about Pericles in the *Epitaph*. There he remarks on "how great an abundance there was at Pericles' disposal then through which he foresaw that the city would very easily prevail in the war over the Peloponnesians alone" (τοσοῦτον τῷ Περικλεῖ ἐπερίσσευσε τότε ἀφ' ὧν αὐτὸς προέγνω καὶ πάνυ ἂν ῥᾳδίως περιγενέσθαι τὴν πόλιν Πελοποννησίων αὐτῶν τῷ πολέμῳ, 2.65.12). In these hypotheticals however, Thucydides makes clear that with only a little more backbone, the Spartans might have "easily" (ῥᾳδίως) captured the Piraeus and won the war in 411 or in 428. They did not do so then, of course. The Spartans were not daring enough at that time. Nevertheless, Thucydides' repetition of that "easily" underscores that the Athenians did not "prevail" and suggests it was never likely that they would prevail "very easily," as Pericles had claimed they would.

Of course, the Athenians in Attica did have more daring enemies than the Spartans in 411. They were in danger from the men on Samos, and an *Athenian* attack on the Piraeus lurks behind Thucydides' discussion of the Spartans' missed opportunity there. Thucydides writes that when the Spartans failed to sail on the Piraeus, they "proved not on this occasion alone, but also on many others that the Lacedaemonians were the most convenient for the Athenians to fight against" (8.96.5). If readers did not know the outcome of the war, they would judge from this passage that the Spartans will not defeat the Athenians, for this passage suggests that the only thing that could defeat the Athenians is an attack by an enemy more like them – if, for example, they attacked themselves. This, of course, the men in the fleet on Samos had almost done when they twice proposed to attack the Piraeus. Thucydides' discussion here calls to mind a hypothesis related to that possibility: "but if the active innovative men from Samos had attacked the Piraeus, then. . . ." Thucydides' judgment about the slow and obliging character of the Spartans, therefore, serves again to underscore the danger that the Athenians faced from their fleet and the danger they had brought on themselves through *stasis.*

THE CITY IS IN ATTICA

Quite abruptly, however, Thucydides changes tack and begins to focus on reconciliation. In the earlier hypothetical sentence in book 8 (8.86.4–5), when Alcibiades prevented the city on Samos from attacking the city in Attica, Thucydides concluded that if Alcibiades had failed, although the men from Samos might have taken the Athens in Attica, "the enemy would have occupied Ionia and the Hellespont immediately" (8.86.4). For preventing this and thus preventing the attack, Thucydides praised Alcibiades for his great "benefit to his city" (τὴν πόλιν ὠφελῆσαι, 8.86.4). Here, however, although Thucydides indicates that an attack from Samos was part of what the Athenians in Attica feared ("since it was unclear when they would fight themselves," ἄδηλον ὂν ὁπότε σφίσιν αὐτοῖς ξυρράξουσι, 8.96.2), Thucydides does not repeat his speculation about what would have happened if the quick Athenians, instead of the slow Spartans, had attacked the Piraeus. Instead, he takes a different and very surprising approach:

> if the Spartans had been more daring they could easily have [sailed into the Piraeus] and if they lay at anchor they would have thrown the city still more into *stasis* or if they remained and undertook a siege, they would have compelled the ships from Ionia – however much they were enemies of the oligarchy – to aid their own home-mates and the entire city. And in that event, the Hellespont and Ionia and the islands and everything up to Euboea, that is the whole empire of the Athenians, would have been the Spartans (8.96.4).

These comments merit careful analysis. First, Thucydides undercuts the symbolism of the Attic Athenians' going on board ship to defend Euboea "with our whole people" (πανδημεί) when he cavalierly declares that the Peloponnesians might have further divided the city just by their appearance. Although the Athenians joined together "with their whole people" to resist the Peloponnesians, the fissures in the city were not gone, he implies, just filled in for the present crisis, ready to reopen should the situation get a bit worse. The paradigm is, again, Corcyra, where democrats and oligarchs together "went on board ship" to fight the external enemy only to return quickly to internecine slaughter. Any reconciliation that had occurred, Thucydides suggests, was weak and temporary.

Nevertheless, Thucydides goes on to say that if the Peloponnesians had remained to put Athens to siege, the fleet in Ionia would have put aside their hostility to the oligarchy. He seems certain that the city on Samos would come to aid what he calls "their own home-mates" and "the entire city" (τοῖς σφετέροις οἰκείοις καὶ τῇ ξυμπάσῃ πόλει βοηθῆσαι). He says, in fact, that the situation would have "compelled" them (ἠνάγκασαν) to come to the aid of Athens. Furthermore, Thucydides claims that helping the city in Attica would help "the entire city" (τῇ ξυμπάσῃ πόλει βοηθῆσαι) even though it might lose "the whole Athenian *arche*" (ὡς εἰπεῖν ἡ Ἀθηναίων ἀρχὴ πᾶσα). The Athenians on Samos, however, before Alcibiades forced a compromise on them, were eloquent in dismissing the men and the city in Attica because of their fixation on democracy. That city meant nothing to them; with their fleet, they could find another city wherever they wished. They were a city themselves. Would those men really judge that saving the oligarchic Attic city was worth losing everything else?

The situation Thucydides imagines here is not much different from his hypothesis from ten chapters earlier (8.86.4). There, Thucydides praised Alcibiades because he prevented the fleet on Samos from sailing to Athens to compel it to be a democracy, "which would certainly have meant the immediate occupation of Ionia and the Hellespont by the enemy" (8.86.4). Thucydides' praise of Alcibiades there suggests that in his eyes, the loss of Ionia and the Hellespont would be too high a price to pay for returning Athens to democracy. Here, Thucydides argues that even the staunch democrats on Samos would have put aside their hatred of oligarchy to preserve the Attic city. His statement that they would have been "compelled" to this choice suggests he thinks it the right one – that they would have been correct to bend from their insistence on "uphold[ing] their ancestral democracy" or "the security of

Athens under democratic government" for which commentators praise them.[55] Athens, Thucydides says, matters more than the form of its government. Furthermore, Thucydides insists on the essential connection between the factioneers despite their political differences. Thucydides says the men on Samos would have been compelled "however much they were enemies of the oligarchy to aid their own home-mates."

Throughout his work, Thucydides suggests that the Athenians failed to judge properly what belonged to them. They had, as we have seen, no proper "home" attachment. Euphemus, furthermore, had argued that denying ties of *philia* or *syngeneia* in making decisions was particularly appropriate to Athens because "to a man who is a tyrant or to a city ruling an empire, nothing is illogical that is expedient nor homelike (οἰκεῖον) that is not trustworthy" (6.85.1). Up to this point, the democratic factioneers on Samos seem to follow Euphemos' logic. They use a calculation of expediency and a focus on the material as they argue the worthlessness of their ancestral city and the men there. They seem, furthermore, to allow Samian democratic foreigners into their ranks as they counsel abandoning the Attic city and the men in it in favor of their new Samian Athens. Thucydides' decision, at this crucial moment, to describe the Athenians in Attica as "their own home-mates" to the fleet insists on the essential connection between the fleet and the men in Attica. The phrase argues that the Athenians on Samos would judge the "homelike" not by expediency or trustworthiness or even politics but by connection to home.

Five times in his *stasis* narrative, Thucydides makes reference to reconciliation. The most overt concerns the aborted oligarchic coup in the *polis* of Samos in 411. When the Samian democrats defeated their opponents, they killed thirty of the three hundred oligarchic conspirators and punished three more with exile, but as for the rest, Thucydides tells us, "they remembered no wrongs against them and lived together as fellow citizens in a democracy for the future" (τοῖς δ' ἄλλοις οὐ μνησικακοῦντες δημοκρατούμενοι τὸ λοιπὸν ξυνεπολίτευον, 8.73.6).[56] With

[55] Westlake 1989, 188; Connor 1984, 221.

[56] Bearzot (2006b, unpaginated) assigns the proposal of this idea to Thrasybulus, but Thucydides gives no hint of this. In Thucydides, the Samians are the actors. They are aided by the Athenians, but they seem in charge. They are the subject of the crucial sentence, and the idea of "not remembering wrongs" against

regard to the Athenian *stasis* opponents, both Alcibiades and Thucydides himself (twice) each insists that the two groups, Samian-Athenians and Athenians in Athens, despite their political differences, are not distinct groups but rather "themselves" (σφᾶς αὐτούς 8.86.4, 8.86.7, 8.96.2). Finally, Thucydides says that the Samian-Athenians, despite the loss of empire that it would probably entail, would have been "forced" to come to the aid of "their own home-mates and the entire city" (8.96.4).

In his account of the *stasis* that convulsed Corcyra, Thucydides remarks that "the cities that came late to *stasis*, by hearing of what had been done before, greatly added to the excess of the revolution in thinking both in the extraordinary cunning of the attacks and in the extraordinary nature of the revenge" (τὰ ἐφυστερίζοντά που πύστει τῶν προγενομένων πολὺ ἐπέφερε τὴν ὑπερβολὴν τοῦ καινοῦσθαι τὰς διανοίας τῶν τ'ἐπιχειρήσεων περιτεχνήσει καὶ τῶν τιμωριῶν ἀτοπίᾳ, 3.82.3). He thus leads the reader to expect that Athens, which came to *stasis* years after Corcyra, would be even more violent in *stasis* than Corcyra and that the *stasis* would be even more destructive. But in 411, at least, this was not the case. Alcibiades calmed the fleet with political compromise and they did not attack "themselves." Furthermore, the Athenians in Athens united to face the Peloponnesians and ended their *stasis* with the introduction of the rule of the Five Thousand. Eventually, city and fleet reintegrated. In 404–403, too, although the rule of the Thirty Tyrants was very violent, the end result of the *stasis* was peaceful. The democrats, in victory, did not in their turn slaughter hundreds of their political opponents, but proclaimed an amnesty that declared "and of things in the past it is not permitted for anyone to remember wrongs against another (τῶν δὲ παρεληλυθότων μηδενὶ πρὸς μηδένα μνησικακεῖν ἐξεῖναι) except in the case of the Thirty, the Ten, the Eleven, and the governors of the Piraeus" (*Ath. Pol.* 39.6).

Aristotle uses the same verb Thucydides uses to describe the restraint of the Samian democrats of 411: "they did not remember any wrongs against the rest" (τοῖς δ' ἄλλοις οὐ μνησικακοῦντες 8.73.6).[57] Andrew

the Samian oligarchs is intimately tied to "living together as fellow citizens," showing that it is the Samians and citizens of the Samian polis who are being discussed.

[57] Thucydides also uses the phrase μὴ μνησικακῶ (4.74.2) when he describes an (ultimately failed) agreement between Megarian factions (4.66–74), but the

Wolpert notes that Thucydides' readers "cannot help but be surprised" at the eventual outcome of the Athenian Civil War and the Athenian reconciliation agreement in part because "we are taught by the Corcyran revolution the difficulty of stopping violence once *stasis* erupts." Wolpert suggests that "if Thucydides wrote much of his work after the Peloponnesian War, perhaps he expected his account of Corcyra to draw to the reader's attention the uniqueness of Athens."[58] The emphasis that Thucydides places on reconciliation toward the end of book 8 strongly supports this suggestion. Thucydides' readers are meant to be impressed by the uniqueness of Athens not just in 403 but also in 411, when the Athenians on Samos and the Athenians in Athens reconciled with "themselves." The emphasis of the account we have suggests, further, that if Thucydides had lived to write up an account of the *stasis* of 403, he would have been wary of all zealots, democratic and oligarchic alike, and would have praised the Athenians' agreement "not to remember wrongs" against each other.[59]

Any discussion of how Thucydides might have written about the end of the war must confront a major paradox in Thucydides' account of the war. Thucydides claims in the *Epitaph* that it was because of *stasis* that Athens lost the war: "they did not give in until falling afoul of each other in their private disagreements they were overthrown" (οὐ πρότερον ἐνέδοσαν ἢ αὐτοὶ ἐν σφίσι κατὰ τὰς ἰδίας διαφορὰς

events on Samos are particularly noteworthy because of the close connection Thucydides forges between the Samians and the Athenians at this time. This at least suggests that the Samian-Athenians approved and supported the Samians' decision to act generously toward their former opponents. The Athenians seem to have taken the restraint of the Samians toward their fellow citizens as a model in their own later *stasis*.

58 Wolpert 2002, xi. We do not know how or when Thucydides died. I agree with Hornblower (2000, 372) that "the material about Archelaos of Macedonia at 2.100 virtually compels a terminal date [for Thucydides' life] later than 399, the known date of Archelaos' death." This means that he lived to see the reign of the Thirty and makes likelier the apparent echo here.

59 It is not clear, of course, if Thucydides intended to write an account of the *stasis* of 403. The "second preface" makes it seem that Thucydides conceived of his narrative extending only until the defeat by Sparta. However, the judgment in the *Epitaph* that it was *stasis* that ultimately destroyed Athens suggests that perhaps Thucydides saw the story he told extending through the *stasis* of 403.

περιπεσόντες ἐσφάλησαν, 2.65.12). This presentation, however, does not accurately reflect the military reality of Athens' final defeat at Aegospotami in 405 and its surrender to the Spartans after a long siege.[60] As Andrewes remarks, Thucydides' judgment in the *Epitaph* "would mislead us totally on how the Peloponnesian War ended if we were deprived of sources other than Thucydides. . . . The destruction of the Athenian fleet and the subsequent reduction of Athens by starvation are entirely suppressed."[61] Thucydides instead stresses *stasis*. In this Thucydides seems to follow the tack of many in Athens after the Peloponnesian War who, in effect, praise the Athenians by refusing to admit that any enemy defeated them. Instead, the Athenians were betrayed or defeated themselves with *stasis*.[62] This is how Andrewes interprets Thucydides' comment in the *Epitaph*: "it is possible that Thucydides wanted the critical approval of his countrymen more than other people's" and so "he preferred in 2.65 to exploit a prevailing idealization of ὁμόνοια ["concord"] and guilt over failure to achieve it."[63] Similarly, Nicole Loraux argues that Thucydides gives "an Athenian version of the facts" which he "shares with the orators" and "adopts a quasi-official explanation for the defeat of 404, attributing the victory of the Lacedaemonians, who did not expect it, to the city's internal dissensions; Athens, then, *has been defeated only by itself*."[64]

The alternative to this approach is to interpret "private disagreements" very broadly. Thus Kagan judges that the events of the end of the war "support [Thucydides'] opinions in general." But his ultimate

[60] De Romilly (1962b, 49, n. 1) notes that Thucydides' claim "approaches paradox."

[61] Andrewes in Gomme et al., 1981, 424.

[62] Xenophon 2.1.32 reports that Adeimantus was accused of betraying the fleet to Lysander. Lysias 14.38 recounts the treachery of Adeimantus (together with Alcibiades) as fact. As Levy (1976, 36) notes, the Athenians saw in the treachery of their generals a way to "exculpate" themselves. "The treason of their generals allows them to judge that their defeat was not on the level." The argument that the Athenians defeated themselves with *stasis* also serves the same purpose. Cf. Levy (1976, 39): "like the idea of treason, it suggests that they did not succumb to their adversaries."

[63] Andrewes in Gomme et al., 1981, 424.

[64] Loraux 1981/1986, 139. Italics Loraux.

conclusion is that "Athens' hope for victory or survival lay in the cooperative leadership of Theramenes and Thrasybulus, but the disgrace of Alcibiades removed them from the leading positions." Thus only "in that very important sense, but in no other," in Kagan's view, did "private disagreements" lead to Athens' defeat.[65] Even more generally, Price argues that Thucydides, "far from viewing the Athenian *stasis* as beginning and ending with a particular oligarchical government in 411, interpreted the internal condition of Athens after Pericles' death as one of prolonged and ever deepening *stasis*." According to Price, Thucydides "thought the condition of *stasis* to have held its grip in Athens until the very end of the war, with milder or more serious outbreaks."[66] In this view, *stasis* ended the war because Athens was in *stasis* from Pericles' death onward.

It seems highly unlikely that in order to curry favor at home, Thucydides consciously endorsed Athens' self-deluding claims after the war that only Athenians and not the Lacedaemonians defeated Athens. As Connor perceptively warns,

> Thucydides is often at play with his readers, challenging and subverting attitudes, including those widely held within his own socioeconomic class, and those which had initially been assumed, affirmed, or sympathetically represented within the *Histories*. . . . The narrative frequently seems at first to accept or justify one assessment – often a conventional one – then new considerations emerge and new responses are evoked.[67]

The disagreement between Thucydides' judgment in the *Epitaph* and what we know of the facts of Athens' defeat, together with the different ways scholars interpret that discrepancy, urge us to read Thucydides' statement about *stasis* in the *Epitaph* with caution.

Even if the *Epitaph* "was necessarily written after the war" because it refers to its end and so, as Price argues, "reflects Thucydides' ultimate thoughts," this need be the case only with regard to the time of

[65] Kagan 1987, 418 and 421.

[66] Price 2001, 326–27.

[67] Connor 1984, 240. Cf. Perry (1937, 427): "Thucydides has the strange faculty of seeing and telling the plain truth of a matter without trying in any way to bring it into line with the cherished beliefs of men."

writing.[68] The *Epitaph* should not be read as Thucydides' last word on the defeat of Athens any more than it should be read as his last word on Pericles. Thucydides, of course, did not call chapter 65 of book 2 an *Epitaph*. Nevertheless, the summing-up nature of the chapter and the fact that it shares an argument about the defeat of Athens with the orators and with Lysias's *Epitaphios* suggests that, perhaps, it shares with real *Epitaphioi* and eulogies an interest in euphemism. Furthermore, its purpose may be to reflect, and so to comment on, the arguments Athenians made to themselves about the war while leaving Thucydides' own views obscure. Plato wrote a parody of a funeral oration in the *Menexenus* which follows the tradition of exculpating the Athenians' for their defeat but pushes that tradition "to the absurd."[69] As Loraux describes it, the *Menexenus* "immortalizes" the last Athenian victory at Arginussae by "declaring that Athens won the war."[70] Plato claims that "by their virtue we won not only the sea-battle then but also the whole war" (243d).

Recently, Morrison has compared Thucydides' *History* with Plato's early "aporetic" dialogues, which "are left in an important sense without resolution." Morrison argues that Thucydides' *History* and the early dialogues share a "special quality of eliciting the reader's engagement."[71] As Morrison notes, Thucydides regularly displays a "*lack of closure* in rhetorical and military conflict." In fact, "if there is to be any resolution, it is the reader who must provide it."[72] Morrison does not discuss the *Epitaph* in these terms, but it seems possible that, like Plato, Thucydides expected his readers to recognize (as indeed they have) that the explanation for the defeat of Athens he gives in the *Epitaph* is not entirely satisfactory. But rather than argue that Thucydides wished to soothe his shattered countrymen with falsehoods rather than accept an interpretation of his words so broad that they become almost meaningless, we should entertain the possibility that Thucydides is, once again, writing with irony.

[68] Price 2001, 369.

[69] Levy 1976, 39.

[70] Loraux 1981/1986, 140.

[71] Morrison 2006, 5.

[72] Morrison 2006, 19. Morrison's perceptive description of Thucydides' technique is antithetical to an acceptance of the *Epitaph* as the last word on anything.

Thucydides certainly seems to endorse the "quasi-official" view that only Athens could defeat Athens when he writes of the Peloponnesian (non)raid on the Piraeus in 411 and comments on what "obliging" enemies the Athenians had in the Lacedaemonians. However, if Thucydides did intend to write about the whole war, as he indicates in the second preface when he announces that he continued "until the Lacedaemonians and their allies put an end to the empire of the Athenians and occupied the Long Walls and the Piraeus" (5.26), he would have had to write about the defeats at Notium and Aegospotami. He would have had to write about the arrival of Lysander's fleet at the Piraeus (which Thucydides takes care to underline in his second preface). It would therefore have been obvious to any reader that if *stasis* played a part in defeat, it at least went hand in hand with military failure.

Furthermore, even Thucydides' comparison of Athenian and Spartan character in relation to the Peloponnesian (non)raid of 411, which seems to endorse the idea that Athens defeated itself, actually gives the lie to its own argument. If the Peloponnesian (non)raid on the Piraeus in 428 lies behind Thucydides' description of the (non)raid in 411, suggesting that the Spartans are ever and always the same, and if the Samian-Athenian (non)raid of 411 lurks behind it as well, suggesting that only the quick Athenians could defeat themselves, there looms also the actual appearance of Lysander at the Piraeus in 404. Eventually, even the slow Spartans made it to the Piraeus. If *stasis* destroyed Athens, it came with military defeat, and it is, as Price remarks, not a clearly defined outbreak like that in 411 but something more diffuse, general, and long-term. Price argues that Athens was in *stasis* since Pericles' death. I suspect Thucydides would put its genesis much earlier.

At the end of his *stasis* narrative, Thucydides has strong words about the city. As we have seen, in his earlier hypothesis in book 8, Thucydides argued that the loss of Ionia and the Hellespont would have been too high a price to pay to return the Attic Athens to democracy. In his later hypothesis, Thucydides suggests that such a loss would be worth it – indeed, compulsory – if it was required to preserve that city from the Spartans. The fleet had said that Athens was nothing. Pericles had suggested that Athens was a technicality, that what Athens really consisted of was the empire, the fleet, and power. The physical spot that grounded these was essentially interchangeable with any other. In his last hypothesis, however, Thucydides contends that the fleet would have rejected their own earlier judgment and Pericles' disdain for Athens and would have chosen, even at the loss of the empire, to save the Attic city. Foster notes that Pericles "refuses to think of Attica as anything other than property." She describes this as "logical" because "a different value might easily conflict with the fixed value of the empire. If Attica is worth having, then the empire is a relative value, and can be drawn back out into the sphere of real life in which it is compared to other good or bad things."[73] This might, in turn, lead to a reevaluation of the relative worth of Attica and the empire. This is exactly what Thucydides does in his final hypothesis. He places in stark contrast the city in Attica and the empire and says that in their reevaluation, the men of the fleet would have chosen that Attic city even over the empire.

Thucydides does not expressly state whether the decision of the fleet would have been wise or not (although his judgment that they would be "compelled' to their choice implies he thought it was). However, his emphatic use of the words "the whole city" (ἡ ξύμπασα πόλις) to describe what the fleet would have been saving (despite its sacrifice of "the whole empire of the Athenians," ὡς εἰπεῖν ἡ Ἀθηναίων ἀρχὴ πᾶσα), strongly suggests that nothing but an entity grounded in the Attic city can be "the city." It suggests that Thucydides would say the fleet would be right to abandon the empire to save the Athens in Attica. Would that not imply that Pericles was wrong all along?

Thucydides does not mention Pericles by name in his account of the Athenian *stasis* of 411, but an important echo of Pericles in Thucydides' *stasis* narrative suggests that Thucydides wishes his readers to think of Pericles and his radical ideas about the city as they contemplate Athens in *stasis*. Thucydides gives his ironic comment that it was no easy matter to deprive the Athenian people of their liberty (8.68.4) in order to explain why there was any difficulty at all in introducing oligarchy to Athens, given the powers of the oligarchic conspirators Peisander, Antiphon, Phrynichus, and Theramenes that he details immediately before this comment (8.68.1–4). Thucydides says that of the four, Antiphon was "the one who had planned the whole affair to get it to

[73] Foster 2001, 169.

this point and had taken greatest care of it." Thucydides then describes Antiphon as "second to none of the men of his time in *arete*, and most able both to form plans and to explain his judgments" (8.68.1). As Connor noted, "the wording used to praise Antiphon's rhetoric echoes Pericles' description of himself as someone 'inferior to none both to devise what is necessary and to communicate it'" (2.60.5). Connor deems it crucial to assessing the difference between Antiphon and Pericles that Pericles "immediately added two further considerations; he was, he said 'devoted to my city and incorruptible'" (φιλόπολίς τε καὶ χρημάτων κρείσσων, 2.60.5). In Connor's view, "the implicit comparison to Pericles helps us assess Antiphon's accomplishments and deficiencies. His rhetorical skill is almost Periclean but to stop the comparison at this point draws attention to Antiphon's lack of devotion to his city."[74]

Connor writes as if "devotion to one's city" is a straightforward idea without ambiguity or irony. But Thucydides' whole narrative shows that it is not, especially when attributed to a man like Pericles, who so radically redefined his city. Antiphon, after all, presumably felt devoted to the vision of the city that he, Peisander, Phrynichus, and Theramenes were trying to bring to birth. In fact, the wording of Thucydides' description of Pericles urges the reader to carefully ponder Pericles' devotion to his city and the difference between a Pericles and an Antiphon. When Pericles calls himself "devoted to my city," he uses the word *philopolis* (φιλόπολις). Thucydides' only other use of this word is in the mouth of Alcibiades at Sparta. "The true lover of his city," Alcibiades said, "is not the one who does not attack his city when he has lost it unjustly, but the one who, because of his longing, attempts to recover it in any way possible" (φιλόπολις οὗτος ὀρθῶς, οὐχ ὃς ἂν τὴν ἑαυτοῦ ἀδίκως ἀπολέσας μὴ ἐπίῃ, ἀλλ' ὃς ἂν ἐκ παντὸς τρόπου διὰ τὸ ἐπιθυμεῖν πειραθῇ αὐτὴν ἀναλαβεῖν, 6.92.4). Price contends that "whereas Pericles uses the term straightforwardly, Alcibiades contorts it in a breathtaking way."[75] Yet the echo is more complex that this. It encourages us to ask if Pericles' love of his city was really so very different from that of Alcibiades. Pericles' protestations of his "love for

[74] Connor 1984, 225
[75] Price 2001, 260.

his city," after all, like those of Alcibiades, appear in a speech in which he dramatically and unilaterally redefines the city he loves as he alone sees fit. Pericles professes his "love for his city" just a few breaths before he reveals to the Athenians that their *arche* consists not in their allies, as they think (much less in their houses and cultivated land), but in the whole of the nautical part of the world (2.62.4). This reveals that for Pericles, the "city" he loves and that inspires him to "patriotism" is the imperial, nautical city that has abandoned Attica in favor of control of half the world. If Alcibiades is, as Michael Palmer argues, "the true political heir of Periclean Athens," he is the successor to Pericles not least in his ability and willingness to reject the Athens that is in favor of a city that he likes better.[76] If being "devoted to his city" distinguishes Pericles from Antiphon, then it links Pericles to Alcibiades and so to faction fighting. For it is devotion to one's own personal definition and vision of the city that leads to and exacerbates *stasis*.[77]

Hornblower judges that Thucydides attributed the downfall of the Athenian empire to "greed or *pleonexia*." However, according to Hornblower

> personal prejudice – the spell of Pericles and the nostalgia for Pericles induced by experience of his less stylish successors – stood between Thucydides and a correct assessment of the moment at which *pleonexia*, which had been there from the Periclean period, and indeed from 479 and the beginning of the empire, began to have effects which would be fatal.[78]

On the contrary, this study of Thucydides' use of city and home imagery indicates that far from being under the "spell" of Pericles, Thucydides saw Pericles' culpability for Athens' *pleonexia*. Pericles' culpability is not total, of course, and he is hardly responsible for everything that happened in the war. Nevertheless, this study has shown that Thucydides connected the Athenians' *pleonexia* to their reconceptualization of the

76 Palmer 1992, 42.

77 Hobbes remarked, "a faction, therefore, is, as it were, a city in a city" (Hobbes *De Cive* XIII.13 in Hobbes 1983). The Samian "patriots" were *philopoloi* and devoted to their idea of a democratic city. Only because they were willing to compromise on that point could they hope to save "the whole city."

78 Hornblower 1987, 174–75.

city and to their inability to focus on their own home territory instead of lusting after the faraway, characteristics that (although he did not create them) Pericles certainly fostered. These characteristics are what, according to Thucydides, make Athenians Athenians. They led to their downfall, but they are the same characteristics that led them to imperial triumph. That is, Thucydides identified the fall of Athens with its rise; he saw the downfall in the pursuit (and conquest) of empire itself.

Works Cited

Abbott, G. F. 1925. *Thucydides: A Study in Historical Reality*. London: G. Routledge and Sons.

Adams, C. D., trans. 1919. *The Speeches of Aeschines*. Cambridge, Mass.: Harvard University Press.

Adcock, F. E. 1932. "Alcidas ἀργυρολόγος," in *Mélanges Gustave Glotz* I. Paris: Les Presses universitaires de France.

———. 1947. "EPITEIXISMOS in the Archidamian War," *The Classical Review* 61: 2–7.

———. 1951. "Thucydides in Book 1," *The Journal of Hellenic Studies* 71: 2–12.

Allison, J. W. 1983. "Pericles' Policy and the Plague," *Historia* 32: 14–23.

———. 1989. *Power and Preparedness in Thucydides*. Baltimore: Johns Hopkins University Press.

———.1997. "Homeric Allusions at the Close of Thucydides' Sicilian Narrative," *American Journal of Philology* 118: 499–516.

Amit, M. 1962. "The Sailors of the Athenian Fleet," *Athenaeum* 40: 157–178.

———. 1968. "The Melian Dialogue and History," *Athenaeum* 46: 216–235.

———. 1973. *Great and Small Poleis. A Study in the Relations between the Great Powers and the Small Cities in Ancient Greece*. Vol. 134 of Collection Latomus. Brussels: Latomus.

Andrewes, A. 1960. "The Melian Dialogue and Perikles' Last Speech," *Proceedings of the Cambridge Philological Society* n.s. 6: 1–10.

———. 1992. "The Spartan Resurgance. II. The Beginnings of the Athenian Revolution," in *The Cambridge Ancient History*. 2d ed., Vol. V. *The Fifth Century* B.C., ed. D. M. Lewis, J. Boardman, J. K. Davies, and M. Ostwald, 471–74. Cambridge: Cambridge University Press.

Avery, H. C. 1973. "Themes in Thucydides' Account of the Sicilian Expedition," *Hermes* 101: 1–13.

Badian, E. 1988. "Towards a Chronology of the Pentekontaetia Down to the Renewal of the Peace of Callias," *Echos du monde classique/Classical Views* 32 n.s. 7: 289–320.

———. 1993. *From Plataea to Potidaea. Studies in the History and Historiography of the Pentecontaetia*. Baltimore: Johns Hopkins University Press.

Bakker, E. 2006. "Contract and Design: Thucydides' Writing," in *Brill's Companion to Thucydides*, ed. A. Rengakos and A. Tsakmakis, 109–29. Leiden: Brill.

Balot, R. 2001. *Greed and Injustice in Classical Athens*. Princeton: Princeton University Press.

Bauslaugh, R. A. 1991. *The Concept of Neutrality in Classical Greece*. Berkeley: University of California Press.

Bearzot, C. 2001. "Στάσις e πόλεμος nel 404," in *Il pensiero sulla guerra nel mondo antico (Contributi dell'istituto di storia antica 27)*, ed. M. Sordi, 19–36. Milan: Vita e Pensiero.

———. 2006a. "Atene nel 411 e nel 404. Tecniche del colpo di stato," in *Terror et pavor. Violenza, intimidazione, clandestinità nel mondo antico (Atti del convegno, cividale del friuli, 22–24 Settembre)*, ed. G. Urso, 21–54. Pisa: ETS.

———. 2006b. "Memoria e oblio, vendetta e perdono nell'Atene del 403 A.C.," *Rivista online 4* (n.p.).

Berent, M. 1998. "*Stasis* or the Greek Invention of Politics," *History of Political Thought* 19: 331–62.

Bétant, E. A. 1843–1847. *Lexicon Thucydideum.* 2 vol. Geneva: É. Carey.

Bischoff, H. 1932. *Der Warner bei Herodot*. Ph.D. diss., Philipps-Universität Marburg.

Bleckmann, B. 1993. "Sparta und seine Freunde im dekeleischen Krieg. Zur Datierung von *IG* V 1, 1," *Zeitschrift für Papyrologie und Epigraphik* 96: 297–308.

Bloedow, E. F. 1981. "The Speeches of Archidamus and Sthenelaidas at Sparta," *Historia* 30: 129–43.

———. 2000. "The Implications of a Major Contradiction in Pericles' Career," *Hermes* 128: 295–309.

Bosworth, A. B. 1993. "The Humanitarian Aspect of the Melian Dialogue," *The Journal of Hellenic Studies* 113: 30–44.

———. 2000. "The Historical Context of Thucydides' Funeral Oration," *The Journal of Hellenic Studies* 120: 1–16.

Bowersock, G. W. 1968. "Pseudo-Xenophon. Constitution of the Athenians," in *Xenophon in Seven Volumes. VII. Scripta Minora*, ed. E. C. Marchand and G. W. Bowersock. Cambridge, Mass.: Harvard University Press.

Bruell, C. 1974. "Thucydides' View of Athenian Imperialism," *The American Political Science Review* 68: 11–17.

———. 1981. "Thucydides and Perikles," *The St. John's Review* 32: 24–29.

Brunt, P. A. 1965. "Spartan Policy and Strategy in the Archidamian War," *Phoenix* 19: 255–80.

Buck, R. J. 1998. *Thrasybulus and the Athenian Democracy* (*Historia einzelschriften, Heft* 120). Stuttgart: Franz Steiner Verlag.

Buffière, F. 1962. *Héraclite. Allégories d'Homère*. Paris: Les Belles Lettres.

Cagnazzi, S. 1986. "L'Αρχαιολογειν di Nicia (Tucidide VII 69, 2)," *Athenaeum* 64: 492–97.

Cagnetta, M. 1977. "Fonti oligarchiche nell' VIII di Tucidide," *Sileno* 2–4: 215–19.

———. 1980. "Due 'agoni' nell'ottavo libro di Tucidide," *Quaderni di Storia* 12: 249–58.

Camp, J. McK. 2000. "Walls and the *Polis*," in *Polis and Politics. Studies in Ancient Greek History*, ed. P. Flensted-Jensen, T. H. Nielsen and L. Rubinstein, 41–58. Copenhagen: Museum Tusculanum Press.

Campbell, D. A. trans. and ed. 1982. *Greek Lyric. I. Sappho and Alcaeus*. Cambridge, Mass.: Harvard University Press.

Canfora, L. 1970. *Tucidide continuato*. Padua: Atenore.

———. 2006. "Biographical Obscurities and Problems of Composition," in *Brill's Companion to Thucydides*, ed. A. Rengakos and A. Tsakmakis, 3–32. Leiden: Brill.

Classen J., and J. Steup. 1900. *Thukydides*. Vierter Band. Viertes Buch. Berlin: Weidmannsche Buchhandlung.

———. 1912. *Thukydides*. Fünfter Band. Fünftes Buch. Berlin: Weidmannsche Buchhandlung.

———. 1922. *Thukydides*. Achter Band. Achtes Buch. Berlin: Weidmannsche Buchhandlung.

Cogan, M. 1981a. *The Human Thing. The Speeches and Principles of Thucydides' History*. Chicago: University of Chicago Press.

———. 1981b. "Mytilene, Plataea, and Corcyra. Ideology and Policy in Thucydides, Book Three," *Phoenix* 35: 1–21.

Cohen, D. 1956. "*IG* I² 86 and Thucydides V, 47. (Treaty of Athens, Argos, Mantinea and Elis, 420/19 B.C.)," *Mnemosyne* 9: 289–95.

Connor, W. R. 1971. *The New Politicians of Fifth Century Athens*. Princeton: Princeton University Press.

———. 1979. "Thucydides 2.65.12," in *Arktouros. Hellenic Studies Presented to Bernard M. W. Knox on the Occasion of His Sixty-Fifth Birthday*, ed. G. W. Bowerstock, W. Burkert, and M. C. J. Putnam, 269–71. New York: W. De Gruyter.

———. 1984. *Thucydides*. Princeton: Princeton University Press.

———. 1985. "The Razing of the House in Greek Society," *Transactions of the American Philological Association* 115: 79–102.

———. 1991. "Polarization in Thucydides," in *Hegemonic Rivalry from Thucydides to the Nuclear Age*, ed. R. N. Lebow and B. S. Strauss, 53–69. Boulder: Westview Press.

Cornford, F. M. 1907. *Thucydides Mythistoricus*. London: E. Arnold.

Crane, G. 1992. "The Fear and Pursuit of Risk: Corinth on Athens, Sparta and the Peloponnesians (Thucydides 1.68–71, 120–121)," *Transactions of the American Philological Association* 122: 227–56.

———. 1996. *The Blinded Eye. Thucydides and the New Written Word*. Lanham, Md.: Rowman and Littlefield.

Debnar, P. 2001. *Speaking the Same Language. Speech and Audience in Thucydides' Spartan Debates*. Ann Arbor: University of Michigan Press.

Delebecque, E. 1965. *Thucydide et Alcibiade*. Aix-en-Provence: Éditions Ophrys.

Dewald, C. 2005. *Thucydides' War Narrative. A Structural Study*. Berkeley: University of California Press.

Dobree, P. 1874. *Adversaria*. I. Berlin: S. Calvary.

Dover, K. J. 1965. *Thucydides. Book VII*. Oxford: Oxford University Press.

———. 1981. "Thucydides' Historical Judgment: Athens and Sicily," *Proceedings of the Royal Irish Academy* 81: 231–238.

Eberhardt, W. 1959. "Der Melierdialog und die Inschriften ATL A9 (*IG* I^2 63 +) und *IG* I^2 97 +," *Historia* 8: 284–314.

Edmunds, L. 1975. *Chance and Intelligence in Thucydides*. Cambridge, Mass.: Harvard University Press.

Edwards, M. 1995. *Greek Orators. IV. Andokides*. Warminster: Aris and Phillips.

Erbse, H. 1989. *Thukydides-Interpretationen*. Berlin: W. De Gruyter.

Euben, J. P. 1986. "The Battle of Salamis and the Origins of Political Theory," *Political Theory* 14: 359–90.

Finley, J. H. 1938/1967. *Three Essays on Thucydides*. Cambridge, Mass.: Harvard University Press, (reprinted from *Harvard Studies in Classical Philology* 49 [1938] and 50 [1939] and from *Athenian Studies Presented to*

William Scott Ferguson: Harvard Studies in Classical Philology Suppl. Vol. 1 (1940).

———. 1963. *Thucydides*. Ann Arbor: University of Michigan Press.

Finley, M. I. 1954. "Appendix 3" in *Thucydides. History of the Peloponnesian War*, trans. R. Warner, New York: Penguin.

———. 1971. *The Ancestral Constitution*. Cambridge: Cambridge University Press.

———. 1985. *Democracy Ancient and Modern*. Rev. ed. New Brunswick: Rutgers University Press.

———. 1986. *Ancient History. Evidence and Models*. New York: Viking Press.

Flory, S. 1988. "Thucydides' Hypotheses about the Peloponnesian War," *Transactions of the American Philological Association* 118: 43–56.

———. 1993. "The Death of Thucydides and the Motif of 'Land on Sea,'" in *Nomodeiktes. Greek Studies in Honor of Martin Ostwald*, ed. R. Rosen and J. Farrell, 119–23. Ann Arbor: University of Michigan Press.

Fontenrose, J. 1978. *The Delphic Oracle*. Berkeley: University of California Press.

Forde, S. 1986. "Thucydides on the Causes of Athenian Imperialism," *The American Political Science Review* 80: 433–48.

———. 1989. *The Ambition to Rule. Alcibiades and the Politics of Imperialism in Thucydides*. Ithaca: Cornell University Press.

Foster, E. 2002. *Material Culture in Thucydidean Narrative*. Ph.D. diss., University of Chicago.

Fowler, D. P. 1989. "First Thoughts on Closure: Problems and Prospects," *Materiali e discussioni per l'analisi dei testi classici* 22: 75–122.

Frisch, H. 1942. *The Constitution of the Athenians*. Copenhagen: Gyldendal.

Garlan, Y. 1968. "Fortifications et histoire grecque," in *Problèmes de la guerre en Grèce ancienne*, ed. J.-P. Vernant, 245–60. Paris: La Haye, Mouton and Co.

———. 1974. *Recherches de poliorcétique grecque*. Athens: École française d'Athenes.

Goldhill, S. 1990. "The Great Dionysia and Civic Ideology," in *Nothing to Do with Dionysos?*, ed. J. J. Winkler and F. Zeitlin, 97–129. Princeton: Princeton University Press.

Gomme, A. W. 1945. *A Historical Commentary on Thucydides*. Vol. I. Book I. Oxford: Oxford University Press.

———. 1951. "Four Passages in Thucydides," *The Journal of Hellenic Studies* 71: 70–80.

———. 1956a. *A Historical Commentary on Thucydides*. Vol. II. Books II-III. Oxford: Oxford University Press.

———. 1956b. *A Historical Commentary on Thucydides.* Vol. III. Books IV-V.24. Oxford: Oxford University Press.

———, A. Andrewes, and K. J. Dover. 1970. *A Historical Commentary on Thucydides.* Vol. IV. Books V.25-VII. Oxford: Oxford University Press.

———, A. Andrewes, and K. J. Dover. 1981. *A Historical Commentary on Thucydides*. Vol. V. Book VIII. Oxford: Oxford University Press.

Goodhart, H. C. 1893. *The Eighth Book of Thucydides' History*. London: Macmillan Co.

Green, P. 1970. *Armada from Athens*. London: Hodder and Stoughton.

Greenwood, E. 2006. *Thucydides and the Shaping of History*. London: Duckworth.

Grene, D., and R. Lattimore, eds. 1954. *The Complete Greek Tragedies. Sophocles.* Chicago: University of Chicago Press.

Gribble, D. 1998. "Narrator Interventions in Thucydides," *The Journal of Hellenic Studies* 118: 41–67.

———. 1999. *Alcibiades and Athens. A Study in Literary Presentation.* Oxford: Oxford University Press.

———. 2006. "Individuals in Thucydides," in *Brill's Companion to Thucydides*, ed. A. Rengakos and A. Tsakmakas, 439–68. Leiden: Brill.

Grundy, G. B. 1948. *Thucydides and the History of his Age*. 2d ed. Vol. I. Oxford: Blackwell.

Hammond, N. G. L. 1973. "The Particular and the Universal in the Speeches in Thucydides with Special Reference to that of Hermocrates at Gela," in *The Speeches of Thucydides*, ed. P. A. Stadter, 49–59. Chapel Hill: University of North Carolina Press.

Hemmerdinger, B. 1948. "La division en livres de l'oeuvre de Thucydide," *Revue des études grecques* 61: 104–17.

Henderson, J., ed. and trans. 1998. *Aristophanes. Clouds. Wasps. Peace.* Cambridge, Mass.: Harvard University Press.

Hignett, C. 1952. *A History of the Athenian Constitution to the End of the Fifth Century*. Oxford: Oxford University Press.

Hobbes, T. 1843. *English Works*. Vol. 8, ed. Sir William Molesworth. London: J. Bohn.

———. 1983. *De Cive*, ed. H. Warrender. (Clarendon Edition of the *Philosophical Works of Thomas Hobbes*, Vol. III.) Oxford: Oxford University Press.

Holzapfel, L. 1893. "Doppelte Relationem im VIII. Buch des Thukydides," *Hermes* 28: 435–64.

Hornblower, S. 1987. *Thucydides*. Baltimore: Johns Hopkins University Press.

———. 1991. *A Commentary on Thucydides*. Vol. I. Books I-III. Oxford: Oxford University Press.

———. 1992. "Thucydides' Use of Herodotus" in *ΦΙΛΟΛΑΚΟΝ: Lakonian Studies in Honor of Hector Catling*, ed. J. M. Sanders, 141–54. London: British School at Athens. (Reprinted as Appendix A in Hornblower 1996.)

———. 1994. "Narratology and Narrative Techniques in Thucydides," in *Greek Historiography*, ed. S. Hornblower, 131–66. Oxford: Oxford University Press.

———. 1996. *A Commentary on Thucydides*. Vol. II. Oxford: Oxford University Press.

———. 2000. "The *Old Oligarch* (pseudo-Xenophon's *Athenian Politeia*) and Thucydides. A Fourth-Century Date for the 'Old Oligarch'?" in *Polis and Politics. Studies in Ancient Greek History*, ed. P. Flensted-Jensen, T. H. Nielsen, and L. Rubinstein, 363–84. Copenhagen: Museum Tusculanum Press.

———. 2004. *Thucydides and Pindar. Historical Narrative and the World of Epinikian Poetry.* Oxford: Oxford University Press.

Hude, C., ed. 1927. *Scholia in Thucydidem*. Leipzig: Teubner.

Hudson-Williams, H.L. 1950. "Conventional Forms of Debate and the Melian Dialogue," *American Journal of Philology* 71: 156–69.

Hunt, P. 2006. "Warfare," in *Brill's Companion to Thucydides*, ed. A. Rengakos and A. Tsakmakis, 385–413. Leiden: Brill.

Hunter, V. J. 1973. *Thucydides. The Artful Reporter*. Toronto: Hakkert.

Hussey, E. 1985. "Thucydidean History and Democritean Theory," in *Crux. Essays in Greek History Presented to G.E.M. de Ste. Croix on his 75th Birthday*, ed. P. Cartledge and F. D. Harvey, 118–138. London: Duckworth.

Jameson, M. 1960. "A Decree of Themistokles from Troizen," *Hesperia* 29: 198–223.

———. 1963. "The Provisions for Mobilization in the Decree of Themistokles," *Historia* 12: 385–404.

Jordan, B. 2000. "The Sicilian Expedition was a Potemkin Fleet," *Classical Quarterly* 50: 63–79.

Kagan, D. 1969. *The Outbreak of the Peloponnesian War*. Ithaca: Cornell University Press.

———. 1974. *The Archidamian War*. Ithaca: Cornell University Press.

———. 1987. *The Fall of the Athenian Empire*. Ithaca: Cornell University Press.

Kallet, L. 2001. *Money and the Corrosion of Power in Thucydides: The Sicilian Expedition and its Aftermath*. Berkeley: University of California Press.

Kallet-Marx, L. 1993. *Money, Expense, and Naval Power in Thucydides' History 1-5.24*. Berkeley: University of California Press.

Kelly, T. 1982. "Thucydides and Spartan Strategy in the Archidamian War," *The American Historical Review* 87: 25–54.

Kitto, H. D. F. 1966. *Poiesis: Structure and Thought*. Berkeley: University of California Press.

Konishi, H. 1987. "Thucydides' History as a Finished Piece," *Liverpool Classical Monthly* 12.1: 5–7.

Koster, W. J. W., ed. 1978. *Scholia in Aristophanem. Pars. II. Fasc. I: Scholia Vetera et Recentiora in Aristophanis Vespas.* Groningen: Booma.

Lang, M. 1948. "The Revolution of the 400," *American Journal of Philology* 69: 272–89.

———. 1967. "Revolution of the 400: Chronology and Constitutions," *American Journal of Philology* 88: 176–87.

Lateiner, D. 1985. "Nicias' Inadequate Encouragement (Thucydides 7.69.2)," *Classical Philology* 80: 201–13.

———. 1998. "Review Discussion of Simon Hornblower, *A Commentary on Thucydides*, Volume II: Books IV-V.24," *Histos* 2, http://www.dur.ac.uk/Classics/histos/ 1998/lateiner.html.

Lattimore, R. 1939. "The Wise Advisor in Herodotus," *Classical Philology* 34: 24–35.

Lattimore, S., trans. 1998. *Thucydides. The Peloponnesian War*. Indianapolis: Hackett.

Lawton, C. L. 1995. *Attic Document Reliefs. Art and Politics in Ancient Athens.* Oxford: Oxford University Press.

Lévy, E. 1976. *Athènes devant la défaite de 404. Histoire d'une crise idéologique.* Athens: École française d'Athènes.

Liebeschuetz, W. 1968. "The Structure and Function of the Melian Dialogue," *The Journal of Hellenic Studies* 88: 73–77.

Lintott, A. 1982. *Violence, Civil Strife and Revolution in the Classical City.* Baltimore: Johns Hopkins University Press.

Longo, O. 1974. "Atene fra polis e territorio: in margine a Tucidide 1.143.5," *Studi Italiani di filologia classica* 46: 5–21.

———. 1975. "La polis, le mura, le navi (Tucidide, 7.77.7)," *Quaderni di Storia* 1: 87–113.

Loomis, W. T. 1992. *The Spartan War Fund. IG V 1, 1 and a New Fragment. (Historia einzelschriften, Heft 74)*. Stuttgart: Franz Steiner Verlag.

Loraux, N. 1981/1986. *The Invention of Athens. The Funeral Oration in the Classical City.* Cambridge, Mass.: Harvard University Press. (First published as *L'invention d'Athènes: Histoire de l'oraison funèbre dans la "cité classique."* Paris: Editions de l'Ecole des hautes études en sciences sociáles 1981.)

———. 1986. "Thucydide et la sedition dans les mots," *Quaderni di Storia* 23: 95–134.

———. 1991. "Reflections of the Greek City on Unity and Division," in *City States in Classical Antiquity and Medieval Italy*, ed. A. Molho, K. Raaflaub, and J. Emlen, 33–51. Stuttgart: Franz Steiner Verlag.

———. 1993. "Corcyre 427, Paris 1871. La 'guerre civile grecque' entre deux temps," *Les temps modernes* 49 (no. 569): 82–119.

———. 1997/2002. *The Divided City. On Memory and Forgetting in Ancient Athens.* New York: Zone Books. (First published as *La cite diviseé: L'oubli dans la mémoire d'Athènes.* Paris: Payot 1997.)

Luginbill, R. D. 1999. *Thucydides on War and National Character*. Boulder: Westview Press.

MacDowell, D. M. 1985. "Review of M. J. Osborne, *Naturalization in Athens*," *Classical Review* 35: 317–20.

Mackie, C. J. 1996. "Homer and Thucydides: Corcyra and Sicily," *Classical Quarterly* n.s. 46: 103–13.

Macleod, C. W. 1974. "Form and Meaning in the Melian Dialogue," *Historia* 23: 385–400. (Reprinted in C. W. Macleod, *Collected Essays*. Oxford: Oxford University Press 1983, 52–67.)

———. 1977. "Thucydides' Plataean Debate," *Greek Roman and Byzantine Studies* 18: 227–46. (Reprinted in C. W. Macleod, *Collected Essays*. Oxford: Oxford University Press 1983, 103–22.)

———. 1983a. "Thucydides and Tragedy," in C. W. Macleod, *Collected Essays*, 140–58. Oxford: Oxford University Press.

———. 1983b. *Collected Essays*. Oxford: Oxford University Press.

Marinatos, N. 1980. "Nicias as a Wise Advisor and Tragic Warner in Thucydides," *Philologus* 124: 305–10.

Marinatos Kopff, N., and H. R. Rawlings. 1978. "Panolethria and Divine Punishment. Thucydides 7.87.6 and Herodotus 2.120.5," *Parola del Passato* 182: 331–37.

Maurer, K. 1995. *Interpolation in Thucydides* (*Mnemosyne* Suppl. 150). Leiden: Brill.

McCoy, W. J. 1970. *Theramenes, Thrasybulus and the Athenian Moderates*. Ph.D. diss., Yale University. Non vidi.

McGregor, M. F. 1956. "The Politics of the Historian Thucydides," *Phoenix* 10: 93–102.

———. 1973. "The 'Non-Speeches' of Pisander in Thucydides, Book Eight," in *The Speeches in Thucydides. A Collection of Original Studies with a Bibliography*, ed. P. Stadter, 78–89. Chapel Hill: University of North Carolina Press.

McKechnie, P. R., and S. J. Kern, eds. and trans., 1988. *Hellenica Oxyrhynchia*. Warminster: Aris and Phillips.

McNeal, R. A. 1970. "Historical Methods and Thucydides 1.103.1," *Historia* 19: 306–25.

Meiggs, R. 1972. *The Athenian Empire*. Oxford: Oxford University Press.

Meiggs, R., and D. Lewis, eds. 1988. *A Selection of Greek Historical Inscriptions*. Rev. ed. Oxford: Oxford University Press.

Meritt, B. D. 1937. *Documents on Athenian Tribute*. Cambridge, Mass.: Harvard University Press.

———, H. T. Wade-Gery, and M. F. McGregor, eds. 1939–1953. *The Athenian Tribute Lists*. Vols I – IV. Princeton: Princeton University Press.

Moggi, M. 1975. "ΣΥΝΟΙΚΙΖΕΙΝ in Tucidide," *Annali di scuola normale superiore di Pisa* 5: 915–24.

Monoson, S. S. 1994. "Citizen as *Erastes*. Erotic Imagery and the Idea of Reciprocity in the Periclean Funeral Oration," *Political Theory* 22: 253–76.

———, and M. Loriaux, 1998. "The Illusion of Power and the Disruption of Moral Norms: Thucydides' Critique of Periclean Policy," *American Political Science Review* 92: 285–97.

Morrison, J. V. 2000. "Historical Lessons in the Melian Episode," *Transactions of the American Philological Association* 130: 119–148.

———. 2006a. *Reading Thucydides*. Columbus: Ohio State University Press.

———. 2006b. "Interaction of Speech and Narrative in Thucydides," in *Brill's Companion to Thucydides*," ed. A. Rengakos and A. Tsakmakis, 251–77. Leiden: Brill.

Mossé, C. 1963. "Armée et cité grecque (A propos de Thucydide, VII, 77.4–5)," *Revue des ètudes anciennes* 65: 290–97.

———. 1964. "La role de l'armée dans la révolution de 411 à Athènes," *Revue historique* 231: 1–10.

———. 1973. *Athens in Decline 404–86* B.C. London: Routledge.

Munn, M. 2000. *The School of History. Athens in the Age of Socrates*. Berkeley: University of California Press.

Nevett, L. 2005. "Between Urban and Rural: House-form and Social Relations in Attic Village and *Deme* Centers," in *Ancient Greek Houses and Households. Chronological, Regional and Social Diversity*, ed. B. A. Ault and L. Nevett, 83–98. Philadelphia: University of Pennsylvania Press.

Nietzsche, F. 1997. *Daybreak*, trans. R. J. Hollindale. Cambridge: Cambridge University Press.

———. 1998. *Twilight of the Idols*, trans. D. Lange. Oxford: Oxford University Press.

Nisbet, R. G. M., and M. Hubbard. 1970. *A Commentary on Horace: Odes. Book I.* Oxford: Oxford University Press.

Nisetich, F. J., trans. 1980. *Pindar's Victory Songs.* Baltimore: Johns Hopkins University Press.

Ober, J. 1985. "Thucydides, Pericles, and the Strategy of Defense," in *The Craft of the Ancient Historian: Essays in Honor of Chester G. Starr*, ed. J. W. Eadie and J. Ober, 171–88. Lanham, Md.: University Press of America.

———. 1991. "National Ideology and Strategic Defense of the Population, from Athens to Star Wars," in *Hegemonic Rivalry from Thucydides to the Nuclear Age*, ed. R. N. Lebow and B. S. Strauss, 251–67. Boulder: Westview Press.

———. 1998. *Political Dissent in Democratic Athens. Intellectual Critics of Popular Rule.* Princeton: Princeton University Press.

———. 2005. *Athenian Legacies. Essays on the Politics of Going On Together.* Princeton: Princeton University Press.

Orwin, C. 1984. "Democracy and Distrust: A Lesson from Thucydides," *The American Scholar* 53: 313–25.

———. 1988. "*Stasis* and Plague: Thucydides on the Dissolution of Society," *Journal of Politics* 50: 831–847.

———. 1994. *The Humanity of Thucydides*. Princeton: Princeton University Press.

———. 2000. "Review Essay on Thucydides," *Political Theory* 28 no. 6: 861–69.

Osborne, M. J. 1981. *Naturalization in Athens*. Vol. I. Brussels: Palais der Academiën.

———. 1982. *Naturalization in Athens*. Vol. II. *Commentaries on the Decrees Granting Citizenship.* Brussels: Palais der Academiën.

Page, D. 1955. *Sappho and Alcaeus*. Oxford: Oxford University Press.

Palmer, M. 1982a. "Alcibiades and the Question of Tyranny in Thucydides," *Canadian Journal of Political Science* 15: 102–24.

———. 1982b. "Love of Glory and the Common Good," *American Political Science Review* 76: 825–836.

———. 1989. "Machiavellian *virtù* and Thucydidean *arete*: Traditional Virtue and Political Wisdom in Thucydides," *The Review of Politics* 51: 365–85.

———. 1992. *Love of Glory and the Common Good. Aspects of the Political Thought of Thucydides.* Lanham, Md.: Rowman and Littlefield.

Parke, H. W., and Wormell, D. E. W. 1956. *The Delphic Oracle.* Vol. II. *The Oracular Responses.* Oxford: Blackwell.

Parry, A. M. 1981. *Logos and Ergon in Thucydides.* New York: Arno Press.

Paul, G. M. 1982. "*Urbs Capta*: Sketch of an Ancient Literary Motif," *Phoenix* 36: 144–55.

Pelling, C. B. R. 1991. "Thucydides' Archidamus and Herodotus' Artabanus," in *Georgica. Greek Studies in Honour of George Cawkwell*, ed. M. A. Flower and M. Toher, 120–42. London: University of London, Institute of Classical Studies.

———. 1997. *Greek Tragedy and the Historian.* Oxford: Oxford University Press.

———. 2000. *Literary Texts and the Greek Historian.* London: Routledge.

Perry, B. E. 1937. "The Early Greek Capacity for Viewing Things Separately," *Transactions of the American Philological Association* 68: 403–427.

Piérart, M. 1984. "Deux notes sur la politique d'Athènes en mer égée (428–425)," *Bulletin de correspondance hellénique* 108: 161–76.

Pleket, H. W. 1963. "Thasos and the Popularity of the Athenian Empire," *Historia* 12: 70–77.

Plenio, W. 1954. *Die letzte Rede des Perikles (Th. II.60–64).* Ph.D. diss., Universität zu Kiel. Non vidi.

Pouncey, P. R. 1980. *The Necessities of War. A Study of Thucydides' Pessimism.* New York: Columbia University Press.

Price, J. 2001. *Thucydides and Internal War.* Cambridge: Cambridge Unversity Press.

Pritchett, W. K. 1975. *Dionysius of Halicarnassus: On Thucydides.* Berkeley: University of California Press.

Ptaszek, I. 1994. "Thucydides 8.86.4. An Interpretation," *Eos* 82: 207–212.

Pusey, N. M. 1940. "Alcibiades and τὸ φιλόπολι," *Harvard Studies in Classical Philology* 51: 215–31.

Quinn, T. J. 1981. *Athens and Samos, Lesbos and Chios.* 478–404 B.C. Manchester: Manchester University Press.

Raaflaub, K. 2006. "Thucydides on Democracy and Oligarchy," in *Brill's Companion to Thucydides*, ed. A. Rengakos and A. Tsakmakis, 189–224. Leiden: Brill.

Rackham, H., trans. 1932. *Aristotle in Twenty-three Volumes.* Vol. XXI. *Politics.* Cambridge, Mass.: Harvard University Press.

Rasmussen, A. H. 1995. "Thucydides on Pericles (Thuc. 2.65)," *Classical and Mediaevalia* 46: 25–46.

Raubitschek, A. E. 1941. "Two Notes on Isocrates," *Transactions of the American Philological Association* 72: 356–64.

_______ (with L. H. Jeffery). 1949. *Dedications from the Athenian Akropolis.* Cambridge, Mass.: Archaeological Institute of America.

_______. 1963. "War Melos tributpflichtig?" *Historia* 12: 78–83.

Rawlings, H. R., III. 1981. *The Structure of Thucydides' History.* Princeton: Princeton University Press.

Rengakos, A. 1984. *Form und Wandel des Machtdenkens der Athener bei Thukydides.* (*Hermes einzelschriften, Heft* 48). Stuttgart: Franz Steiner Verlag.

_______, and A. Tsakmakis, eds. 2006. *Brill's Companion to Thucydides.* Leiden: Brill.

Rhodes, P. J. 1972. "The Five Thousand in the Athenian Revolutions of 411 B.C.," *The Journal of Hellenic Studies* 92: 115–27.

Rogers, B. B. 1910. *The Acharnians of Aristophanes.* London: Bell.

Rood, T. 1998a. "Thucydides and his Predecssors," *Histos* 2, http://www.dur.ac.uk/Classics/histos/1998/rood.html.

_______. 1998b. *Thucydides. Narrative and Explanation.* Oxford: Oxford University Press.

_______. 1999. "Thucydides' Persian Wars," in *The Limits of Historiography: Genre and Narrative in Ancient Historical Texts*, ed. C. S. Kraus, 141–68. Leiden: Brill.

De Romilly, J. 1947/1963. *Thucydides and Athenian Imperialism*, trans. P. Thody, Oxford: Blackwell. (Originally published as *Thucydide et l'imperialisme athénien. La pensée de l'historien et la genèse de l'oeuvre.* Paris: Les Belles Lettres, 1947.)

_______. 1962a. "Les intentions d'Archidamos et le livre II de Thucydide," *Revue des études anciennes* 64: 287–299.

_______. 1962b. *Thucydide. La guerre du Péloponnèse. Livre II.* Paris: Les Belles Lettres.

_______. 1965. "L'optimisme de Thucydide et le jugement de l'historien sur Périclès (Thuc., II.65)," *Revue des études grecques* 78: 557–75.

Rusten, J. S., ed. 1989. *Thucydides. The Peloponnesian War. Book II.* Cambridge: Cambridge University Press.

Schwartz, E. 1929. *Das Geschichtswerk des Thukydides.* Bonn: Hildesheim.

Sealey, R. 1976. *A History of the Greek City-States. ca. 700–338* B.C. Berkeley: University of California Press.

Seaman, M. G. 1997. "The Athenian Expedition to Melos in 416 B.C.," *Historia* 46: 385–418.

Seltman, C. 1955. *Greek Coins. A History of Metallic Currency and Coinage down to the Fall of the Hellenistic Kingdoms.* 2d. ed. London: Methuen.

Shipley, G. 1987. *A History of Samos. 800–188* B.C. Oxford: Oxford University Press.

Sicking, C. M. J. 1995. "The General Purport of Pericles' Funeral Oration and Last Speech," *Hermes* 123: 404–25.

Silk, M. S. 1974. *Interaction in Poetic Imagery (with Special Reference to Early Greek Poetry).* Cambridge: Cambridge University Press.

Skydsgaard, J. E. 2000. "The Meaning of *Polis* in Thucydides 2.16.2. A Note," in *Polis and Politics. Studies in Ancient Greek History*, ed. P. E. Flensted Jensen, T. H. Nielsen, and L. Rubinstein, 229–30. Copenhagen: Museum Tusculanum Press.

Smith, B. H. 1968. *Poetic Closure. A Study of How Poems End.* Chicago: University of Chicago Press.

Sordi, M. 2000. "Trasibulo e la contorivoluzione di Samo: l'assemblea del popolo in armi come forma di opposizione," *Contributi dell'Istituto di storia antica* 26: 103–9.

———. 2001. *Il pensiero sulla guerra nel mondo antico.* (*Contributi dell'Istituto di storia antica* 27). Milan: Vita e Penstero.

Spratt, A. W. 1905. *Thucydides. Book VI.* Cambridge: Cambridge University Press.

Stadter, P. A., ed. 1973. *The Speeches in Thucydides. A Collection of Original Studies with a Bibliography.* Chapel Hill: University of North Carolina Press.

———. 1993. "The Form and Content of Thucydides' Pentecontaetia (1.89–117)," *Greek, Roman and Byzantine Studies* 34: 35–72.

Stahl, H.-P. 1966/2003. *Thucydides. Man's Place in History.* Swansea: The Classical Press of Wales. (Originally published as *Thukydides. Die Stellung des Menschen im geschichtlichen Prozess.* Munich: Beck, 1966.)

———. 1973. "Speeches and Course of Events in Books Six and Seven of Thucydides," in *The Speeches in Thucydides. A Collection of Original Studies with a Bibliography*, ed. R. Sadter, 60–77. Chapel Hill: The University of North Carolina Press.

De Ste. Croix, G. E. M. 1972. *The Origins of the Peloponnesian War.* Ithaca: Cornell University Press.

Steiner, D. T. 1994. *The Tyrant's Writ. Myths and Images of Writing in Ancient Greece.* Princeton: Princeton University Press.
Strasburger, H. 1958. "Thukydides und die politische Selbstdarstellung der Athener," *Hermes* 86: 17–40.
Strauss, B. S. 1986. *Athens After the Peloponnesian War. Class, Faction and Policy, 403–386* B.C. Ithaca: Cornell University Press.
Strauss, L. 1964. *The City and Man.* Chicago: University of Chicago Press.
Stroud, R. 1971. "Greek Inscriptions. Theozotides and the Athenian Orphans," *Hesperia* 40: 280–301.
Taylor, M. C. 2002. "Implicating the *demos*: A Reading of Thucydides on the Rise of the Four Hundred," *The Journal of Hellenic Studies* 122: 91–108.
Thompson, N. 2001. *The Ship of State. Statecraft and Politics from Ancient Greece to Democratic America.* New Haven: Yale University Press.
Tod, M. N. 1946. *Greek Historical Inscriptions to the End of the Fifth Century.* Vol. I. Oxford: Oxford University Press.
Tompkins, D. 1972. "Stylistic Characterization in Thucydides: Nicias and Alcibiades," *Yale Classical Studies* 22: 181–214.
———. 1993. "Archidamus and the Question of Characterization in Thucydides," in *Nomodeiktes. Greek Studies in Honor of Martin Ostwald*, eds. R. Rosen and J. Farrell, 99–111. Ann Arbor: University of Michigan Press.
True, M. 1953. "Athen und Melos und der Melierdialog des Thukydides," *Historia* 2: 253–73.
———. 1954. "Nachtrag zum Athen und Melos und der Melierdialog der Thukydides," *Historia* 3: 58–59.
Tsakmakis, A. 2006. "Leaders, Crowds and the Power of the Image: Political Communication in Thucydides," in *Brill's Companion to Thucydides*, ed. A. Rengakos and A. Tsakmakis, 161–188. Leiden: Brill.
Wade-Gery, H. T. 1970. "Thucydides," in *The Oxford Classical Dictionary*, ed. N. G. L. Hammond and H. H. Scullard. Oxford: Oxford University Press.
Walters, K. R. 1981a. "Four Hundred Athenian Ships at Salamis?" *Rheinisches Museum für Philologie* 124: 199–203.
———. 1981b. "'We Fought Alone at Marathon': Historical Falsification in the Attic Funeral Oration," *Rheinisches Museum für Philologie* 124: 204–211.
Walker, H. J. 1995. *Theseus and Athens.* Oxford: Oxford University Press.
Wasserman, F. 1947. "The Melian Dialogue," *Transactions of the American Philological Association* 78: 18–36.

———. 1953. "The Speeches of King Archidamos in Thucydides," *Classical Journal* 48: 193–200.

———. 1964. "The Voice of Sparta in Thucydides," *Classical Journal* 59: 289–97.

Weil, R. 1972. *Thucydide. La guerre du Péloponnèse. Tome V. Livre VIII.* Paris: Les Belles Lettres.

West, III., W. C. 1973a. "The Speeches in Thucydides. A Description and Listing," in *The Speeches in Thucydides*, ed. P. Stadter, 3–15. Chapel Hill: University of North Carolina Press.

———. 1973b. "A Bibliography of Scholarship on the Speeches in Thucydides. 1873–1970," in *The Speeches in Thucydides*, ed. P. Stadter, 124–61. Chapel Hill: University of North Carolina Press.

Westlake, H. D. 1945. "Seaborne Raids in Periclean Strategy," *Classical Quarterly* 39: 75–84.

———. 1958. "Thucydides 2.65.11." *Classical Quarterly* n.s. 8: 102–10.

———. 1968. *Individuals in Thucydides*. Cambridge: Cambridge University Press.

———. 1989. "The Subjectivity of Thucydides: His Treatment of the Four Hundred at Athens," in *Studies in Thucydides and Greek History*, 181–200. Bristol: Bristol Classical Press.

Wettergreen, J. A. 1980. "On the End of Thucydides' Narrative," *Interpretation* 9: 93–110.

Whitehead, D. 1986. *The Demes of Attica, 508/7–ca. 250* B.C. *A Political and Social Study*. Princeton: Priceton University Press.

———. 2001. "Athenian Demes as *Poleis* (Thuc. 2.16.2)," *Classical Quarterly* 51: 604–7.

Will, W. 2003. *Thukydides und Perikles. Der Historiker und sein Held.* Bonn: Habelt.

Wilson, J. R. 1989. "Shifting and Permanent 'Philia' in Thucydides," *Greece and Rome* 36: 147–151.

Wolpert, A. 2002. *Remembering Defeat. Civil War and Civic Memory in Ancient Athens*. Baltimore: Johns Hopkins University Press.

Young, D. C. 1968. *Three Odes of Pindar. A Literary Study of Pythian 11, Pythian 3 and Olympian 7*. (*Mnemosyne* Suppl. 9). Leiden: Brill.

Yunis, H. 1996. *Taming Democracy. Models of Political Rhetoric in Classical Athens.* Ithaca. Cornell University Press.

Ziolkowski, J. E. 1981. *Thucydides and the Tradition of Funerary Speeches at Athens*. New York: Arno Press.

General Index

Index Locorum